The Darker Side of Western Modernity

A book in the series

LATIN AMERICA OTHERWISE *Languages, Empires, Nations*

Series editors
WALTER D. MIGNOLO, Duke University
IRENE SILVERBLATT, Duke University
SONIA SALDÍVAR-HULL, University of Texas, San Antonio

THE DARKER SIDE OF WESTERN MODERNITY

Global Futures, Decolonial Options

Walter D. Mignolo

DUKE UNIVERSITY PRESS Durham & London 2011

© 2011 Duke University Press All rights reserved

Printed in the United States of America on acid-free paper ∞
Designed by Jennifer Hill. Typeset in Minion Pro by Achorn International

Library of Congress Cataloging-in-Publication Data
appear on the last printed page of this book.

Once again, to Andrea and Alexander. Life continues, and so the conversations.

And to Reynolds Smith, for twenty years of conversation and the more than a decade of working on Latin America Otherwise.

CONTENTS

Part Four

Latin America Otherwise: Languages, Empires, Nations is a critical series. It aims to explore the emergence and consequences of concepts used to define "Latin America" while at the same time exploring the broad interplay of political, economic, and cultural practices that have shaped Latin American worlds. Latin America, at the crossroads of competing imperial designs and local responses, has been construed as a geo-cultural and geopolitical entity since the nineteenth century. This series provides a starting point to redefine Latin America as a configuration of political, linguistic, cultural, and economic intersections that demands a continuous reappraisal of the role of the Americas in history, and of the ongoing process of globalization and the relocation of people and cultures that have characterized Latin America's experience. *Latin America Otherwise: Languages, Empires, Nations* is a forum that confronts established geo-cultural constructions, rethinks area studies and disciplinary boundaries, assesses convictions of the academy and of public policy, and correspondingly demands that the practices through which we produce knowledge and understanding about and from Latin America be subject to rigorous and critical scrutiny.

In this pathbreaking work, Walter D. Mignolo further pierces the surface episteme of rationality marking Western modernity to reveal its terrible and hidden underside. Western modernity, he shows convincingly, is inseparable from the logic of coloniality: modernity's elaborate façade of "civilizing" and "civilization" covers its necessary foundation in the terror-logic of imperial rule. Not only a critique of dominant Western paradigms of knowledge, but of so-called critical studies, Mignolo's volume exposes the pervasiveness of Western epistemic "rationalities" along with their self-congratulatory sentiments. But *The Darker Side of Western Modernity* goes beyond revealing the limitations of Western epistemic rationality and its geopolitical genesis. Mignolo's extraordinary contribution is to present and strategize a "decolonial" epistemology or ways of being in the world—a route to agency through decolonial thinking and decolonial transformative being. This is thinking "otherwise."

What actual significance do you think there is in discussing the question of modernity? Discussing the significance of the question of modernity involves many dimensions. These include, for instance, the relation between contemporary nationalism and modernity, the question of globalization, consumerism, the theory of modernization, and West-centrism. If we are talking about the direct significance of this question, however, then I think that the critique of developmentalism is a very important aspect. The reconsideration of developmentalism is a very important aspect. The reconsideration of developmentalism is specially urgent today. I am not an expert on this matter but I am still willing to go over a cursory discussion of these perspectives.
WANG HUI and KE KAIJUN, "An Interview Concerning Modernity," 2009

THE STRUCTURE of the argument and therefore of the book is built on the premises that currently there are three types of critique to modernity. One type is internal to the history of Europe itself and in that sense these premises are a Eurocentered critique of modernity (for example, psychoanalysis, Marxism, poststructuralism, postmodernity), and the other two types emerged from non-European histories entangled with Western modernity. One of them focuses on the idea of Western civilization (for example, dewesternization, Occidentosis), and the other on coloniality (such as postcoloniality, decoloniality). The three types of critiques are analyzed in relation to their point of origination and their routes of dispersion. Postmodernity originated in Europe but dispersed around the world. Decoloniality originated among Third World countries after the Bandung Conference in 1955, and also dispersed all over the world. Dewesternization originated in East Asia, but the dewesternizing argument can be found in other parts of the world.

The unfolding of the book's argument is not linear but spiral, a mode of exposition that I have already practiced in two previous books (*The Darker Side of the Renaissance* and *Local Histories/Global Designs*), both of which form a trilogy with this one. As in jazz, I have a leitmotif and several formulaic sentences that the reader will encounter once and again in the preface and introduction, and which will reappear in each chapter and the afterword. Leitmotif and formulaic sentences are not "facts" or "principles" that once announced need not reappear. They have to reemerge, not only to illuminate the topic of a given chapter but also to be empowered by the issues, topics, and problems examined in each chapter.

The initial idea of the book, which dates back to around 2002, was to show that the belief in one sustainable system of knowledge, cast first in theological terms and later on in secular philosophy and sciences (human and natural sciences; nomothetic and ideographic sciences, as Wilhem Dilthey distinguished the "science of the spirit" from the hard sciences), is pernicious to the well-being of the human species and to the life of the planet. Such a system of knowledge, referred to here as the "Western code," serves not all humanity, but only a small portion of it that benefits from the belief that in terms of epistemology there is only one game in town. The "code" has been preserved in the security box since the Renaissance. Diverse knowledge has been generated from that secret code in six European modern or imperial languages: Italian, Spanish, Portuguese, French, German, and English. One may discern a hierarchy within modern European languages when it comes to epistemology. Certainly, theology was grounded in Latin and translated to vernaculars, while romance languages enjoyed a certain respectability in terms of knowledge making. However, after the Enlightenment, French was the romance language that led the second modernity, while German, and more recently English, have come to be the language that preserves and hides the code.[1]

One last observation: in the epigraph above, Wang Hui connects modernity with development. One will not find such a connection among the thousands of pages written and published in Europe and the U.S. about modernity. In the same vein the question about modernity and the geopolitics of knowledge is not being asked. In sum, when I say that decoloniality and postcoloniality did not originate in Europe but in the Third World, I am reminded that Aimé Césaire and Frantz Fanon, for instance, were in France where they wrote their influential books. Fanon actually was in Algeria when he wrote *The Wretched of the Earth* (1961). The point, however, is not where you *reside* but where you *dwell*. Césaire and Fanon, both Martinican, dwelled in the history of the Middle Passage, of the plantations, of slavery and of the runaway slaves. Furthermore, the spirit of the Bandung Conference showed that there is a horizon to explore beyond capitalism and communism: decolonization. Decolonization is the horizon of thinking and being that originated as response to the capitalist and communist imperial designs.

On the Historical Foundation of Western Civilization, Modernity, and the Economy of Accumulation

There is a story behind the process of compiling material for and writing this book. The first version of this manuscript was delivered to Duke University Press in May 2006. Revision, after the outside evaluations came in, began sometime in the spring of 2007, a time which also marked the beginning of the massive Wall Street–self-inflicted destructions that, more than 9/11, generated a global *Pachacuti*, a turnaround, and a point of no return: the five-century cycle of Western civilization—its foundation, hegemony, and dominance—came to an end. Global futures are already being built by the emerging political society (of which I will say more in chapter 1), while the G7 to G20 are too busy to prevent the present collapse, the consequences of 500 years of Western hegemony and dominance. However, processes of decoloniality breaking the Western code are already underway building global futures where the communal should obtain over the liberal commonwealth, the neo-liberal elite wealth, the Marxist commons, and the Christian afterworld. This book is intended as a contribution to thinking and building such global futures.

"Western modernity" has been an addition and also an enormous contribution to the many histories of cultures and civilizations that have appeared since *homo erectus* began to walk around the planet, to use his or her hands, and to think while doing. But it by no means should be taken as the point of arrival of human existence on the planet. The history of Western civilization was conceived in the period between the Renaissance and the Enlightenment, and this conception continued and was reinforced in the Enlightenment era. It was during the Renaissance that the invention of the Middle Ages and the invention of America appropriated the idea of history, colonized time, and space and located Europe as the point of reference of global history (see chapter 4). The fact that Western civilization was the most recent civilization in human history doesn't mean that it was the best, that the rest of the world should follow suit. However, the idea that European modernity was the point of arrival of human history and the model for the entire planet came to be taken for granted. The darker side of modernity materialized in this belief. I explain it as "the logic of coloniality" (see chapter 1, "The Roads to the Future: Rewesterniation, Dewesternization, and Decoloniality").

The distinction between "les anciens et les moderns" was in retrospect the time-pillar in building the idea of modernity and of Western civilization. The distinction between "the civilized and barbarians" was the space-pillar. However, in the process, the architects of Western civilization capitalized on many previous achievements and in five hundred years achieved a grandeur equal to great civilizations like Ancient China and Ancient Egypt; like Ancient Greece and Ancient Rome; like the civilization east of Greece that is today incorrectly referred to as the "Persian Empire" (the ruler was designated shah, not emperor); like the Incas and the Aztecs. It doesn't, of course, make sense to be "against European modernity." However, while European modernity should be admired for its many virtues, its imperial bent to "save the world" by making of the world an extended Euro-America is unacceptable. The problems of the present and of the future will be played out between a successful European-American modernity that is taken as a global model and "the rest of the world," which refuses to be told what to do (see chapter 1).

The idea I wanted to argue—in this book I address it chiefly in chapters 2 and 3 (although the idea appears in every chapter)—is that we (on the planet) have entered into an irreversible polycentric world order currently based on a type of economy that in liberal and Marxist vocabulary is described as "capitalism." The polycentric aspect is constituted by the *commonality* of the global economy and by *disputes* for the control of other domains of what I describe as the "colonial matrix of power" (see introduction). In the disputes for the control of knowledge, of authority, of the economy of the norms regulating gender and sexuality, and the assumptions regulating racial classification of people and of regions, there are several options (that in this argument I define as "epistemic and political projects"), and each option has several avenues—all outlined in chapter 1. Such an outline of options and avenues is helpful for clarifying what the decolonial option offers and what is necessary for distinguishing the polycentric world order in the making from the pluriversal world orders to which trajectories of the decolonial option aspire. The decolonial option, in the singular, as in many other cases a sphere of believers and actions that orient our thinking (such as for instance the Christian option, liberal option, the Marxist option, the Islamic option, the feminist option, etc.), means that, while simultaneously none of these options are uniform and homogenous, they are diverse and polemical between themselves. There are many options within Christianity. That one person could somehow be liberal and Christian means only that he or she can be both and not that liberalism and Christianity are one and the same. By the same token, no one at present is likely to confuse the Islamic with the Christian or Marxist options (although one can surmise that alliances working toward an ethical and just world should be welcome).

I argue that one of the defining features of decolonial options is the analytic of the construction, transformation, and sustenance of racism and patriarchy that created the conditions to build and control a structure of knowledge, either grounded on the word of God or the word of Reason and Truth. Such knowledge-construction made it possible to eliminate or marginalize what did not fit into those principles that aspired to build a totality in which everybody would be included, but not everybody would also have the right to include. Inclusion is a one-way street and not a reciprocal right. In a world governed by the colonial matrix of power, he who includes and she who is welcomed to be included stand in codified power relations. The locus of enunciation from which inclusion is established is always a locus holding the control of knowledge and the power of decision across gender and racial lines, across political orientations and economic regulations.

The decolonial option starts from the analytic assumption that such hierarchies are constructed, as the dictum goes, and specifically that they have been constructed in the very process of building the idea of Western civilization and of modernity. As the decolonial option proceeds from the prospective assumption that locus of enunciations shall be decentered from its modern/colonial configurations and limited to its regional scope. Decoloniality shall dispel the myth of universality grounded on theo- and ego-politics of knowledge. The open questions are then: what kind of knowledge, by whom, what for?

To dispel the myth that there are global needs but only one (diverse) center where knowledge is produced to solve the problem of every body, and to contribute to breaking the Western code, I began to argue (in seminars, articles, lectures) that the anchor of decolonial epistemologies shall be "I am where I think" and better yet "I am where I do and think," as they become synonymous. What that means is not that you "think where you are," which is common sense, but that you constitute yourself ("I am") in the place you think. And that place is not, in my argument, a room or office at the library, but the "place" that has been configured by the colonial matrix of power. In 2006 Évelyne Trouillot opened her intervention in the Sixteenth International Conference of the Academy of Latinity in Lima by saying, "I am a woman, I am black, and I am Haitian."[2] Her talk was thus announced as a confrontation with patriarchy (I am a woman), with racism (I am black), and with imperial geopolitics (I am Haitian). The announcement was not just stating the obvious, what every one of the 250 or so people in the audience already knew, although they may not have brought that knowledge to the foreground or even thought it important, but was a succinct way of saying (in my interpretation): Be advised that I am not just transmitting to you my thoughts about "subjectivity." I am telling you that whatever I say on "subjectivity" is located beyond, next to, tangential to, diagonally to the Western code. By saying I am Haitian, I move away, delink, from imperial imaginary, and engage in knowing-making as a Haitian, which doesn't mean that I represent all Haitians. It means that I have the right to speak as a Haitian, disregarding the fact of whether I "represent" the Haitians. And since I have the right, I do so. By telling you I am a woman but also black, I am telling you that I am speaking as a black woman and, by so doing, breaking the Western code that has denied women and blacks both humanity and intelligence. But I am not saying this to tell you that I am intelligent and that I deserve the recognition of those who disavowed blacks and women and asked them to sit in the background, as though blacks and women could not think. Could really black women think? I am telling you that because I am engaging in breaking the Western code. Thus, I am telling you that by disengaging, I am breaking away from the Western code and enrolling in knowledge making among all those "who are where they think/do" (like Descartes was where he thought). I am telling you that the "universal epistemic code," the *hubris of the zero point*, still has its believers, but the illusion that the Western code is the only game in town has certainly been broken.

On the Meaning of "Western Code": The Trilogy

Since the report written by the Franciscan Diego de Landa, *Relación de las Cosas de Yucatán* (1556), decipherment of the Maya script has been a constant preoccupation.[3] The story has been told by Michael D. Coe's book *Breaking the Maya Code*.[4] Curiously enough, and in another domain of knowledge, Roberto Mangabeira Unger's also classic book, *Knowledge and Politics* (1975), confronted a similar problem. But in this case, the code to be broken was "the unity of liberal thought," which is the main thesis of the book. I offer a quote to explain Mangabeira Unger's thesis, which is not easy to summarize.

> Thus, the house of reason in which I was working proved to be a prison-house of paradox whose rooms did not connect and whose passageways led nowhere. . . . The premises of this vision [the unified vision of a liberal system of ideas] of the world are few; they are tied together; and they are as powerful in their hold over the mind as they are unacknowledged and forgotten. They took their classic form in the seventeenth century. For reasons that will become clear, I resolved to call them the liberal doctrine, even though the area they include is both broader and narrower than the one occupied by what we now ordinarily take for liberalism. This system of idea is indeed the guard that watches of the prison house.[5]

What I wish to highlight is not Mangabeira Unger's thesis, but the fact that he intends not only to decipher, but to break the liberal code. Coe reported on the effort by Western scholars to break the writing-system code of a non-Western society. Mangabeira Unger aimed at breaking the code of a system of thought to which he, as scholar and intellectual, belonged.

I thought of titling this book *Breaking the Western Code* since I am here pursuing a line of reflection that started with *The Darker Side of the Renaissance* (1995) and continued with *Local Histories / Global Designs* (2000). But many of my friends and colleagues voted against this title, so I changed it to *The Darker Side of Western Modernity*. Common to my previous two books in the trilogy was an effort to anchor the argument in a perspective similar to that of those who attempted to break a code (the Maya code in the case of Coe; the liberal code in the case of Ungar). While I sympathize with Mangabeira Unger's thesis (the unity of liberal thought and the attempt to break the code that sustains it), my attempt is not only to break the liberal code but to make a contribution toward breaking the Western code sustained by and anchored in the rhetoric of modernity and the logic of coloniality, which I explain in the introduction. That means that my focus is the "unity" of the colonial matrix of power, of which the rhetoric of modernity and the logic of coloniality are its two sides: one constantly named and celebrated (progress, development, growth) and the other silenced or named as problems to be solved by the former (poverty, misery, inequities, injustices, corruption, commodification, and dispensability of human life). Research grants are not offered to pursue this kind of investigation. Furthermore, I do not ground my critique on the universality of "human nature," but lean toward embracing the perspective on "human nature" of those whose humanity has been called into question.

At this point a clarification and a disclaimer are in order. The clarification, which will regularly reappear during my argument, concerns the often-asked question about the distinctions between the decolonial and the Left, that is, the Marxist-oriented Left. In a nutshell, the difference is this: the Marxist Left confronts capitalism first within Europe itself; with the imperial expansion and the exportation and importation of Marxism to the colonies, the confrontation of capitalism and the focus on social class was simply adapted to the new context. The decolonial confronts all of Western civilization, which includes liberal capitalism and Marxism. And it does it from the perspective of the colonies and ex-colonies rather than from the perspective internal to Western civilization itself, be it Spengler's decay of Western civilization or the postmodern critique of Western modernity.

Western civilization is deployed here in its underlying structure: the colonial matrix of power. The main thesis of this book is that while capitalist economy is globally shared, the colonial matrix of power—created and controlled by Western imperial countries (from Spain and Portugal, to Holland, France, England, and the United States)—is today disputed (by

China, Russia, some Islamic countries, India, Union del Sur). The dispute over the control of the colonial matrix impinges and transforms the uses and reasons to maintain globally an economy of accumulation and growth and to avoid engaging in a noncapitalist economy instead of focusing on maintaining it with better distributions and lessened exploitation of human beings and their labor. The competition for the control of authority and knowledge by state, corporations, and religious institutions, simultaneous to the disputes for liberation from that control in the spheres of sexuality, gender, and subjectivities growing daily around the world, including "minorities" in Western Europe and the United States (for example, the emerging global political society), indicates that what is being contested is not only the control of authority in inter-state relations (and therefore in political theory and in human-rights regulations), but also the control of the sphere of knowledge and subjectivity. Gender, racial, and sexual liberations take a central role next to, but also beyond class struggles. The dispute of knowledge in this sphere is being fought not only in mainstream and independent media, but also in higher education through the creation of programs and departments focusing on ethnic/racial and gender/sexuality issues.

The disclaimer is about the title "The Darker Side of Western Modernity." I have been asked through the years if I feel comfortable with the word *darker* in the *Darker Side of the Renaissance*. The first time was by a student who pointed to Joseph Conrad's *Heart of Darkness* and to references to Africa as the "Dark Continent." While the argument in the *Darker Side of the Renaissance* lays ground for disputing common knowledge in which Africa is seen as "dark" and "dark" is seen as bad, I selected the adjective precisely in contradistinction to the image of the "Dark Age" that the Renaissance projected toward the Middle Ages. The "Dark Age" in Europe was that period between the white columns of Greece's Parthenon, the blue and sunny sky of Mediterranean Rome, and the light, of course, of the Enlightenment. But if that "darkness" was recognized by European men of letters, one of its "darker sides," slavery, was not acknowledged as such, but portrayed as bringing "light" and civilization to the colonies, as a necessary step toward progress and civilization and good business for merchants from Portugal, Spain, France, Holland, and England. After pondering these issues and looking for alternatives, I realized that the image of Africa as the "Dark Continent" is indeed one of the many hypocrisies of Western modernity. It is, in terms that will become clear below, part of the rhetoric of modernity (geographic racism) hiding the logic of coloniality (legitimization of either to disregard racialized places or to justify the "saving missions," implied in the rhetoric of modernity, from religious orders to philanthropic billionaires and institutions working to end poverty in Africa). After much debate with myself and consultations with Reynolds Smith, I decided to name this book *The Darker Side of Western Modernity*.

The Darker Side of Western Modernity is indeed the third installment of a trilogy that was not planned as such. But, in retrospect, perhaps it might be better understood as the fourth volume of a tetralogy that began in the early 1980s. The first "volume" was not a book but a series of articles exploring issues that later came together in *The Darker Side of the Renaissance*. One set of issues were explorations on semiotics, hermeneutics, epistemology, discourse analysis, and literary theory. Two examples of this line of investigation are "Semiosis y universos de sentido" (1983), which explores the concept of "semiosis" in the frame of semiotic theory and discourse analysis, and "La semiosis colonial" (1992), which introduces "colonial semiosis" into the field of colonial studies.[6] The argument was, in a nutshell, that while the field presupposed lines of inquiry such as "colonial economy," "colonial literature," "colonial historiography," "colonial society," and so on, there was not yet a concept that captured the domain of interactions, at different semiotic levels (verbal, visual, dialogical communication), between the diversity of Spaniards landing in the New World and the diversity of ab-original civilizations and cultures being invaded by strangers.

The second line of investigation focused on, in the vocabulary of the time, "historiographic narratives" and was inaugurated by an article and a monograph that appeared within one year of each other. The article is "El metatexto historiográfico y la historiografía Indiana" (1981), and the monograph, "Cartas, crónicas y relaciones del descubrimiento y de la conquista" (1982).[7] By the late 1980s and early 1990s, my research and thinking on historiographic narratives joined my work on semiotics and was channeled toward the concept of colonial semiosis. Thus, when in the second half of the 1990s I became aware of Anibal Quijano's explorations on "coloniality" (which he had introduced by 1989–90), it was just like meeting a kindred soul.[8]

While in *The Darker Side of the Renaissance* the concepts of "colonial semiosis" and, consequently, of "pluritopic hermeneutics" were the two anchors, in *Local Histories/Global Designs*, "border thinking" (border gnosis, border epistemology, border hermeneutics, colonial difference) was the compass that directed my exploration of new paths. At that time, as I had already encountered Quijano, I learned that hidden behind modernity was the agenda of coloniality; that coloniality was constitutive of modernity; that coloniality was the secret shame of the family, kept in the attic, out of the view of friends and family. Thus, the slash ("/") between, which both unites and divides modernity and coloniality (modernity/coloniality), was an invisible dwelling place, the place of the divide between *humanitas/anthropos* (an equation I will return to several times). Thus, Gloria Anzaldúa's epistemic construction coupling the Mexico/U.S. border with the colonial wound ("The U.S.-Mexican border *es una herida abierta* where the Third World grates against the first and bleeds"), an idea that contributed to shape the argument in *The Darker Side of the Renaissance*, acquired a new dimension in *Local Histories/Global Designs*, where it encountered the concept of "coloniality."[9] At that point, border thinking was extended to understand all those places, through the expansion of Western civilization, where "the open wound, the colonial wound, where modernity grates against coloniality and bleeds." At that point, two additional concepts appear to describe *la herida abierta* in its global dimension: colonial and imperial differences. Both concepts are also central to the argument that I unfold below.

As I mentioned before, the trajectory after the publication of *Local Histories/Global Designs*, with the interregnum of *The Idea of Latin America* (2005), started with an article published in 2002, "Geopolitics of Knowledge and the Colonial Difference."[10] The series of investigations that followed were developed in a lengthy article published in 2007, "Delinking: The Rhetoric of Modernity, the Logic of Coloniality, and the Grammar of Decoloniality."[11] The trajectory between the former and the latter article was the complementation of geopolitics with bio-graphic, where the geopolitics and the body-politics of knowledge reinforces each other in decolonial thinking. This trajectory can be understood when we move from Anzaldúa's "herida abierta" to the slash between modernity/coloniality. The former brings forward bio-graphic (body-politics of knowledge), while the second underlines geopolitics of knowledge. Both are intertwined, of course, since the imperial classification and ranking of regions (for example, developed/underdeveloped or First/Second/Third Worlds, where the imperial and the colonial differences can be seen working in tandem) goes hand in hand with classification and ranking of people (for example, civilized/barbarians, humanitas/anthropos; black, yellow, brown, white; heterosexual/gay and man/woman in the First, Second, or Third Worlds, etc.).

What is relevant in the two concepts that I explore in more detail in the subsequent chapters is that both are decolonial concepts that coexist and confront the imperial assumptions constructed around theo- and ego-politics of knowledge (which I also introduced and explored in detail in "Delinking: The Rhetoric of Modernity, the Logic of Coloniality, and the Grammar of Decoloniality"). Thus it is crucial to distinguish bio-politics from bio-graphic or body-politics of knowledge. Bio-politics (or bio-power) is a concept that has served to analyze state-oriented strategies (and now used by the corporations) to manage and control the population. My use of bio-graphic or body-politics of knowledge describes instead the responses, thinking and action, of the population who do not want to be managed by the state and want to delink from the technologies of power to which they are being summated. Both concepts affirm thinking and doing in regions and bodies who were disqualified from thinking. Geo- and body-politics of knowledges are, in my argument, always ingrained in decolonial thinking or, vice versa, decolonial thinking is at once geo- and body-political (see Franz Fanon's work). For example, it is not common to find critiques of Westernization among white scholars and intellectuals in Western Europe and the United States in which the racialization of geo-historical locations and of lesser human beings (those who inhabit "underdeveloped areas") is brought into question. Why? Because historically Western Christianity and Western Europe were successfully constructed as the geo-historical places where specific bio-graphies of Christian and European men were thinking and building knowledge. The rest of the world was to be civilized.[12] Successfully constructing locations of knowledge doesn't mean that in those locations there were and are always consensus. On the contrary, there is diversity of opinions, but the diversity has a common system of belief, languages, and categories of thoughts. Now the location of knowledge cannot longer be controlled by the languages, actors, institutions, and categories of thought on which Western civilization and Western modernity were imagined, described, and built. For these reasons, the investments and the stakes are different, even if the "enemy" is the same: capitalism. But capitalism is not experienced in the same way in Paris and in La Paz. To name and unveil the hidden geo- and body-politics of the Western code is already a decolonial move that legitimizes, at the same time, geo-historical locations and bio-graphic stories that were delegitimized and pushed on the side or outside of the house of knowledge.

The argument herein, very much like that in *The Darker Side of the Renaissance* and in *Local Histories/Global Designs*, unfolds in a spiral rather than linear way. For that reason you will find the same paragraph text quoted or rephrased in two chapters, the point being that the same text or paragraph is taken from a different perspective in each case, at the same time that they reinforce each other. That is the case, for instance, with Kant in chapter 5 and in chapter 7; and with Ali Shari'ati and Lloyd Best in chapter 1 and the afterword. A linear argument cannot capture the nuances, since once a name or a paragraph is mentioned or quoted in a linear flow, it does not return: repetitions are not good in English composition but are important in decolonial thinking.

The Postcolonial and the Decolonial

A frequently asked question is what is the difference between postcoloniality and decoloniality? I have responded to the question in writing, elsewhere.[13] Here I will summarize the arguments, in the hope that the distinction will be clarified in the subsequent chapters.

To start with, both projects take on the meaning of "decolonization" after the Bandung Conference (1955) and the Conference of the Non-Aligned Countries, during the Cold War. In the first conference twenty-nine Asian and African countries participated. The second meeting of the nonaligned countries took place in Belgrade in 1961. The idea of the "Third World" was a French invention prompted by the initiative of nonaligned countries.

Although both projects drink from the same fountain they are grounded in a different genealogy of thoughts and different *existentia* (in the sense that Lewis R. Gordon conceptualizes *existentia Africana*).[14] By this I mean that geo-historical and bio-graphical genealogies of thoughts are at the very inception of decolonial thinking. Frantz Fanon closes his essay *Black Skin, White Masks* (1952) with a prayer: "O my body, makes of me always a man who questions!"

The challenge is radical. If you take Fanon's request, then you may not feel comfortable analyzing Fanon from an epistemic perspective in which your body doesn't call your mind into question. What are the connections between your body, bio-graphically and geo-historically located in the colonial matrix of power, and the issues you investigate? Here Horkheimer's (1937) critical theory will be taken a step further. Horkheimer rightly argued that it is not possible to detach the knowing subject from the known object. Thus traditional theory is charged with believing that knowledge can be objective. However, in making this charge Horkheimer still assumed that the knower is a disembodied subject beyond location. His shortcoming was not to question the ego-politics of knowledge that underlines both traditional and critical theory. The problem with Horkheimer's argument is that his subject is a modern subject, de-racialized, de-sexualized, gender-neutral, and unaware that such a subject dwells in Europe, better yet, Germany, and not in the City of Singapore, Tehran, or La Paz, where the issues, problems, and knowledge-making have different needs, genealogies of thoughts, affects, and problems. It is from the body, not the mind, that questions arise and answers are explored. What calls for thinking is the body, rather than the mind, and the questions that Fanon's Black body asks are not prompted because the body is Black, but because Black bodies have been denied or questioned Humanity in the imperial rhetoric of modernity. Fanon's responses, through his work, were responses to a long-lasting memory of racism, but also to the present conditions of the Cold War and the struggles for decolonization in Africa. Decolonial thinking materialized, however, at the very moment in which the colonial matrix of power was being put in place, in the sixteenth through the eighteenth centuries. And decolonial thinking is always synonymous with decoloniality, to distinguish the new meaning from the legacies of the concept of decolonization. There is not a question of choosing which one is best or more exact, because they both carry their respective meaning toward decolonial futures. Were there problems with the output of decolonization during the Cold War? Sure there were. And so you have the choice: if you are leaning toward postmodern thinking you would try to dismiss it. If you are a decolonial thinker you would try to recast it.

That is, decolonial thinking goes hand in hand with modernity/coloniality in this way: the rhetoric of modernity is a rhetoric of salvation (by conversion yesterday, by development today), but in order to implement what the rhetoric preaches, it is necessary to marginalize or destroy whatever gets in the way of modernity. It so happens that not everyone believes in the salvation being proposed, and those who don't either react against (resistance) or engage in a critical analysis of the situation in order to move in a different direction (re-existence).[15] That was the case of Guaman Poma de Ayala, in the colonial Viceroyalty of Peru, and of Ottobah Cugoano, through his experience of being captured and enslaved, working in Caribbean plantations, and moving to London, in the mid-eighteenth century, with his master, where he engaged in articulating decolonially a critique of slavery and in a concept of sovereignty that first considers people, not the institution. That means that instead of proposing a transformation of the state to solve the problem of slavery (and also save the state as an institution), Cugoano placed sovereignty among people: no human being has the right to enslave other human beings. Therefore, the question is not to reform the state to comply with this principle (which always ends up in formality), but to create institutions that will respond to this basic principle of "human sovereignty."[16]

Now, when Anibal Quijano introduced the concept of *coloniality*, and suggested disengaging and delinking from Western epistemology, he conceived that project as decolonization: decoloniality became an epistemic and political project. Quijano's references at that point were, on the one hand, José Carlos Mariátegui's *Siete ensayos de Interpretación de la realidad peruana* (1927), where Mariátegui introduced several issues that had not been considered seriously, up to that point, by dissenting creole and mestizo intellectuals: the questions of colonialism, of racism, of land appropriation and expropriation, of the university, of religion in Tawantinsuyu, and so on. On the other hand, Quijano had been involved since the 1970s in the heated debates on "dependency theory." "Coloniality" was his way to move to a third stage (Mariátegui in the 1920s, dependency theory in the 1970s, coloniality/decoloniality in the 1990s). At that point, Quijano engaged Wallerstein's world-system analysis, not as a "model" to be imitated, but because Wallerstein himself draws on "dependency theory" to conceptualize world-system analysis. Indeed, Wallerstein's world-system analysis has three references: his training as an Africanist and, because of it, his proximity with Frantz Fanon; the influence of dependency theory in Wallerstein's thoughts; and, finally, the influence of Fernand Braudel, which became of primary importance in relation to the other two. Thus, Wallerstein deemed

"Fernand Braudel" the Center of World-System Analysis, which he created at the University of New York at Binghamton. Quijano's coloniality, however, is a concept that one will not see in Wallerstein's writing. The difference is that while Wallerstein critically analyzes the rhetoric of modernity and the devastating consequences for many people and regions, Quijano introduced the hidden side of modernity and of the modern world-system. In a nutshell, Wallerstein was looking at the modern world-system critically, but from the perspective and experience of the First World, while Quijano was looking at coloniality from the receiving end, from the perspective of the Third World. And here we again encounter the relevance of the geo- and body-politics of knowledge in decolonial thinking.

Postcoloniality has a different genealogy of thought. In terms of existence, it emerged from the experience of British colonization (of Egypt and India and of the Palestinian question) and, obviously, after the concept of postmodernity was introduced by the late 1970s. In that line of thought and concerns, South Asia, Australia, South Africa, and other former British colonies naturally joined postcoloniality, but the English- and French-speaking Caribbean did not. In this case, there is a long tradition of decolonial thought that goes back to C. L. R. James, Aimé Césaire, and Frantz Fanon, emerging long before French poststructuralism and postmodernism that made the idea of postcolonialism and postcoloniality possible. Antonio Gramsci informed South Asian subaltern studies, and he was influential before the emergence of Caribbean thinkers, but he was mainly part of poststructuralist debates inasmuch as he offered an alternative to Louis Althusser's recast of Marx's theoretical revolution. Nevertheless, colonial English was—in general—the "natural" language in the foundation of postcolonial studies and theories; or, if you wish, of the vocabulary of postcoloniality. If you consider, instead, that decolonial projects that emerged in South America, the Caribbean, and among Latinos/as in the United States, and that the concept is of currency among Arabo-Muslim intellectuals, then you have also a linguistic-religious-epistemic issue to consider.[17]

I do not see decoloniality and postcoloniality campaigning for election to win the voting competition that decides which is the best, but as complementary trajectories with similar goals of social transformation. Both projects strive to unveil colonial strategies promoting the reproduction of subjects whose aims and goals are to control and possess. It may happen that, as everything else, either postcoloniality and decoloniality (as they become "popular") will be used by individuals to increase personal gains at the institution or in the public sphere. I cannot speak for postcolonialist, but I can tell you that the aims of decolonial thinking and the decolonial option (even when it appears in a book by Duke University Press written by a professor at Duke University) joint the aims of the political society for whom the decolonial is a question of survival rather than promotion. The American and the European Academy are not hubs of the decolonial. In any event, the post- and the decolonial are two different projects that have in common the concern with colonialism, colonial legacies, and above all for decolonial thinkers, coloniality. We, humans in the planet, cannot avoid conflictive coexistence and the solution is not to eliminate the difference but to decolonize the logic of coloniality that translated differences into values. Unless you believe that consolidating and eliminating options (which is one feature of neo-liberal politics) is preferable to multiplying options (see afterword), and you would like to subsume (or merge) the decolonial into the postcolonial or vice versa, there is nothing wrong with having several approaches as guides for action to confronting the historical legacies of colonialism and the logic of coloniality. On the contrary, each approach carries with it a way of being in the world and not just a way of operating with concepts or telling stories about colonialism. "Consolidating" (that is, eliminating options in order to maintain control, which has been obvious in the neo-liberal doctrine and the Washington Consensus) would be a modern/colonial objective and desire, not a decolonial one. I see more advantages than problems in accepting and working with and in coexisting compatible options and sharing similar goals while taking different roads toward achieving those goals. I would not argue that decoloniality is moving "beyond" postcoloniality or vice versa. Global histories would tell in what direction global futures would be moving. But of course history is not an agent in itself. It moves because of the doing of human beings. To argue for one or the other also would be a modern/colonial way of framing the issue. That is, the bend toward eliminating options.

Decoloniality means decolonial options confronting and delinking from coloniality, or the colonial matrix of power. While the decolonial option is not proposed as *the* option; it is an option claiming its legitimacy among existing ones in the sphere of the political, in the same way that Christianity,

Marxism, or liberalism house many options under the same umbrella (I will come back to this point in more detail in chapter 1). And it is an option claiming its legitimacy among existing academic projects, such as postcoloniality, ethnic studies, gender studies, the social sciences and the humanities, and the professional schools; but also it is an option among options offered by macro-narratives such as Christianity, liberalism, and Marxism. The decolonial option also doesn't mean "decolonial mission(s)." Missions implied projects of conversion of achieving and end programmed in the blueprint. Options are the antithesis of missions. We—decolonial intellectuals—are not missionaries going to the field to convert and promote our form of salvation. What we—and by "we" I refer here to all those who share decolonial projects—put on the table is an option to be embraced by all those who find in the option(s) a response to his or her concern and who will actively engage, politically and epistemically, to advance projects of epistemic and subjective decolonization and in building communal futures.

That is why my argument is built on "options" and not on "alternatives." If you look for alternatives you accept a point of reference instead of a set of existing options among which the decolonial enters claiming its legitimacy to sit at the table when global futures are being discussed. For that reason, the first decolonial step is delinking from coloniality and not looking for alternative modernities but for alternatives to modernity. Not only are postcoloniality and decoloniality two different options within the same set (like it happens within Christianity, Marxism, Islamism, Buddhism, and the like, where the names encompass unity in diversity), having modern/colonial histories and experiences in common, but both are options offered in diverse universes of discourse and sensing. Postcoloniality, for example, emerged as an option to poststructuralism and postmodernity, but decoloniality emerged as an option to the rhetoric of modernity and to the combined rhetoric of "development and modernization" (from 1950 to 1970), re-converted to "globalism" during the Reagan years. Decoloniality came to light also as an option to the discourse of decolonization during the Cold War and as a critical option in relation to Marxist-dialectical materialism.

Let's explore further "options" and "alternatives": if you argue for "alternative modernity or modernities" or "alternative development," you are already accepting that there is *a* modernity and *a* development to which nothing but alternatives could exist. You lose the match before starting the game. Arturo Escobar shifted the expression to "alternative to modernities," which comes very close to "option." Thus, if you say that modernity is an option and development is an option, then decoloniality is also an option, and as "options," all are at the same level. By the same token, you highlight the privileging of one option (modernity or development) in its appearance as *the* option. Alternatives to modernity will be one step toward decolonial options building transmodern rather than postmodern global futures.[18]

And what about the decolonial option and the Left, meaning the Marxist-oriented Left? (I will expand on this topic in chapter 1.) The distinction between the two was introduced in the 1960s by Fausto Reinaga, in Bolivia, and by Ali Shari'ati, in Iran. Reinaga admired Marx and referred to him as "el moro genial" ("the genial Moor").[19] At the same time, Reinaga despised the Bolivian Left of his time, whose interests were closer to those of the ruling elite and less concerned with Indians. Indeed, the Bolivian Left did not see Indians. They saw peasants and workers.

> El Manifesto del Partido Indio de Bolivia (pib) no tiene por qué sujetarse a un modelo real o lógica formal e intelectual de los partidos politicos del cholaje blanco-mestizo de Bolivia y de Indoamérica. No es un manifesto de una clase social. Es un Maifiesto de una raza, de un pueblo, de una nación; de una cultura oprimida y silenciada. No se puede establecer paragón ni con el Manifesto Comunista de Marx. Porque el genial "moro" no se enfrentó al Occidente. Enfrentó la clase proletaria con la clase burgues; y propuso, como solución de la lucha de clases, dentro de a civilización occidental, la Revolución Comunista.
>
> En tanto que el manifiesto del pib plantea la revolución India contra la "civilización" occidental.
>
> El Manifiesto Indio no es un documento que trata de la formación y propósito de un partido político por venir [. . .] es un **ser**, un ser social vale decir, hecho vital. Y como toda agrupación de esclavos ha tenido y tiene un proceso sui generis, un proceso inmanente a la "naturaleza humana" del indio.[20]

There is no reason or obligation for the Manifesto of Partido Indio de Bolivia (pib) to follow an existing model or the formal and intellectual logic of the political parties created by the white-mestizo "cholaje" in Bolivia and Indoamérica. This is a Manifesto of a race, of a people, of a nation; of an oppressed and silenced culture. A parallel cannot be made with Marx's Communist Manifesto for Marx confronted the proletarian class with the bourgeoisie and proposed, as a solution, a class struggle within Western civilization, that is the Communist Revolution.

Whereas the PIB Manifesto proposes the Indian revolution against Western "civilization."

The Indian Manifesto is not a document about the formation and goals of a forthcoming political party [. . .] It is a **being**; it is a social being that is a vital event. And as the statement of any community of slaves went through a sui-generis process, it is an immanent process about "the human nature" of the Indian.

Two aspects of Reinaga's thought are of interest for my argument. The first is that, as he himself expressed it, his thought changed after visiting and returning from Europe. His politics between 1940 and 1960 promoted the assimilation of Indians to Bolivian society. After returning from Europe, he became a promoter of the Indian revolution. The second aspect is connecting and at the same time distancing himself from Marx, and most definitively from the Bolivian Left.[21] Shari'ati, the Iranian intellectual and activist, was much younger than Reinaga (and his life was shorter). Reinaga was born in 1906 and died in 1994, while Shari'ati was born in 1933 and died in 1977. However, the classic works of each author were published two years apart. *La Revolución India* was published in 1969, and Shari'ati's *Eslam Shenasi* was published in 1971.[22] Shari'ati confronted the Left supported by the Soviet Union, Western imperialism, and the Shah of Iran's ties with U.S. politics; he was critiqued by conservative Islamists. He advanced a new perspective on Islamism that today can be understood as a struggle for decolonization of knowledge and of being.[23] Both men used and rejected Marxism—Reinaga in the name of Indianism and Shari'ati in the name of Islamism confronted Marxism, liberalism, and Occidentalism. What saved them from falling into a plain fundamentalism was for both the "making of the Third World."

The Bandung Conference of 1955 allowed them to link Islam and the Indian cause with the struggle for decolonization in Africa and Asia. At both ends of the spectrum, both were confronting not capitalism as a type of economy, but the West as a lifestyle very much shaped of course by capitalism—but not *only* by capitalism. Shari'ati was in Paris when the Bandung Conference took place in Indonesia. Reinaga arrived a few years later, when the struggle for liberation in Algeria was in full bloom and just as Frantz Fanon published *Les damnés de la terre* (1961). A new horizon was opening up beyond capitalism and communism, between the West and the Soviet Union: it was decolonization. Half a century later it mutated into decoloniality. This book is also about this mutation.

Acknowledgments

Some of the material in this book has been published previously in different form. While in earlier printings the argument of each article was framed according to the general issue of the collection for which the contribution was requested, the articles herein have been modified to fit the overall argument of this book. However, and since these articles were written while I was working on this manuscript, they were already casting the net wide and addressing different audiences.

My thanks to all conference organizers and editors of special volumes and edited books for their invitations and for their permission to reprint.

The introduction, "Coloniality: The Darker Side of Western Modernity," was requested by Sabine Breitwieser, curator of the exhibit "Modernology/ Modernologías: Contemporary Artists Researching Modernity and Modernism," held at the Museum of Contemporary Art of Barcelona in the fall of 2009. The article was published in English and Spanish.

Chapter 2 was originally a lecture delivered at the Mellon Postdoctoral Program in the Humanities at the University of California at Los Angeles. The theme of the Postdoctoral Program was "Cultures in Transnational Perspective," 26 November 2007. The title of my lecture was "Global Futures and the Decolonial Option"—the anticipated title of the book. The lecture was later written for a collection edited by Shu-mei Shi and Françoise Lionnet, *Creolizing Theory* (Duke University Press, 2011).

Chapter 3, originally titled "Epistemic Disobedience, Independent Thoughts, and Decolonial Freedom," was published in *Theory, Culture and Society* 26, nos. 7–8 (December 2009): 159–81.

Chapter 4, "(De)Coloniality at Large: Time and the Colonial Difference," has a long history. It was presented and published for the first time, in 1999, in Rio de Janeiro, at the conference "Time in the Making and Possible Futures," which took place at the Candido Mendes University. The original title "Coloniality at Large: Time and the Colonial Difference" was intended to address and acknowledge the presence, at the same conference, of Arjun Appadurai. And it was simultaneously published in a collection of conference papers as "texts of reference." Several years later, it was picked up by Saurabh Dube and appeared in the collection *Enchantments of Modernity: Empire, Nation, Globalization*, published by Routledge in the "Critical Asian Studies" book series. This article was perhaps, in retrospect and without knowing it, the seed that ended up in this book.

Chapter 6, "The Zapatistas' Theoretical Revolution: Its Historical, Ethical, and Political Consequences," has also a long history. At the invitation of José David Saldívar, I presented it for the first time, in June 1997, at the department of ethnic studies at the University of California at Berkeley. I subsequently read it, in a modified version, at the conference "Comparative Colonialisms: Preindustrial Colonial Intersections in Global Perspective" at the Center for Medieval and Renaissance Studies Thirty-First Annual Conference (Binghamton University, State University of New York), 31 October–1 November 1997. It appeared, in 2002, in *Review* 25.3: 245–75 (a publication of the Fernand Braudel Center, the University of New York at Binghamton).

Chapter 7 was written at the request of Torrill Strands, editor of a special issue of *Studies in Philosophy and Education* (29.2: 111–27) titled "Cosmopolitanism in the Making." I expanded this version with and through a series of investigations on the "communal" (and, of course, the "cosmopolitan"). Some of this new research found in the afterword was published as "The Communal and the Decolonial" in *Turbulence* 5 (November 2009). It was printed in a German translation in *Analyse und Kritik* (April 2010).

Ideas and arguments are not formed in scholarly isolation, but in constant interaction with colleagues who share, challenge, or oppose the ideas one puts forward. This installment is no exception. The argument presented here took almost ten years of research and elaboration. The starting point was "The Geopolitics of Knowledge and the Colonial Difference," published in 2002, with the interregnum of *The Idea of Latin America* (2005).[24] First and foremost, I am indebted to some participants in the collective modernity/colonality/decoloniality, with whom I have an ongoing collaboration. Beyond the regular communication among participants in the collective, we engage in a series of workshops co-organized with other institutions, coedit volumes, discuss ideas and current world affairs, and so on, through which interactions the present version of my argument was shaped.[25] I have described elsewhere the participants in the project and my debt to them.[26] Significant publications by members of the collective that are related to or relevant for my argument here include, in chronological order, *La ley del Ayllu: Práctica de jach'a justicia y jisk'a juticia (Justicia Mayor y Justicia Menor) en comunidades aymaras* (2000), by the Aymara scholar, activist, and intellectual Marcelo Fernández-Osco;[27] Edgardo Lander's crucial article "Eurocentrism, Modern Knowledge and the 'Natural' Order of Capital" (2002), in which he inserted the question of "nature" into the overall picture of coloniality. Also Lander's *Desarollo, Eurocentrismo y economía popular: Más allá del paradigma neo-liberal* (2006), in which he brings together various ideas exploring coloniality and decoloniality; "Mestizaje Upside-Down: Aesthetic Politics in Modern Bolivia" (2002), by Javier Sanjinés, the Bolivian scholar and intellectual, trained in law and political theory; and *La hubris del punto cero: Ciencia, raza e ilustración en la Nueva Granada (1750–1816)* (2005), by the Colombian philosopher Santiago Castro-Gómez. The *hubris of the zero point*, or epistemology of the zero point, is a key concept to understand how the theo- and ego-politics of knowing and knowledge operate, and to grasp the challenge presented by the emergence of the geo- and body-politics of knowledge, which delink from the hubris of the zero point. Zulma Palermo, the Argentine literary and cultural critic, published *Desde la otra orilla: Pensamiento crítico y políticas culturals en América Latina* (2005); Enrique Dussel came up with a decolonial political manifesto, *20 Tesis de politica* (2006);[28] and Agustín Lao-Montes has introduced into the collective the question of Afro-Latinidad in several articles, but chiefly in "De-colonial Moves: Trans-locating African Diaspora Spaces" (2007). Nelson Maldonado-Torres published a groundbreaking book wherein he connects the project modernity/coloniality/decoloniality with the project of the Caribbean Philosophical Association, of which he became president in 2008; this book, *Against War: Views from the Underside of Modernity* (2008), explores in detail issues of the (de)coloniality of being and the meaning of the decolonial turn. I have worked in collaboration with Catherine Walsh for several years now, chiefly in the doctoral program she created and directs, at the Universidad Andina Simón Bolívar.[29] She recently published a book based on years of fieldwork *with* indigenous and Afro communities, as well as a compendium of her theoretical reflections over the past ten years: *Interculturalidad, estado, sociedad: Luchas (des) coloniales en nuestra época* (2009). Although the book itself reached me only at the end of my journey with this manuscript, I was familiar with Walsh's thesis through years of collaboration and from having read many of the articles she wrote and published in the preceding decade. I have an intellectual debt also to María Lugones, having collaborated with her in her superb translation and edition of Rodolfo Kusch's *Indigenous and Popular Thinking in America* ([1973] 2010) as well as in conversations of one of her ongoing projects of coloniality and gender and in the institute of Decolonial Thinking that she initiated in Binghamton. The wide-ranging intellectual drive and generosity of Colombian philosopher Eduardo Mendieta have always been a source of inspiration and encouragement. For years, he has been a partner in conversation, in the exchange of articles and ideas, and has always been encouraging and pushing me to take the next step.

At Duke University and the University of North Carolina, the collaboration with Arturo Escobar (the Colombian and anthropologist), and several graduate students in the working group on "Globalization, Modernity and Geopolitics of Knowledge," has been another site of debate and exchange of ideas that helped me in structuring the argument.[30] One result of this collaboration was the coedited volume *Globalization and the Decolonial Option* (2010), which is the first volume in English to profile the work of the collective.

I am indebted also to friends and colleagues elsewhere who have been conversant and have joined the modernity-coloniality project. Among them is Heriberto Cairo Carau, a political theorist at the Universidad Complutense de Madrid. Our collaboration started around 2005–06 when I had the first draft of this manuscript ready. This collaboration also included our coedited volume *Las vertientes americanas del pensamiento y el proyecto des-colonial* (2008). With Madina Tlostanova, a cultural critic who presently holds a position in the department of history of philosophy at Peoples' Friendship University of Russia (Moscow), I have been collaborating since the beginning of this century, and bringing into conversation the issues of coloniality (and the imperial and colonial differences) from the existence and experiences of Central Asia and the Caucasus (vis-à-vis the Russian empire, Soviet Union, and Russian Federation) and of South America and the Caribbean (vis-à-vis Europe and the United States). Resulting from that collaboration were two coauthored articles, an edited volume of *South Atlantic Quarterly* (2006), and a coauthored book, *Learning to Unlearn: Thinking De-colonially in Eurasia and Latin/o America* (forthcoming).[31]

A dialogue that started around 2005 between the collective modernity/coloniality/decoloniality and the project of the Caribbean Philosophical Association was indeed crucial. It was crucial because here I was able to see at work two decolonial projects grounded in distinct historical memories and our present inscription in those memories, and both were foundational in the history of the Americas and the Caribbean: the history of displaced people of European descent (including the massive migration at the end of the nineteenth and beginning of the twentieth centuries) and the history of forced displacement of people of African descent. Particularly beneficial and illuminating are the conversations that I have continued to have, since 2005, with Lewis Gordon and Nelson Maldonado-Torres (who participated in both projects) and, more sporadically, with Paget Henry. During this period, I also engaged in conversations with Jean Casimir, whose classic book *La culture de l'opprimé* (1982) has not achieved the recognition that it deserves. His view on Haiti and the Caribbean are strikingly similar to the views of the collective project modernity/coloniality/decoloniality. This should not be surprising: Casimir's intellectual and scholarly experience coincided with those of Anibal Quijano and Enrique Dussel: colonialism and dependency theory were common threads for all of them. But certainly many of the most rewarding experiences I have had since 2004 have been due to the intellectual generosity of Cândido Mendes, who has invited me to many of the international encounters of UNESCO/Académie de la Latinité. Through the encounters in the southeast Mediterranean (Alexandria, Egypt; Ankara/Istambul, Turkey; Baku, Azerbaijan; Amman, Jordan, and Rabat, Morocco) and in the Caribbean (Haiti), South America (Quito, Ecuador; Lima, Peru), and in North America after NAFTA (Mérida, Yucatán), I have had the opportunity to test many of the ideas discussed herein with variegated audiences in ten different countries.[32]

I benefited from colleagues and friends with whom I share interests and concerns beyond the specificities of the modernity/decoloniality project. At Duke University, Margaret R. Greer, Maureen Quilligan (Romance studies and English, respectively), and I coedited *Rereading the Black Legend: The Discourse of Religious and Racial Difference in the Renaissance Empires* (2007). I also benefited greatly from the experience of co-teaching with Bill Reddy (2004–05), whose main work focuses on eighteenth-century France, two seminars (graduate and undergraduate) on "Translations and the Limits of Globalization." Since I link translation with border thinking and border epistemology, these two seminars were extremely helpful in clarifying many ideas I unfold in this book. With Roberto Dainotto conversations continue in many directions. One conversation especially relevant for my argument involves the Southern Question, particularly in the way Dainotto has framed it in the last chapter of his book *Europe* (*In Theory*) (2007). The second conversation involves his passion for the work of Antonio Gramsci and in the dialogue between Gramsciam Marxism and decolonial thinking—ideas that we explored in a graduate seminar, "The Right, the Left, and the De-colonial," we taught together in the fall of 2009, which coincided with the last stage of preparation of this volume.

In the past five years I have benefited also from all the graduate students who attended my seminars on "decolonial thinking"; from my collaborative work with the Institute for Postcolonial and Transcultural Studies (INPUTS) at the University of Bremen, particularly with Sabine Broeck and Gisella Fabel; and in the past two years from my collaborative work with NiNsee, in Amsterdam, and in particular with Kwame Nimako and Artwel Campbell. Adriana Muñoz, a curator at the Museum of World Culture, in Goteborg, gave me the opportunity to work with Kallawaya Walter Alvarez Quispe, from Bolivia, and Carmen Beatriz Loza. Together, we authored a report about "Niño Korin," a collection of Aymara medicinal knowing and doing, acquired by Henry Wassen in the 1970s. The report examined the museum politics of labeling and the confrontation between the collector's knowledge (Wissen) and the Kalawaya's knowledge (Quispe). The experience went to the heart of the coloniality of being and knowledge, and to the need of decolonial knowing to undo unilateral Western epistemology in all spheres of life and institutions. I owe much to the late collaboration with Ovidiu Tichindeleanu, editor of the Rumanian journal *IDEA. Arts + Society*; he showed me what decoloniality means in a post-Soviet context. In Vienna the contact and collaboration with Therese Kauffman, who collaborates with eipcp (european institute for progressive cultural policies) and is coeditor of the multilingual Web journal *transversal*, allowed me to understand how to think decoloniality over the ruins of the Austria-Hungarian empire. My close work with Jens Kastner and Tom Waibel, during the translation into German of *Epistemischer Ungehorsam. Rhetorik der Moderne, Logik der Kolonialität und Grammatik der Dekolonialität* (Vienna: Turia und Kant, 2011), makes me appreciate their generosity with their time and their involvement with decoloniality. In this domain, I have also learned from Dalida Benfield, who edited a special dossier of *Worlds and Knowledges Otherwise*, "Decolonizing Digital Media/De-colonial Digital Media."

Last but not least, special thanks goes to Fred Wilson for allowing me to use his *The Unnatural Movement of Blackness* (2006) on the cover of the paperback and also for his unyielding work decolonizing the museum, the visual imaginary of modernity, and, more generally, for decolonizing aesthetics.

Needless to say, none of those mentioned above is responsible for how I interpreted what I learned from them. I remain forever thankful to them for constantly nourishing my thinking.

I will also remain forever thankful to Tracy Carhart. She endured version after version of chapters that, after being carefully edited, were not included and chapters that, after being edited, were totally remodeled. And as ever, my recognition goes to Andrea and Alex, always involved in conversations related to this or that part of the book or on disseminating ideas through the Web.

The Darker Side of Western Modernity

Coloniality

The Darker Side of Western Modernity

I WAS INTRIGUED, many years ago (around 1991), when I saw on the "news" stand in a bookstore the title of Stephen Toulmin's latest book: *Cosmopolis: The Hidden Agenda of Modernity* (1990). I went to a coffee shop, across the street from Borders, in Ann Arbor, and devoured the book, with a cup of coffee. What was the hidden agenda of modernity?—was the intriguing question. Shortly after that I was in Bogotá and found a book just published: *Los conquistados: 1492 y la población indígena de las Américas*, edited by Heraclio Bonilla (1992). The last chapter of that book caught my attention. It was by Anibal Quijano, of whom I had heard, but with whom I was not familiar. The essay, also later published in the journal *Cultural Studies*, was titled "Coloniality and Modernity/Rationality." I got the book and found another coffee shop nearby, where I devoured the essay, the reading of which was a sort of epiphany. At that time I was finishing the manuscript of *The Darker Side of the Renaissance* (1995), but I did not incorporate Quijano's essay. There was much I had to think about, and my manuscript was already framed. As soon as I handed the manuscript to the press, I concentrated on "coloniality" which became a central concept in *Local Histories/Global Designs: Coloniality, Subaltern Knowledge and Border Thinking* (2000). After the publication of this book, I wrote a lengthy theoretical article, "Geopolitics of Knowledge and the Colonial Difference," which appeared in *South Atlantic Quarterly* (2002). For Toulmin, the hidden agenda of modernity was the humanistic river running behind instrumental reason. For me, the hidden agenda (and darker side) of modernity was coloniality. What follows is a recap of the work I have done since, in collaboration with members of the collective modernity/coloniality.[1]

The Hidden Agenda

"Coloniality," as I explained in the preface and hinted at in the previous paragraph, was a concept introduced by the Peruvian sociologist Anibal Quijano in the late 1980s and early 1990s, that I further developed in *Local Histories/Global Designs* and other publications that followed. Coloniality has been conceived and explored as the darker side of modernity since then. Quijano gave a new meaning to the legacy of the term *colonialism*, particularly as it was conceptualized during the Cold War in tandem with the concept of "decolonization" (and the struggles for liberation in Africa and Asia). Coloniality names the underlying logic of the foundation and unfolding of Western civilization from the Renaissance to today of which historical colonialisms have been a constitutive, although downplayed, dimension. The concept as used herein, and by the collective modernity/coloniality, is not intended to be a totalitarian concept, but rather one that specifies a particular project: that of the idea of modernity and its constitutive and darker side, coloniality, that emerged with the history of European invasions of Abya Yala, Tawantinsuyu, and Anahuac; the formation of the Americas and the Caribbean; and the massive trade of enslaved Africans. "Coloniality" is already a decolonial concept, and decolonial projects can be traced back to the sixteenth through the eighteenth centuries. And, last but not least, "coloniality" (e.g., *el patrón colonial de poder*, the colonial matrix of power) is unapologetically the specific response to globalization and global linear thinking that emerged within the histories and sensibilities of South America and the Caribbean. It is one project that does not pretend to become the project. Thus, it is one particular option among those that I call here decolonial option(s). More straightforwardly: the argument that follows takes as its core the colonial matrix of power, and as such, the argument is one among several decolonial options at work (see afterword).

The basic thesis—in the specific universe of discourse as just specified—is the following: "modernity" is a complex narrative whose point of origination was Europe; a narrative that builds Western civilization by celebrating its achievements while hiding at the same time its darker side, "coloniality." Coloniality, in other words, is constitutive of modernity—there is no modernity without coloniality. Hence, today's common expression "global modernities" implies "global colonialities" in the precise sense that the colonial matrix of power is shared and disputed by many contenders: if there cannot be modernity without coloniality, there cannot either be global modernities without global colonialities. Consequently, decolonial thinking and doing emerged and unfolded, from the sixteenth century on, as responses to the oppressive and imperial bent of modern European ideals projected to and enacted in, the non-European world. However, as it was pointed out in the preface, the "awareness and the concept of decolonization," as a third option to capitalism and communism, materialized in the Bandung and Non-Aligned countries conferences. This is the scenario of the transformation from a polycentric and noncapitalist world before 1500 to a monocentric and capitalist world order from 1500 to 2000 (a topic I explore in chapters 1 and 2).

The Advent of a Four-Headed and Two-Legged Monster

I will start with two scenarios—one from the sixteenth century and the other from the late twentieth century and the first decade of the twenty-first.

First, let's imagine the world around 1500. It was, in brief, a polycentric and noncapitalist world. There were several coexisting civilizations, some with long histories, others being formed around that time. In China, the Ming dynasty ruled from 1368 to 1644. China was a center of trade and a civilization with a long history. Around 200 B.C., the Chinese Huángdinate (often wrongly called the "Chinese empire") coexisted with the Roman empire. By 1500, the former Roman Empire became the Holy Roman Empire of the German Nations, which still coexisted with the Chinese Huángdinate ruled by the Ming dynasty. Out of the dismembering of the Islamic caliphate (formed in the seventh century and ruled by the Umayyads in the seventh and eighth centuries, and by the Abassids from the sixth to the thirteenth centuries) in the fourteenth century, three sultanates emerged. The Ottoman Sultanate, in Anatolia, with its center in Constantinople; the Safavid sultanate, with its center in Baku, Azerbaijan; and the Mughal

Sultanate, formed out of the ruins of the Delhi Sultanate that lasted from 1206 to 1526. The Mughals (whose first sultan was Babur, descendent of Genghis Kan and Timur) extended from 1526 to 1707. By 1520, the Moscovites had expelled the Golden Horde and declared Moscow the "Third Rome." The history of the Russian tsarate began. In Africa, the Oyo Kingdom (around what is today Nigeria), formed by the Yoruba nation, was the largest kingdom in West Africa encountered by European explorers. The Benin and the Oyo Kingdoms were the two largest in Africa. The Benin Kingdom lasted from 1440 to 1897, and the Oyo from 1400 to 1905. Last but not least, the Incas in Tawantinsuyu and the Aztecs in Anáhuac were both sophisticated civilizations by the time of the Spaniards' arrival. What happened, then, in the sixteenth century that would change the world order, transforming it into the one we live in today? The advent of "modernity" could be a simple and general answer, but . . . when, how, why, where?

In the second scenario, at the beginning of the twenty-first century, the world is interconnected by a single type of economy (capitalism) and distinguished by a diversity of political theories and practices.[2] Dependency theory should be reviewed in the light of these changes. But I will limit myself to distinguishing two overall orientations. On the one hand, globalization of a type of economy known as capitalism (which by definition aimed at globalization from its very inception) and the diversification of global politics are taking place. On the other, we are witnessing the multiplication and diversification of anti-neo-liberal globalization (e.g., anti-global capitalism) movements, projects, and manifestations.

With regard to the first orientation, China, India, Russia, Iran, Venezuela, and the emerging South American Union have already made clear that they are no longer willing to follow uni-directional orders coming from the International Monetary Fund (IMF), the World Bank, or the White House. Behind Iran is the history of Persia and the Safavid Sultanate; behind Iraq, the history of the Ottoman Sultanate. The past sixty years of Western entry into China (Marxism and capitalism) has not replaced China's history with the history of Europe and the United States since 1500, nor has that occurred with India. On the contrary, Western encroachment has reinforced China's aim for sovereignty. Post-national is a Western expression that conveys the dreams of and desire for the end of nation-state boundaries and opens doors to free trade. But in the non-European world, post-national means the affirmation of an identity that preceded the birth of nationalism in Europe and its dispersion around the world. Nationalism is one form of identification confronting the homogenizing forces of globalization. Globalization has two sides: that of the narrative of modernity and that of the logic of coloniality. Those narratives engender different responses; some are being described here as dewesternization and others as decoloniality. Postnationalism in the West means the end of nationalism, while in the non-European world it means the beginning of a new era in which the concept of nationalism serves to reclaim identities as the basis of state sovereignty. The imperial partition of Africa among Western countries between the end of the nineteenth century and the beginning of the twentieth (which provoked the First World War) did not replace the past of Africa with the past of Western Europe. And thus in South America: five hundred years of colonial rules by peninsular officers and, since the early 1900s, by creole and mestizo elites did not erase the energy, force, and memories of the Indian past (compare with current issues in Bolivia, Ecuador, Colombia, southern Mexico, and Guatemala); nor have the histories and memories of communities of African descent in Brazil, Colombia, Ecuador, Venezuela, and the insular Caribbean been erased.

With regard to the second orientation, I am witnessing many nonofficial (rather than nongovernmental) transnational organizations not only manifesting themselves "against" capitalism and globalization and questioning modernity, but also opening up global but noncapitalist horizons and delinking from the idea that there is a single and primary modernity surrounded by peripheral or alternative ones. While not necessarily rejecting modernity, these organizations are making clear that modernity goes hand in hand with coloniality and, therefore, that modernity has to be assumed in both its glories and its crimes. Let's refer to this global domain as "decolonial cosmopolitanism" (to which I return in chapter 7).[3]

What happened in between the two scenarios outlined above, between the sixteenth century and the twenty-first? The historian Karen Armstrong—looking at the history of the West from the perspective of a historian of Islam—has made two crucial points. Armstrong underscores the singularity of Western achievements in relation to known history until the sixteenth century, noting two salient spheres: economy and epistemology. In the sphere of economy, Armstrong points out, "the new society of Europe and its American colonies had a different economic basis," which consisted in reinvesting the surplus in order to increase production. The first transformation, according to Armstrong, was thus the radical shift in the domain of economy that allowed the West to *reproduce its resources indefinitely*" and is generally associated with colonialism.[4] The second transformation, epistemological, is generally associated with the European Renaissance. Epistemological here shall be extended to encompass both science/knowledge and arts/meaning. Armstrong locates the transformation in the domain of knowledge in the sixteenth century, when Europeans "achieved a scientific revolution that gave them greater control over the environment than anybody had achieved before."[5] No doubt, Armstrong is right in highlighting the relevance of a new type of economy (capitalism) and the scientific revolution. They both fit and correspond to the celebratory rhetoric of modernity—that is, the rhetoric of salvation and newness, based on European achievements during the Renaissance.

There is, however, a hidden dimension of events that were taking place at the same time, both in the sphere of economy and in the sphere of knowledge: *the dispensability* (or expendability) *of human life* and of life in general from the Industrial Revolution into the twenty-first century. The Afro-Trinidadian, politician, and intellectual Eric Williams succinctly described this situation by noting that "one of the most important consequences of the Glorious Revolution of 1688 . . . was the impetus it gave to the principle of free trade. . . . Only in one particular did the freedom accorded in the slave trade differ from the freedom accorded in other trades—the commodity involved was man."[6] Thus, hidden behind the rhetoric of modernity, economic practices dispensed with human lives, and knowledge justified racism and the inferiority of human lives that were naturally considered dispensable.

In between the two scenarios described above, the idea of "modernity" came into the picture. It appeared first as a double colonization, of time and of space. I am also arguing that the colonization of space and time are the two pillars of Western civilization, and so I discuss these two crucial concepts in chapters 4 and 5. Colonization of time was created by the Renaissance invention of the Middle Ages, the colonization of space by the colonization and conquest of the New World.[7] However, modernity came along with coloniality: America was not an existing entity to be discovered. It was invented, mapped, appropriated, and exploited under the banner of the Christian mission. During the time span 1500 to 2000 three cumulative (and not successive) faces of modernity are discernible: the Iberian and Catholic face, led by Spain and Portugal (1500–1750, approximately); the "heart of Europe" (Hegel) face, led by England, France, and Germany (1750–1945); and the U.S. American face, led by the United States (1945–2000). Since then, a new global order has begun to unfold: a polycentric world interconnected by the same type of economy.

Another version of what happened between 1500 and 2000 is that the great transformation of the sixteenth century—in the Atlantic that connected European initiatives, enslaved Africans, dismantled civilizations (Tawantinsuyu and Anáhuac, and the already-in-decay Maya), and encompassed the genocide in Ayiti (which Columbus baptized Hispaniola in 1492)—was the emergence of a structure of control and management of authority, economy, subjectivity, gender and sexual norms and relations that were driven by Western (Atlantic) Europeans (Iberian Peninsula, Holland, France, and England) both in their internal conflicts and in their exploitation of labor and expropriation of land.[8] Ottobah Cugoano vividly depicted this scenario, in the late eighteenth century, when he described the imperial organization of the slave trade inscribed in the emergence of the triangular Atlantic economy.

> That traffic of kidnapping and stealing men was begun by the Portuguese on the coasts of Africa, and as they found the benefit of it for their own wicked purposes, they soon went on to commit greater depredations. The Spaniards followed their infamous example, and the African slave-trade was thought most advantageous for them, to enable themselves to live in ease and affluence by the cruel subjection and slavery of others. The French and English, and some other nations in Europe, as they founded settlements and colonies in West Indies, or in America, went on in the same manner, and joined hand in hand with the Portuguese and Spaniards, to rob and pillage Africa, as well as to waste and desolate the inhabitants of the Western continent.[9]

The narrative stages a dramatic scenario behind which an enduring structure of management and control was being put in place as these kinds of events unfolded in the sixteenth and the seventeenth centuries. Control and management means here that the actors and institutions engineering the game were establishing its rules on which the struggles for decision-making would unfold. Africans and Indians did not participate in the process. Global designs and their implementation were an affair of European Atlantic nations (those mentioned by Ottobah Cugoano). In the process, internal conflicts of interest emerged among Spain, Portugal, Holland, France, and England in connection with their vested interest in the African slave trade and Indians' land and labor. Thus, in the process the rules of the imperial internal differences (among European imperial states) were established (e.g., the invectives launched by Elizabeth I against the brutality of the Spaniards in the New World that became known as "the Black Legend").[10] These were the conditions that prompted the emergence of a colonial matrix of power.

The Formation and Transformations of "Patrón colonial de poder"

In its original formulation by Quijano, the "patrón colonial de poder" (colonial matrix of power) was described as four interrelated domains: control of the economy, of authority, of gender and sexuality, and of knowledge and subjectivity (see fig. 1). The events unfolded in two parallel directions. One was the struggle among European imperial states, and the other was between these states and their enslaved and exploited African and Indian colonial subjects.

What supports the four "heads" or interrelated spheres of management and control (the world order) are the two "legs," that is, the racial and patriarchal foundation of knowledge (the enunciation in which the world order is legitimized). I explain below—and often return to the idea in subsequent chapters—that the historical foundation of the colonial matrix (and hence of Western civilization) was theological: it was Christian theology that located the distinction between Christians, Moors, and Jews in the "blood." Although the quarrel between the three religions of the book has a long history, it has been reconfigured since 1492, when Christians managed to expel Moors and Jews from the peninsula and enforced conversion on those who wanted to stay. Simultaneously, the racial configuration between Spanish, Indian, and African began to take shape in the New World. By the eighteenth century, "blood" as a marker of race/racism was transferred to skin.

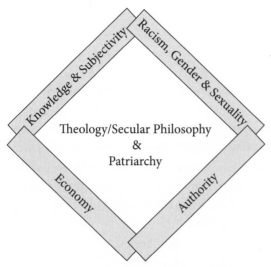

Knowledge & Subjectivity
Racism, Gender & Sexuality
Theology/Secular Philosophy
&
Patriarchy
Economy
Authority

1 Schematic visualization of the colonial matrix of power.

And theology was displaced by secular philosophy and sciences. The Linnaean system of classification helped the cause. Secular racism came to be based on the ego-politics of knowledge; but it so happened that the agents and institutions that embodied secular ego-politics of knowledge were, like those who embodied theo-politics of knowledge, mostly white European males. So, the struggle between *theologism* (I need this neologism here) and *secularism* was a family feud. Proponents of both were Christian, white, and male, and assumed heterosexual relations as the norm—consequently they also classified gender distinctions and sexual normativity.

In both cases, geo- and body-politics (understood as the biographic configuration of gender, religion, class, ethnicity, and language) of knowledge-configuration and epistemic desires were hidden, and the accent placed on the mind in relation to God and in relation to Reason. Thus was the enunciation of Western epistemology configured, and thus was the structure of the enunciation holding together the colonial matrix. Consequently, decolonial thinking and doing focus on the enunciation, engaging in epistemic disobedience and delinking from the colonial matrix in order to open up decolonial options—a vision of life and society that requires decolonial subjects, decolonial knowledges, and decolonial institutions.

Decolonial thinking and options (i.e., thinking decolonially) are nothing more than a relentless analytic effort to understand, in order to overcome, the logic of coloniality underneath the rhetoric of modernity, the structure of management and control that emerged out of the transformation of the economy in the Atlantic, and the jump in knowledge that took place both in the internal history of Europe and in between Europe and its colonies, as we will see below. Needless to say, it is not this book, nor any other or many of them, on decoloniality that will make the difference, if we (intellectuals, scholars, journalists) do not follow the lead of the emerging global political society (referred to as "social movements"). Take, for instance, the question of "nature" (which could also be flagged as the fifth domain of the colonial matrix, rather than consider it as part of the economic domain). During the past ten years, the question of nature has been debated in the collective modernity/coloniality. Shall we consider nature as a fifth sphere or, as Quijano suggested, as part of the economic sphere? It so happened that the contemplation of Pachamama (for Western minds "nature") in the new constitutions of Bolivia and Ecuador was incorporated not due to green movements, to the theology of liberation, or to Marxist anti-capitalism, but because of the simple fact and thinking of indigenous communities, leaders, and indigenous intellectuals. Now, this is part of the struggle for the control of the colonial matrix of power based on the concept of "nature" or, on the contrary, delinking from it by arguing decolonially on the basis of the concept of "Pachamama." There is no entity out there that is "better" understood as one or the other. There are different epistemic and political conceptualizations in the struggle for global futures. Thus the question is not so much where do we "file" nature as what are the issues that emerge from the analytic of the coloniality of nature (that is, its control and management) and in decolonial thinking and doing on environmental issues. There are joint efforts to contemplate, in the sense that scholarly decolonial thinkers contribute through our limited experiences and areas of knowledge to decolonial thinkers in the field, that is, in the political society and in the state, as the cases of Bolivia and, in a certain sense, of Ecuador illustrate.

We, scholars and decolonial thinkers, can contribute not by telling indigenous scholars, intellectuals, and leaders what the problem is, since they know it better than we do (and better than Al Gore does, for that matter), but by acting in the hegemonic domain of scholarship, wherein the idea of nature as something outside human beings has been consolidated and persists. Decolonizing knowledge consists precisely in this type of research. The next step would be to build decolonial options on the ruins of imperial knowledge. Two examples come to mind.

First, when in 1590 the Jesuit Father José de Acosta published *Historia natural y moral de las Indias*, "nature" was, in Christian European cosmology, something to know; understanding nature was tantamount to understanding its creator, God. But the Aymaras and Quechuas had no such metaphysics; consequently, there was no concept comparable to the Western concept of "nature." Instead they relied on "Pachamama," a concept that Western Christians did not have. Pachamama was how Quechuan and Aymaran *amauta* and *yatiris—amautas* and *yatiris* were the silenced intellectual equivalents of *theologian* (Acosta)—understood the human relationship with life, with that energy that engenders and maintains life, today translated as mother earth. The phenomenon that Western Christians described as "nature" existed in contradistinction to "culture"; furthermore, it was conceived as something outside the human subject. For Aymaras and Quechuas, more-than-human phenomena (as well as human beings) were conceived as Pachamama; and, in this conception, there was not, and there is not today, a distinction between "nature" and "culture." Aymaras and Quechuas saw themselves *in* it, not separated *from* it. As such, culture was nature and nature was (and is) culture. Thus the initial moment of the colonial revolution was to implant the Western concept of nature and to rule out the Aymara and Quechua concept of Pachamama.[11] This was basically how colonialism was introduced into the domain of knowledge and subjectivity. Twenty years after Acosta, Sir Francis Bacon published his *Novum Organum* (1620), in which he proposed a reorganization of knowledge and clearly stated that "nature" was "there" to be dominated by Man. During this period, before the Industrial Revolution, Western Christians asserted their control over knowledge about nature by disqualifying all coexisting and equally valid concepts of knowledge and by ignoring concepts that contradicted their own understanding of nature. At the same time, they engaged in an economy of brutal resource extraction (gold and silver and other metals) for a new type of global market. They also undertook a macroeconomy of plantation, harvest, and regeneration (sugar, tobacco, cotton, etc.) and did so without transgenic incentives, which engrossed the banks of Manchester, Liverpool, and London such that taking loans from Genoa bankers (as was the norm in Spain in the first half of the sixteenth century) was unnecessary.

Second, once "nature" became an established concept, the relation of man to nature displaced the European medieval concept of labor as well as all other ideas and uses of labor in Tawantinsuyu (to which Guaman Poma de Ayala devoted the last forty or so drawings of his *Nueva corónica y buen gobierno* [1616]). Working to live (or living labor, in Marx's conceptualization) began to mutate into enslaved and then waged labor. Similar cases can be found (beyond the history of Europe and its colonies) in the Islamic world and in China. All these cases worldwide had two features in common: labor was necessary to live and was not engulfed in the colonial matrix of power that transformed living labor into slavery and waged labor (enslaved and waged labor became naturalized in the process of creating an economy of accumulation that is today recognized as capitalist economic mentality). Before this, living was the necessary precondition to work. This transformation resulted in extensive enslaved trade that transformed human life into a commodity—for the owner of the plantation, of the mine, and, later on, of the industry.

The next step was the Industrial Revolution: the meaning of "nature" in Acosta and Bacon changed, coming to refer to "natural resources," the food necessary to nourish the machines of the Industrial Revolution that produced other machines (railroad and automobile) that required more food, charcoal, and oil. "Environmental catastrophe" started at this moment. While regeneration of life before the Industrial Revolution still sustained a friendly relation between the Western man of culture and the integration of labor and nature on which he built his culture, the distance grew after the Industrial Revolution and all other civilizations were relegated, in the eyes of Western men, increasingly to the past. "Nature"—broadly conceived— mutated into "natural resources": while "nature"—as a concrete noun that names the physical non-human world—became in the New World the basis for the cultivation of sugar, tobacco, cotton, and so forth. In other words, the concept mutated into one referring to the source of natural resources (charcoal, oil, gas) that fueled the machines of the Industrial Revolution; that is, "nature" became a repository of objectified, neutralized, and largely inert materiality that existed for the fulfillment of the economic goals of the "masters" of the materials. The legacy of this transformation lives today, in our assumption that "nature" is the provider of "natural resources" for daily survival: water as a bottled commodity. The mutation of nature into natural resources in the West was a sign of progress and modernization and at the same time a sign that other civilizations stagnated and were falling behind the West. Such images were pure and simple narrative constructions; that is, they were assumed to be realities represented in the domain of knowledge, and knowledge was the basic and powerful tool used both to control authority and to be transferred as a commodity. Knowledge in the colonial matrix of power was a double-edged sword: on the one hand, it was the mediation to the ontology of the world as well as a way of being in the world (subjectivity). On the other hand, as far as knowledge was conceived imperially as true knowledge, it became a commodity to be exported to those whose knowledge was deviant or non-modern according to Christian theology and, later on, secular philosophy and sciences. This combination was successful enough, in terms of the amassing of wealth and power, that by the end of the nineteenth century China and India had to confront the fact that Western men and institutions saw them as (i.e., built knowledge in such a way that they came to be regarded as) lagging behind historically; and history, for the West, was equal to modernity. Consequently, Western knowledge became a commodity of exportation for the modernization of the non-Western world.

Coloniality wrapped up "nature" and "natural resources" in a complex system of Western cosmology, structured theologically and secularly; it also manufactured an epistemological system that legitimized its uses of "nature" to generate massive quantities of "produce," first, and massive quantities of "natural resources" after the Industrial Revolution. The first was still the period of regeneration; with the second we entered the period of recycling. The industrial and the technological revolution also made possible the industrialization of "produce" and the mercantilization of food and life.[12]

It is already possible, through the research conducted recently, to trace the stages and transformations of the colonial matrix over the past five hundred years, in each of its spheres and in mutual relations of interdependence. I will offer you more examples that I have developed elsewhere.[13]

First, the logic of coloniality (that is, the logic that held together the different spheres of the matrix) went through successive and cumulative stages presented positively in the rhetoric of modernity: specifically, in the terms salvation, progress, development, modernization, and democracy. The initial stage deployed the rhetoric of modernity as salvation. Salvation was focused on saving the souls through conversion to Christianity. The second stage involved the control of the souls of the non-European through the civilizing mission outside Europe and management of bodies in emerging nation-states through the set of techniques that Foucault analyzed as bio-politics. Thus, coloniality was (and still is) the missing complementary half of bio-politics. This transformation of the rhetoric of salvation and the logic of control became prevalent during the period of the secular nation-state. Theo-politics mutated into ego-politics. The third stage—a stage that continues today—began the moment the corporations and the market became dominant; biotechnology displaced eugenics; and advertising bombarding TV, on the streets, on newspapers, and the internet, displaced the radio. Consequently, the healthy European citizen and the healthy minority in the colonies, who were managed and controlled through eugenics in the nineteenth century and the first half of the twentieth, have now been converted into "consumer entrepreneurs" of their own health by the uses of bio-technology complicit with pharmacology. The well-known insistence of former president George W. Bush to privatize health insurance and to make each citizen a private entrepreneur and a consumer of pharmaceutical and biotechnological "advancement" has been very well documented, in facts and arguments, by Nikolas Rose's description of the politics of life itself.[14] One consequence of the corporate stage in controlling bodies and converting citizens into health-consumers (that is, the politics of life itself, rather than bio-politics) is that it has engendered the "medical mafia." The stage of the politics of life itself in developed countries is indeed quite different. Here modernity cannot be separated from development, as we saw in the epigraph by Wang Hui. Rose, sometimes apologetically and sometimes in bad faith, recognizes that the politics of life itself is basically implemented in developed countries; that is, it is marketed to the minority of Western Europe and U.S. elite middle-class consumers. For the rest of the world (with the exception of each country's elite in the circle of westernization), the mutation has been from civilization to development: salvation by conversion to Christianity or assenting to Western civilization as it mutated into economic development, which was a conversion to Western economic principles, such as those of the Washington Consensus.

Second, in the sphere of epistemology, coloniality had its foundation in theology, that is, in the theo-politics of knowledge. Secularism displaced God as the guarantor of knowledge, placing Man and Reason in God's stead, and centralized the Ego. Ego-politics (the overarching cosmology on which bio-politics was founded) then displaced theo-politics (whose concern was the control of the soul, not of the body), but, in the last analysis, both joined forces to maintain the epistemic and political control of the colonial matrix. Carl Schmitt saw it clearly: political theology, said Schmitt, is not a metaphysical issue, but rather a well-grounded structure based on categories of knowledge, vision, and institutional configuration.[15] The technological revolution together with the corporate values that were prioritized in Western Europe and the United States (I leave Japan in suspension for the time being) made management itself the prime center of social life and knowledge. Corporate values require efficiency—the more you produce, the larger the gains, the happier you are supposed to be. And technology has trained its own experts who are paid to "improve" technological management of everything. In the case of nurturing and education, the technological revolution is creating a new type of subject whose "knowledge" consists in spending time to package "knowledge" according to the technological options on the menu. "Technological thinking" takes the place of thinking in general and of disciplines like philosophy and the philosophical aspect of all knowledge, reducing them to a technological packaging of options. Nevertheless, this is happening to only a small percentage of the global population: the population that has the "privilege and the benefit" of economic and energy resources that enable them to "enjoy" technology. There is perhaps 80 percent or so of the world population for whom technology is not available, and the question for the future would be whether they would have access to technological menus. Will there always be at least an 80 percent rate of exclusion? Or will the 80 percent become aware that they form the majority of the population of the planet and perhaps build a world in which technology will be at the service of humanity, instead of men and women being at the service of technology. These will be the first moments of the decolonial education.[16] In the meantime rewesternization (see chapter 1) means that human beings will continue to be at the service of technology and therefore the reproduction of the colonial matrix of power (CMP) will continue.[17]

I have provided two hindsights on the logic of coloniality, a scheme of its structure, and a few examples of its historical foundation and transformation through five hundred years of the birth and histories of Western civilization and its imperial expansion. Needless to say, I am stating that the colonial matrix of power is the very foundational structure of Western civilization. Let me now give some more specific details of the levels at which the logic of coloniality operates. It is possible to identify a number of specific historico-structural nodes in which we can see the hierarchical structure of each node. Quijano's concept of heterogenous historico-structural nodes will be understood as a state wherein any pair of items is likely to be related in two or more differing ways. In a pedagogical formula it could be said that historico-structural nodes are heterarchical, but to say so we have to decolonize the concept of heterarchy (which is defined in universal terms) and understand heterarchies crossed by the colonial and imperial differences. Once we do that, decolonized heterarchy mutates into heterogenous historico-structural nodes, crossed by colonial and imperial differences.[18] We have thus changed epistemic terrain to further describe the colonial matrix as a logical structure that underlines the totality of Western civilization; it is a managerial logic that by now has gone beyond the actors who have created and managed it—and, in a sense, it is the colonial matrix that has managed the actors and all of us. We are all in the matrix, each node is interconnected with all the rest, and the matrix cannot be observed and described by an observed located outside the matrix that cannot be observed—that observer will be either the God of Christian theology or the Subject of secular Reason.

Coming back to the heterogenous historic-structural nodes by which I have displaced heterarchy and changing epistemic terrain: I will first enumerate such nodes and then follow up with a few examples to illustrate their inter-relations. The order in which I will present them can be modified, for some will argue that economy and class relations are the foundation of hierarchies in societies, and others will argue that it is racial classification and the particular subjectivity and control of knowledge that makes possible such hierarchy through colonial and imperial differences. The colonial matrix (which manifests itself in the rhetoric of modernity that hides the logic of coloniality), remember, is tantamount to Western civilization as built in the past five hundred years, originating in the Atlantic, then expanding and encroaching on other civilizations justified by the colonial and imperial differences. Thus, the colonial matrix is built and operates on a series of interconnected heterogenous historico-structural nodes, bounded

by the "/" that divides and unites modernity/coloniality, imperial laws/co-
lonial rules, center/peripheries, that are the consequences of global linear
thinking in the foundation of the modern/colonial world (see chapter 2). Its
legitimacy is anchored in the principles of diverse knowledges as well as in
the apparatus of enunciation, which consists of categories of thought, social
actors, and institutions held together through the continuity of education.
Decolonial thinking and doing starts from the analytic of the levels and
spheres in which it can be effective in the process of decolonization and
liberation *from* the colonial matrix.

CMP then operates in a series of interconnected heterogenous historico-
structural nodes crossed by colonial and imperial differences and by the
underlying logic that secures those connections: the logic of coloniality,
which I hope will become more visible in the remaining pages of this book.
Historico-structural nodes mean that no one is independent of any other,
as any node is likely to be related in two or more differing ways. The analytic of coloniality (decolonial thinking) consists in the relentless work of
unveiling how the matrix works. And the decolonial option is the relentless project of getting us all out of the mirage of modernity and the trap of
coloniality. They all connect through the logic that generates, reproduces,
modifies, and maintains interconnected hierarchies. For that reason, I start
with the racial historico-structural node in which the colonial and imperial
differences have been anchored. Colonial and imperial differences have also
shaped patriarchal relations since gender and sexual hierarchical relations
very much depend, in the modern/colonial world, on racial classification.
A white woman in the colonies, for example, is in a position to dominate a
man of color. And a woman of color, in the colonies, would most likely join
her ethnically exploited male companion rather than join the white woman
who exploits and dominates him. Let's then enumerate some historico-
structural nodes, keeping in mind that each node is not a universal instance
but that each of them are constantly being articulated through the colonial
and imperial difference.[19]

1   A global racial formation whose point of origination was Christian Spain
    in its double and simultaneous classification: the Moors and the Jews in
    Europe and the Indians and Africans across the Atlantic.[20]
2   A particular global class formation where a diversity of forms of labor (slav-
    ery, semi-serfdom, wage labor, petty-commodity production, etc.) were to

coexist and be organized by capital as a source of production of surplus value through the selling of commodities for a profit in the world market. This particular global structure originated in the sixteenth century.

3 An international division of labor of core and periphery where capital organized labor at the periphery around coerced and authoritarian forms.[21] International division of labor was supported by the ordination of international law (de Vitoria, Grotius) in the sixteenth and seventeenth centuries.[22]

4 An inter-state system of politico-military organizations controlled by Euro-American males and institutionalized in colonial administrations (comparable to NATO).[23]

5 A global racial/ethnic hierarchy that privileged European people over non-European people.[24] While politico-military organizations were known in Europe and other parts of the world, in the sixteenth century politico-military organizations became entrenched with international law.[25]

6 A global gender/sex hierarchy that privileged males over females and European patriarchy over other forms of gender configuration and sexual relations.[26] A system that imposed the concept of "woman" to reorganize gender/sexual relations in the European colonies, effectively introducing regulations for "normal" relations among the sexes and the hierarchical distinctions between "man" and "woman."[27]

7 Consequently, the colonial system invented also the categories "homosexual" and "heterosexual" (e.g., Las Casas's [in]famous expression "el pecado nefando"), just as it invented the category "man" and "woman." This invention makes "homophobia" irrelevant for describing Maya, Aztec, or Inca civilizations, since in these civilizations gender/sexual organizations were cast in different categories, which Spaniards (and Europeans, in general, whether Christian or secular) were either unable to see or unwilling to accept. There was no homophobia, as indigenous people did not think in these types of categories.[28]

8 A spiritual/religious hierarchy that privileged Christian over non-Christian/non-Western spiritualities was institutionalized in the globalization of the Christian (Catholic and later Protestant) Church; by the same token, coloniality of knowledge translated other ethical and spiritual practices around the world as "religion," an invention that was also accepted by "natives" (Hinduism was invented as religion only in the eighteenth century).[29]

9 An aesthetic hierarchy (art, literature, theater, opera) that through respective institutions (museums, school of beaux arts, opera houses, glossy paper magazines with splendid reproductions of paintings) manages the senses and shapes sensibilities by establishing norms of the beautiful and the sublime, of what art is and what it is not, what shall be included and what shall be excluded, what shall be awarded and what shall be ignored.[30]

10 An epistemic hierarchy that privileged Western knowledge and cosmology over non-Western knowledge and cosmologies was institutionalized in the global university system, publishing houses, and *Encyclopedia Britannica*, on paper and online.[31]

11 A linguistic hierarchy between European languages and non-European languages privileged communication and knowledge/theoretical production in the former and subalternized the latter as sole producers of folklore or culture, but not of knowledge/theory.[32]

12 A particular conception of the "modern subject," an idea of Man, introduced in the European Renaissance, became the model for the Human and for Humanity, and the point of reference for racial classification and global racism.[33]

Let's take the example of language, knowledge, racism, authority, and economy creating heterogenous historico-structural nodes that transform themselves and yet remain, maintaining the logic of coloniality: the context and the content changes, but the logic remains (see afterword). I have argued this point several times in the past. Following up on Quijanos's statement that Eurocentrism is a question not of geography but of epistemology, I have backed up this dictum with the observation that Western knowledge is founded in two classic languages (Greek and Latin) and unfolded in the six modern/colonial and imperial European languages: Italian, Spanish, and Portuguese (the vernacular languages of the Renaissance and early foundation of modernity/coloniality) and French, German, and English (the three vernacular languages that have dominated from the Enlightenment to this day).[34] Eurocentrism (as imperial knowledge whose point of origination was Europe) could be found and reproduced in the colonies and ex-colonies, as well as in locales that have not been directly colonized (routes of dispersion). Eurocentrism is, for example, easily found in Colombia, Chile, or Argentina, in China or in India, which doesn't mean that these places are, in their entirety, Eurocentric. Certainly not. One will not say that Bolivia is in totality Eurocentric. However, it couldn't be denied that traces of Eurocentrism are alive and well in Bolivia, in both the Right and the Left, politically and epistemically. The same considerations could be made with respect to China. It will be difficult to convince any one that China is a Eurocentered country, although no one will dispute that the traces of Eurocentrism are still alive and well in China. The linguistic hierarchy in which Eurocentrism has been founded—which leaves out of the game Arabic, Hindi, Russian, Urdu, Aymara, Quechua, Bambara, Hebrew, and so on—controls knowledge not only through the dominance of the languages themselves, but through the categories on which thought is based. Therefore, border epistemology emerges from the exteriority (not the outside, but the outside invented in the process of creating the identity of the inside, that is Christian Europe) of the modern/colonial world, from bodies squeezed between imperial languages and those languages and categories of thought negated by and expelled from the house of imperial knowledge. If we explore how aesthetics have been conceived and defended and art practiced in the eighteenth century, we will see that the hierarchy of languages goes hand in hand with the hierarchy of knowledge and of art and literature. However, and since the Renaissance, literature and painting held hands in the concept of "representation" and in the belief in the direct connection between "words and things," as Foucault explained. Consequently, literature and painting set the rules by which to judge and evaluate written expressions and visual figurations not only in Europe, but, above all, in the non-European world. While arts and literatures were already flourishing in Italy in the fifteenth century, this flourishing was connected to the economic well being of Italy, which was based on three financial and commercial cities: Florence, Venice, and Genoa. That foundation was crucial in the sixteenth century, when European men and institutions began to populate the Americas, founding universities and establishing a system of knowledge, training Indians to paint churches and to legitimize artistic principles and practices that were connected with the symbolic in the control of authority and with the economic in the mutual complicity between economic wealth and the splendors of the arts. From the seventeenth century, European colonies provided the raw material for the foundation of museums of curiosities (Kunstkamera), which later on divided pieces from the non-European world (museums of natural history, of anthropology) from museums of art (primarily European, from the Renaissance on).

The Argument to Come

Chapter 1 lays out the groundwork, outlining five wide trajectories that will shape global futures for many decades to come, perhaps the entire twenty-first century. I describe these five projects as rewesternization, the reorientation of the Left, dewesternization, decoloniality or the decolonial option, and spirituality or the spiritual option. I am not looking for a winner. These trajectories and options coexist and will coexist in conflictive and/or diplomatic relations, some will be compatible with others and others will be incompatible. I am just saying that there is not and cannot be a winner anymore. "Terrorism" and "Wikileaks" are two examples of the point of no return, and the point of no return is that there is no longer a place in this world for one and only one trajectory to reign over the others. *Imperium* has run its course and global futures are being built in which many trajectories and options will be available; however, there will be no place of one option to pretend to be *the* option. The decolonial option is not aiming to be *the* one. It is just an option that, beyond asserting itself as such, makes clear that all the rest are also options, and, not simply the irrevocable truth of history that has to be imposed by force and fire. That is simply the political treatise, in one sentence, written by the EZLN: a world in which many worlds will coexist. Chapters 2 and 3 move toward decolonial thinking, the historical foundation of decoloniality, and the decolonial option. Both chapters 2 and 3 explore in depth geopolitics and body-politics of knowledge confronting (e.g., looking into the eyes of) theo- and ego-politics of knowledge (that is, modern/imperial knowledge). Chapters 4 and 5 offer decolonial readings of two basic concepts in the rhetoric of modernity and the logic of coloniality: space and time. Colonization of time and space are foundational for the rhetoric of modernity: the Renaissance colonized time by inventing the Middle Ages and Antiquity, thus placing itself at the unavoidable present of history and setting the stage for Europe becoming the center of space. Hegel concluded this narrative by having a main character, the Spirit traveling from the East and landing in the presents of Germany and Europe, the center of the world. The rhetoric of modernity displaces previous similar conceptions of space and time, the many "firsts" *nomos* of the earth: Beijing was the middle kingdom, as were Jerusalem and, later on, Mecca and Medina for Islam; Cuzco for the Incas; and Tenochtitlan for the Aztecs. Chapter 4 delves into coloniality and colonization of time—that is, Western time. If the Renaissance invented the Middle Ages and Antiquity, installing the logic of coloniality by colonizing its own past (and stored it as its own tradition), the Enlightenment (and the growing dominance of the British) invented Greenwich, remapping the logic of coloniality and colonizing space, with Greenwich as the zero point of global time. Chapter 5 follows up by examining the coloniality (the logic) and colonization (the enactment) of space in Immanuel Kant's *Geography*. It also follows up on chapters 5 and 6 in *The Darker Side of the Renaissance*, in which I previously examined the colonization of space. At the time Kant was delivering his lessons in geography (in the second half of the eighteenth century), the feeling that Hegel developed a few decades later was already in place: Germany was for both Hegel and Kant the equivalent of what Cuzco was in the organization of Tawantinsuyu or Beijing as the Middle Kingdom of the China Dynastic organization. Germany was, in other words, the Cuzco and Beijing of Europe. Kant and Hegel placed themselves and are well installed in the secularization of the epistemology of the *zero point* (see chapters 2 and 3 herein): the observers observing the valley from the top of the mountain. Shall I call this *panopticon*? Not necessarily: decolonially I am talking about the *hubris of the zero point*. I am talking about different histories, conditions, sensibilities, and epistemologies, since I do not believe in the universality of concepts that have been useful to account for a local history, even if that local history is the history of the point of origination of the idea of modernity and of the imperial routes of dispersion. Once again, geopolitics and body-politics of knowledge coexist with ego-politics, in which language and experience—the panopticon—was brought into the picture. Chapters 6 and 7 continue the decolonial argument that was introduced in chapters 2 and 3, and advanced in chapters 4 and 5. Chapter 6, on the Zapatista's theoretical revolution, highlights the unity of *doing through thinking* and *thinking through doing*, replacing and displacing the distinction between theory and practice. There are many issues that have unfolded since the initial Zapatista uprising, within the movement itself, within Mexico (e.g., *la otra campaña*, the creation of Caracoles, the Festival de la Digna Rabia, etc.), and outside the borders of Mexico (the government of Evo Morales, the indigenous movements in Ecuador).[35] My argument is not historical or sociological, but theoretical. Chapter 6 prepares the terrain for chapter 7 on cosmopolitanism and the decolonial option. The point is that while Kant's cosmopolitanism was conceived centrifugally (e.g., a cosmopolitan world designed and lead by and from Europe), the future demands decolonial cosmopolitanism, rather than imperial cosmopolitanism, for who will indeed take to the field and map, from the top of the hill, a new and good cosmopolitan order? Decolonial cosmopolitanism should be thought of as cosmopolitan localism, an oxymoron for sure, but an oxymoron that breaks away, delinks, from the imperial bend of Kantian cosmopolitan legacies. Cosmopolitan localism names the connector for global and pluriversal projects, where all existing nation-states and future organizations that will replace, displace, or redo current forms of nation-states, as well as the emerging political society will participate (by whatever form of organization) to a truly cosmopolitan world. This global project, without a single leader, without the G7, G8, or G20, would be—contrary to Kant— pluriversal rather than universal.

The afterword is both a conclusion and an opening up to the decolonial option and to planetary communal orders. Planetary communal "orders" are based on pluriversality as a universal project, as argued in the chapters 6 and 7, rather than on a "communal global order" (a commonwealth or a universal commons) that would be monocentric, universal, and endorse the imperiality of objectivity and truth without parenthesis. This premise is crucial to understanding my argument, for if you read my argument with the expectations created by modernity (from the Left and from the Right)— that a global order is necessary and that global order is equated with *one* project, then you will miss the main point and get derailed in your interpretation. The global order I am advocating is pluriversal, not universal. And that means to take pluriversality as a universal project to which all contending options would have to accept. And accepting it only requires us to put ourselves, as persons, states, institutions, in the place, as Ottobah Cugoano stated, no human being has the right to dominate and be imposed over other human being. It is that simple and it is so difficult. To move in that direction we need to change the terms of the conversation. Changing the terms, and not just the content, of the conversation means to think and act decolonially. Much has to be done, but the growing global political so-ciety indicates that decolonial options will increase exponentially and by so doing will contribute to remapping the end of the road to which Western civilization and the colonial matrix of power has led us.[36] Once again, the goal of decolonial options is not to take over, but to make clear, by thinking and doing, that global futures can no longer be thought of as one global future in which only one option is available; after all, when only one option is available, "option" entirely loses its meaning.

Part One

CHAPTER ONE

The Roads to the Future
Rewesternization, Dewesternization, and Decoloniality

When one puts objectivity in parenthesis, all views, all verses in the multiverse
are equally valid. Understanding this, you lose the passion for changing the other.
One of the results is that you look apathetic to people. Now, those who do not
live with objectivity in parentheses have a passion for changing the other. So they
have this passion and you do not. For example, at the university where I work,
people may say, "Humberto is not really interested in anything," because I don't
have the passion in the same sense that the person that has objectivity without
parentheses. And I think that this is the main difficulty. To other people you may
seem too tolerant. However, if the others also put objectivity in parentheses,
you discover that disagreements can only be solved by entering a domain of co-
inspiration in which things are done together because the participants want to do
them. With objectivity in parentheses, it is easy to do things together because one
is not denying the other in the process of doing them.
HUMBERTO R. MATURANA, "Biologie der Sozialität," 1985

IN THE SECOND EDITION of *The* Nomos *of the Earth in the International Law of the* Jus Publicum Europaeum (1974), Carl Schmitt
traces three possible future scenarios. His vision of the future is,
naturally and correctly, grounded on his view of the past: the history of *nomos* and linear global thinking (see chapter 2 in this
book).

The history of *nomos* is divided into two distinct eras: before
1500 and after 1500. "There always has been some kind of *nomos* of
the earth," observes Schmitt in a sweeping view of planetary history before 1500: "In all the ages of mankind, the earth has been
appropriated, divided and cultivated. But before the age of the

great discoveries, before the sixteenth century of our system of dating, men had no global concept of the planet on which they lived. Certainly, they had a mythical image of heaven and earth, and of land and sea, but the earth still was not measured as a globe, and men still had not ventured onto the great oceans."[1]

I agree with Schmitt on this count. But instead of linking and anchoring this period in planetary history to the Greek nomos, I prefer the decolonial version of "a polycentric world in which no one civilization is imposed over all the rest." There are many explanations for such state of affairs, but the fact remains that, in the sixteenth century, European men reached, for the first time in the history of humankind, a planetary view as depicted by, among many others, the Flemish cartographer Rumold Mercator, in 1587.[2] Before 1500 there was no reference point to which "alternatives" could be imagined. There were many options and interactions among people from different languages, religions, and territories. There were conflicts, of course. But the conflicts remained at local levels. Briefly stated: before 1500 the world order was polycentric and noncapitalist. After 1500 the world order entered into a process in which polycentrism began to be displaced by an emerging monocentric civilization (e.g., Western civilization). Western civilization emerged not just as another civilization in the planetary concert, but as the civilization destined to lead and save the rest of the world from the Devil, from barbarism and primitivism, from underdevelopment, from despotism, and to turn unhappiness into happiness for all and forever. In the name of modernity (the Renaissance version), colonization of space first and of time later (see chapter 4) were the two main strategies (or technologies if you wish) of management and control. Tied to both colonization of space and time, the colonial and imperial differences came into being. Through a long process, over five hundred years (1500–2000, roughly), a monocentric world order took precedence over the polycentric one. How did that happen? According to Schmitt,

> The first *nomos* of the Earth was destroyed about 500 years ago, when the great oceans of the world were opened up. The earth was circumnavigated; America, a completely new, unknown, not even suspected continent was discovered. *A second* nomos *of the earth arose from such discoveries of land and sea.* The discoverers were not invited. They were made without visas issued

by the discovered peoples. The discoverers were Europeans, who appropriated, divided and utilized the planet. Thus, the second *nomos* of the Earth became Euro-centric. The newly discovered continent of America first was utilized in the form of colonies. The Asian landmasses could not be appropriated in the same way. The Eurocentric structure of *nomos* extended only partially, as open land-appropriation, and otherwise as protectorates, leases, trade agreements and spheres of interests; in short, in more elastic forms of utilization. Only in the nineteenth century did the land-appropriating European powers divide up Africa.[3]

There are several issues with which decolonial perspectives would be in harmony with Schmitt's narrative. The difference lies in the geo- and body-politics of knowing and knowledge. That is, the concerns of a given scholar, politician, activist, banker, journalist, farmer, former slave, and so on do not meet in the universal house of knowledge where truth without parenthesis is disputed and conflict of interpretations arises. Geo-historical and biographical locations are not naturally ranked in their privilege, but they are located by the colonial matrix of power and the imperial/colonial differential order of knowledge. For example, during the same years that Schmitt published the books and the articles added to the second edition, Edmundo O'Gorman, in Mexico (precisely between 1950 and 1960), published two equally groundbreaking books: *La idea del descubrimiento de América* (1952) and *La invención de América* (1958). In both cases, the basic and strong argument is that America was not *discovered*, because there was no such entity thus named, but *invented*. It is as if Schmitt and O'Gorman were facing each other at two ends of the Atlantic, looking at how things had happened since the sixteenth century. One was looking at dwelling in the imperial history of Europe, while the other was dwelling in the colonial history of the Americas and the Caribbean. This argument has been familiar in the South American history of thought for six decades, and I have stressed the point on several occasions.[4] You may prefer Schmitt's option; but at this point it would be difficult to deny that O'Gorman has an equally valid option that has been obscured by the coloniality of knowledge that made Schmitt the quantitatively preferred option.

More relevant, however, is what one can call "Schmitt's trick," although I am persuaded that it was not intentional. That means that Schmitt took for granted that once the "new nomos" emerged, all the others vanished. He was taking for granted the very modern idea that history is singular, that there is only one historical line so that once something new appears, what existed before is superseded and relegated to the past—to history, precisely. But even if we accept this view, we have to account for two different types of erasure: first, the new nomos erased the previous nomos that had been incorporated in the history of Europe (that is, the Greek nomos); but, second, the Incas and the Aztecs did not belong to that trajectory, and their nomos (if you wish to look at their sense of territoriality in this term) was negated and discarded, not incorporated. Today we see that "the first nomos" of the earth was not "destroyed." Because they were not destroyed they are re-emerging in the twentieth-first century in different guises: as religious and ancestral identities re-articulated in responses to and confrontation with Western global designs (globalism rather than globalization). This is not, of course, to propose a return to the past but, precisely, to open up the roads toward global futures. So, let's get back to Schmitt's trick, which is in part responsible for our blindness regarding the co-existence of global histories hidden under the illusion (Schmitt's trick) that once the second nomos of the earth came, the first ceased to exist, or was left out of history and put into the museum. First Schmitt tells us that there were many nomos, which he reduces to "the first nomos." That is, he aligned the diversity of the polycentric world with a single line of Western history. For that reason, when he was imagining the future he was unable to imagine that "the first nomos" (in plural) had never been destroyed, had always coexisted along-side the "new nomos," and that now they have reemerged. Beyond the lin-earization of nomos diversity before 1500 that is Schmitt's story, there is in front of him (like O'Gorman) the view of the coexistence of non-European nomos with the linearization of time (global linear thinking) and the empty space (in the Americas and in Africa, but not in India and China—"The Asian landmasses could not be appropriated in the same way"). These no-mos that never were destroyed (e.g., think of the persistence of Tawantin-suyu in Bolivia today, grounding the revival of indigenous political society; or the reframing of Confucius's legacy in modern China; or in the attempts by Muslim intellectuals to decolonize Western translations of Shari'a and Jihad and to restore them as a proper foundation for Muslim ways of life), and they never vanished either. Thus, we all are returning to a polycentric world order only that today—contrary to the world before 1500—it is poly-centric and capitalist.

Decolonizing the Second Nomos of the Earth

The future is bound to the chains of the past. Thus, Schmitt states,

> The main characteristics of *this second nomos* of the earth lay first in its Eu-rocentric structure and second in that, *different from the first*, in its mythical image of the world, it encompassed the oceans. . . . The Eurocentric *nomos* of the earth lasted until World War I (1914–1918). It was based on a dual bal-ance; first, the balance of land and sea. England alone dominated the sea, and allowed no *balance* of sea power. By contrast, on the European continent there existed a balance of land powers. Its guarantor was the sea power of England.[5]

The Eurocentric nomos may have lasted until the First World War, but its agony extended until the Second World War, when Europe suffered the consequences of its own imperial history: the vacuum left by the collapse of *jus publicum Europaeum* was taken up by Adolf Hitler, who, as Aimé Cés-aire noted, applied to white men the same racial principles that Europe has applied, for five centuries, to the non-European population.[6] The entry of the United States as an emerging world leader after the Second World War initiated the Cold War with the Soviet Union. In that context, Schmitt was forecasting the future. If the second *nomos* ended, what would be the new *nomos*? He saw, as I have mentioned, three possible scenarios.

The first scenario, according to Schmitt, would depend on who suc-ceeds and comes out of the Cold War as the new hegemony. The divide between East (at that time, the Soviet Union) and West would be the last stage before the unification of the world—a possibility celebrated by Francis Fukuyama immediately after the collapse of the Soviet Union. But, appar-ently, this scenario did not obtain. Schmitt saw a second possibility based on the concept of *balance* of the nomos previously described: "That would mean that England's former domination of the oceans be expanded to a joint domination of sea and air, which only the United States is capable of doing. America is, so to speak, the great island that could administer and guarantee the balance of the rest of the world."[7] One could say that this is the scenario that was viable, particularly from the Reagan-Thatcher years, until the combined collapse of events that were contributed to by the Bush administration (the invasion of Iraq and the collapse of Wall Street) showed this scenario as unviable. The third scenario, for Schmitt, was no longer based on a viable and possible balance of England and the United States (which would have required a sort of transnational and transimperial hegemony), but from a combination and balance "of several independent *Großraume* or that blocs could constitute a balance, and thereby could precipitate a new order of the earth."[8] This seems to be the situation today. But it complicates the question of a "new nomos." Therefore, I turn now to explore this scenario from a decolonial perspective. What follows is the overall historico-theoretical frame in which the following chapters are connected.

Let's start in agreement with Schmitt and say that the Eurocentered nomos of the earth between 1500 and 1914–18/1945 was indeed the result of a project of Westernization (which went hand in hand with the process of building on the idea of Western civilization) that grew and expanded consistently for four and a half centuries. The process and project of Westernization did not stop with the crisis of the second nomos of the earth, between the First and Second World Wars. It continued not by appropriating land, but by managing finances and natural resources through the project of development and modernization, in two stages: from 1950 to 1970, when the project collapsed, and from 1980 to 2008, when the project revived. In the second stage, development was translated into globalism, the conceptual tool of neo-liberal designs.[9]

However, by 2000, the world was changing and those changes are clear today. The world order in which we are living is polycentric, as it was before 1500, but unlike that world order, today the various centers share the same economic principles: capitalism.[10] You can say that U.S. capitalism is not the same as European or Chinese capitalism, but the fact remains that the differences are superficial, not of the deep structure; the economic rules and principles continue to be oriented to the horizon of accumulation of wealth, which anchors the power of decisions. Some are attempting to impose, and others reject, the imposition (e.g., China's recent recasting of international relations; the Egyptian people reaching the limit of state imposition). Which means that—in the sphere of the state and the corporations—the struggle that is being fought is located in the domain and control of authority and the control of knowledge (political and epistemic struggles). "Capitalism" is not only a domain of economic transactions and exploitation of labor, but of control and management of knowledge and subjectivities. A second significant change was the emergence and growth of a global political society (often referred to as social movements) unknown during the second half of the twentieth century. During the Cold War, industrial-worker struggles beyond the United States and the Soviet Union were the most visible manifestation of dissent with governments and industries. Today, claims for economic and other material benefits go hand in hand with claims for dignity and the rights (human rights) to re-inscribe the active participation of the political society and to be in and out of the colonial matrix of power, like La Via Campesina, moving toward decolonial horizons. Decolonial horizons in the domain of the state have been at work in Bolivia under the presidency of Evo Morales, and appear in the written constitution of both Bolivia and Ecuador. In both cases the very concept of a plurinational state (with all the complications that it entails) is a clear decolonial formulation, since modern/colonial states outside Europe (where the modern/imperial state was founded) intend to displace the ethno-class of European descent that created and managed the modern/colonial state (since its inception in the early nineteenth century), and that lived behind and outside citizenship in the vast population of Indians and Afro descendants. Bolivia and Ecuador are the only two states, to my knowledge, that opened up the decolonization of the modern/imperial model of the state by introducing the crucial concept of a "plurinational state."[11] In these two cases, certain collaboration exists (amid many conflicts) between the political society and the state.

Today the historical scenario has changed, as have the perspectives through which one feels and understands the present. I do not see the future in terms of the three scenarios drawn by Schmitt (or any other alternatives), as these have proposed terms of "either/or." Schmitt's forecast presupposes that one of the three would obtain and hold the world together. The argument of this book is predicated on the belief that, in the forthcoming decades, the world order will be decided in the struggles, negotiations, competitions, and collaborations between five different and coexisting trajectories—without a winner. If there is a winner it would be the agreement that global futures shall be polycentric and noncapitalist. Which means that a struggle for world domination that was based on wealth accumulation, military power, and the pursuit of a form of supremacy that could impose its own notion of universality would yield to pluriversality as a universal project.

The first of the five trajectories is rewesternization, which has become clear since the failure in Iraq and the collapse of Wall Street. The later was manifested in the multitude of articles devoted to how to save capitalism and the future of capitalism. The second trajectory, a response to the first, I call the reorientation of the Left. The third one is dewesternization, the project that has emerged in East and Southeast Asia since the late 1990s, but that has gained strength through the support of China, not only in economic growth, but primarily in political, epistemic, and subjective confidence. Dewesternization is not an anti-Western move, but, on the contrary, a moving in a different direction, a regaining of the confidence that the West took away from it first by classifying them as the "yellow race" and second by the humiliating experience and the colonial wound impinged through the Opium War. Dewesternization is also a deracializing move by actors of the "yellow race," whose existence was not due to biological laws but to the fact that the "white race" controlled the discourse of science and of politics. I will return frequently throughout the book to discuss this trajectory. The fourth trajectory is the decolonial option, generically expressed, and decolonial options in their historical enactments, which is the topic of this book. And the fifth trajectory, akin with decolonial options, is the spiritual option. The spiritual option, offers responses not only to the materiality and efficiency of secular modernity, but also to the institutionalization and colonization of the spirituality of the institutionalized religions.[12] The decolonial and spiritual options have their domain of action and interaction in the political society, except in the Andes, where the decolonial and the spiritual options come together in the revamping of concepts like "the right of Pachamama" and "Sumak Kawasy-Sumaq Kamaña" (to which I will return in the afterword) and are being explored and enacted in the process of decolonizing the state and in the radicalization of critiques to developmental policies in the domain of economy.[13]

In what follows I describe one trajectory at a time keeping in mind, first, that each trajectory displays and discloses a series of options, and, second, that trajectories and options are not closed systems: actors can move from one to the other; the "core" of one trajectory can incorporate the "context"

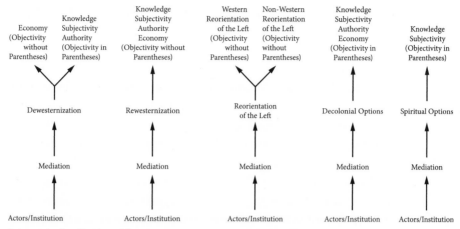

2 Schematic visualization of five current trajectories of the global order that are shaping global futures.

of another trajectory (e.g., multiculturalism in United States or Europe) means that the "context" of immigrant cultures is included without endangering the political and economic "core." In another scenario it could be that one element of the "core" of one trajectory (e.g., rewesternization) is adapted to a different trajectory (dewesternization) (as it is in the case of China incorporating a Western economy of growth and accumulation, without losing the "core" of their own identity. That means that adapting an element that is the "core" of one trajectory doesn't mean to adopt also its "context" (neoliberalism). It means that the "core" elements are not the same for each trajectory. (I will return to these issues in the afterword.) In the remainder of this book I will focus on rewesternization, dewesternization, and decoloniality.

Rewesternization

Let's start with the graphic overview of the five trajectories by examining rewesternization.

The government of George W. Bush contributed to erasing the leadership image that the United States had succeeded in building since the end of the Second World War. The three pillars of the Bush administration that contributed to its own demise were the invasion of Iraq, unilateralism in many global issues, and the collapse of Wall Street. The end of Bush's government also coincided with the end of the neoliberal Washington Consensus and the kingdom of the neo-con that had consolidated from the Reagan-Thatcher team to the Bush-Blair team. One of the many tasks of Barack Obama's administration is to rebuild the confidence the world had in the United States. I call this project rewesternization. Rewesternization touches all the levels of the colonial matrix of power. In the sphere of economy, the task is to "save capitalism," to re-imagine the "future of capitalism." In the sphere of authority, the United States is trying to maintain its leadership in international relations. In the sphere of knowledge, the United States is promoting what the country has done best—science and technology—now clearly oriented toward the corporations, which means knowledge to revamp the economy. "Knowledge for development" is the unquestioned orientation of the United States in its current project of rewesternizing the world, which is also transparent in the initiation of the World University Forum, in Davos. Of particular interest is the call for papers for Davos University 2010.[14] In the sphere of subjectivity, the financial crisis made evident how important it is for the future of capitalism to have "consumers." Consumer-subjects live in a special world and possess a certain psychology: they live to work and work to consume, instead of working and consuming to live. Working and consuming to live is a basic principle of the decolonial option, moving toward and building psychologies and subjectivities consistent with communal and pluriversal futures.

President Barack Obama's move, in July 2009, to look for a partnership with China was well in line with the trajectory of rewesternization. In March 2010, and in the same project, President Obama visited three countries in Latin America (Colombia, Brazil, and Chile), the three countries that are, in the view of the United States, the most plausible candidates to support the project of rewesternization. Brazil, however, may be not in that line but leaning toward dewesternization. As we will see below, China is already well advanced in its process of dewesternization. This also presents a good case for understanding how dewesternization works. That China acquiesced to Obama's move doesn't mean that China will follow Obama's (or the IMF's or the World Bank's) instructions; it also doesn't mean that Chinese leaders are succumbing to Obama's magic. It means that the "partnership" is for the U.S. government a move toward rewesternization; but, for Chinese leaders, it is a move of dewesternization. In a decolonial analysis of the confrontation between rewesternization and dewesternizaton, both sides of the coin shine at the surface: the hegemonic and/or dominant views can no longer erase the "de" responses, either dewestern or decolonial. This reordering of global forces, between rewesternization and dewesternization, seems to suggest a twenty-first-century tendency toward building a capitalist global order and a polycentric world. The major conflict in this scenario will be played out in the domain of authority and of subjectivity at once, for control of authority could hardly be asserted without a radical transformation of subjectivities responding to imperial differences: that is, the Western imperial idea that the yellow race is inferior to the white race could only work in the process of rewesernization but has already ended from the perspective of dewesternization. The section below will clarify what I mean.

Reorientations of the Left

Responses to rewesternization are coming from the "reorientation of the secular Left," where I see at least four internal trajectories. The secular Marxist Left has one important element in common with the "theological Left" of both Western Christianity and Islam. While in both Christianity and Islam you can find arguments showing that religion and capitalism are compatible, there are also strong arguments in Christianity and Islam arguing that capitalism is simply evil. This is a scenario in which noncapitalist futures have to be thought out in terms of pluriversality, truth in parenthesis and the coexistence of the secular and the theological (Christianity and Islam), the decolonial and the communal, and the neither secular nor theological Confucian legacies.[15] However, while theological Islam is critical of Western secularism, of the life style prompted by capitalism, and of Christianity (seen as different faces of Western civilization), theological Christianity is critical of capitalism and of secularism and of Islamism as well. And if Christianity is critical of Western civilization, it will necessarily be self-critical as well, since Christianity is one of Western civilization's basic pillars. Coexistence and cooperation would be impossible, however, if the agents in each of the theological and secular "leftist" orientations see their own as the one and only trajectory. At that point, the future will be envisioned as "my own good and best universal." For the Left, the crisis was not caused by the invasion of Iraq, Bush's unilateralism, and the collapse of Wall Street. Iraq and Wall Street are merely signposts of the crisis of capitalism and its companions, the liberal state and international imperial relations. For the secular Left, the crisis manifested itself in the collapse of the

Soviet Union. For those who subscribe to the theology of liberation, there is instead a continuity of victims of capitalism and of the poor. However, if the fall of the Soviet Union was not as critical for theology of liberation as it was for the secular Left, its demise created the conditions to increase the victims of capitalism and the levels of poverty.[16]

In between, but perhaps also continuing after 9/11, the expression "global Left" began to take hold.[17] To be sure, the spectrum of the "Left" is very wide. I would mention a few cases in which remapping the Left in global perspectives is taking place in the Western (Euro-American) and in the non-Western world. While the *history* of the Left in the non-Western world lies in the shadow of the Communist Party (that reproduced in secular fashion what Christian missionaries did in the sixteenth century, changing the content by maintaining the terms of the conversation), the Left has been reorienting itself according to their local histories, which were interfered with by global designs of the European Left. Such is the case with the New Left in China and Bolivia, and before that, the Nationalist Left in Argentina in the 1960s. The common ground among these trajectories is not only their dispensation of the directives of the Communist Party (or, in the case of China, of Mao's legacy) but also in their successful detachment from the guidance of the Euro-American Left. Today the Euro-American Left is inverting the process. Instead of positing itself as the guiding light of the Third World, it is looking for cooperation and dialogue across secular and theological lines; for example, dialogues that have opened up between Muslim intellectuals and the European and U.S. Left. They are also networking between leftist nodes established in Europe, the United States, and the Global South (for example, the World Social Forum). In this respect, this particular version of the global Left as well as the New Left in China could be conversant with decolonial projects, although each project cannot be subsumed into the other. The differences are significant, and most prominent in the decolonial rejection of any option that claims universality, or that has not yet clearly rejected the legacies of universalism in their own trajectory. Decolonial projects coexist with other trajectories, sometimes in tension sometimes in collaboration, but always stressing its distinctiveness. Why would the rhetoric of sameness prevail over that of difference? Why one would prefer "what all humans have in common is our differences" to "because we are all the same and equal we have the right to difference." Who benefits from one or the other formula? Conversations and collaborations across the aisle are possible and desirable, but the differences between projects are also crucial. Not understanding this point leads to misunderstandings and conflicts instead of collaborations.

The European Left in revamping the idea of "the commons" allows for the reorientation of previous concepts of communism and socialism. As the proletariat was reconceptualized in terms of the multitude, socialism and communism are replaced by the idea of the common: the construction of the public space as alternative to the dominion of the private in a capitalist-oriented society.[18] Proposals of the Left around the idea of "the common" shall be distinguished from decolonial ideas of "the communal" as has been argued by Aymara intellectuals in Bolivia (to which I shall return in the afterword), as well as from liberal notions of the commonwealth.[19] In a nutshell, we are facing here three similar concepts, but each is attached to three different genealogies of thought, trajectories, sensibilities, and local memories. Decolonially, there are three options that could lead to a world ruled by the assumptions that truth is always in parenthesis. And once again, there is no reason to think that one has the right to be the universal that the seven billion people in the world shall accept and run with it. They can hardly be "consolidated" or subsumed into one another. The multiplication of options, rather than the elimination of them, is, again, the road to global futures. The decolonial option is one among many existing options whose destiny would be traced by the very unfolding of different trajectories looking toward a non-exploitative world ruled by the ones who need to appropriate and exploit to live. However, the decolonial option is the one that informs this book in both its analytic and prospective aspects.

A tendency of the Euro-American Left has been to turn toward an encounter with Islamic progressive thinkers, an alliance that right-wing activist David Horowitz has looked at with suspicion.[20] Susan Buck-Morss, in her paper for the 11ème Colloque International de l'Academie de la Latinité, in Ankara (2005), asked herself and the audience: "Can there be a global Left?" The question had already a frame, and the frame was the paper she had presented the year before, titled "The Post-Soviet Condition" (2004). By this she meant not just the post-Soviet condition in Russia but also globally, since the Soviet Union was not merely a communist and imperial nation-state but one that continued the legacies of the Russian Empire after Peter and Catherine the Great. In this sense it was similar to its Western liberal enemies. In fact, capitalism and communism are both anchored in the philosophy of the European Enlightenment. As such, the fall of the Soviet Union had global consequences; one was the short-lived belief that human history had arrived at its end and from then on would be Western modernity all the way down. Therefore, Buck-Morss has alerted us that the world order in its entirety was and is living in the post-Soviet condition. It is in that context in which she asked the question. Both of Buck-Morss arguments, furthermore, were related to another awakening for the Marxist Left: 9/11. At that point, Buck-Morss made a valiant effort to extend her hand toward the Islamic world and join the rethinking of Islam, and not just the Western Left. She stated her project in a telling metaphor: thinking past terror.[21] Can it be possible, I now ask, to bring together some expressions and projects of the Western Left with progressive Islamics, after Ali Shari'ati, an intellectual leader of the Iranian revolution, questioned both the Western Right and the Left in his well-known argument on Marxism and other Western fallacies?[22] Whether some branches of the Western Left can or cannot work with Islamic progressive intellectuals is a question that would be decided in the process. What remains crucial is that progressive Islamism and the progressive Western Left are two distinct projects that cannot be subsumed into the other; neither one could be the guiding light of the other. I would be surprised if actors of the Western Left decided to follow the ideas, terms, and content of the struggles, concerns, and vision of a progressive Islamist. As for the inverse situation, Shari'ati has already spoken.[23]

A third clearly identifiable trajectory in the reorientation of the Left has emerged in and with the World Social Forum. Two of its most consistent advocates are Walden Bello from the Philippines and Boaventura de Sousa Santos from Portugal. For them it was not 9/11 that called for remapping the Left, but rather the foundation of the WTO (World Trade Organization), which began in 1995 and was of course a consequence of the fall of the Soviet Union. The WSF (World Social Forum) was a response to the remapping of imperial designs by the WTO. In the case of Boaventura de Sousa Santos, his most explicit statement bringing together the agenda of the WSF and the global Left can be found in his article "The World Social Forum and the Global Left" (2008).[24] De Sousa Santos's work in Portugal's former colonies, as well as his relentless work in Latin America, has allowed him to extend his arms, as Buck-Morss did with Islam, and work with those who struggle in Portugal's and Spain's former colonies for dignity and social justice. Lately de Sousa Santos has been very much engaged in, and in conversations with, the governments of Bolivia (particularly through García Linera) and Ecuador, conversant with President Rafael Correa's government and with Indigenous organizations.[25] For that reason his work bridges the gap between the European Left and non-European projects of epistemic decoloniality, with political implications. By this I mean, endorsing the claim of Maori anthropologist and activist Linda Tuhiwai Smith, that "decolonization, once viewed as the formal process of handing over the instruments of government, is now recognized as a long-term process involving the bureaucratic, cultural, linguistic and psychological divesting of colonial power."[26]

Walden Bello, a senior analyst of Focus on the Global South, is well known for his advocacy for economic justice. He is one of the leading critics of the current model of economic globalization. Combining the roles of intellectual and activist, he is a singularly noteworthy figure in the reorientation of the Left. His project of *deglobalization*, launched in 2003, is very much akin to many projects of decoloniality. The difference lies in the focus and in the local histories in which deglobalizing and decolonial projects are thought out and enacted. Bello's focus on the economy moved away from classic Marxist analysis. His innovative thinking and his interest in and vision for the Global South, as well as his analysis of neo-liberal globalization and the food crisis, is informed by the very history of Maritime South East Asia (next to Indonesia and Singapore) that the thinking subject inhabits. Walden Bello's work as scholar and activist is an exemplary case of the reorientation of the Left—first in his engagement with the cause of the Global South and secondly in his active role in the WSF.[27]

A fourth path within the reorientation of the Left can be found in "the modern/colonial Left," distinguished from the "modern European Left" (and always keeping in mind that I am arguing the geopolitics of knowledge and the enunciation of rather than focusing on the "universalism" of the content and the enunciated); this is an important distinction for decolonial thinking and the relevance that the geo-historical and bio-graphical politics of knowing and knowledge. By "modern/colonial Left" I mean the Left from a Marxist background, as was introduced and unfolded in colonial countries and subcontinents (South America, Caribbean, India, the Middle East, etc.). A well-discussed case at this point is the reorientation of the Left in South America, internationally known as "the turn to the Left." The figures most visible today are Luiz Inácio Lula da Silva, in Brazil, Vice President Álvaro García Linera, in Bolivia, and Hugo Chávez in Venezuela. However, the international enthusiams for the turn to the Left in "Latin" America doesn't account for Evo Morales's proximity (in his own discourses) with Indianismo and decoloniality and for Lula da Silva's joining the projects of dewesternization rather than turning to the Left.[28] In fact, the most significant effort in Lula da Silva's government is his growing role in international relations and his alignment of Brazil with the general premises of dewesternization. His role in working out a proposal for a nuclear fuel swap with Prime Minister Recep Tayyip Erdogan, of Turkey, beyond the intervention of the United States and the European Union, clearly speaks of Lula's alignment with the politics of dewesternization. Lula's diplomatic relations with Chávez, as well as those very supportive of Evo Morales, shall not obscure the most relevant decision he took in international relations. Interestingly enough, the European Left (as well as a significant number of Latinoamericanists) cannot read this move as dewesternization, but interprets it instead through the lens of the Eurocentered concept of post-occidental—the limits of the European Left to see beyond their own belly.[29]

In Bolivia, García Linera's efforts to understand the country's history and present conditions have been clearly expressed in the collection of articles *La potencia plebeya: Acción colectiva e identidades indígenas obreras y populares en Bolivia*.[30] However, by the spring of 2010, what many of us had suspected from the very beginning of the Evo Morales–García Linera government had become clear. While seeing Evo Morales's good choice appointing García Linera as vice president, we also sensed that the danger of a split and the Left's attempting to lead with the self-reassurance and belief that it "understands" Indian's demand. Today it is clear that this is not the case. As of December 2010 that tension is increasing and the split between "Indianismo" and "Marxismo" (as he himself puts it) may have reached a point of no return. Which is not surprising, indeed. The positive side of the tension is that Indian intellectuals, activists, and organizations are gaining ground and confidence in building and affirming their place in the emerging plurinational-state. Which shows once again the limits of the Marxist

Left (and white Left in general) to transcend and supercede its Eurocentrism. This shall give us pause in relation to the intellectual reorientation of the Latin American Left congregated around Consejo Latinoamericano de Ciencias Sociales (CLACSO) and expressed through several of its publications (e.g., OSAL, *Crítica y Emancipación*, and *Cuadernos de Pensamiento Crítico*) and the project Sur-Sur.[31]

Much has been said and written about the turn to the Left in Latin America. Following the patterns I am outlining here, the scenario looks different. With regard to the Left, yes, there is a clear reorientation, led first by Hugo Chávez and his advisors in pursuit of "socialism of the twenty-first century." Evo Morales appointed Alvaro García Linera to give more visibility and increase the range of influence of the Bolivian Left grouped around the organization called *Comuna*, which had been developed before the advent of Evo Morales. On one hand, both Venezuela and the Bolivian Left encouraged a revision by intellectuals and scholars of countries that had not received much attention in the past. On the other hand, Igacio Lula da Silva in Brazil and Rafael Correa in Ecuador turned their attention toward dewesternization, rather than to the Left, as I am arguing here.

The politics of both Correa and Lula make clear the ambiguous lines that Hugo Chávez has been following. They help us to understand the tensions in Chavez's rhetoric of socialismo of the twenty-first century and his politic of dewesternization; that is, between his maintaining a capitalista economy along with a decisive confrontation with the West and a leaning toward China, Russia, and Iran. Evo Morales's goverment, on the other hand, doesn't fit the politics of the Left, in spite of the orientation of his vice-president and notwithstanding that Morales was the leader of a coca labor union before the Indianist's decolonial discourse and direction began to take hold. Alongside Evo Morales's efforts, and his difficult situation in the government, the Indian nations (*pueblos originarios*) in Boliva, Ecuador, Chiapas, and Guatemala are moving in clear decolonial directions parallel to the state and are creating a strong decolonial political society.

These are some of the options and quarrels facing the non-European Left and its equivalent—progressive Muslims and radical political organizations like Hamas and Hezbollah. These same challenges face scholars based in non-Western countries, who must consider to what extent Western political theories and political economy and Western universities (as institutions and curricula) shall be the model for socio-economic organization and education (and certainly the corporate university is there in tension with dewesternization): parents belonging to the elites in non-Western countries would prefer their children to have a Western education, which would make them "successful," rather than an education that emphasizes training "good and critical" citizens. All these options are at work, in different places and in many complex ways. The diversity of trees, however, shouldn't prevent us from trying to develop a sense of the forest.

The roads to global futures shall be thought out in the scenario of inter-actions, conflicts, and dialogues among coexisting options, without hoping that one of them will overcome the other and impose itself on the rest. "Hegemony" may no longer be the success of one of the options, but the acceptance of the notion that no single option would provide all the needs to satisfy the vision of all members subscribing to other options. Thus hege-mony in the future may be precisely in the common acceptance that there cannot be one hegemonic option. The desirable hegemony is the hegemony of truth in parenthesis that defines the horizon of pluriversality as a univer-sal project. The main tasks of decolonial thinking and doing lie precisely in advancing this project, as I explain below and argue in the rest of the book.

Dewesternization

Since I will come back to this trajectory often in several of the follow-ing chapters, I will present here what I see as the overall design of dewest-ernization. The point of origination of this trajectory is not the West, but East and Southeast Asia. In this respect, it is clearly a response to West-ern modernity. Dewesternization was forecast by Samuel P. Huntington, in his book *The Clash of Civilizations and the Remaking of the World Order*.[32] Huntington saw it as an unavoidable challenge to the West, but he focused on Islam. Dewesternization includes Islam, particularly Islamic countries like Malaysia and Indonesia, but it also encompasses India and China. Al-though Huntington foresaw dewesternization as a challenge to the West, its most ardent advocate, Kishore Mahbubani, turned the plate around and appropriated the term in a radical and confrontational way that Huntington may not have anticipated.[33]

In December 2007 the editorialist Philip Stephens published in the *Fi-nancial Times* an op-ed titled "Encounter with History that Resonates Today" (see fig. 3). "Why are Chinese yellow?" Stephens asks ironically; the answer is that they are not, he replied to himself. The evidence, however, did not stop countless generations of (white) Europeans from classifying the Chinese and Japanese by the supposed hue of their skin. By the same token Native Americans have never been red nor South American and Latinos and Latinas brown before Western racial classification. I will come back to this issue. What they have in common, though, is that they fill the spectrum between white and black, reflecting a process that in the sixteenth century mapped slavery with blackness and master with whiteness. Classification of the global population by skin color was not undertaken by blacks, yellows, reds, and browns. Nor were they consulted. The process of classification was initiated and sustained by white men of letters and scientists who were the gatekeepers of Western and modern knowledge. This is not a simple curiosity, but a fundamental pillar of Western civilization and, therefore, epistemology: the geo-historical and bio-graphic foundation of modern epistemology (that is, of the idea of modernity and its darker side, coloniality). Notice the epistemic privilege of white actors and their institutions: while whiteness is one of the colors identifying certain actors among others in the global classification by skin color, it is only whites and their institutions who have established the categories and the institutions of "sustainable" knowledge; it is whites who constitute the only knowing subject who can determine classification. What I mean is that actors could be black or yellow or mestizos/as educated, trained, and assimilated to Western concepts and ways of knowing, but the constitution and the configuration of modern epistemology (sciences, philosophy, the arts, preceded by Christian theology) were a business conducted by white men and continue to be managed accordingly. Dewesternization is calling into question not just the content of Western epistemology but its very foundation: the structure of enunciation.

Stephens was careful to emphasize that those who have been classified as *yellow* by *white men* do not forget that they have been classified, while those who belong to and dwell in the memories that made possible the classification often forget. The observation is relevant on several counts. It helps in countering current universalistic claims that differences shall be forgotten because we, humans, are all equal. Generally, such claims are made by those who belong to the ethno-class that feels in possession of truth without

3 A cartoon illustrating Philip Stephens's commentary "Encounter with History that Resonates Today," which appeared in the *Financial Times*, in December 2007. Confucius, bearing a Linnaeus text under his arm, greets an oblivious Western executive or politician. Permission granted by the *Financial Times, Ltd.*

parenthesis, and who regard themselves as the embodiment and guardians of knowledge; for to classify is not only a naming of what is there but an epistemic classification and ordering of the world. The claim made by Linnaeus and taken to a hierarchical level by Kant was devised by *Homo sapiens europaeus*, who found out, in the process of classifying, that he himself was the master of knowledge and was on top of the chain of being. Kant's ethno-racial tetragon owes much to Linnaeus's classification of four human species of the genus primates: *Homo sapiens europaeus*, *Homo sapiens afer*, *Homo sapiens asiaticus*, and *Homo sapiens americanus*. Is all of this relevant today, in a world in financial crisis, a world on fire, increasing pauperization, exuberant advances in biotechnology, global warming, and so on?

What was indeed behind the scenario illustrating Stephens's argument (see fig. 3)? Behind Stephens's editorial was the two hundred and some years that elapsed between Linnaeus's classification and Kant's recasting of it (see chapter 4 of Kant's *Géographie*). There was also a shorter history behind this scenario, around ten years old: first the lecture, then the paper that was collected in Kishore Mahbubani's *Can Asians Think?* (1998).

Dewesternization is not anti-West and, consequently, its program is not to end, supercede, or replace Western hegemony with East Asian hegemony.[34]

Dewesternization is a project of conflictive coexistence between forces that share common economic principles that in the Left and Right vocabulary are called "capitalism." In decolonial vocabulary, "capitalism" is one sphere in the colonial matrix of power, as explained in the introduction that became predominant after the Second World War. While dewesternization shares with rewesternization the "survival of capitalism," the confrontation takes place at other levels of the colonial matrix of power: the sphere of authority, of knowledge, and of subjectivity. Briefly, it is not a movement of anti- but of self-affirmation. The distinction between modernization and dewesternization is clearly stated by Mahbubani: "Modernization means that you want to have a comfortable, middle-class existence with all the amenities and attributes that go along with it—clean water, indoor plumbing, electricity, telecommunications, infrastructure, personal safety, rule of law, stable politics and a good education system. As these societies modernize and become more confident, they are rejecting the Western frame of mind and cultural perspectives they have accepted, or been forced to accept, for the past 200 years."[35] The main difference between dewesternization and decolonization, and the main challenge, is not that decolonization rejects what Mahbubani describes as "modernization." Instead, the issue and the challenge are, first, to have that level of comfort in a noncapitalist economy, that is, how to modernize, in Mahbubani's word, without reproducing coloniality in such a way that not only the middle class enjoys certain basic standards of living, but also the entire planet. The second issue is that there is no essential connection between electricity, clean water, telecommunication, and so forth, and modernity. These connections are not essential, but arbitrary. For Mahbubani the problem is that these arbitrary connections have been naturalized; their arbitrary nature has been obscured and, within the ideological projects of westernization, has been made to appear part of the natural unfolding of history (e.g., modernity).

The struggle for control of the colonial matrix of power and the authority that attends such control was on display when China and India rejected Washington's instructions, thus causing the failure of the seven Doha round—which was a failure for the project of rewesternizing the world and a victory for the projects of dewesternization. These events were well publicized and helped build the confidence of both countries. In the last meeting of the G20, in London, a meeting designed to solve the global financial crisis, the self-affirmation of non-Western nations was again on display. In late 2010, while reviewing the copyedited manuscript for this book, and commenting on the failure of the Cancun Climate-Change Summit of 2010, China's leaders were shown by the media to have remained firm in their positions in the decision making that affects the global economic order. What this means is that Chinese leaders' growing self-confidence in their global role is a clear sign that the process of dewesternization is not only clearer rhetorically, but is also being enacted, for example, in disputing the control of the colonial matrix of power in Western hands since its formation.[36]

That means also that subject formation is changing not only among the governed, but also among those who govern and feel that they have been underestimated in the international order. Of course, you can rightly point out that making this argument is like noting that due to the Wall Street crisis Bill Gates and Warren Buffet had to declare losses of about $50 billion—one hardly feels sorry for them. However, in the domain of the dispute for the control of knowledge and authority, dewesternization can make a difference beyond the fact that the economy of accumulation and development is not questioned. For over four hundred years, since the arrival of Jesuits in China in 1582, the West elaborated a discursive formation that moved from a short period of admiration to a long period of disavowal.[37] Now the question is no longer about "China in the Western mind" (what the West thinks and writes about China) but about China (and East and Southeast Asia) and Chinese (and East and South Asian) minds in their relations with Western civilization (that is, what Chinese, East and South East Asian leaders and intellectuals think about themselves and about their relation to a civilization that has been encroaching upon theirs at least since the Opium War). Dewesternization means the end of a long history of Western hegemony and of racial global discrimination projecting the image and the idea that Asians are yellow and that yellow people cannot think. Like many others, East and Southeast Asians have come out of the closet, and in this regard dewesternization means economic autonomy of decision and negotiations in the international arena and affirmation in the sphere of knowledge, subjectivity. It means, above all, deracialization: it is the moment in which the yellow-other takes the field, and by taking the field vanishes as "other," because the "other" has become the "same" but with a difference: the wounds inflicted over time by the imperial difference. This means that it is not sameness by inclusion (which is the Western dream) but rather equal and separate, discrete and equivalent in power and authority, without forgetting the colonial wound inflicted by the imperial racial diffeence; the sameness lies in their equivalent autonomy, power of self-determination, and economic influence. Bearing this in mind, dewesternization and decoloniality are processes in which the distinctive features of a (formerly subjugated) culture remain in the memories of colonial subjects. The distinctive histories, cultural achievements, and unique sensibility are celebrated; at the same time, connotations of inferiority, or residual assumptions of subordination are erased. There is no attempt to return to the past, but to reinscribe the past in the present toward the future. When those who have been the target of colonial and imperial subjugation and made "others" and "barbarians" assert themselves in fullness, their claim is not to be integrated into the Western proclaimed "humanity of the same" but to delink and assert "humanity in difference." Dewesternization means, without questioning capitalist economy, that the era of "the other" has ended and that the era of "thinking without the other" has began. Thus, the affirmation of subjectivity leads to the dispute for the control of knowledge parallel to the dispute for the control of authority—that is, the management of the colonial matrix is disputed in the terrain of politics and epistemology.

Now, in the struggle for the control of knowledge, there are three domains of thought: the human sciences, or, if you prefer the U.S. classification, the social sciences and the humanities (including here all the arts); then, there are the hard sciences and technology; and finally, the professional schools that are leading the way of the corporate university. Modern epistemology is the common ground of the three dimensions and, since the Renaissance, the West has led the way in establishing its epistemic standards globally. But today dewesternization's main goal is no longer to catch up, but rather to catch up and move in a different direction. Furthermore, and as I heard it in Germany in the summer of 2007, agents of rewesternization know that the control of scientific and technological knowledge is the card the West shall play. However, the field of the human sciences is, so to speak, up for grabs, and in this regard dewesternization does not have to bend to the rules of Western social sciences, except in cases in which, in the non-Western world, the myth of scientific knowledge is still kept as a security blanket for internal colonialism (we will return to this in chapter 3). It doesn't mean that discourses of dewesternization are promoting sloppiness; it only means that there is no one way, or truth without parenthesis, of what constitutes "valid" knowledge. In fact, they ask for whom, why, when, and what kind of knowledge fulfills the needs of the community. They are appropriating English, discourses are cast in good English, they follow scholarly argumentative structures, with footnotes and bibliographies and so on and so forth. This is the terrain of scholarship. In the case of official and state discourses by prime ministers or other functionaries, the discourses follow their respective appropriate protocols, which doesn't mean that they must follow the blueprint determined by the IMF or Washington. From there to bend to the Western norms of, say, sociology, economics, political sciences, diplomacy, or nanotechnology there is a world of difference. This is a case in which the human sciences are put at the service of the issues, rather than making the issues fit the norms of the human sciences. And it is the case in which official state discourses are structured in a way that diplomatic relations have to be pursued with only one set of rules. Delinking is already taking place in this sphere. I will come back to these issues in subsequent chapters.

With the fall of the Soviet Union (and the free flight of neo-liberal globalism as one of its consequences) and the re-entry of Islam in numerous ways after 9/11 (from radical anti-Westernization to the remapping of the future of Islam) various strategies have been deployed to follow Western democratic rules of voting; some of these efforts have resulted in the democratic election of candidates from the political organizations Hamas and Hezbollah, which are not seen as democratic by the West.[38] For some in the industrialized West, democracy is a one-way street only. Facing such scenarios in contradiction with the rhetoric of global democracy, what are the options for the reactivation—let's say—of Mao's leftist program in China, since dewesternization does not question capitalism? Would such a program oppose dewesternization and support rewesternization? Would it be against both, and if that is the case, what would such a Left stand for? Would it be for re-Maoizing, so to speak? Perhaps the riddle is more difficult to solve for adherents of a global Left in East and Southeast Asia than it is for progressive Muslims rebuilding the categories of thought embedded in their languages and histories. And perhaps this is one reason why Confucianism is returning both in the sphere of the state and among the New Left.[39]

While in their search for justice progressive Muslims lead—on the one hand—a struggle parallel to Western Marxists (and I am using this expression in its most generous and ample meaning) and its non-Western adherents, they are—on the other—squarely apart from it: the histories and subjectivities of Marxism and Marxists and Islamism and Muslims are strikingly dissimilar. Muslims have a memory and a way of life, language, and religion to reinscribe into global futures, while Western Marxists belong to the same history of languages and memories as Christians, liberals, and neo-liberal. Marxism, in other words, is an outgrowth of Western civilization. East and Southeast Asian Marxists have to deal with a system of ideas that came from afar (to reject some, to adopt and adapt others) and local histories, languages, and systems of sacred and moral belief that conformed to their subjectivities.[40] It is always possible to suppress or repress feelings and to replace them with conceptual structures. It is certainly possible but it is not necessary, and it may be painful to be forced to inhabit memories that are not the ones inscribed in your body (the so-called colonial wound) since birth.

Dewesternization also permeates the public sphere, through that engine of public-sphere opinion that is the media. Debates about "dewesternizing media studies" and focusing on the "parochialism of Western media theory" entered the academy as well, not only in international relations, but in the domestic states. The dispute for control of knowledge is widespread, and with it comes the releasing of colonized subjectivities.[41]

Trajectories toward dewesternization and decolonization can be found in the wide spectrum of the Islamic world. By Islamic world (and I would use an equivalent expression to refer to the wide spectrum of the Christian world or the Marxist world or the Science world, the latter often being referred to as the "scientific community"), I mean memories and ways of living, cosmologies (e.g., Christian or Marxist or liberal or Confucian) that have been established through centuries, sometime millennia of human effort around the planet. Thus, in that wide horizon of progressive Muslims, we find that, for instance, the former prime minister of Malaysia, Mahathir Mohamad, took a definitive dewesternizing stand during his mandate, while Syed Naquib al-Attas, also in Malaysia, called for the "Islamization of knowledge" to come closer to the idea of "decolonizing knowledge" in the collective project of modernity/decoloniality (in which this book is inscribed) as well as closer to Native American claims for "indigenizing the university."[42] Or "decolonizing methodologies."[43]

Briefly, all are open questions prompted by the radical shifts that we, all, are witnessing in the world order: the dispute of the colonial matrix of power and the coming into being of strong actors, around the world, in the spheres of the state, of knowledge, and of political society.

The Decolonial Option

Decoloniality, in my argument, means "long term processes involving the bureaucratic, cultural, linguistic, and psychological divesting of colonial power," as I quoted Linda T. Smith above. These processes should lead to the "new humanity" claimed by Frantz Fanon within the genealogy of Black Caribbean thinkers. They should lead also, as a consequence, to social organizations centered on the indigenous notions of "the communal" (see afterword). The "communal" (as well as the "common" in the Left genealogy of thought, and the "commonwealth" or "common good" in the liberal universe of discourse) could coexist in a pluriversal world, a world in which truth and objectivity in parenthesis is sovereign. For there is no entity that can be represented by the common, the common good, or the communal. Neither of them shall be seen as the ultimate blueprint for the future. Instead they shall be seen as concurrent projects that could either endorse universal and totalitarian conceptions based on truth without parenthesis or could turn into the pluriversality and promote truth in parenthesis. The future of the planet, not just of Western civilization, can hinge on whether the balance is tilted in one or the other direction.

I have already mentioned the coming into being of "decolonization" in the language of the Bandung Conference (1955) and the first meeting of the Non-Aligned Countries (1961) during the Cold War. Non-alignment was already a sign of the need to delink, to break away from the idea that the world is managed by two imperial powers. "Non-alignment" and "Third World" became almost synonymous terms. They made visible the hidden face of modernity, that is, *coloniality*. Therefore decolonization became a choice by those who needed to delink rather than a decision of those who were in a condition to marginalize. In this respect Anibal Quijano redefined decolonization in terms of decoloniality when he affirmed: "It is necessary to extricate oneself from the linkages between rationality/modernity and *coloniality*, first of all, and definitely from all power which is not constituted by free decisions made by free people."[44] How to understand this proposal? Not in terms of a "decolonization as revolution" in which the state will be taken and the project of the previous state replaced by the revolutionary one without a questioning of the theory of the state and the economic rules.

It is not in that direction that, in my view, decoloniality works. Quijano's claims would be better understood by remembering the closing paragraph in Lewis Gordon's article "Fanon and Development: A Philosophical Look": "When the people are ready, the crucial question will be of how many ideas are available for the reorganization of social life. The ideas, many of which will unfold through years of engaged political work, need not be perfect, for in the end, it will be the hard, creative work of the communities that have taken them on. That work is the concrete manifestation of political imagination" (92).[45]

At this point it becomes necessary to make a distinction between decolonization and decolonialty. "Decolonization" describes, from the perspective of non-aligned states, their struggles to detach themselves from both capitalism and communism. Decolonization is a "third option," but not in between democracy and socialism, capitalism and communism. It is an option that implies the decolonization of democracy and socialism and, hence, capitalism and communism. It describes a period and refers to a complex scenario of struggles that today have become an object of study for historians, political scientists, economists, and international law scholars. Decoloniality is, instead, the term preferred by the collective modernity/coloniality (and my argument is cast within the spirit of such project) for two reasons.

The first reason involves distinguishing the historical experiences to which the term *decolonization* responded and the goals it implied (e.g., to expel the imperial administration from the territory, in order for the local elites to govern themselves). In the early nineteenth century the words employed in the colonies referring to the same ends were *independence* and *revolution*, as per the American and Haitian Revolutions or the Mexican and Argentine Independence. Toward the end of the Cold War, decolonization mutated into decoloniality (without, of course, losing its historical meaning), to highlight "decolonization of knowledge" and to cast

Eurocentrism as an epistemic rather than a geographical issue. The conditions have changed. Colonizers were no longer occupying countries. Imperialism without colonies that started in the nineteenth century became the norm toward the end of the twentieth century. Decoloniality redirected the orientation established at the Bandung Conference and that of the non-aligned countries. The focus was on epistemology rather than on taking the state. The focus became the decolonization of knowledge rather than of expelling the colonizer from the territory, and delinking from the colonial matrix of power (once again, Quijano's "extrication"; *delinking* in my vocabulary). At this point decoloniality became synonymous with being epistemically disobedient. The Zapatistas taught many of us that to change the world as it is may be an impossible task, but to build a world in which many worlds would coexist is a possible task. In order to move in that direction, of building other worlds, which are and will be coexisting in conflict with the existing dominance of the colonial matrix: to the current world order, peaceful worlds built without "their authorization" are dangerous for the sheer reason that building a world in which many worlds will coexist demands epistemic disobedience and epistemic delinking: that is precisely the irrevocable contribution of the Zapatistas' theoretical revolution (see chapter 6).

The second reason why "decoloniality" is the term preferred in the collective has to do with the complex concept of modernity/coloniality/decoloniality. "Decoloniality" makes clear that any act and project of decolonization refers to the colonial matrix of power, rather than to any indeterminate domain of "reality": "Decoloniality" is part of the triad. Decolonial doing and thinking (doing while thinking, thinking while doing) means to address the four spheres and the many layers in which the colonial matrix operates (see above). The specific meaning that the word acquires in this project distinguishes it from several other contexts in which "decolonial" is increasingly used to indicate political and epistemic projects, rather than a disciplinary field of study. Once again, it is not our (e.g., the collective's) intention to argue that our definition is the best and should replace all others. On the contrary, we (the collective) are putting a specific option on the table, the decolonial option. Decoloniality, therefore, means both the analytic task of unveiling the logic of coloniality and the prospective task of contributing to build a world in which many worlds will coexist. In that respect I am aware of the many contexts and universes of meaning in which "decolonization" is today used. My attempt is not to propose the "right one" but to be clear on "the one I embody."

I return here to the compatibilities and differences between postcoloniality and decoloniality already introduced in the preface. First of all, they have distinct points of origination. The decolonial originated during the Cold War, as explained above, and from the experience of decolonization in the Third World and in the works of Afro and Afro-Caribbean intellectuals and activists. The point of origination of the postcolonial is the experience of decolonization of British India and owes much to Edward Said's influential *Orientalism* (1978), published the same year François Lyotard's *The Postmodern Condition* (1978) appeared. Both trajectories have in common the specter of the colonial experience in the modern world, the first of the Spanish/Portuguese inauguration and the second of the British and French following up and taking over the first. The historical presence of "pueblo originarios" (ab-origines) and the massive African slave trade are two of the radical historical experiences that differentiate the decolonial from the postcolonial. Remember, I am arguing from the assumption of the geo- and bio-graphical configuration and enactment of knowledge and understanding. I am not a judge to evaluate who has more points and who is leading the competition. Although I have explored the issue elsewhere, I would just address here some of the basic features that distinguish both projects—postcolonial and decolonial—starting from the fact that both walk in the same direction, following different paths.

In South America (more precisely, the Andean region), where the modernity/coloniality/decoloniality found its point of origination (which was not the point of origination of postcolonialism) in the early 1990s, the question of colonialism was a well-established concern. José Carlos Mariátegui, laid the groundwork between 1920 and 1930. Mariátegui's referents were the history of Spanish colonialism and the indigenous question; the period of England's imperialism without colonies in Latin America; and the displacement of England by the United States, at the beginning of the twentieth century, also as an empire without colonies. The Peruvian scholar and cultural critic Sara Castro-Klárén reported that for Latin American intellectuals the publication of Said's *Orientalism* was met with mixed reactions. After enumerating a significant number of well known and influential intellectuals in South America and the Caribbean histories of thought, which starts with decolonial responses to the Spanish invasion in the sixteenth century, to José Carlos Mariátegui in the 1920s (already mentioned), and to Edmundo O'Gorman (in Mexico) in the 1950s, Castro-Kláren observes that given that background, it should not be surprising that Said's book was received with mixed reactions. It was a sort of déjà-vu although in reverse: the genealogy of thought Castro-Kláren enumerated was a response to Occidentalism (the European invention of the West Indies after the "discoveries"), and Occidentalism was the necessary condition of Orientalism—without Occidentalism, Orientalism is unthinkable. She observes:

> On the one hand, the thesis advanced in *Orientalism* seemed similar to the claims made in O'Gorman's own thesis on the "invention"—the non-referential disposition of the epistemological object—of America by the historiography of the sixteenth century. Said's sweeping inquiry was a brilliant investigation of Europe's invention of the Orient as its nineteenth-century other, and it rang surprisingly familiar themes of scholars in the Latin American field. Reading *Orientalism* produced in students of Latin America "the shock of recognition," an effect that postcolonial theory claims, takes place in the consciousness of postcolonial subjects as they assess their experience of coloniality in comparison with other colonial subjects.[46]

Thus while O'Gorman was the counterpart of Schmitt, he was at the same time advancing the line of argument that Said would popularize twenty years after O'Gorman's groundbreaking work. However, in the geopolitical ranking of knowledge, both the history and the scholarship of core imperial languages (English, French, and German) are more visible, which doesn't mean that they are more relevant. Relevant to whom? We should not remain caught in the intellectual market-bubble but remember instead the geopolitics and coloniality of knowledge.

I have already reported in *Local Histories/Global Designs* on Fernando Coronil's argument in his classic essay on Occidentalism, wherein he reminds us of a simple forgotten truth: in order to imagine Orientalism in the eighteenth century you have to have Occidentalism as a point of reference. And Occidentalism, in its specific relation to Orientalism, is a sixteenth-century invention. I will repeat more than once in the following chapter that we should get used to the fact that modern history does not go directly from Greece and Rome to France, England, and Germany, but takes a detour, the Atlantic detour. And in the Atlantic detour *Occidentalism was invented*. Following in Coronil's steps, I have claimed that the argument from Latin America should be not postcolonialism but post-Occidentalism.[47]

Recently Coronil has made a second pitch in regionalizing postcolonialist claims to—if not universality—at least to globality. He devotes some pages to exposing the imperial postcolonial appropriation of Latin America in Robert Young's global account from above.[48] None of the long history of thought that Castro-Kláren mentions is to be found in Young's account. As was and is the case with Western knowledge-making about the world (disciplinary or journalistic), seldom, if ever, are intellectual debates in the regions being reported taken into account. Beyond Europe, things also happened and people continued to think in their accustomed ways. The colonial experience in South America and the Caribbean did not have to wait until the word *postcolonialism* entered the U.S. academy in the early 1980s, after the word *postmodernism* was introduced in France. However, very much like natural resources, Third World thoughts are processed in European intellectual factories. A vigilant postmodern reader could wonder how come a professor at Duke University in the United States could have the authority to voice this opinion. Well, I am here, and here I am writing as a Latino or Hispanic, whatever you prefer. But at the same time that I am here, I am also there, and when I am there I am writing as a South American of European descent; northern-Italian to be more specific. The point of Coronil's argument has been made in the title: "Elephants in the Americas?: Latin American Postcolonial Studies and Global Decolonization."[49] We could expand the title to "Elephants, Camels, and Aberdeen Angus in Latin America?" Aberdeen Angus, yes they can be found abundantly, especially in Argentina, because of England's economic control of the region since the mid-nineteenth century; but elephants and camels, no. The problem is that if indeed postcolonial theories claim globality, if not universality, it may be problematic. For such a claim will reset the imperial pretensions that postcolonial studies critiques imperialism for. It would become an imperial design as any other. If that were the case, if postcolonial studies in England were to replicate the underside of imperial England, postcolonial studies would then compete with Marxism for global dominance! If something like that were the argument or the hidden expectation of postcolonial studies and theory, then the subtitle of Coronil's article is right to the point: "global decolonization," including decolonizing postcolonial studies.[50] Let's say that both postcoloniality and decoloniality were built on a common legacy: coloniality. In this regard there is a similarity between Protestantism and Catholicism: both belong to Christianity, but they are irreducible to each other.

However, decoloniality departs from postcoloniality as we know it today in its work beyond the U.S. academy and beyond the academy in non-Euro-American countries. Postcolonial studies has been accepted in the American academy and bounced to Germany, where by the first decade of the twenty-first century it was becoming the talk of the town. So here we need to come back to the distinction between decoloniality in *sensu stricto* (within the modernity/coloniality project) and in *sensu largo*. The term is used—in *sensu largo*—beyond the academy to project and enact (as in the case of Bolivia) the decolonizing of the state, the economy, and education—common expressions but not "applications" of decoloniality. On the contrary, the sense and the force of decoloniality come from its being used to articulate new politics of knowledge rather than new contents. The term (decoloniality or decolonization, but in the sense the word acquired at the end of the twentieth century) is used among Indigenous intellectuals around the world (from continental America to Australasia), African as well Latinos/as, intellectuals and activists, and in the United States. Indigenous leaders and intellectuals do not need white Latin Americans (that is, people of European descent) to tell them what coloniality is and what decoloniality means. In *sensu strictu*, the term is used in scholarly works and is connected with scholarly activism—a legitimate activity that should bring and is bringing fruitful collaborations between critical thought in the academy and political society, as we will see in the afterword of this book. As a matter of fact, scholars and activists are not necessarily different persons—these two are often embodied in the same person. For example, the recent publication of Kuan-Hsing Chen's, *Asia as Method: Toward Deimperialization*, introduces a new dimension in the debates on the decolonial and the postcolonial. Although the title emphasizes deimperialization, decolonization is a crucial component of the argument.

The arguments advanced in the book originated in the 1990s, the same years that the project of modernity/(de)coloniality was emerging in the Andean region of South America. In Taiwan, the creation of the journal *Inter-Asian Studies*, masterminded by Chen, marks a turning point in scholarly activism. This project makes clear that deimperialization and de-colonization (in Chen's vocabulary) emerged from the histories of the non-European world: they are not concepts that originated in Germany, France, or England and were then exported/imported to Asia. I mentioned above that the Bandung Conference was a landmark not only for decolonial struggles of the moment but also in the emergence of decolonial discourses. The epistemic break introduced by "decolonization" was spatial rather than temporal. Decolonization departed from both capitalism and communism and opened up a disobedient "third way" delinking from both. The aim of the conference was to promote economic and cultural cooperation and to oppose colonialism. China was an important player and strengthened its friendly relations with other Asian nations. However, South Africa, Israel, Taiwan, South Korea, and North Korea were not invited to the conference. The non-aligned movement was established in 1961, but the historical un-folding of world histories eroded the solidarity and the commonality of goals expressed in the conference. *Asia as Method* invites all of us to review that history, particularly because the book is structured around three main axes: imperialism, colonization, and the Cold War through which three interrelated projects emerge: deimperialization, decolonization, and de-Cold War.

Chen traces a genealogy of thought of those who addressed and still address the very history of Asia and of Western interference after 1848 in a critical vein. Prominent among these thinkers, critical border thinkers indeed, are Lu Xun in China and Partha Chatterjee and Ashis Nandy in India. But his genealogy is not an essentialist one and reaches out to the French and English thinkers in the Caribbean: to the works of Frantz Fanon and Stuart Hall. *Asia as Method* makes geopolitics of knowledge a central concern: "Asia as method recognizes the need to keep a critical distance from uninterrogated notions of Asia, just as one has to maintain a critical distance from uninterrogated notions of the nation-state. It (the method) sees Asia as a product of history, and realizes that Asia has been an active participant in historical processes" (214–15).

The statement is a corollary of a shift in the geography of knowing that the book's argument proposes: "Asian studies," in its several denominations, has been mainly carried out in the First World as "area studies." Such a division of scientific labor presupposed that knowledge existed in the First World, while the cultures being studied were in the so-called Third World.

And Asia was part of it. Now there are Asians who are doing "Asian studies" and Asia, at the same time, is no longer an object but a method, a way of looking and understanding the world. Which doesn't mean that Asians have the truth or epistemic privileges. They simply have the right to think for themselves. Chen asserts:

> The implication of Asian studies in Asia is clear. If "we" have been doing Asian studies, Europeans, North Americans, Latin Americans, and Africans have also been doing studies in relation to their own living spaces. That is, Martin Heidegger was actually doing European studies, as were Michel Foucault, Pierre Bourdieu and Jurgen Habermas. European experiences were their system of reference. Once we recognize how extremely limited the current conditions of knowledge are, we learn to be humble about knowledge claims. The universalist assertions of theory are premature, for theory too must be deimperialized." (3)

Now, what does Chen mean by decolonization and deimperialization, two concepts that are crucial to understand the significance of the two previous statements?

> By decolonization, I do not simply mean modes of anticolonialism that are expressed mainly through the building of a sovereign nation-state. Instead, decolonization is the attempt of the previously colonized to reflectively work out a historical relation with the former colonizer, culturally, politically and economically. . . . If decolonization is mainly active work carried out on the terrain of the colonized, then deimperialization, which is no less painful and reflexive, is work that must be performed by the colonizer first, and then on the colonizer's relation with its former colonies." (3, 4)[51]

Hence, when I use the term *decoloniality*, in sensu largo, I am not engaging in describing "postcolonial situations around the world," ignoring how those situations were thought out, debated, and evaluated. Rather I enter into social and cultural configurations through discourses (in words, painting, film, video, web pages, etc.) that are being produced in situ, or at a distance, although engaged with the debates in situ and not only with the events. How to get out of the illusion that if "we talk about" something beyond our experience and know only from afar (which is not wrong in itself), then we achieve a theoretical, objective, or scientific perspective that is above the closer and experiential understanding of the actors involved? The first perspective was strongly argued against, and the second in favor of, on several occasions, by Raymundo Panikkar, reflecting on his experience (as Catalan) investigating East and South Asian religions. His position is summarized in the following statement: "Diatopical hermeneutics stands for the thematic consideration of understanding the other without assuming that the other has the same basic self-understanding as I have. The ultimate human horizon, and not only different contexts, is at stake here."[52] In other words, my understanding of the other may be, and often is, irrelevant to how the ones understood by me understand themselves and of how they would understand me trying to understand them. When in this particular hermeneutic conundrum the imperial and colonial differences are at stake, the coloniality of knowledge and being comes in full force and slaps us in the face (I will come back to this issue in chapters 2 and 3).[53]

Monotopic hermeneutics assumes that objectivity and truth are without parenthesis (see section "A Summary of Coexisting Options" below). Monotopic hermeneutics and epistemology are pervasive in the project of Westernization common to the Right and to the Left. The epistemology of the zero point stems from the same belief. The Right and the Left are the two pillars of Western knowledge making that sustain academic disciplines, science, and technology; but they also support political ideologies. Decolonial projects imply border thinking. Border thinking is a particular version of diatopical thinking (or pluri-topic, if you see problems in being dia-topic and are willing to risk falling into dichotomies, as in dia-lectics); and its hermeutics articulate the particular version of experience that operates on the awareness and power differential. And the power differentials we are talking about here are the imperial and colonial differences. Monotopic hermeneutics and epistemology assumes instead that if my truth and objectivity is not that of others, then those others should be converted to my own objectivity in religion, economy, politics, knowledge, and so on, or be put out of the way by other means.

Taking the events into account and rendering them into one's own epistemic and hermeneutic frame may justify claims of "objectivity" by a social scientist who "observes" during fieldwork and who "describes and evaluates" the situation, addressing not those who are engaged in the situation, but to a community of scholars who are debating what "they" are doing and what they should really do. I am attempting to shift from the ego-politics of knowledge (e.g., the knower and the known); I am attempting to *link* (instead of delinking) with knowers who are dealing with conditions of coloniality and projects of decoloniality. Or if you wish, I am making an effort to link with all those who are delinking from truths without parenthesis.

The Spiritual Option

The spiritual option is the fifth trajectory that has to be mentioned, although I cannot at this point go into any detail. Briefly stated, the spiritual option advocates decolonizing religion to liberate spirituality. It operates mainly at the level of knowledge and subjectivity (in the scheme of the colonial matrix), but it is fundamental to the decolonization of economy and politics, since both—political theory and political economy—have become imperial tools in the formation of the subjectivity of consumers and voters that nourish and support imperial actors and institutions in the states and corporations. These trajectories (spiritual options) can be found today not only in the "religions" invented in the eighteenth century (Hinduism, Buddhism, Taoism, and the non-religions of South and North American Indians) simultaneous with the colonization of aesthesis, its mutation into aesthetics, and its *imprissonement* in the concept of the beautiful and the sublime (and then further limited to art). "Religions" can be dangerous, secular modern and postmodern thinkers state. Yes, modernity and post-modernity can be dangerous too. There is no safe place. Spirituality can be found beyond religions (in the etymological sense of the word, which means "community building," not only in its sacred dimension) and can also be found in hip-hop and in Latinas' "artistic" expressions.[54] The common ground for all these re-inscriptions of spirituality is the desire to find ways of life beyond capitalism and its magic of modernity and development that keep consumers caught in the promises of dreamworlds. What the spiritual option offers is the contribution of opening up horizons of life that have been kept hostage (that is, colonized) by modernity, capitalism, and the belief in the superiority of Western civilization. Hardcore materialists tend to look at spirituality as related to "new age" or to soft and romantic revolutionaries. By such arguments, progressive secular intellectuals indirectly support capitalist's arguments for modernity and development. I see the spiritual option differently. My own view has been informed, among others advancing the spiritual option, by Native American epistemology. Andrea Smith provides, for instance, a succinct and groundbreaking connection between spirituality and land that neither Christians, liberals, nor Marxists may be ready to accept. Summarizing Gabrielle Tayat, she says, "Intolerance toward Indian religions cannot be addressed by educating white people about our spiritual beliefs, because our religious oppression is not based on ignorance but on the seizure of Indian lands upon which Indian spiritualities are based."[55]

There are many threads through which the spiritual option is being re-inscribed into the global debates toward equal, equitable futures in search of fullness and plenitude without the anxiety of being surrounded by commodities and being the first in whatever sphere of life. I would limit myself to a few cases. The most striking and less understood by liberal, neoliberal, postmodern, and Marxist tendencies (in general), are indigenous/Native American sustained decolonial arguments that connect land with spirituality and not with commodity, and which also disconnect "buen vivir/to live in harmony" from development. On this last topic I will return in the afterword. On spirituality and the land I would like to remind you of Reverend Steven Charleston, a man of spoken rather than written words. One of his influential essays, "From Medicine Man to Marx," has caught the attention of the FBI. Subsequently, Charleston seemed to show regret for using Marxist terminology to express Indians concerns. Certainly he did not need Marx to make his point. He did it, I surmise from his argument, to connect with black theology, through Cornel West. But instead of getting the attention of Marxist and black theologians, he got the attention of the FBI.

The main point of the essays should not be dismissed, as Reverend Charleston is not the only one who has been connecting land and ecology to spirituality. As Charleston observes in his essays, Native Americans are pleased when Anglo-white New Age followers approach Indian spirituality to weaken the guilt of an affluent society; but when it becomes clear that the spirituality is connected to land and that that land is not conceived as a commodity nor as private property nor as provider of natural resources, then spirituality changes face. It is an-other spirituality, a decolonial spirituality that is not only confronting modernity but also proposing to delink from it. The problem is that the democratic forces of capitalist and modern societies won't allow any lifestyle that is not capitalist to prosper. Even progressive intellectuals support capitalism by critiquing the outmoded, traditional, romantic, Arcadian potentials of indigenous spirituality. After all, we know that since 1492, indigenous people all around the world have been thought of as barbarians; and furthermore, in the eighteenth century they became primitives.[56] Many people still think so today.

Smith adds, "Spirituality, then, is not something to be purchased by paying $300 for a pipe ceremony. Instead, it is a way of living in 'right relations' with the awareness that everything one does affects everything else."[57] It is a road to re-existence delinking from the beliefs that modernity and development are the only way to the future. In the South American Andes, the expression *sumak kawsay* (see afterword) expresses a similar philosophy. If this philosophy were to guide the behavior of decision makers, if "we" were to move to become decision makers, then the world would no longer have to endure slavery, holocausts, corporate-based environmental disasters (e.g., BP in the Gulf of Mexico), or Wall Street philosophies of life that consist in making money by taking it away from people and by exploiting natural resources to produce artificial commodities. That land goes hand-in-hand with spirituality should be the starting point of the spiritual option. Briefly, if some doubt remains that "spirituality" today is being recast among radical indigenous intellectuals (in North, Central, and South America), I would refer, in the United States, beyond Reverend Steven Charleston, already mentioned, the arguments advanced by Vine Deloria, Jr, the Reverend George E. Tinker, and educator Gregory Cajete.[58] In South America, spirituality is being recast in a different vocabulary, that of "Sumak Kawsay" and the "right of Pachamama" issues. Monica Chuji, an indigenous Kichua activist from the Amazon and ex-assembly member of the Rafael Correa government in Ecuador, is one of the strongest advocates of a line of reasoning akin to Native Americans and Maories in New Zealand; hers is an activism of many oral and written discourses.[59]

Among the religious unfoldings of the spiritual option, Nurculuk should be mentioned. Nurculuk originated in Turkey, after the formation of the republic and in dissidence with the extreme Westernizing influence of Said Nursî (1877–1960). Nurculuk's current leader is Fetullah Gülen, inarguably the most influential Muslim scholar and activist today. He has been deemed by *Public Policy* to be among the "Top 100 Public Intellectuals." If the point of origination of Nurculuk is Turkey, the routes of the project's dispersion can be located in more than one hundred countries, in several hundred educational institutions, and in its millions of followers around the world. Basically, Nurculuk has become a "faith-inspired collectivity." Gülen has been so influential that the Nurculuk project has come to be known as "the Gülen movement."[60] One line of thought and struggle that nourishes the movement is, in the words of its leader, that community's survival depends on idealism and good morals, as well as on being able to reach the necessary level in scientific and technological progress: that dominant Western civilization has lost the good morals, and that many Muslim movements lack the necessary interest in science and technology. This is another scenario in which the spiritual option is being played out.

A Summary of Coexisting Options

Figure 2 (page 35) summarizes what I described in the previous section as the five trajectories toward the future.

At the bottom of the five trajectories we have *actors* and *institutions*, each of them inserted in regional histories that could last either millennia or just four or five centuries. In order to implement each project, each trajectory has to go through *mediations*. By mediations, I mean knowledge in its most general sense. Westernization, the historical unfolding since the sixteenth century, and the invention of Indias Occidentale (later on renamed America), went hand in hand with the coming into being of the colonial matrix of power. Knowledge in its most general sense means the complex of knowledge-made, but also the basic principles by which knowledge is made. In the sixteenth century, Westernization had two complementary epistemic trajectories. One trajectory was internal to the history of Europe itself—Europe as the land of Japheth at the West of Jerusalem upon which the idea of the West and of Western civilization rest (see map 1 on page 66).

The other trajectory unfolds in the process of conquering and colonizing Indias Occidentales. These two broad trajectories of knowledge supported arguments that oriented and justified the actions of Western expansion that in their turn reverted to the need for further knowledge making and leadership from the Renaissance to the Enlightenment. Westernization (the expansion of the West) means, in the realm of mediation, that the control

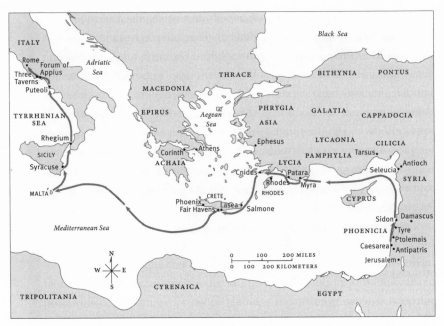

Map 1 Saint Paul's journey to "the West" of Jerusalem, A.D. 58–63.

of knowledge implies and disavows other forms of knowing and living. Dewesternizaton and decolonization operate at the level of mediations and the control and management of knowledge. Both projects' goal is to delink from it. But they (heterogeneous, complex, and diverse as they are) have to build on what Westernization disavowed by in-corporating Western contributions to human civilization into dewesternizing and decolonial projects. Thus, border thinking (or border gnosis or border epistemology: three different expressions, one overall meaning) is common to both dewesternization and decoloniality. The aims of each trajectory, however, are not.

Thus the fundamental component of mediation in the trajectory of Westernization was and still is the colonial matrix of power, which emerged in the process of European conquest and colonization of Indias Occidentales/America and reverted in the making of Europe itself. There would be no Europe without the discovery and conquest of America and the colonial matrix of power. That is why modernity/coloniality are two sides of the same coin. The colonial matrix is therefore a structure not only of management and control of the non-Euro-American world, but of the making of Europe itself and of defining the terms of the conversations in which the non-Euro-American world was brought in. Modernity/coloniality brings forward the complex entanglement of heterogenous historico-structural nodes, rather than a dichotomy between the West and the rest. Hence, both dewesternization and decoloniality have to acknowledge that if Western civilization and hence modernity are not the totality, they defined the terms of the conversations with which both "Ds" (dewesternization and decolonization), and, consequently, the reorientation of the Left have also to deal. Aimé Césaire saw it clearly, explaining that for Europeans the horror of Nazism was the horror not only of killing, but of killing white people based on the arguments and strategies that Europe had applied for 450 years to the non-European world. In this sense, Europe (and its extension to America) is not a direct line (as I said, and will keep reminding you, the direct line goes from Athens and Rome to Western Europe), but a detour line that deviates toward the Atlantic and reverts to Europe. John Locke and Immanuel Kant are not deriving their thoughts directly from Greek political theory and philosophy but from the enormous consequences of the "detour" through the Atlantic in Western and world history.

Disputes for knowledge are fought at the level of mediations. For it is in knowledge-making and argument-building that decisions take place. Westernization was on its own for five hundred years, building knowledge and expanding, disavowing all other mediating epistemologies. Today this is no longer possible, because the set of mediations (the rhetoric of modernity and the logic of coloniality) on which the West built itself as such and by which it expanded, were protested but not contested. Today they are not only protested, but also contested: dewesternization and decolonial knowledge-making and delinking from Westernization (e.g., the celebration of "development" in Western mediations and growing epistemic contestations of development as understood in Western terms, from the perspective of both dewesternization and decoloniality, as I describe in the afterword). This means that the colonial matrix of power is no longer totally managed by Western states and corporations. Because the dispute for the control of authority and of knowledge will be the battlefield of the twenty-first century, both at the spheres of the states and of the global political societies, sometimes confronting the state, sometimes moving along with the state (like in Bolivia today), there is the need to *rewesternize*.

Rewesternization is moved by two impulses: one is its own internal crisis of mismanagement, miscalculation, and misunderstanding (e.g., the invasion of Iraq, the collapse of Wall Street): Western leaders in all fields reached the limits of their own political decisions manifested in their own incapacity to anticipate the consequences of supporting a type of economy that encourages outlaw procedures in order to increase gains (e.g., the conditions leading to the collapse of Wall Street). And the second is to understand and repair the consequences of Western aggression (many times in complicity with local leaders): violent anti-imperialism, dewesternization, decoloniality, and the reinscription of spirituality are among the most striking responses to date. These are the conditions today not just to imagine but to understand that the world is moving toward a polycentric third nomos. It means that "the first nomos of the earth" (in Schmitt's one-line chronology following the appearance of the "second nomos") is being reinscribed at once incorporating the contributions of Western modernity—chiefly the idea of emancipation and of independent thoughts—and detaching from its imperial antitotalitarian dreams. And here lies the radical difference between Schmitt's third scenario toward the future, in which the polycentric balance did not take into account the reinscription of the plurality of existing nomos before the coming of the "second" one, in 1500.

Epistemic struggles take place in the spheres of epistemic mediations and geopolitics of knowledge—for example, the cosmology upon which corporations justify the expropriation of lands, and the cosmology upon which Indigenous projects of resistence and re-existence build their arguments. Violent physical responses to the physical violence of the corporations had to be mediated by strong arguments delinking from the knowledge upon which the corporations justify their actions. It is not just the action of the corporations. Arguments are built, for example, in economic knowledge stating that economic growth is necessary for the well-being of humanity but that at the same time developing underdeveloped lands that indigenous people do not develop (developing here understood in terms of Western mediating discourse and cosmology of development) is detrimental for humanity. We can cite many examples, including the recent oil spill in the Gulf of Mexico by BP, and the long-lasting lawsuit of Chevron/Texaco in Ecuador, or the Shell pipelines in Rossport, Ireland, etc., over their serious damages to local populations, all in the name of improving economic and human conditions. Here is where you see the rhetoric of modernity and the logic of coloniality working at their best to the benefit of the corporations. On the other side of the spectrum, indigenous intellectuals and leaders dispute the universality of that knowledge, and build counter-arguments based on their own conception of living in harmony and in fullness (Sumak Kawsay) rather than in competition to be the best, the first, and the richest. The horizon of the communal emerges as a distinctive orientation toward possible futures in which decolonial options are embedded.

Dewesternizing arguments build on over five centuries of Western suspicion and denial of Asians' mediations while decoloniality builds on five centuries of Western denial of African humanity in Africa and Indian humanity in the "New" World. In between dewesternization and decoloniality, sectors of Islam can be identified that are in confrontation with Western modernity and that are leaning either toward dewesternizing (like in Malasya and Indonesia) or into decolonial arguments (mostly emerging among Iranian intellectuals based in Iran or abroad), depending on their attitude toward the compatibility, or lack thereof, between Islamic and Western liberal worldviews.

Actors can move and institutions engage in many different and complex interactions. However, the distinctiveness of the five trajectories should not be lost. For example, there is no obligation of divine deterministic forces that will push a given actor who was educated in the trajectory of Westernization to remain in it and be loyal to it. Actors have many options. Actors formed and educated in Western cosmology can support Westernization and rewesternization, or they could become decolonial thinkers and actors. Similarly, actors born and educated in Eastern cosmology and colonial histories can opt to move and endorse Westernization in the past and rewesternization in the present and future. There is no one-to-one relation between actors and trajectories, although actors make their options at the intersections of their biography, their desires, and the available option. The same could be said with respect to decoloniality. Trajectories are not *essentially* linked to actors, and actors could move from one trajectory to the other during their life, although they are marked, in a sense, with collective and individual identities by their imperial and colonial differences. However, because trajectories are options and not essential forces, we are here moving toward the terrain of *identity in politics*, rather than *identity politics* (which, of course, is another option).[61] A key factor for distinguishing between the five complex trajectories, beyond their configuration in the materiality of cultures (ethno-racial, gender, class, institutional belonging and inscription, and so on) and how actors respond to this racial configuration and manage institutions accordingly (compare Condoleezza Rice and Barack Obama), are the assumptions related to the scope of "objectivity" and "truth."

The argument I'm working on builds on the distinction already mentioned above, made by the Chilean neurophysiolist and philosopher Humberto Maturana, between "objectivity without parentheses" and "objectivity in parentheses." His basic argument is that objectivity without parentheses leads to an epistemology of management, on the one hand, and of obedience on the other; the result is a closed political system ready to be taken by totalitarian regimes and fertile for an economy in which increases of production and wealth take priority over human lives and life in general. Inter-cultural dialogue, or inter-epistemic dialogue between epistemologies, based on the premise of objectivity without parentheses, could prove deadly when agencies defending opposite objectivities without parentheses confront each other. Dialogue becomes unsustainable. Objectivity in parentheses, on the other hand, opens up the doors for true inter-epistemic (and intercultural) dialogues. The realization of objectivity in parentheses, however, is predicated on the difficult task of overcoming objectivity without parentheses. In a world where objectivity in parentheses is hegemonic, the observer accepts that explanatory paths, political organizations, and economic philosophies are secondary to life, to human lives as well as life in general. If the final horizon is the flourishing of creativity and fullness (in the sense of Sumak Kawsay), and not the imperial management of authority, economy, subjectivity, knowledge, and gender/sexuality, predicated on an objectivity and truth without parenthesis as the primary ends to insure the flourishing of life, then objectivity in parentheses would be the necessary path to insure true inter-epistemic conversations and cooperation in building a non-imperial world order. Humberto Maturana writes,

> There are two distinct attitudes, two paths of thinking and explaining. The first path I call objectivity without parentheses. It takes for granted the observer-independent existence of objects that—it is claimed—can be known;

it believes in the possibility of an external validation of statements. Such a validation would lend authority an unconditional legitimacy to what is claimed and would, therefore, aim at subjection. It entails the negation of all those who are not prepared to agree with the "objective" facts. One does not have to listen or try to understand them. The fundamental emotion reigning here is powered by the authority of universally valid knowledge. One lives in the domain of mutually exclusive transcendental ontologies: each ontology supposedly grasps objective reality; what exists seems independent from one's personality and one's actions.[62]

The other attitude is defined as objectivity in parentheses. In this attitude,

> the emotional basis is the enjoyment of the company of other human beings. The question of the observer is accepted fully, and every attempt is made to answer it. The distinction between objects and the experience of existence is, according to this path, not denied but the reference to objects is not the basis of explanations, it is the coherence of experiences with other experiences that constitutes the foundation of all explanation. . . . We have entered the domain of constituted ontologies: all Being is constituted through the Doing of observers. If we follow this path of explanation, we become aware that we can in no way claim to be in possession of the truth, but that there are numerous possible realities. . . . If we follow this path of explanation, we cannot demand the subjection of our fellow human beings, but will listen to them, seek cooperation and communication.[63]

It would take too long to explore the political and ethical consequences of a world in which objectivity and epistemology in parentheses would be hegemonic. But I could add that Maturana's reflections from the sphere of sciences states in a different vocabulary the Zapatistas' dictum: a world in which many worlds would coexist. The realization of that world, built on interepistemic relations, will require the hegemony of an epistemology in parentheses. Maturana has conceived it as "multi-verse," the Zapatistas as "a world in which many worlds will coexist." In our project, modernity/coloniality, we talk about "pluriversality as a universal project." No need to debate which one is the best, the correct, and the right one. Such a debate will place us squarely into the epistemology without parentheses, where each of us wants "to win." Notice also that "multi-verse" and "pluriversality" are quite different from the idea of "pluralism" in the vocabulary of the liberal political theories critiqued by Carl Schmitt. And both concepts are quite different from Schmitt's "pluriverse," which he conceives as a plurality of states. Both liberal political theory and Schmitt's theory are based on the paradigmatic example of modern-imperial societies (England, France, Germany), while Maturana's multiverse, our (the collective) "pluriversality," and the Zapatistas' conceptualization are based on the experiences of modern/colonial societies (see chapter 6). The former takes the modern states as a model; the latter takes as a model the colonial states. I suggest a thought experiment: take the pluralism of liberal political theory and "apply" it to Bolivia, and see what you get. And take Schmitt's pluriverse, and "apply" it to Latin America, and see what you get. To move from the liberal to the decolonial is necessary to shift the geography of reasoning and begin the argument from the project of plurinational states inscribed in the Constitution of Bolivia and Ecuador. If you start from here and then look at Schmitt's pluriverse you will become aware of the regional and limited scope of liberal political pluralism.[64]

Let's come back—in closing this chapter—to the five trajectories and the distinctions, compatibilities, and incompatibilities among them. Rewesternization, in its liberal and neo-liberal orientations, operates on the assumption of objectivity without parenthesis. In general, the Marxist Left and the theology of liberation are not exempt from the belief that truth and objectivity are always without parenthesis. Even when theologians of liberation place Bartolomé de Las Casas next to Karl Marx, one has the impression that there is no other option. As options contesting hegemony and dominance (let's limit our consideration here to the Atlantic world) Marxism and the theology of liberation have twisted criteria of objectivity and truth toward their own windmill: Las Casas is a ferocious critic of the imperiality of the Church (the legacy of institutional theology and the papacy), and Las Casas and Marx are both critics of secular liberal/neo-liberal imperiality. In fact, the future of the global Left, in the three directions I summarize below, will depend on where the Left locates itself in the spectrum between objectivity without parenthesis and objectivity in parenthesis. Moving to the extreme, the Euro-American Left will recognize that it has a role to play, and that that role should be global but not universal, for there are many other options, global projects, and trajectories (including those within the

Left itself) in the making, each with its own agenda. This is precisely the road toward pluriversality promoted by decolonial options.

Speculating from the two epistemic categories introduced by Maturana, the Soviet Union was a paradigmatic example of changing the content (objectivity and truth without parenthesis), but not questioning the terms of the conversation. However, in the recent self-remapping of the Left (as when Buck-Morss became open to conversations with Muslim history of thought and to the current intellectual revitalization of critical Islamism; and as with García Linera opening up to Indigenous nations on the move due to his close and long interaction with indigenous leaders and intellectuals), one sees that the Left of European "descent" in the former American colonies of Europe is moving toward an epistemology in parenthesis that is becoming conversant and collaborative with decolonial projects. Perhaps the exemplary cases are the work and the publications of Boaventura de Sousa Santos in Portugal and Walden Bello in the Philippines. Two key concepts introduced by de Sousa Santos, "epistemology of the south" and "oppositional postmodernity," certainly are akin to border thinking (border epistemology, border gnosis) and to the decolonial option.[65] "Deglobalization," argued by Walden Bello, is a road companion of decolonization and deimperialization. These four examples illustrate how the global Left could make a signal contribution in building futures without falling into totalitarian dreams backed up by the imperial belief that truth and objectivity must be without parenthesis. De Sousa Santos's work and experience in Africa and Latin America are breaking new ground in reorienting and opening up the Left from the south of Europe, where a turning point is taking place.[66] In all these cases, lines of contact emerge that are delinking from liberal and neoliberal rewesternization and opening new paths, connecting at some level with dewesternization (the spheres of objectivity in parenthesis in dewesternization) and connecting more fully, in the case of de Sousa Santos, with an epistemology in parenthesis.

Within these five trajectories and the disputes for the control of the colonial matrix of power, dewesternization juggles objectivity and truth without parenthesis, embracing the idea of "development," while taking a clear stance for an objectivity in parenthesis in the spheres of knowledge and in decolonization of being (e.g., liberating subjectivities from the enduring racial classification of "yellow"). On the contrary, dewesternization as formulated by Muslim thinkers during the Cold War period, when the confrontation with Occidentalism was grounded both in Islamic and Third World perspectives, epistemologies, and affects, moves more decisively toward an epistemology in parenthesis and closer to both dewesternization, in its more recent East Asian formulation, and decoloniality. All three share, for different reasons, similar experiences of dwelling in the border and border thinking when the moment comes to confront the imperial bent and the darker side of Western modernity. I would stress that both—critical dewesternization and decoloniality—are compatible projects, marching in the same direction, distinguished by where we dwell in relation to the colonial/imperial differences. Hence, the relevance of the Euro-American Left opening to dialogue with Islamic and former Third World projects of dewesternization. In this regard, Brazil's stance in the global order, as defined by Ignacio Lula's government—as one of the BRIC (Brazil, Rusia, India, China) countries—is akin to dewesternization and conversant with the modern/colonial Left in Latin America (and by that I mean actors of European descent, not Indians and Africans whose concerns are not the same— they are mainly decolonial rather than leftist concerns).

In the next two chapters I focus on particular versions of decolonial options: decoloniality in the specific sense of delinking from the colonial matrix of power. I focus on geo- and body-politics of knowledge in two complementary directions: decolonizing imperial knowledge and building decolonial knowledges. Epistemic geo- and body-politics contest and shift the geography of reasoning controlled by the theo- and ego-politics of knowledge—that is, the two anchors of imperial epistemology that Schmitt saw as the two branches of political theology. The next two chapters explore the epistemic, historical, and political foundations (foundations in an architectural sense, like the foundations upon which a building is built) of decolonial thinking and the decolonial option(s), in conflictive and/or collaborative relations with the general trajectories outlined in this chapter.

Part Two

CHAPTER TWO

I Am Where I Do

Remapping the Order of Knowing

Colonialism is the very base and structure of the West Indian's cultural awareness.
. . . I am not so much interested in what the West Indian writer has brought to
the English language; for English is no longer the exclusive language of the men
who live in England. That stopped a long time ago; and it is today, among other
things, a West Indian language. What the West Indians do with it is their own
business. . . . A more important consideration is what the West Indian novelist has
brought to the West Indies. That is the real question; *and its answer can be the
beginning of an attempt to grapple with that colonial structure of awareness which
has determined West Indian values* (emphasis added).
GEORGE LAMMING, "The Occasion for Speaking"

THE PREVIOUS CHAPTER ended with a description of possible future scenarios described in five trajectories, building on
Carl Schmitt's predictions—during the Cold War—on the future
world order. His predictions were derived from his story—in his
words—of the second nomos of the earth. The second nomos is,
from a decolonial perspective, the nomos of modernity or better
yet of modernity/coloniality. This chapter takes Schmitt's story in a
different direction: on the one hand, it looks at the type of decolonial responses that global linear thinking elicited and, on the other,
it insists on both the geo-historical and bio-graphical foundations
of knowledge in the spectrum of modernity/coloniality. By the
spectrum of modernity/coloniality I mean, for instance, that *there
is no* ontological reality such as modernity or tradition. Modernity

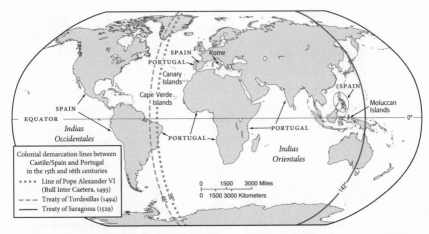

Map 2 The Treaties of Tordesillas and Saragossa by simply dividing and appropriating the globe by the Pope's dictate, set the historical foundations of global linear thinking, the pillars of Western civilization, and the imperial march of modernity and coloniality. After W. Mignolo, published with permission of the *Journal of Anthropological Research* 67, no. 2 (2011): 175.

and tradition are *both Western and modern concepts* by means of which "West" and "modernity" became the very definition of the enunciation that invented "tradition" and the "Orient." This chapter sets up the scenario through Schmitt's narratives and then invites decolonial characters who are dealing with the consequences of global linear thinking to sit at the table and enter in dialogue.

Global Linear Thinking and Global Decolonial Thinking

An unintended consequence of global linear thinking was the coming into being of decolonial thinking. Global linear thinking (one of the basic historical foundations of international law and Westernization) describes—in Carl Schmitt's conceptualization of history—the imperial partition of the world since the sixteenth century.[1] From the Treaty of Tordesillas (1494), by which Pope Alexander VI created an imaginary line that divided the Atlantic from north to south and settled the dispute between Spain and Portugal for the possessions of the New World and the Treaty of Saragossa (1529) that divided Indias Orientales among the same emerging empires, until the end of the nineteenth century and beginning of the twentieth, when the scramble for Africa among Western European states led toward the First

World War, global linear thinking mapped not only the land and waters of the planet, but also the minds.

Schmitt's analytical narrative of global linear thinking and international law has several important consequences for the imperial foundations of the (modern/colonial) world order and the imperial foundation of knowledge. The authority of the pope to divide the planet and to offer it to Spanish and Portuguese monarchs was indeed an act of sovereign authority, not only political but epistemic. For the act of tracing a line dividing the Atlantic means that there is an epistemic sovereign: God has the knowledge backing up the legality of the decision, and He is also in control of the rules and acts of knowing. Although by the mid-sixteenth century the authority of the pope and the monarchs began to be disputed by a group of legal theologians in Salamanca, who called into question the limits of divine and natural law (and of course of divine and natural knowing) in favor of human law (which opened up the doors toward the secular move we encounter in the eighteenth century), the fact remains that global linear thinking, as Schmitt himself specifies in the subtitle of his book, goes hand in hand with the origin of international law. I underline this point: the origin of international law lies in the constitution of the modern/colonial world and of Western civilization.

The new nomos of the earth, in Schmitt's own formulation, was based, therefore, in the pontifical partition of the earth and international law as the necessary consequence: who has the right indeed, and what are those rights that Europeans may have over non-European lands and people? A second consequence after the partition and the origin of international law was the depiction of the planet on the world map of which Abraham Ortelius's *Theatrus Orbis Terrarum* (1570) remains the paradigmatic example[2]—never before Ortelius had the planet Earth been seen from "above," and the sea and landmasses seen at a glance. But above all, the main issue is not that the observer observes the planet from above, but that the observer is "above" the earth and can map the world with the Atlantic, not the Pacific, at its center. The *new nomos* of the earth comes with a *new observer and a new epistemic foundation*. This sense of "newness" will become one of the anchors of all rhetoric of modernity, from the sixteenth century to the twenty-first. The Colombian philosopher Santiago Castro-Gómez described it as the hubris of the zero point.[3] This second consequence sets the stage for the imperial control and colonization of knowledge and of being.

The co-existence of diverse ways of producing and transmitting knowledge is eliminated because now all forms of human knowledge are ordered on an epistemological scale from the traditional to the modern, from barbarism to civilization, from the community to the individual, from the orient to occident. . . . By way of this strategy, scientific thought positions itself as the only valid form of producing knowledge, and Europe acquires an epistemological hegemony over all the other cultures of the world.[4]

Basically, zero point epistemology is the ultimate grounding of knowledge, which paradoxically is ungrounded, or grounded neither in geo-historical location nor in bio-graphical configurations of the bodies. The geopolitical and bio-graphic politics (e.g., body-politics, not bio-politics) of knowledge is hidden in the transparency and the universality of the zero point. It is grounding without grounding; it is in the mind and not in the brain and in the heart. Every way of knowing and sensing (feeling) that do not conform to the epistemology and aesthesis of the zero point are cast behind in time and/or in the order of myth, legend, folklore, local knowledge, and the like. Since the zero point is always in the present of time and the center of space, it hides its own local knowledge universally projected. Its imperiality consists precisely in hiding its locality, its geo-historical body location, and in assuming to be universal and thus managing the universality to which everyone has to submit.

The zero point is the site of observation from which the epistemic colonial differences and the epistemic imperial differences are mapped out. Latin absorbed and recast knowledges that were either translated from Greek to Arabic or that were cast in the Arabo-Islamic tradition. While of course Arabic remained crucial locally, it lost its global influence once that modern/European language—derived from Greek and Latin—became the language of sustainable knowledge, disavowing the epistemic insights of non-European languages. Being where one thinks has become since then a fundamental concern of those who have been mapped out by the colonial and imperial differences and, therefore, relegated to a second or third place in the global epistemic order. "I am where I think" sets the stage for epistemic affirmations that have been disavowed. At the same time, it creates a shift in the geography of reason for the affirmation "I am where I think." From the perspective of the epistemically disavowed colonial subjects (now migrants in Western Europe and the United States), the affirmation implies "And you too," addressed to believers in the epistemology of the zero point. In other words, "we all are where we think," but only the European system of knowledge was built on the basic premise "I think, therefore I am," which was a translation of the theological foundation of knowledge, in which the privilege of the soul over the body was translated into the secular mind over the body and on the premise that love should be global currency, and that every one in the world should believe (after Descartes) that they think and therefore exist.

"By way of this strategy," Castro-Gómez observes, "scientific thought positions itself as the only valid form of producing knowledge, and Europe acquires *an epistemological hegemony* over all the other cultures of the world."[5] From the fact that Western epistemology—that is, the epistemology of the zero point—became hegemonic, it doesn't follow that whoever was and is not thinking in those terms is not thinking. There is ample evidence to the contrary, evidence that is kept silenced both in the academic world and in mainstream media. The democratization of epistemology is under way (my argument intends to contribute to it), and "I am where I think" is one basic epistemic principle that legitimizes all ways of thinking and de-legitimizes the pretense of a singular and particular epistemology, geo-historical and bio-graphically located, to be universal.

Humanitas and Anthropos, Modernity and Tradition: Two Western Civilizational Concepts to Rule the World[6]

Schmitt's *The Nomos of the Earth* is more than a scholarly book concerned with the discipline of international law. On the contrary, it is through the history and the discipline of international law that Schmitt reflects on the situation of Europe after the Second World War and forecasts the future. He was not a Nigerian scholar looking at how international law and the nomos of the earth affected Africa; nor was he an Aymara scholar in Bolivia reflecting on the origin of international law and the Spanish justification for appropriating their land. By spatializing the sites of knowledge and linking them through the colonial epistemic power differential, the process of decolonizing knowledge and being is underway. While zero point epistemology is and shall be recognized in its splendors, it shall also be recognized in its miseries and arrogance.

Decolonizing Western epistemology means to strip it out of the pretense that it is the point of arrival and the guiding light of all kinds of knowledges. In other words, decolonizing knowledge is not rejecting Western epistemic contributions to the world. On the contrary, it implies appropriating its contributions in order to then de-chain from their imperial designs. "Humanitas" and "modernity" are concepts that do not emerge from an ontology wherein entities carry with them the essential being of humans and modernity; instead, they are concepts allowing those who manage categories of thought and knowledge production to use that managerial authority to assert themselves by disqualifying those who ("anthropos" who at once are barbarians and traditional) are classified as deficient, rationally and ontologically. Once you realize that true values and objectivity without parenthesis are only true values and objectivity for those who believe in them (as in the case of religion or any other ideology that holds to truth and objectivity without parenthesis), you are ready to delink, to free yourself from the imperial magic of "modernity" sustained by the epistemology of the zero point. Humanitas and modernity, then, are two companion concepts and central concepts of Western civilization. Such an epistemic style of thinking hides coloniality and prevents pluriversal, dialogic, and epistemically democratic systems of thought from unfolding. Two choices are given to the anthropos: to assimilate or to be cast out. In other words, universal options are options based on truth without parenthesis and cannot admit the difference. As a matter of fact, differences are created in order to eliminate other options.

This argument is being structured from anthropos's perspectives. That means that it builds and is built on an enunciation grounded on geo- and body-politics of knowledge, while humantitas's arguments build and are built on theo- and ego-politics of knowledge,[7] that is, on zero point epistemology.

In a scenario composed of options working toward the communal world order and the hegemony of truth in parenthesis, Ancient Greece and Christian Paradise lose their privileges as the secular and sacred origin; they become just options among others, and other-beginnings are becoming more visible and gaining in legitimacy. The same considerations shall be made chiefly about economy. Capitalist economy is only one option, but an option that is posited by the believers to be the only possible option. People

dwelling in legacies alien to the Greco-Christian and suffering the consequences of capitalist economy are gaining confidence in their own narratives and feeling positive in *their* dwelling, rather than feeling ashamed by
believing the narratives of modernity that put them outside of history and
behind modernity—that made them anthropos. The scenario I am proposing here begins neither in Ancient Greece nor in the Biblical Paradise but
in the sixteenth century, in the Atlantic; and, it connects three continents
and many civilizations.

The Atlantic in the sixteenth century marks a discontinuity with the classical tradition on which Western Europe built itself.[8] Accepting that "we are
where we think" and that the place we are follows from the place we occupy
in the new nomos of the earth (that is of the modern/colonial world), then
several epistemic trajectories emerge that escape the control of global linear
thinking. I understand these trajectories, loosely, as decolonial.

Rational classification meant racial classification. And rational classifications do not derive from "natural reason," but from "human concepts" of
natural reason. Who establishes criteria of classification and who classifies?
Those who inhabited the epistemic zero point (*humanitas*) and were the
architects of global linear thinking. And who are classified without participating in the classification? People who inhabit the *exteriority* (the outside
invented in the process of defining the inside) created from the perspective
of the zero point of observation (*anthropos*). To manage, and to be in a
position to do so, means to be in control of knowledge—to be in the zero
point. That is precisely what global linear thinking was. Global linear thinking since the sixteenth century has been imperial; it is imperial thinking
that I described elsewhere as the rhetoric of modernity and the logic of
coloniality.[9]

While global linear thinking is imperial, the consequences of tracing
lines to divide and control the world are not the same everywhere. I see
at least three dimensions of global linear thinking that prompted, non-
intentionally, the emergence of decolonial thinking.

First, "nodes" in global linear thinking have the particularity of breaking
up "linear time," dividing space "by means of lines." Thus, the imperialism
of time in linear historical narratives is undermined and its control of time
is shaken up by the emergence of coexisting options, decolonial options being among them, that put forward coexisting time lines (see chapter 5). The

building of narratives which incorporate "nodes" that have been silenced by imperial narratives invites us to see the past and the present as "heterogeneous historic-structural nodes" of imperial/colonial space—that is, the exteriority where the anthropos dwells and where decolonial thinking emerges. This book is a case in point. This book is intended as a contribution to building decolonial nodes, the nodes of "other histories," which will allow us also to make educated guesses about the future other than those predicted by Schmitt, as outlined at the end of the previous chapter. For example, the partition of India (decolonization) and the creation of the State of Israel (nation-state building) took place in 1947 and 1948. In China Mao Zedong dethroned Chiang Kai Shek (revolution). How do you connect and make sense of these three simultaneous events in a linear global chronology? By simultaneous, I do not mean the same day, the same month, and the same hour. However, you cannot deny that these three events are strictly co-related in global linear thinking—linear not in the chronological sense, but by horizontally coexisting in space. To see the interconnections between these spatially located events, we need to look at the changes in the colonial matrix, drawing lines and creating nodes: by interconnecting these three events in the colonial matrix of power, decolonial thinking marks indeed the final limits of global linear thinking and doing.

Second, global linear thinking from its beginning in the late fifteenth century (Tordesillas and Saragossa Treaties) played two simultaneous roles. On the one hand, the *raya* divided the operational space or imperial formations and conflicts between themselves (e.g., Spain and Portugal in the sixteenth century); between the former and France, England, and Holland in the seventeenth century; between the former and the United States, since the nineteenth century, when the idea of a Western Hemisphere affirmed the United States as an imperial contender—none of the South American and Caribbean countries having any say in the line that divided the Western Hemisphere from Europe. On the other hand, the raya divided imperial states (monarchic or secular nation-states) from their colonies. The first introduced the internal imperial differences within Western civilization, the second the colonial differences between Western modern/imperial subjects and their colonial subjects. When colonies became "independent states" (in South America and the Caribbean, for example, through the nineteenth and twentieth centuries), or overseas departments of France, or "estado libre asociado" of the United States (like Puerto Rico), the raya was redrawn, allowing certain former colonies to cross the line and to get "inside"; however, it also reinforced the fact that, say, South America, although in the Western Hemisphere, became a region of the Third World. This is why today, for example, Samuel Huntington puts Australia and New Zealand in the First World and South America in the Third World[10]—who is in and who is out of the *raya* of Western civilization is a constant process of remapping *exteriority* and the *anthropos*.

Third, the geopolitical consequences of the line in the reconfiguration of the nomos of the earth went beyond geography proper. Space went hand-in-hand with people inhabiting it. Land and people became "packaged" by imperial global linear thinking and the invention of the *humanitas* and *anthropos*. Anthropos doesn't refer literally to the native barbarians of the sixteenth century or the naked primitives of the eighteenth, but to every instance in which people, institutions, and disciplines where knowledge is managed and controlled, defines humanitas and uses the definition to describe the place they inhabit. Since humanitas is defined through the epistemic privilege of hegemonic knowledge, anthropos was stated as the difference—more specifically, the epistemic colonial difference. In other words, the idea was that humans and humanity were all "human beings" minus the anthropos. Anthropos, then, is as much the barbarian or the primitive as the communist, the terrorist, all those who can be placed in the axis of evil, and those who are friends of the Devil. Illegal immigrants and homosexuals are today within the realm of the anthropos. The domain of humanitas is con-substantial with the management of knowledge and of global linear thinking—the lines have been traced from the perspective of humanitas, and it is in the humanities where the control of knowledge resides.

Before continuing, and in order to clarify my point, I would like to remind you that I am talking within (enunciation) and about (enunciated) a complex unit of three dimensions: the rhetoric of modernity telling the triumphal narratives of Western civilization; the logic of coloniality, which is the hidden and darker side of the rhetoric of modernity and constitutive of it; and the grammar of decoloniality, which is the task in the present toward the future. Put more simply, there is no modernity without coloniality, and because of it, modernity/coloniality engenders responses that have taken the form of the grammar of decoloniality.[11] The rhetoric of modernity and the logic of coloniality embodied global designs thought out and implemented in and by actors in the metropole and dispersed over the colonies. Decoloniality, instead, in the colonies and ex-colonies, and because of immigration, disperses and is becoming a matter of daily life in Europe and the United States.[12] Parallel phenomena are being witnessed all over the world, including in the former Soviet Union, where migrants from the ex-Soviet colonies are descending on Moscow, provoking (in December 2010) riots and violent persecutions of non-Slavic and non-Orthodox people.

Colonial and Imperial Differences:
The Dwelling of Decolonial Thinking

My goal here is not to redraw the map traced by Schmitt, but to decolonize and make understandable two crucial functions of global linear thinking. The first was to establish the criteria for the making and remaking of *imperial differences*; the second for the making and remaking of *colonial differences*. They are both crucial to understanding the world order of the past five hundred years (1500–2000) and the radical transformations we (all us living) have been witnessing since 2000, of which 9/11, the collapse of Wall Street, and the Israeli massacre in Gaza are telling signs (I will come back below to these issues).

We can locate the founding moment of both imperial and colonial differences in the canonical work by the legal theologian Francisco de Vitoria, alluded to in the introduction and the starting point of Schmidt's argument. We have already noticed that de Vitoria had to solve two sides of one problem. On the one hand, he needed to debunk the sovereignty of the pope and the monarch and their privileges in appropriating lands inhabited by non-Christians and to deal with the question of jurisdiction. To cut off the authority of the pope and the monarch, he stated that all nations on the planet (but in this case, the Spanish nation and the Indian nations in the New World) were endowed with *ius gentium*, the rights of nations. Since Indians belong to the human community and were endowed with ius gentium, neither the pope nor the monarch could have *dominium* over them. Now the second step was to deal with the Spaniards and the Indians, face-to-face in the New World. Since Spaniards and Indians were equal according to the principle of ius gentium, how could Spaniards justify their interventions in the life and habitat of the New World (from the perspective of Europe) people? Francisco de Vitoria ended up, after recognizing that Indians had the rights of nations, demonstrating their deficiencies in rationality (although they possessed reason) and maturity (although they were human). Once de Vitoria determined Indians to be somehow inferior (although people with rights), he built up his argument on racial epistemic hierarchies, placing himself at the zero point of observation—the epistemic colonial difference was established. The idea of "private property" emerged from this confrontation between, on the one hand, "cancellation" of divine law and the rights of the pope and the monarch to possess and dispossess the natives and, on the other, the "limitations" of the natives with regard to their right to benefit from the land over which they had entire disposition before the arrival of Europeans. This idea appears in Francisco de Vitoria, re-emerges in Hugo Grotius, and is fully developed by John Locke.[13]

Once Indians were endowed with "rights," rights which were meaningful in the European world, but not in Tawantinsuyu and Anáhuac (and there was nothing wrong at that point when rights were not needed), the question became what to do with them, since they have rights but at the same time are rationally deficient. Remember that this was a problem for the Spaniards, not for the New World people, who were not participating in the conversation. Francisco de Vitoria and the Spaniards—and, in the twentieth century, the French, the British, and the Americans—attributed to themselves the right to be where they think and to think that other people are uncivilized, underdeveloped, or that they are becoming, just emerging. However, from the sixteenth century to the twenty-first, many who were and are considered anthropos from the perspective of the humanitas (be it de Vitoria and the Church, scientific disciplines, or the World Bank that appropriates the language of the anthropos to remain itself as savior and not to allow self-determination) took and are taking their epistemic destinies in their own hands: anthropos becomes humanitas not by conversion, civilization, or developments by humanitas, but by assuming their humanity *and being where they think*—humanity is appropriated by the anthropos rather than being endowed by *humanitas* to the anthropos. When that happens we become all anthropos or humanitas, since the privilege of zero point epistemology that built such distinctions is erased and displaced by the geo- and body-politics of knowledge, that is, the epistemology of dewesternizing and decolonial anthropos.

A few decades after these debates in Spain, the Quechua Guaman Poma de Ayala was living in Tawantinsuyu, the territory of the Incas being replaced by the Viceroyalty of Peru. Guaman Poma was experiencing a radical transformation of his civilization. He was (existed) where he was doing and thinking through his doing; and what he was thinking responded to needs, desires, and visions grounded in the history of the Tawantinsuyu, not in the history of Western Christians, as it was the case for de Vitoria.[14] While de Vitoria participated in a discussion among Spaniards about the Indians, Guaman Poma addressed Philip III from the perspective of Tawantinsuyu. He did not represent all Indians, as de Vitoria did not represent all Spaniards. Undeniably, however, de Vitoria was speaking in the middle of heated debates and issues affecting Spanish society and life. He was more concerned about Spain than about Tawantinsuyu. Guaman Poma's concern was instead Tawantinsuyu. However, de Vitoria has been recognized, praised, critiqued, and enthroned, whereas Guaman Poma was despised, ignored, and silenced until recently, and his work is still recognized only as a document, not as political treatise at the same level as de Vitoria's. You see here at work the epistemic colonial difference supported by the ontological colonial difference: Indians do not think, therefore they are ontological inferior human beings, and whatever they do is assumed to be doing without thinking, or at best, of doing and thinking wrongly or deficiently. The very names "Indian" and "Indias Occidentales" denied them the possibility of being were they where (Tawantinsuyu, Anáhuac, Abya-Yala). That long history of racial epistemic prejudice is at work today in Bolivia, both nationally and internationally.[15] Decolonial thinking and decolonial option(s) work toward redressing not only a long history, but also the intractable logic on which modern imperial epistemology was founded and is maintained.

That was yesterday, the late sixteenth and early seventeenth centuries. Today decolonial thinking confronting global linear thinking is alive and well, although generally silenced or marginalized by the institutional coloniality of knowledge as well as the hegemonic priorities of modern Western idea knowledge in practices and education. *Global* is appropriated by decolonial thinkers and twisted, for it is not used to defend a new "imperial globalism," but on the contrary to confront global modernity with global decolonialities. In spite of differences we can identify and analyze in the rhetoric and narrative of modernity, both spatially and chronologically, from the sixteenth century to today, between the European Union and the United States, or between England and France, those internal imperial differences are not of the same kind as the differences that modernity created by expanding and extending to the non-European world, either by manipulating external colonial and imperial differences (e.g., the classical difference between the West and Islam). Because of the similarities in the internal imperial differences among Atlantic European imperial countries, it was possible to maintain Western imperial dominance. However, the differences at the borders of Euro-American modernity (e.g., the borders between Europe and Africa; or between the United States and South/Central America and the Caribbean; or between the European Union/United States and East Asia) created the conditions for the emergence of decolonial thinking, both as epistemic and political projects. Thus, there cannot be a monotopic history of decolonial options. They emerge in diverse local histories and have in common the experience of being interfered by the colonial matrix of power and therefore Western civilization. You may be thinking that Euro/America epistemology is also diverse. But it is not the same as the diversity of decolonial thinking. The diversity of European thinking is contained within cohesive narratives of Western civilizations.[16] Decolonial thinking cannot be contained in cohesive macro-narratives because it emerges in diverse local histories entangled with Western civilization. The first are grounded on theo- and ego-politics of knowledge, that is, in zero point epistemology while the second are calling for geo- and body-political epistemic foundations and political orientations. Pluriversal global futures are born from the common experience the non-Western world had with the expansion of the West. Sure, there were local agents who facilitated the expansion. But that is not a solution; it is part of the problem itself. Pluriversal global futures require epistemic democratization, which is to say the decolonization of democracy.

A system of sorts has been outlined in the previous paragraphs, an underlying structure that connects global linear thinking with cartography and the world map, the idea of human and humanitas, and a zero point of observation (the invisible knower, God, or the transcendental secular subject), that not only observes but also divides the land and organizes the known. Carl Schmitt's *The* Nomos *of the Earth* has been written from that point of observation and with the concern of imperial countries, particularly after the humble crisis of the Second World War and the Holocaust. The line of colonial differences traced the separation between "humanitas" and "anthropos," and therefore was the necessary condition for inventing the epistemic and ontological differences and then making the lines appear neutral and objective[17]—objectivity without parenthesis at its best. Thus the "/" between modernity/(de)coloniality is the site, as I said and will repeat, where modernity/coloniality unite and divide, where imperial and colonial differences dwell, where decoloniality and dewesternization emerge, where spiritual options flourish. Who introduced decolonial thinking was the anthropos not the humanitas; humanitas can think decolonially by joining the body politics of the anthropos, for you can not think decolonially and remain within the value frame of humanitas. That will mean that you appropriate the anthropos contributions and reproduce coloniality.

What does the anthropos do? He or she can surrender, assuming his or her inferior epistemic and ontological status vis-à-vis the model of humanitas. The anthropos can fight back and show that he or she is also human, claiming recognition. This is the path of assimilation, of being happy to be accepted in the palace of humanitas. By following this path, he or she admits defeat, represses what he or she was, and embraces something that he or she was not by the fact of belonging, by birth, education, language, sensibility, to the anthropos. The third possibility, and the most rewarding and hopeful, is for the anthropos to unveil the pretentious sense of superiority of those who inhabit the humanitas—not to claim recognition, but to show how insane the inhabitants of the house of humanitas are, that they still believe that Humanity is divided between humanitas and anthropos, and to show that the control of knowledge gives them the privilege of seeing themselves as humanitas and not as anthropos. In other words, the task of the anthropos is to claim and assert, through argumentation, his and her epistemic rights, to engage in barbarian theorizing in order to decolonize humanitas and in knowledge-building to show that the distinction between anthropos and humanitas is a fiction controlled by the humanitas. Engaging in decolonial thinking means confronting the imperial privileges of imperial/global linear thinking, not to resist but to re-exist in building decolonial futures. This is the beginning from which decolonial subjects engage in the process of decolonizing authority (e.g., the modern state, and the modern/colonial states in the anthropos side of the linear divide) and decolonizing economy—that is, imagining global futures in which the complicities between the state, market, and epistemic imperial hubris (e.g., global linear thinking, hubris of the zero) will be accepted as a historical moment in the life of the planet and of the species, the right of Western civilizations to exist among others, but not longer to posit itself as the savior of the other. That belief that lasted five hundred years is no longer sustainable.

The first step in decolonial thinking is to accept the interconnection between geo-history and epistemology, and between bio-graphy and epistemology that has been kept hidden by linear global thinking and the hubris of the zero point in their making of colonial and imperial differences. That is, the first step is to assume the legitimacy of "I am where I think" and not be afraid of inquisitorial corporate and/or postmodern thinkers. By revealing geo-history and bio-graphy configurations and heterogenous historico-structural nodes in the historical frame created by global linear thinking, decolonial thinking and doing performs two operations at once: it anchors new epistemic and ontological sites; and it contextualizes Descartes's claim, which by requiring the awareness of thinking in order to be aware of its existence, narcotized the historical geo- and body-political motivations of his own thinking. Descartes was unaware or did not pay attention to his awareness in the last analysis that his philosophy contributed to secularizing the zero point of observation and to anchoring his thought in the imperial domain secured by global linear thinking. While we cannot consider Descartes guilty for doing what he felt he was supposed to do, we should not take for granted that 80 percent of the population of the world, beyond Europe, shall be jumping for joy because Descartes discovered that "one thinks, therefore one is."

My purpose here is to articulate a discourse, the discourse of the anthropos in the process of appropriating humanitas in order to become something other than humanitas—the humanitas of the anthropos that enveils the anthropos in the humanitas. In the process of so doing I attempt to show the illogic rationality of the hubris of the zero point and of the humanitas placing itself in a position of domination through the partition of the earth and the classification of its people. Border thinking is of the essence as we switch from imperial and territorial epistemology (e.g., global linear thinking) to an epistemology emerging from the places and bodies left out of the line (e.g., the anthropos, the Orientals, the Third World, etc.). And I take "I am where I think" as the basic proposition of such reasoning, both epistemically and politically.

Decolonizing Knowledge and Being: Thinking Decolonially during the Cold War and After (Bennabi, Kusch, Wynter)

In the first two sections I mapped the imperial/colonial scenarios in which zero point epistemology emerged and was consolidated. "Imperial/colonial" doesn't refer only to conservative or right-wing ways of thinking. Let's take theology, for example, Christian theology. While there is a history of theology obviously linked to imperial designs and interests, the papacy being an obvious example, there are theologies of liberation in South America, North America, and Africa, as well as a Jewish theology of liberation. My claim is that, as in the disputes between (neo)liberalism and (neo) Marxism, both sides of the coin belong to the same bank: the disputes are entrenched within the same rules of the game, where the contenders defend different positions but do not question the terms of the conversation. In this section I will argue that shifting from "I think, therefore I am" to "I am where I do and think" (meaning that thinking derives from doing in the same proportion that doing is guided by thinking) is a shift in the geo- and body-politics of knowledge that focuses on changing the rules of the game rather than its content. We can call it decolonizing epistemology or, if you wish, working toward epistemic decolonial democratization. Decolonizing is nothing more and nothing less than taking democracy seriously instead of using it to advance imperial designs or personal interests. We cannot leave the word *democracy* only in liberal and neo-liberal hands. If used, it will belong to all of us, to the anthropos and the humanitas, as that is precisely what democracy means. "We" (members of the political society, who are not in the sphere of the state or the corporations and that were cast in the scale of the anthropos) are claiming democracy beyond its Greek origins and its imperial appropriation in eighteenth-century Europe; we (the anthropos) are working toward decolonizing knowledge and therefore decolonizing Western interpretations of democracy.

In what follows I explore and explain what decolonizing knowledge and being may mean not in definitional terms (since once the definition is read, it is forgotten), but as the seed from where collective decolonial reasoning and options grow, unfold, spread, and transform our (those involved in it) thinking and doing decolonially toward global decolonial futures.

My aim is to work out genealogies of thought across national and regional histories; non-national genealogies that are connected through the common experience of the colonial wound—of sensing that, in one way or another, one belongs to the world of the anthropos. The awareness of being on the side of anthropos leaves a bad taste in the mouth. However, if those of us who have been seen and classified as anthropos want to join humanitas, the bad taste in the mouth persists, although it is a different taste. Someone who has been classified as anthropos will choose which of the two bad tastes he or she prefers, and then decide what to do. And if you do not feel that you are on the side of anthropos—either because you belong to humanitas or because you prefer to ignore your situation and to fool yourself, pretending that you belong to humanitas—that is of course your responsibility. Ethics comes into the picture at this point; that is where responses to historical realities are unavoidable. What are the possible responses, what are the options? One option is to ignore it, thus lying to oneself and living in a state of bad faith. Another option is to assimilate, to do the best we can to be accepted. The third is the decolonial option: to fight the inhumanity of the humanitas, the irrationality of the rational, the despotic residues of modernity. The three thinkers I comment on in the following pages dwelled in exteriority. Their thinking assumed that experience, and as a consequence they built on the decolonial option, being where they did and thought, not looking for assimilation in or recognition by the humanitas. One of them is an Algerian, the other an Argentine, and the third an Afro-Caribbean thinker; through them I further explore the interconnections between geo- and body-politics of knowledge. Malik Bennabi (the Algerian) and Rodolfo Kusch (the Argentine) share in different places the common experience of colonial legacies of the Cold War. Sylvia Wynter (the Afro-Caribbean) lived through the Cold War, but her most recent works were written after the end of it. She shares with Bennabi and Kusch knowing through bodies marked by colonial legacies, by knowing and sensing the gaze of the Master: being through the gaze of humanitas. Sociogenesis was Fanon's response, and Wynter capitalized on it.

"Being" (in the sense of "I am where I do and think") here doesn't mean that I am now at my house in North Carolina, or that you are in a café in

Paris, but where we are, each of us, located in the house of modernity/coloniality: that means that we have been born and raised, and therefore seen and classified, from the perspective of the zero point among the humanitas or the anthropos (and of course all the intermediate cases that the categories allow us to make). Are we anthropos or humanitas, black or Indian, developed or underdeveloped, Jews or Muslims, Christians or Israelites? I am not saying either that there is modern/colonial determinism, for I am talking about built-in constructions of modern epistemology. I am saying that it just is, and it is our ethical responsibility to know and understand the house of modernity/coloniality (the colonial matrix of power) we all inhabit. My task here is to help in cleaning up and restoring the house of knowledge that has been knocked down by the global storm blowing from the paradise of linear thinking.

That is precisely the point of bringing Algerian, Argentinean, and Afro-Caribbean thinkers into the conversation. Algeria, to make a long story short, was conquered by the Ottomans, shortly after the completion of the Spanish Reconquista (in 1492); Ottoman rule lasted until approximately 1830, when Algeria fell into French hands. That period ended with the decolonial liberation of Algeria, in 1961. Quite simply, if your body came to this world before 1961 and lived through the war of decolonization in Algeria during the Cold War, your feelings and intellectual, ethical, and political concerns would have been very different from someone whose body came to this world at the beginning of the twentieth century in Germany, that is, in Europe, who went through the First and Second World Wars, and through Hitler. Thus, there is no reason to take for granted that thinking in the German language and dwelling in German history has epistemic privileges over thinking in a Francophone language and dwelling in colonial history; or, yet, has epistemic privileges over thinking in Arabic at the crossroad of Islamo-Arab history, Western interventions, and the Three Worlds configuration (as Algeria was classified, from the perspective of zero point epistemology, which of course was located in the First World, but pretended not to be located and just to reflect an objective state of things). Being where you think means, first and foremost, to delink from the epistemic mirage that you can only be if you think as someone else (who is precisely where he or she thinks) told you (and get rewards by funding institutions whose funds come from unequal distributions of wealth), directly or indirectly, that you should think and therefore what you should be: do not remain as anthropos and therefore deficient in your being; you have to abandon that state of immaturity (as Kant defined *enlightenment*) and be like me as I am already inhabiting the house of humanitas. If you do not follow the instructions, you do not get rewarded. Your reward shall be instead the decolonial process itself, which by definition will not be rewarded by today's existing hegemonic institutions reproducing the coloniality of knowledge and of being.

A similar argument can be made in the case of the Argentine thinker of German descent Rodolfo Kusch. After independence from Spain (1810), and indirectly ruled by England (economy) and France (ideology), Argentina was controlled by the Creole elite of Spanish descent, who implemented ideas and public policies that originated in England. Notice that toward 1830, when Algeria was invaded and colonized by France, Argentina was at the inception of building a modern/colonial state. I said "modern/colonial" because the independence from Spain meant the continuation of indirect imperial ruling by England and France. This situation called for the concept of "internal colonialism" introduced in the late sixties and early seventies. From 1860 on, Argentina's wealth increased due to its commerce with England. The installation of railroads through the second half of the nineteenth century and the exportation of corned beef generated the golden years of the economy. The cycle of increasing wealth and prosperity lasted until 1930, when Argentina suffered the consequences of the stock-market collapse. The crisis opened up the doors for a radical transformation that created the conditions for the ascent of Juan Domingo Perón, in 1945. Rodolfo Kusch's first book (*La seducción de la barbarie* [*The Seduction of Barbarism*]) was published in 1953. The book's title is indicative of the shift in the geography of reasoning: "civilización y barbarie" was the enduring opposition on which the process of nation building—which ensued independence from Spain in 1810—unfolded. It is not necessary to go into elaborated arguments and overwhelming evidence to argue that "civilización y barbarie" is the colonial-state formula, in Argentina, of the overarching distinction between humanitas and anthropos. Peronism brought the masses (anthropos) into the picture, and Kusch picked up on that shift, on the potential of popular and indigenous thinking confronting the privilege of civilized (e.g., progress, development) thinking. The anthropos not only took the streets, but also took the word. And Kusch's sensitivity picked up from there: it was enactment of the anthropos (from the perspective of Argentine white elite of European descent) that was bringing forward their being and their thinking. As we will see, another of Kusch's books was titled *Pensamiento indígena y pensamiento popular en América* (*Indigenous and Popular Thinking in America*),[18] a book in which he explores the commonalities between these two types of thinking, not in opposition but complementing each other. In so doing Kusch removes himself from the role as observer (the humanitas); his thinking then becomes complicit with popular and indigenous thinking. A shift in the geography of reasoning has begun to take place and shape.

Sylvia Wynter's dwelling place (Jamaica colonial history and then through England and the United States) in the modern/colonial world has been framed by the history of slavery in the Caribbean and by the confluence of racism and patriarchy. There is a pervasive concern among black Caribbean thinkers—from the Haitian Anténor Firmin to the Trinidadian C. L. R. James—and that is the question of humanity, of being human. The fact that this concern is crucial among Afro-Caribbeans more than among African intellectuals (and, of course, even more than among Europeans) has its reason: if Africans were cast as descendents of Ham (the derailed Noah's son), black Africans since the sixteenth century came to be equated with slavery and slaves' lives became also expendable, both as commodities and as labor force. Humanitas was the point of reference, and those who fell into the domain of anthropos suffered the consequences. Wynter confronts this issue through Frantz Fanon, and thus appropriates the humanity of being, dwelling, and thinking in the location of the anthropos.[19] In the process, the anthropos of the humanitas is being unveiled at the same time as its epistemic limitations: while humanitas attributes to itself epistemic privileges, anthropos operates in the epistemic potential that comes from knowing both the reason of humanitas and the reason of those who in the eyes of humanitas are anthropos. Now, let me insist that anthropos is assumed as such, not as an ontological category, but as an epistemic one: I know that from the perspective of the humanitas *I am an anthropos*—which doesn't mean of course that I am, but it means that once I acknowledge it, my thinking is no longer located in the zero point, but in the geo- and body-politics of knowing and being. It means that I know that you classified me among the anthropos and as such, I will respond by questioning and delegitimizing your claims to the universality of your classification. Being where one thinks implies, first and foremost, recognizing and confronting both imperial categorizations of being and universal principles of knowing; it means engaging in epistemic disobedience, in independent thoughts, in decolonial thinking (see chapter 3).

Malik Bennabi's Dead and Deadly Ideas and the Quest for Independent Thought

Malik Bennabi (1905–73), in Algeria, and Rodolfo Kusch (1920–79), in Argentina, did not know each other, although they were both living, writing, and thinking during the trying years of the Cold War.[20] Their works are two monumental examples, taking on subjects parallel to crucial issues in the imperial world to which Darwin and Freud devoted their lives and intellectual energy. Bennabi went through the hard years of Algerian decolonization (1954–62). Kusch went through the trying years of the rise and fall of Juan Domingo Perón (1946–55). They were one generation apart. However, both were mature persons and intellectuals during the demanding and frustrating decades from 1945 to 1970, from the end of the Second World War (1945) until the end of the period of the welfare state and the global commotion from Beijing to Prague, from Paris to Mexico (late 1960s). As far apart as they seem, Bennabi and Kusch had a similar concern sprouting from their awareness of being where they were thinking, thrown as they were into their respective imperial/colonial countries (Algeria; Argentina) and regions (Maghreb and the Middle Eastern Islamic world; South America—or América, as Kusch preferred to say).

Both historical processes were points of non-return; processes in which no one in the societies affected by the turmoil could remain the same during his or her life; processes that would also remain in the memory of the community for years to come and will imprint the subjectivity of the generations born after the fact. Both sets of processes affected people differently in different places, although they are connected through the colonial wound. In the case of the decolonization of Algeria, French citizens were no doubt distressed, surprised, and taken aback. Beyond the human tragedy, French national spirit suffered the consequences of a loss of a colony. The imperial pride, however, is different from the colonial wound and therefore the responses are of a different nature. Postcolonialism in Algeria is not the same as postcolonialism in France. Christians, Marxists, and liberals all have their view and their frames within which to account for the events. Influential intellectuals in France like the Algerian-born Albert Camus and the French native Jean-Paul Sartre, had conflicting views of the events. Bennabi's reflections before, during, and after the eight years of the Algerian War transcended the events and brought the discussion back home to Algeria, rather than letting it remain in Paris, counting in France's history. Bennabi's frame of thought is not fashioned from Western philosophical thinking, as was Sartre's; instead, his thought existed in tense relation with Western humanism. Bennabi was, like Camus, a secular colonial subject. Bennabi asked questions and developed arguments that were very different from those of the French intellectuals. Their thinking was limited simply because the meaning of the Algerian War in France was embedded in the history of France and of European imperialism, while the meaning of the Algerian War in Algeria was embedded in the history of North Africa and the enduring histories of colonialism. The same event had different meanings for different thinkers and depended on their cultural background: their geo-historical and bio-graphic configurations crossed by colonial and imperial differences.

Bennabi asks and addresses a set of well-qualified questions, all dealing with knowledge and subjectivity in the history of Algeria and North Africa, in the density of layers from Islamization before the Ottomans ruled the area and then after the French displaced the Ottomans. In that displacement a radical change took place: Algeria entered, through French imperialism, the imperial domains of Western capitalism (e.g., it was enmeshed in the spreading tentacles of the colonial matrix)—which of course the Ottoman Sultanate had not been. In other words, what happened in 1830 was not just a change of rulers and sultans by modern presidents or prime ministers of imperial states. It was not similar to what happened in France after the revolution, when the bourgeoisie displaced the monarchy, but all belong to the same cosmology, albeit to different social strata. In this case those who disputed political and economic control were mostly of Gallic descent; they became French citizens, and they were all white and all Christians. In Algeria they were not: they were Arabs and Berbers, Jews and Muslim, black and brown, and had been ruled by the Ottoman Sultanate for several centuries. Dwelling in that history, during the challenging years between wars in Europe and through the critical years of decolonization in Asia and Africa (between 1947 and 1971 approximately), Bennabi wrote two short and crucial pieces that are particularly germane to my argument: *The Question of Ideas in the Muslim World*, conceived in late 1960 and 1961, but finished and published a decade later; and *The Question of Culture*, originally published in 1954.[21] Both pieces respond to a common concern among "Third World" intellectuals: gaining independence from a long history of coloniality of knowledge and of being, that is, decolonizing being and knowledge by being where one thinks and does. Bennabi describes the state of Islamic civilization at the moment of writing, comparing it with a rider losing control:

> Like a rider who has lost control over the stirrup and failed to recapture it, it has been struggling to attain its new equilibrium. Its secular decadence, condemning it to inertia, apathy, impotence and *colonizability*, has nonetheless preserved its traditional values in a more or less fossilized condition. It has emerged under such conditions at the time when the twentieth century reaches the peak of its material power but when all the moral forces have started disintegrating since the First World War.[22]

We shall focus on the enunciation, rather than in the enunciated, of these observations and we will understand that "I am where I do and think" relocates thinking and knowledge at the intersection of the geo- and body-political imperial classification of places and racialization of people, languages, and ideas. But of course, it relocates not only "Third World" thinking, but "First World" as well. If Descartes arrived at the conclusion "I think, therefore I am," it was precisely because he was where he was doing, although he suppressed the materiality of the enunciation; he just took for granted this: if you feel and know that you are humanitas, you most likely will not be concerned about *where* you do and think—you would assume that you inhabit the universal house of knowledge, the epistemic zero point. "I am where I do" flatly rejects the assumptions that rational and universal truths are independent of who presents them, to whom are they addressed, and why they have been advanced in the first place; and that the problems philosophers and thinkers address in Europe shall have "applicability" beyond Europe, so you have to look for problems that more or less fit the theory.

The reader may think at this point, "Oh, I see, you are talking about situated knowledge." Certainly I am, but not about "universal situatedness"; rather, I am talking about situatedness within the colonial matrix of power, and where you are located within the epistemic and ontological racial coordinates of imperial knowledge. To say that knowledge is situated in and of itself doesn't take us too far. It amounts to saying that "reality is constructed." Sure. But once we have beaten the essentialist claim that reality exists, the next step and the most important one is to ask how is it constructed, by whom, why, what for, and whose interest does it serve if we construct reality in A or B manner? And what are these constructions saying to those who are affected by the construction of reality without having the opportunity to participate in such construction?

Thus, three hundred years after Descartes's death (in 1650, in Stockholm), someone like Malik Bennabi, in Algeria, had to deal with the consequences of Descartes's contribution to the foundation of modern philosophy and knowledge. Bennabi now is confronted with a problem similar to the one Descartes had, although it is of quite dissimilar configuration. In fact, while Descartes was dealing with a past framed by theology and Renaissance humanism, both were within their own tradition. While Bennabi dwells in memories embedded in Arabic language and Muslim philosophy (Al Gazhali, Ibn Sina, and Ibn Rush), Descartes was dwelling in memories embedded in Latin and French: he wrote *Discourse on Method* in French and *Meditations on First Philosophy* in Latin.[23] In both traditions, Bennabi's and Descartes's, algebra and geometry were a common ground: Muslim and Christian philosophers around 1200 were drinking from the same Greek fountains. Bennabi, like Descartes, *is where he does and thinks*; his being is formed in a double movement. Understanding, on the one hand, the local history of Algeria at the intersection of the Ottoman Sultanate's rules and French imperial rules, living at the intersection of Arab and French languages and of Islam and Christianity means being in a dense memory in which French, contrary to Descartes's assumption, is a marginal language, experience, and subjectivity. Descartes, in sum, inhabits the epistemology of the zero point and of linear thinking, Bennabi that of border thinking and geo/body politics of knowledge. The first is territorial and the second decolonial thinking.

On the other hand (as with many others in similar human conditions and historical intersections, as I will deal with below), "discourse on method" doesn't begin by looking at the basic, indubitable, simple truth upon which the whole edifice can be built—the whole edifice of truth without parenthesis. Quite the opposite: for Bennabi (and for many decolonial thinkers and artists around the world), the problem is how to disengage from the trap, how to elide the entrapment. The problem is, in other words, how to decolonize knowledge and being by affirming the geopolitical legitimacy of knowledge for "decolonization," rather than knowledge to "control the world" by "knowing" its laws. Paradoxically, Descartes's brilliant move to depart from theology and humanism ended up trapping other knowledges and subjectivities totally alien to the personal and regional forces that motivated his relentless search for "truth." The bottom line: theirs are two different subjectivities, modes of being in the world tilted by coloniality of knowledge and of power. There is no reason, other than the colonial differential of power, to assume that Descartes's thinking is more relevant for the well-being of Humanity than is Bennabi's. Since we are where we think, there is no reason (other than epistemic racism) to believe that, among all forms of creative thinking (not destructive thinking), one mode of being where one thinks is better or preferable to the other. Transcendental truths (God, Reason, Rights, and Knowledge) that are attainable and controlled by one ethno-class result in asserting one mode of being and one mode of thinking—that is, the imperial mode of being where one thinks.

Unlike for Descartes, the problem to solve for Bennabi was not that of the overarching presence of theology and the soft arguments of tolerant humanists (in the middle of religious war and the assassination, in 1610, of Henri of Navarre, founder of the College La Fleche, where Descartes studied), but that of the power of ideas in relation to bilingualism. Remember that one of Bennabi's concerns (which is that of many Arabo-Muslim intellectuals) is, as Moroccan philosopher Mohammed Al-Jabri put it: why, if Ibn-Rushd (1126–1190), sharing his life between Córdoba (today Spain) and Marrakech (today Morocco), reached a level of rational thinking, Arabo-Muslim philosophy "stopped" there and re-emerged, five centuries later, in France and Holland, in the body of Descartes, at the time when Western Greco-Latin Christianity had already silenced Arabo-Islamic philosophy and sciences forever? That is the context in which Bennabi is concerned with the question of *ideas* in the Muslim world.

Bennabi's distinction between "dead ideas" and "deadly ideas" illustrates quite well the type of situation motivating independent thoughts and the need to shift the geography of reasoning and to be where one does and thinks: "A dead idea is an idea whose origins have been betrayed, one that has deviated from its archetype and thus no longer has any roots in its original cultural plasma. In contrast, a deadly idea is an idea that has lost both its identity and cultural value after having been cut of its roots that are left in their original cultural universe."[24] Although in Bennabi's essays there is a larger horizon of humanity and human history, it is the closer horizon that generates his concern: being a Muslim and at the same time a Third World intellectual means to be in two subaltern positions, in relation to imperial Christianity and Western secularism and in relation to the First World. What does someone dwelling in *exteriority* do? There are several possibilities indeed. One would recognize that history is of the winners and to accept and embrace the First World, Western modernity, and secularism. Which of course, ruling elites not only in Arabo-Islamic countries, but also in South America and the Caribbean also did. Let me give you a parallel example (during the Cold War) to get a better sense of the point I am making in reading Bennabi. Would Marxism be of any help here? Perhaps not much.

Instead, we could ask a similar question: what does a Third World and black intellectual dwelling in exteriority do? And we can respond to the question by looking over the shoulder of Lloyd Best (1934–2007).[25] He starts one of his key essays, titled "Independence and Responsibility: Self Knowledge as an Imperative," drawing l'état de la question.

> Since 1962, two visions of the future have been offered to Caribbean peoples. Both have been aborted. The first proved to be an illusion; the second turned into a nightmare. . . . They [the agents of the first vision] . . . urged to produce what we consume and consume what we produce. This strategy involved a sharp increase in government ownership and operation of economic enterprise and hastened the emergence of the omni-competent state.
>
> The second vision was that of the socialist state, with the means of production predominantly owned and controlled by a paramount Leninist party.[26]

What I am driving at is that beyond the significant difference between a Muslim in Algeria and a black in the Caribbean, they are responding to the global entanglements driven by the expansion of the colonial matrix. In many and different local histories, Muslims and Africans were entangled with a myriad of different Western European local histories (mainly that of the Atlantic countries from the Iberian Peninsula to England, going through France and Holland). Best's major concern was "independent thought and Caribbean freedom," as he extensively argued in his essay of this title. The first version of the essay was presented, in 1966, at the Second Conference of West Indian Affairs, in Montreal. The scenario drawn by Best and the description of local elites in their dependency on Western education, technology, and science (which if they are not necessarily deadly by nature, can become deadly—e.g., the idea of development) are similar to the one drawn by Bennabi. Similarly, where Bennabi saw dead ideas in the Muslim world, Best saw not dead ideas of a historical civilization, but disqualified ideas of black communities—no longer in Africa, but in South America and the Caribbean: the communities and emerging civilization formed in the encounter among Africans from different kingdoms, languages, religions, and ways of life. At that crossroads, Lloyd Best claims at the end of his article,

I have argued that we need independent thought. One of the most blatant manifestations of the colonial condition in the Caribbean—of the plantation mind—is the refuge, which our intellectual classes take in a sterile scientism on the one hand, or in a cheap populism on the other. . . . One half of our intellectual classes are a-political. They are engrossed in technical exercises or they are busy dissipating their energies in administration and public relations—running the public service, running the Universities, running this, running that, running in effect, away from the issues.

It is being proposed here, that being who we are, what we are and where, the kind of action to which we must be committed is determinate. . . . To acknowledge this is to set ourselves three tasks. The first is to fashion theory on which may be based the clear intellectual leadership for which the nation calls and which it has never had. The second is to conduct the inquiry on which theory can be soundly based. This is what may be called, in the jargon of my original trade, the creation of intellectual capital goods. Thirdly, we are to establish media by which these goods may be transmitted to the rest of us who are otherwise engaged. . . . We may wish to create a media of direct democratic expression suitable to the native Caribbean imagination.[27]

Where Best saw the failure and the nightmare of solutions for the Caribbean proposed by the national elite in complicity with external-imperial institutions and ideas (mostly Western liberalism and capitalism, rather than

Western and/or Slavic Marxism or Chinese Maoism), Bennabi saw Muslim societies saturated by dead ideas that created the conditions for the advent of deadly Western ideas.

> It is under such circumstances, Bennabi concludes, that the present Muslim society borrows modern and "progressive" ideas from Western civilization! This is a natural outcome of a process determined by the dialectic of things, human beings and ideas that has shaped Muslim history. Nevertheless what is unnatural is its inertia and apathy in this stage, as if it wished to stay there forever. Starting from the same point, other societies such as Japan and China have, on the contrary, succeeded to pull themselves out of their state of inertia by rigorously subjecting themselves to the conditions of new dynamics and new historical dialectics.[28]

Here we have two Third World intellectuals—one Muslim in North Africa, the other black in the Caribbean—looking at the global conditions, being where they think, dwelling in the *exteriorities* of the modern colonial world. These views have not been accounted for in the analysis of globalization and modernity. Certainly Anthony Giddens and Niall Ferguson are where they think: dwelling in the *interiority* of British and imperial European histories.[29] Although they, too, are where they think, their thinking (propelled by the book market and the coloniality of knowledge) generates the effect that in reality they just think, being nowhere, as if instead of inhabiting the interiority of self-fashioned imperial histories, they were standing at the top of the hill looking down and dominating the valley.

The dialectic between dead and deadly ideas tells the story of imperial and colonial differences in the modern/colonial world, for the dialectic is operative not only in the sphere of the liberal state and capitalist economies looking for new surrogate states opening new markets, but also in the internal contestation: Marxism. Bennabi is clear in analyzing the consistency of Marx's ideas within his own cultural sphere, in which industrial capitalism unfolded: "If Marx had analyzed such situations he would certainly have done so based on the logic of a dialectic whose constituent elements were all part and parcel of one and the same cultural universe that was his own universe."[30] In contrast, Bennabi continues, in the colonized and formerly colonized countries, such situations are the complex result of "a

dialectic obtaining in an original cultural universe as well as of the dialecti-
cal relationship between the latter and the alien cultural universe, that of
colonialism."[31]

In my view, Bennabi's *The Questions of Ideas in the Muslim World* is
nothing less than an agonic quest for independent thought. The need and
anxiety has not gone away yet, today, among Muslim intellectuals (as well
as among intellectuals of the former Third World around the globe). Let's
listen to the Iranian scholar Amr G. E. Sabet. In introducing his argument,
Sabet makes clear that in the investigation he presents he is not making any
claim in favor of the "Islamization of knowledge," or for its secularization.
His argument aims, he stresses, at the integration of knowledge, "whether
secular or religious, through a measure of *intersubjectivity*."[32] Furthermore,
and this is crucial for my argument, Sabet notes that beyond looking for an
integration of Islamic thought and social theory, "this study seeks to link
the former (e.g., Islamic thought) with *decolonization* in order to underscore Islam's liberating commitment not only toward Muslims but toward
humanity at large. The decolonization process that had taken place during
the post–World War II era remains, unfortunately, an unfinished, and even
a regressing, project."[33]

Decoloniality refers to a set of projects that, based on border identifications (dwelling in the border between dead ideas and deadly ideas), are
open to humanity at large, in the same way that Christian theology, secular
liberals, and postmodern thinkers (Marxists or not) are. However, the latter
do not recognize their projects emanating from an *identity*. They *identify*
their project as universal. Here lies the conundrum by which postmodern
thinkers chastise identity claims and retain the convenience store of universality. For that reason, Sabet stresses, "in addition to political, as well
as economic, independence there is *the essential need for the independence
of thought, of the mental, the psychological, and the spiritual*; for the exor-
cising and liberating of souls."[34] That means that the decolonization of the
economy and of the state needs a change of terrain. While Adam Smith,
Immanuel Kant, and Karl Marx were where they thought, their thoughts
acquired a universal profile that seemed independent of their geo-historical
and bio-graphical locations and therefore of global import. Geo- and bio-
graphic politics of knowledge materializes the change of terrain, undoing
and moving away from the imperial political theology and its translation

into secular egology. Bennabi's decolonial thinking was enacting this change of terrain.

Rodolfo Kusch: Epistemic Synergy of Immigrant Consciousness

Gunter Rodolfo Kusch was born in Argentina in 1922, and he died in 1979. He was the only child of Ricardo Carlos Kusch and Elsa María Dorotea Tschunke de Kusch, a German couple who moved to Argentina, from Germany, shortly after the First World War ended. He was four years old when his father passed away. At the end of his teen years, Kusch found himself in the middle of an exciting decade in Buenos Aires, from 1940 to 1950, witnessing the end of the Second World War, the Juan Domingo Perón and Eva Perón years, and a very intense intellectual and cultural life. A "native" intelligentsia that was largely of European descent (mainly from Spain, Italy, and Germany) was struggling to found its own ways of thinking and delink from the Argentine intellectual elite reproducing in the country the debates taking place in Europe. The "mestizo consciousness" that Kusch explored in the beginning of his book *La seducción de la barbarie* was a reflection built on the experience of a community of displaced Europeans (immigrants *from* Europe) who coexisted with the dense and strong presence of the indigenous population, which Kusch experienced in northwest Argentina and in Bolivia. By the time of Kusch, the Afro-population had practically vanished from Argentina's imaginary, although he was aware of their presence in America—the consistent name he uses in all his writing; he rarely mentioned "Latin" America. A telling statement that is consistent with the philosophical explorations he conducted throughout his life.

In his second book *América profunda*, published in 1962, Kusch intensified his philosophical reflections anchored in "an-other history." He described that "other history," distinctive in its profile and coexisting with European history, with metaphors such as "seducción de la barbarie," as "América profunda," as "América vegetal," and many others. Crucial to the understanding of Kusch's sustained meditations from *La seducción de la barbarie* to *Geocultura del hombre Americano* (1976) and *Esbozo de una antropología filosófica Americana* (1978) is the coexistence of a European history transplanted and framing the conflicts in/of "América profunda," the legacies of "poblaciones originarias" through the history of conquest and colonization. On the one hand, Kusch felt that Indian memories throughout the Americas needed to be re-inscribed in conflictive dialogue and tension with the existence of people of European descent and institutions (economic, political, and family) modeled on European social organization. He was not Indian, but he was not alien to the fact that Indian legacies are embedded in the history of América. This history could no longer be the narrative of internal transformation, as was the case for the history of Europe. Engaging indigenous thoughts meant to engage an-other epistemology.

It takes several readings to recondition reading habits. One must practice before fully understanding the radical shift in the geography of reasoning that Kusch was engaged in and to grasp his concept of "mestizo consciousness." For, "mestizo" for Kusch doesn't have anything to do with biology, with mixed bloods, with the color of your skin, or the form of your nose. "Mestizo" is for Kusch a matter of "consciousness," not of blood, but of geo-history and bio-graphy—as becomes clear in the last two books he published.

"Mestizo consciousness" is a paradoxical concept in an argument enunciated by Kusch, the son of German immigrants, father and mother. He was clearly not a mestizo by blood but in consciousness, a conceptualization that emerges from a body that experiences *existentia Americana*, similar to what the Jamaican philosopher Lewis Gordon has termed and explored as *existentia Africana*.[35] About fifty years before Kusch's first book, W. E. B. Du Bois introduced the concept of "double consciousness" to articulate his experience and translate it into a term familiar in the human and social sciences.[36] But his "consciousness," that is, the way he was experiencing "consciousness," was different, although from the same source, from the colonial wound: a person of African descent, in the Americas, experiences life and his or her own existence differently from a person of European descent. Both, however, share a common experience, the experience of the displaced in relation to a dominant order of the world to which they do not belong. The consciousness of being-such and the awareness of not-being-such (in the case of Kusch, neither European nor Indian) or sensing a tension between being-such and such (in the case of Du Bois, being black and American, when American was assumed to be white) points toward the sphere of experience that in Gloria Anzaldúa was articulated as "the mestiza consciousness/la conciencia de la mestiza."[37] It is worthwhile to underline the grammatical twist in Anzaldúa. She is talking not about "mestiza consciousness," but about "the consciousness of the mestiza," which is how I would translate the Spanish title she inscribed in the last chapter of her book: "la conciencia de la mestiza." We should also remember at this point that the title of Rigoberta Menchú's narrative, in Spanish, is *Me llamo Rigoberta Menchu y así me nació la conciencia* (1982), dubiously translated into English as *I, Rigoberta Menchú, an Indian Woman from Guatemala*.[38] The English translator (or the editor at the publishing house) preferred exoticism to philosophical and political meaning, and trumpeted Benjamin Franklin's exultation of the first person: "I, Rigoberta Menchú." Last but not least, the Afro-Colombian Zapata Olivella (self-identified as mulatto) conceived a "mestizo consciousness" (notice that "mestizo" acquires, like in Kusch, a meaning that goes beyond the biological) to capture the *historical essence* of the basic three types (Indigenous, European descent, and Afro descent) of languages, religions, cultures, ways of life, sensibilities, and subjectivities that transformed Anáhuac, Abya-Yala, and Tawantinsuyu in what Kusch calls "America."[39]

In retrospect, and in the more recent spectrum in which "consciousness" has been articulated decolonially (Du Bois, Anzaldúa, Menchú), it would be more adequate to rename Kusch's "mestizo consciousness" as "immigrant consciousness," the consciousness of the immigrant of European descent who arrived in the Americas around the end of the nineteenth century and the beginning of the twentieth, and who, instead of assimilating, reacts critically to the displaced conditions of European immigrants in a country that, by that time, is already in the hands of Creoles of Spanish descent and Mestizos with mixed blood and a European soul and mentality. I found in Kusch a particularly apt response to my long-lasting discomfort as an Argentine of European descent. For that experiential reason I am "appropriating" Kusch and following his thoughts rather than "studying" him from the distance of continental philosophy. Appropriation means that I make his thinking mine and continue what he started, in the same way that, say, Martin Heidegger "appropriated" (and not studied) Friedrich Nietzsche to unfold his own thoughts. Here I am imitating what Heidegger did, not what he said. I am not comparing myself with Heidegger here: I am just following the model provided by great European thinkers, a model of what to do, and not of what to think. Regarding what to think I am following Bennabi, Kusch, and Wynter. Decolonial thinking needs to build its own genealogy of thought; otherwise it would fall prey to genealogies of thought already established and would, in the process, disregard and devalue all other possibilities. Decolonization of knowledge and of being requires one to engage in rebuilding what was destroyed and to build what doesn't yet exist.

"Immigrant consciousness," in other words, is the assumed condition of existence, an existence out of place: for people of European descent, for being in a place whose history is not the history of their ancestors; for indigenous or "pueblos originarios," who built their history in the land they inhabited, then found themselves out of place when their form of life and their institutions, education, and economy were displaced, destroyed, and replaced with ways of life and the institutions of migrants from European countries; for Africans coming from several parts of Africa, with their own different languages and beliefs, forms of life, and institutions, who found themselves in a land whose histories did not belong to their ancestors and, in contrast to the Europeans, in a land whose social structures placed them at the very bottom of the social scale. "Immigrant consciousness," double consciousness, mestiza consciousness, mulatto consciousness, inter-cultural consciousness (as indigenous people in Ecuador maintain today), maroon consciousness (as it has been established among Afro-Andeans in Ecuador), all are diverse expressions and experiences of the same condition of existence: the *awareness of coloniality of being*, of being out of place in the set of regulations (e.g., cosmology) of "modernity." Briefly stated, there are different modes of experiencing the colonial wound and of engaging the decolonial option. It is interesting to note that "critical" intellectuals came up with ideas such as peripheral and alternative modernities: a complaisant position that pretends to be dissenting, but ends up reproducing the standards with superficial variations. "Immigrant consciousness" (double, mestiza, indigenous, maroon consciousness) encompasses diverse manifestations of an-other paradigm: the paradigm constituted by forms of decolonial consciousness whose horizon is no longer that of peripheral or alternative modernities but a pluriversal horizon conceived as transmodernity that begins by assuming "our own modernity"[40] (see chapter 3).

Sylvia Wynter: What Does It Mean to Be Human?

Frantz Fanon made a passing observation in *Black Skin, White Masks* (1952) that has become a fundamental proposition being explored in Afro-Caribbean philosophy: "Reacting against the constitutionalist tendency of the late nineteenth century, Freud insisted that the individual factor be taken into account through psychoanalysis. Fanon substituted for a phylogenetic theory the ontogenetic perspective. It will be seen that the black man's alienation is not an individual question. Besides phylogeny and ontogeny stands sociogeny."[41]

The sociogenic principle is one aspect of languaging and knowing.[42] It is therefore crossed by the differential of power embedded in the modern/colonial world order, through the ranking of languages: "To speak means to be in a position to use a certain syntax, to grasp the morphology of this or that language, but it means above all to assume a culture, to support the weight of a civilization."[43] The problem that we confront in this chapter is this: the Negro of the Antilles will be proportionately whiter—that is, he will be closer to being a real human being—in direct ratio with his mastery of the French language. *I am not unaware that this is one of man's attitudes face to face with Being.* A man who has a language consequently possesses the world expressed and implied in that language. What we are getting at becomes plain: mastery of language affords remarkable power.[44]

Sylvia Wynter took Fanon's sociogenic principle to the next step. What is the next step? It is clear after Fanon that we cannot expect Western sciences and political theory to solve the problems created by five centuries of insertion of Western designs into the world beyond imperial Western Europe, and into colonial Europe itself: Ireland and Southern Italy, for example, as well as the Soviet Republics (e.g., colonies) of former Central and Eastern Europe. Briefly, and once more, by imperial Europe and Eurocentrism I mean three aspects, framed spatially, chronologically, and subjectively. They are all three relevant to understand Wynter's decolonization of being.

Spatially, Eurocentrism refers to the Atlantic imperial monarchies, the nation-states (Spain, Portugal, France, Holland, and England), and the supporting cast (Italy and Germany) whose imperial dominions were lesser than the former, although they were not out of the game. It has been pointed out, several times, that the interconnections between marginal-capitalist countries in relation to central-capitalist countries went through a dictatorial political period: Italy and Germany never enjoyed extensive imperial domination; Spain and Portugal did, but had lost it by the nineteenth century, when France and England were in ascendance and "helping" Spanish and Portuguese colonies to "gain" their independence.

Chronologically, Eurocentrism refers to a potent matrix of categories of thoughts that connect and unify all areas of knowledge (what today we describe as natural sciences, the humanities, the social sciences, and the professional schools [medicine, law, engineer, business, computing]). That colonial matrix of power is legitimized on Greek and Latin categories of thoughts and their translation and unfolding in six modern European imperial languages: Italian, Spanish, Portuguese, French, German, and English. Cast, defended, and promoted in the rhetoric of modernity, progress, salvation, development, and so on, that matrix generated the image of its own totality, which authorized its promoter and defender to disregard, marginalize, ignore, deprecate, reprove, rebuke, attack all knowledge that didn't obey the rules and principles of the (post)modern matrix of knowledge. At that point, the modern matrix (Eurocentrism) became also colonial.

Subjectively, the modern/colonial matrix of knowledge (e.g., coloniality of knowledge) has been created, perfected, transformed, expanded, exported/imported by a particular kind of social agent: in general (and we can go through the biography of the great thinkers and scientists in the Western canon), they were male, they were Christians, they were white, and, as we said, they lived in Western Christendom, which, after the sixteenth century, was translated into Europe. That is to say: the modern/colonial matrix of knowledge has been linked to a kind of subjectivity emerging from the lived experience of white and Christian males who lived and studied in the six countries and languages above mentioned. Although someone like Kepler who was born in Cracovia and started his studies at the university in the city he was born, had the chance nevertheless to pursue his learning and lived experience at the University of Bologna. Being one of the first medieval/renaissance universities, Bologna provided Kepler with the institutional push to his personal genius and intellectual impetus. Today the "Plan Bologna" in Europe is closing the cycle that the University of Bologna started.

These three parameters map the hubris of the zero point. Wynter's "next step" is to envision a *scientia* (and I write it in the Renaissance style to distinguish it from the concept of *science* that unfolded from Galileo to Newton and from Newton to Einstein, as well as from Buffon and Linnaeus to Darwin) that disobeys the hubris of the zero point. I see this move as *decolonial scientia* based on Fanon's sociogenic principle. Fanon's hypothesis, Wynter argues, is first of all a hypothesis derived from his awareness of reporting in the third person his own experience in the first person ("Look Mom, a Negro"!). The experience, in other words, of Being through the eyes of the imperial Other; the experience of knowing that "I am being perceived, in the eyes of the imperial Other, as not quite human." Thus, decolonial scientia is the scientia needed not for progress or development, but for liberating the actual and future victims of knowledge upon which progress and development are predicated. It is not the case, most certainly, of studying the Negro problem from the perspective of any of the already established social sciences or humanities. For, if that were the case, sociogenesis would become an object of study rather than being the historical foundation and constitution of future and global epistemic loci of enunciations, geo- and body-politically constituted. This scientia, built on the sociogenic principle (in this case the lived experience of the black man, although this is not the only colonial experience—colonial wound—that would sustain the emerging scientia), makes clear from the start that the mind/body problem (or the soul/body if we take a step back from secularism to Christian theology) only makes sense in the domain of ontogenesis; it is only there that the mind/body problem makes sense.[45] That the sociogenic principle is not an object of knowledge but rather the signpost of a locus of enunciation and the energy that links knowledge with decolonial subjective formations is a conclusion that derived from Wynter's argument.

Unlike the "common reality" of a wave phenomenon, however, the sociogenic principle is not a natural scientific object of knowledge. In that if, in the case of humans, this transcultural constant is that of the sociogenic principle as a culturally programmed rather than genetically articulated "sense of self," with the "property" of the mind or human consciousness being located only in the dynamic processes of symbiotic interaction between the opioid reward and punishment system of the brain and the culture-specific governing code or sociogenic principle (as the semantic activating agent) specific to each of our hybrid nature-culture modes of being, and thereby, of experiencing ourselves as human, then the identification of the hybrid property of consciousness, which such a principle makes possible, would call for another form of scientific knowledge beyond the limits of the natural sciences—including beyond that of neurobiology whose natural-scientific approach to the phenomenon of consciousness is paradoxically based on our present culture's purely biocentric and adaptive conception of what it is to be human.[46]

Long sentences in Wynter's prose are manifestations of her struggle to shift the geography of reasoning. Thus, if modern/imperial epistemology (in its diversity, but always imperial diversity) was spatially, chronologically, and subjectively located, scientia (starting from the sociogenic principle) becomes the project of decolonial scientia setting up new places or nodes of space, time, and subjectivity. That is, while modern/colonial epistemology was based on theology and secular philosophy and the affirmation of Descartes's "I think, therefore I am," geo- and body-politics start by the negation of such propositions by the anthropos. The negation is simultaneously the anthropos's affirmation: the affirmation of being when one thinks and does.

Spatially, decolonial scientia is located at the borders (territorial as well as linguistic, subjective, epistemic, ontological) created by the consolidation and expansion of the modern/colonial epistemic matrix described above. This matrix, which emerged in the sixteenth century, was then folded and unfolded in the hands of England and France and projected itself into Asia and Africa, from the late seventeenth to the mid-twentieth century. The leadership was then taken up by the United States and the basic principle and structure of knowledge were expanded by the use of the English language and the meteoric expansion of scientific knowledge and technology. Consequently, decolonial scientia responding and delinking from coloniality of knowledge is literally all over the globe (in the same way that modern/imperial science is), and it moves constantly from the "third" to the "first" world, and from the latest Western imperial countries to the "emerging empires" (China, Russia, and perhaps in the near future, India and the Islamic Middle East; further in the future, one can see that in the Andes, under the leadership of Bolivia, the model of Tawantinsuyu will interact with the model of the liberal/colonial state).

Chronologically, decolonial scientia denounces—on the one hand—the chronological timeline of the colonial matrix of power and the coloniality of knowledge. And it calls—on the other hand—for rebuilding chronologies of local histories: while in imperial scientia connections through time, including epistemic breaks and paradigmatic changes, followed one another in time, decolonial scientia links nodes in space—the space of colonial histories and decolonial struggles around the world—to which follows today the massive migrations of the "barbarians" to the "civilized regions." If *double consciousness* and *mestiza consciousness* (Du Bois and Anzaldúa) are two key concepts that give substance to the sociogenic principle (for what are double consciousness and mestiza consciousness if not concepts capturing the fact that people who fall on the side of the racially inferior and sexually abnormal—that is, the anthropos—are seeing themselves through the imperial Other?), then the imperial/modern subject holding and controlling knowledge and, therefore, determining who is authorized to know and what knowledge is useful (for whom?) to have loses the magic effect of its universal legitimacy.

Subjectively, decolonial scientia is embraced by people who either suffer the consequence of the colonial wound or by those who, not having had that experience, have experienced the violence of science and embrace the decolonial option not to become a new savior but to twist the politics of knowledge in which they were educated as modern subjects and modern subjectivities. Contrary to the male, Christian, and Eurocentered subjects and subjectivities that dominated the philosophy of modern/imperial knowledge, the decolonial subject is at the border of non-European languages, religions, epistemologies; subjects that have been racialized and/or categorized as sexually abnormal by imperial knowledge. That is, by subjects whose consciousness of the self is reflected on the perception of the imperial Other; subjects that embrace, in other words, the sociogenic principle as a historical foundation of knowledge as well as by imperial subjects who instead of "saving the colonial Other" without questioning the hubris of the zero point join instead and accept the guidance of the decolonial thinkers. It requires an act of humility to realize that there is no longer room for abstract universals and truth without parenthesis. And it takes a moment of rage and of losing fear to move from the colonial wound to decolonial scientia.

Now, decolonial scientia has three types of tasks ahead. One is to show that the hubris of the zero point enacted a geo- and body-politics of knowledge that consisted in denying that geo-historical locations and racial-sexual body configurations were relevant to knowledge. It denied, in other words, the links between geo-history and knowledge and between biography and epistemology. The second task is to explore the consequences that Western expansion (today called "globalization") had for the environment (e.g., natural resources needed by imperial economy) and for the population who were targeted for conversion to Christianity, for civilization, for development, and now for human rights and democracy. That is, to explore global responses, through time (500 years) to globalization, for it is necessary to look at responses globally and avoid the imperial trap that looks at local responses to global designs. The third task is to generate knowledge to build communities in which life (in general, not only human life) has priority over economic gains, economic growth, and economic development, to cultivate knowledge that will subject economic growth to human needs, rather than submit human needs to economic growth and development.

Redrawing the House of Knowledge at the Intersection of Global Linear and Decolonial Thinking

In the twenty-first century, the four spheres of the colonial matrix of power ("coloniality" for short) on which Western civilization built itself as such, and its imperial/colonial legacies all over the non-European world of being, are being disputed, appropriated, and thwarted in two directions: dewesternization and decoloniality. I mean dewesternization in its mainstream discourse (Mahbubani) and its critical dewesternizing one (Shari'ati, Qutb, Komeni), although both types of projects move in quite different directions.[47] What is being claimed is not the end of Western civilization, but its crisis in the process of becoming one among many and not the one that leads the other toward growth, development, modernization, and happiness. Dewesternization, the spiritual option, and decoloniality are three options that are contributing to delegitimize the global designs of rewesternization (from the left or the right, in politics and economy) cast in the language of democracy and development.[48] Needless to say, the trajectories I outlined in chapter 1 are not the equivalent of the architect's plan to build an edifice. They are tendencies that you can hardly find in pure form in any place. However, the trajectories allow us to make distinctions, to understand political and economic orientations in the inter-state system, and to branch into the complexities of always moving borders of colonial and imperial differences, the increasing force and presence of the decolonial political society.

I see two directions in which decoloniality would contribute to eroding and rebuilding the rules of the game and the edifice of Western epistemology. "Disengaging" is not the same as "ignoring." We cannot disengage from something that is in all of us, today, around the world, including, of course, Bennabi, Kusch, and Wynter. By "disengage/delink/epistemic disobedience" I mean and understand a double movement: unveiling the regional foundations of universal claim to truth as well as the categories of thought and the logic that sustain all branches of Western knowledge, from theology to philosophy, from psychology and psychoanalysis to natural science, from political theory to political economy. The problems are places in front of the disciplines rather than the disciplines in front of the problems.

What is the place of decolonial thinking at the time when global linear thinking has been displaced by—on the one hand—global disputes over managing authority and economy that do not depend any more on partition and division of land, but on control of natural resources, military bases, nuclear weapons, and financial transactions and trades and—on the other— by the international conflicts over the control of the colonial matrix of power in a polycentric world united in dispute by capitalist economy? The concentration of decision power in the sphere of authority and economy is more overwhelming today than twenty years ago because, precisely, of the polycentricity of capital accumulation and the devastating consequences for the life of the planet when political and financial leaders and the media are in a blind and wild race toward death, motivated by the belief in economic growth, global development, and happiness.

There are hundreds of cases, examples, every day. I offer just one, from the *New York Times* front page on 17 February 2008, written by Sara Rimer.[49] *The Great Gatsby* is a great piece of literature that deserves to be taught; while there are many ways to teach it, the one celebrated by the *New York Times* and the teacher involves the identification of young students (in their late teen years) with the American Dream and the "fantastic" life that Gatsby made for himself. Other possibilities, some of them hinted at by F. Scott Fitzgerald himself, are the individual and social costs of Gatsby's achievements, costs of which Gatsby himself is well aware. Other readings, still, would be decolonial, helping students to understand what Gatsby means in America and America in the world at the turn of the twentieth century, what America means today at the beginning of the twenty-first century when the enormous costs of a lifestyle based on success are more

obvious, success in personal achievements and personal achievements related to the success of one country at the cost of many others. The young
Chinese student featured in the article has as her goal to attend Harvard,
receive a degree, and return to China to help the country to "have a faster
development."

That, too, is being where one thinks. The "where" is not just a geographical location, but geopolitical in the sense of how imperially made
regions, beyond "natural environment," shape and conform people dwelling in that region. It is not, of course, the physical space of the region that
counts, but the place that the region and its inhabitants occupy in a global
order of coloniality. That regions are no longer there to be known, but are
engendering knowledge necessary to their survival in building global futures and in delinking from the needs of other regions (e.g., the developed
world), for which it is not convenient the people they need to disengage.
There are different agendas confronting each other, one type of agenda aiming at subsuming, managing, and controlling (modernity/coloniality), the
other not wanting to be managed and controlled or to be included (decoloniality). Thus, "I am where I think." The "where" is marked in the map
of desires and aspirations of a civilization driven by economic and social
success, paying enormous costs in wars, refugees, unemployed, new forms
of slavery, rather than a civilization driven by the collective desire for well-
being and the celebration of life in general, not human life as a singular
privilege. Celebrating only the life of a sector we take as "humanitas" at
the cost of other sectors of life is already embedded in the civilization of
death we are immersed in today: firing eight hundred employees to reduce
costs and reward the CEO of a given company is a common procedure of
our time. If nothing else, decolonial thinking and the decolonial option can
contribute in the large sphere of education to understanding the logic of
coloniality driving all of us toward a collective death dressed under the triumphal growth of a global economy.

In this chapter I showed the complementary and conflictive faces of
global linear and decolonial thinking and how the latter presupposes a displacement of the very principles of knowledge and understanding on which
the rhetoric of modernity and the logic of coloniality were constructed,
transformed, and maintained. In the next chapter I examine the pursuit
of freedom and the correlated search for independent thought or, in other
words, for decolonial thinking.

CHAPTER THREE

It Is "Our" Modernity

Delinking, Independent Thought, and Decolonial Freedom

ONCE UPON A TIME scholars assumed that the knowing subject in the disciplines is transparent, dis-incorporated from the known, and untouched by the geopolitical configuration of the world in which people are racially ranked and regions are racially configured. From a detached and neutral point of observation, the knowing subject maps the world and its problems, classifies people, and projects what is good for them. Today that assumption is no longer tenable, although there are still many believers. At stake is indeed the question of racism and epistemology.[1] And once upon a time scholars assumed that if you "come" from Latin America or Algeria, you have to "talk about" Latin America or Algeria, that in such cases you have to be a token of your culture. Such expectations will not arise if the author "comes" from Germany, France, England, or the United States. In such cases it is not assumed that you have to be a token of your culture, but that you are a theoretically minded person. As we know it: the First World has knowledge; the Third World has culture; Native Americans have wisdom; Anglo Americans have science. The need for political and epistemic delinking comes here to the fore, as do decolonizing knowledge and decolonial knowledges as necessary steps to imagining and building democratic, just, and non-imperial/colonial societies.

In the previous chapter my argument focused on redressing imperial disembodied and un-located assumptions about knowing and knowledge-making, both by agents as well as by institutions created to support, promote, and disseminate both principles and results. I argued that decolonial thinking and knowing are contesting that myth, showing the epistemic differential (e.g., coloniality of knowledge) and at the same time unveiling the hidden geo- and bio-graphical politics of knowledge of imperial epistemology. In this chapter I tilt the balance toward understanding and acting on epistemic decoloniality.

Geopolitics of knowledge (the enunciated) is a decolonial concept and goes hand in hand with geopolitics of knowing (the enunciation). Why is this a decolonial concept? Because it was introduced to deal with the epistemic dependency of Third World countries as well as of their scholars and intellectuals. Epistemic dependency was and is parallel to economic dependency. Geopolitics of knowledge was not, and could hardly have been, a concern of Euro-American scholarship and thoughts, for all the reasons explained in the previous chapter. Who and when, why and where knowledge is generated (rather than produced, like cars or cell phones)? Asking these questions means to shift the attention from the enunciated to the enunciation.

The shift I am indicating is the anchor (constructed, of course; located, of course; not just anchored by nature or by God) of the argument that follows. It is the beginning of any epistemic decolonial delinking with all its historical, political, and ethical consequences. Why? Because geo-historical and bio-graphic (constructed, of course, in the same way that zero point epistemology is constructed) loci of enunciation have been located by and through the making and transformation of the colonial matrix of power: a racial system of social classification that invented Occidentalism (e.g., Indias Occidentales); that created the conditions for Orientalism; that distinguished the South of Europe from its center (Hegel); and that remapped the world in First, Second, and Third ranking during the Cold War. Places of non-thought (of myth, non-Western religions, folklore, underdevelopment involving regions and people) today have been waking up from the long dossis of Westernization.[2] As argued in chapter 2, the anthropos, in inhabiting non-European places, discovered that she/he has been invented, as anthropos, by a locus of enunciation self-defined as humanitas. Now the anthropos is inside the space and institutions that created him/her. This book is a case in point.

There are currently two trajectories advanced by the former anthropos, who are no longer claiming recognition by or inclusion in the humanitas, but engaging in epistemic disobedience and delinking from the magic of the Western idea of modernity, ideals of humanity, and promises of economic growth and financial prosperity (*Wall Street Journal* dixit). In a way we, the anthropos, in order to be independent shall not behave like humanitas, for it is humanitas that made us dependent, increasing poverty, leaving people without jobs and health insurance to increase the gains of the company and the awards to their legally delinquent CEO, multiplying wars, and destroying the planet. One trajectory is dewesternization and the other decoloniality. As I mentioned before, one of the strongest advocates of the first is the Singaporean scholar and politician Kishore Mahbubani. But he is not alone in advancing and pushing dewesternizing projects; similar arguments have been advanced by the prime minister of Malaysia, Mahathir Mohamad. In the discourse he delivered to the Tenth Islamic Summit Conference, he advanced clear statements in the line of dewesternization, which, unsurprisingly, were not well received in the West. Let's examine these two paragraphs.

> I will not enumerate the instances of our humiliation and oppression, nor will I once again condemn our detractors and oppressors. It would be an exercise in futility because they are not going to change their attitudes just because we condemn them. If we are to recover our dignity and that of Islam, our religion, it is we who must decide, it is we who must act.
>
> To begin with, the Governments of all the Muslim countries can close ranks and have a common stand if not on all issues, at least on some major ones, such as on Palestine. We are all Muslims. We are all oppressed. We are all being humiliated. But we who have been raised by Allah above our fellow Muslims to rule our countries have never really tried to act in concert in order to exhibit at our level the brotherhood and unity that Islam enjoins upon us.[3]

There are two points in this paragraph defining the compulsion to dewesternize. The first is the sense of humiliation inflicted on the *damnés*; the other is dignity. You have the right to doubt whether Mahatir Mohammed believes in what he is saying or whether he is making a political statement. Whatever the case may be, the conditions are right for him to make such a statement. You should focus on the enunciation rather than on the enunciated. The case illustrates once more the distinction between class and racism. Commonly the damnés are imagined as lower class or, as Fanon correctly put it: I am poor because I am black, I am black because I am poor. In this sphere, the compulsion is toward decolonization. On the other hand, damnés in the sense of humiliating people racially (the colonial epistemic and ontological differences) transcend class, as is clear in Mahbubani (e.g., can Asians think?; and the humiliation Mahatir Mohamad is talking about). You could quibble and interpret it as an "excuse" to justify capitalism in the Eastern and Muslim way. Well, if you need excuses, there are many ways of getting them. However, we do know that yellow people and Muslims have been constantly put down, since 1500, in the growing discourse of Westernization. That is a socially constructed "fact" or, as Fanon would have it, a "socio-genetic" fact: I realize that being yellow or Muslim in your eyes makes me see myself differently in terms of how I conceived myself before realizing what being yellow and Muslim means in your hegemonic system of belief. For sure, dewesternizing rhetoric and projects could be critiqued for remaining within the miseries brought up by capitalism. However, it may not be to the advantage of decolonial projects to throw out the baby with the bathwater and not listen to the epistemic shift that dewesternizing arguments are enacting.

The second trajectory is being advanced by what I am describing as the decolonial option. The decolonial option is the singular connector of a diversity of decolonial paths. Decolonial paths have—as already underlined—one thing in common: the colonial wound, the fact that regions and people around the world have been classified as underdeveloped economically and mentally. Racism affects not only people in the lower class. It affects everyone and also regions or, better yet, the conjunction of natural resources needed by humanitas in places inhabited by anthropos, as we saw in the previous chapter. Decolonial options have one aspect in common with dewesternizing arguments: the definitive rejection of "being told," from the epistemic privileges of the zero point, what "we" are, what our ranking is in relation to the ideal of humanitas, and what we have to do to be recognized as such. However, decolonial and dewesternizing options diverge on one crucial and indisputable point: while the latter does not question the "civilization of death" hidden under the rhetoric of modernization and prosperity, of the improvement of modern institutions (e.g., liberal democracy and an economy propelled by the principle of growth and prosperity), decolonial options start from the principle that the regeneration of life shall prevail over primacy of recycling the production and reproduction of goods at the cost of the regeneration of life. I expand on this point below, commenting on Partha Chatterjee's reorienting of "Eurocentered modernity" toward the future in which "our modernity" (in India in his formulation but we can imagine similar arguments in Central Asia and the Caucasus, in South America, briefly, in all regions of the world in which Eurocentered modernity was either imposed or "adopted" by local actors assimilating to local histories inventing and enacting global designs) becomes the statement of inter-connected dispersal in which decolonial futures are being played out.

Last but not least, my argument doesn't claim originality ("originality" is one of the basic expectations of modern control of subjectivity), but aims at making a contribution to growing global decolonial processes. My claim is that geo- and body-politics of knowledge have been hidden from and not supported by the self-serving interests that promote the promise of growth, excellence, and happiness; or, put another way, that promote with a rhetoric of modernity that manifests in the myriad advertising of people jumping and smiling because of their new credit card, new iPad, or new Toyota. These images contrast with the serious and luxurious looks of handsome models, men and women, announcing Versace and Bulgari commodities. The task of decolonial thinking is that of unveiling the rhetoric and promises of modernity, showing its darker side, advocating and building global futures that aspire to the fullness of life rather than encouraging individual success at the expense of the many and of the planet.

Changing the Terms of the Conversation: What Kind of Knowledge Is Needed and What For?

The introduction of geo-historical and bio-graphical configurations in processes of knowing and understanding allows for a radical reframing (e.g., decolonizing) of the original formal apparatus of enunciation on which zero point epistemology has been built.[4] I have argued in the past (following up on Michel-Rolph Trouillot) that it is not enough to change the content; the terms of the conversation must be changed. Changing the terms of the conversation implies epistemic disobedience and delinking from disciplinary or interdisciplinary controversies and the conflict of interpretations. If you ask me how to do it, I will respond that there is no blueprint: many of us are in the process of doing it, and I provide examples in this book. As far as controversies and interpretations remain within the same rules of the game (terms of the conversation), the control of knowledge is not called into question. And in order to call into question the modern/colonial foundation of the control of knowledge, it is necessary to focus on the knower, rather than on the known. It means going to the very assumptions that sustain locus enunciations.

In what follows I revisit the formal apparatus of enunciation from the perspective of geo- and bio-graphic politics of knowledge. This would be one way of working toward changing the terms of the conversation. My revisiting is epistemic, rather than linguistic, although focusing on "languaging" and the enunciation is unavoidable if we aim at changing the terms and not only the content of the conversation.[5] The basic assumption is that the knower is always implicated, geo- and body-politically, in the known, although modern epistemology (e.g., the hubris of the zero point) managed to conceal both and built the figure of the detached observer, a neutral seeker of truth and objectivity who at the same time controls the disciplinary rules and puts himself or herself in a privileged position to evaluate and dictate.

The argument is structured as follows. In the section "The Semiotic Apparatus of Enunciation," I explore geo- and body-politics of knowledge. In the section "Disciplinary Delinking: Knowing, Sensing, and Understanding," I explore three cases in which geo- and body-politics of knowledge come forcefully to the fore: one from Africa, one from India, and the third from New Zealand. These three cases are complemented by a fourth from Latin/o América: my argument here is not the report of a detached observer, but the intervention of a decolonial project that "comes" from South America, the Caribbean, and Latinidad in the United States. Understanding the argument implies that the reader will shift his or her interpretation and move from the zero point of epistemology and the place of detached observer to the decolonial geo-politics of reasoning. In the section "Geopolitics of Knowing and Sensing: Its Ethical, Theoretical, and Political Consequences," I come back to the geo- and body-politics of knowledge and their epistemic, ethical, and political consequences. In the section "From the Semiotic Apparatus of Enunciation to the Geopolitics of Knowledge," I attempt to pull the strings together and weave my argument with the three cases explored, hoping that what I said will be taken not as the report of a detached observer but as the intervention of a decolonial thinker.

The Semiotic Apparatus of Enunciation

In semiotics, a basic distinction has been made (Emile Benveniste) between the enunciation and the enunciated. The distinction was necessary, for Benveniste, to ground the floating sign central to Ferdinand de Saussure's semiology and its development in French structuralism. Benveniste turned to enunciation and, by doing so, to the subject producing and manipulating signs, rather than to the structure of the sign itself (the enunciated). With this distinction in mind, I would venture to say that the four interrelated spheres of the colonial matrix of power (economy, authority, gender and sexuality, and knowledge/subjectivity) operate at the level of the enunciated, while patriarchy and racism ground the enunciation in both actors and institutions. Let's explore it in more detail.[6]

Benveniste laid out the "formal apparatus of enunciation" that he described on the bases of the pronominal system of any language (although his examples were mainly European languages), plus the temporal and spatial deitics or markers. The pronominal system is activated in each verbal (that is, oral or written) enunciation. The enunciator is of necessity located in the first person pronoun (I). If the enunciator says "we," the first person pronoun is presupposed in such a way that "we" could refer to the enunciator and the person or persons being addressed; or, by "we" the enunciator could mean he or she and someone else, not including the addressee or addressees. The remaining pronouns are activated around the I/we of the enunciation.

The same configuration obtains with temporal and spatial markers. The enunciator can only enunciate in the present. The past and the future are meaningful only in relation to the present of the enunciation. And the enunciator can only enunciate "here," that is, wherever she is located at the moment of enunciation. Thus, "there," "behind," "next to," "left and right," and so on are meaningful only in reference to the enunciator's "here."

Now let's take a second step. The extension of linguistic theory and analysis from the sentence to discourse prompted the introduction of "discursive frames" or "conversation frames."[7] Indeed, engaging in conversation, letter writing, meetings of various kinds, and so on, requires more than the formal-linguistic apparatus of enunciation: it requires a frame, that is, a context familiar to all participants, be they business meetings, casual conversations, Internet messages, or other familiar formats. While in everyday life frames are regulated by consensual loose agreements, there are more complex and regulated frames known today as "scholarly disciplines." In the European Renaissance, the disciplines were classified in the "trivium" and the "quadrivium," while Christian theology was the ceiling under which both the trivium and the quadrivium were housed. "Beyond" that ceiling loomed the world of the pagans, gentiles, and Saracens.

In eighteenth-century Europe, the movement toward secularization brought with it a radical transformation of the frame of mind and the organization of knowledge, the disciplines, and the institutions (e.g., the university). The Kantian-Humboldtian model displaced the goals and the format of the Renaissance university and instead promoted the secularization of the university, founded itself on secular science (from Galileo to Newton) and on secular philosophy, and both declared war against Christian theology.[8] During the first quarter of the nineteenth century, the reorganization of knowledge and the formation of new disciplines (biology, economy, psychology) left "behind" the trivium and the quadrivium and marched toward the new organization between human sciences (social sciences and the humanities) and natural sciences.[9] Wilhelm Dilthey came up with his groundbreaking epistemic distinction between ideographic and nomothetic sciences, the first concerned with meaning and interpretations, the second with laws and explanations.[10] These are still distinctions that hold true today, even if there have been, on the surface, disciplines that have crossed lines in one direction or another and pushed toward an interdisciplinarity that more often than not was based on these distinctions, although not addressing them.

So, then, we have moved from the formal apparatus of enunciation, to frames of conversations, to disciplines, and to something that is above the discipline, a supra frame that I would name "cosmology." The history of knowledge-making in modern Western history from the Renaissance on will have then theology and philosophy-science as the two cosmological frames, competing with each other at one level, but collaborating with each other when the matter is to disqualify forms of knowledge beyond these two friendly competing cosmological frames.

Both frames are institutionally and linguistically anchored in Western Europe. They are anchored in institutions (chiefly, through history, the European universities) and in the six modern (e.g., vernacular) European and imperial languages: Italian, Spanish, and Portuguese, dominants since the Renaissance to the Enlightenment; and German, French, and English, from the Enlightenment. Behind the six modern European languages of knowledge lay their historical foundation: Greek and Latin, and not, for instance, Arabic or Mandarin, Hindi or Urdu, Aymara or Náhuatl. The six mentioned languages, based on Greek and Latin, provided the "tool" to create a given conception of knowledge that was then extended to the increasing, through time, European colonies from the Americas to Asia and Africa. In the Americas, notably, we encounter something that is alien to Asian and African regions: the colonial European university, like the University of Santo Domingo, founded in 1538; the University of Mexico, founded in 1553; the University of San Marcos, Lima, founded in 1551; and Harvard University, founded in 1636.

The linguistic institutional foundation, management, and practices that knowledge-making brings allow me to extend Benveniste's formal apparatus of enunciation and to elaborate on enunciation and knowledge-making, focusing on the borders between the Western (in the precise linguistic and institutional sense I defined above) foundation of knowledge and understanding (epistemology and hermeneutics) and its confrontation with knowledge-making in non-European languages and institutions in China or in the Islamic caliphate or in the educational institutions of Maya, Aztecs, and Incas, which *Encyclopedia Britannica* includes, with great admiration, among their descriptions of "education in primitive and early civilizations."[11]

Perhaps Frantz Fanon conceptualized better than anyone else what I have in mind for extending Benveniste's formal apparatus of enunciation. In *Black Skin, White Masks* Fanon made an epistemic foundational statement about language that no one, in the heated atmosphere of structuralism and poststructuralism, picked up in the 1960s. And it was still ignored by the most semantic and philological orientation of Emile Benveniste's approaches to language. This is what Fanon said.

> To speak means to be in a position to use a certain syntax, to grasp the morphology of this or that language, but it means above all to assume a culture, to support the weight of a civilization. . . . The problem that we confront in this chapter is this: The Negro of the Antilles will be proportionally whiter— that is, he will come closer to being a real human being—in direct ratio to his mastery of the French language.[12]

Fanon's dictum applies to language, but also to the sphere of knowledge in general: the Negro of the Antilles, the Indian from India and from the Americas or New Zealand and Australia, the Negro from sub-Saharan Africa, the Muslim from the Middle East or Indonesia, and so on. Replacing "French language" with "disciplinary norms" we can paraphrase Fanon: the anthropos will come closer to being a real human being in direct ratio to his or her mastery of disciplinary norms. Obviously, Fanon's point is not to be recognized or accepted in the club of "real human being" as defined on the basis of white knowledge and white history, but to take away the imperial/ colonial idea of what it means to be human. This is a case, precisely, in which the assault on the imperiality of modern/colonial loci of enunciations (disciplines and institutions) is called into question. A case in point was the question asked by many philosophers in Africa and South America, during the Cold War, and being asked today by Latinos and Latinas philosophers in the United States where there is an African, South American, or Latino/a philosophy. The question was: Is there African philosophy or philosophy in Africa? Is there philosophy in Latin America or a Latin American philosophy? The question was relevant but poorly formulated. Lately, there was a turnaround in which the question was redressed in decolonial frames of mind that has put "philosophy" in its regional history and has removed it from its universalizing pretensions. While during the Cold War the question was asked with a touch of nostalgia or inferiority complex, in the twenty-first century the question is no longer asked; because, if there is no philosophy in Africa and Latin America in the sense that Greeks and modern continental Europe understand philosophy, the question is moot. People still think. This was one of the great legacies of Rodolfo Kusch's work and the main point of this chapter.

To address this problem I turn once again and in more detail to the concepts of geopolitics, body-politics of knowledge, and the colonial epistemic difference, to which I return below.[13]

Disciplinary Delinking: Knowing, Sensing, and Understanding

If to speak a language means to carry the weight of a civilization, then to engage in disciplinary knowledge-making means to master the language of the discipline in two senses. You can of course do sociology in Spanish,

Portuguese, Arabic, Mandarin, Bengali, Akan, and so on. But doing it in those languages will put you at a disadvantage in relation to mainstream disciplinary debates. It will be a sort of "local sociology." Granted, doing sociology in French, German, or English will also be "local sociology." The difference is that you have a better chance of being read by scholars in any of the languages mentioned, but the inverse will not hold. You will have to get your work translated into French, German, or English. That today would be considered Western sociology, located in the heart of Europe and the United States. There are many variations and the issues have been addressed many times. I provide three examples.

The first cases to be examined are the arguments sustained by two African scholars, sociologists, and philosophers, Paulin J. Hountondji and Kwasi Wiredu. Hountondji addressed head-on a question that has been prominent among Third World intellectuals (from 1950 to 1990) all over the world. However, since it did not receive much attention in mainstream intellectual debates and among publishing houses, it remained a pervasive issue literally in the margins. From 1960 on mainstream debates in the humanities and social sciences focused on structuralism and poststructuralism in its various forms (psychoanalysis, deconstruction, archeology of knowledge, communicative action). The social sciences, on the other hand, were enjoying their promotion after the Second World War and gained a status in the domain of scholarship (in England, Germany, and France) they did not have before the war.

The promotion of the social sciences status was part of a changing leadership hand in the world order, and the United States was taking over the role that Europe (England, France, and Germany) had enjoyed until then. Geopolitically and geo-economically the three world division was parallel to geo-epistemology or the distribution of scientific labor, as Carl Pletsch mapped it in the early 1980s.[14] Yet, Pletsch's landmark article was still centrifugal: it mapped *how* First World scholars thought out the new world order. First World scholars have the privilege of both being in the enunciated (one of the three worlds), but also being the only and one enunciator (the First World). As a consequence, what scholars in the Second and Third World thought of themselves and how they were responding was not taken into account. They (Second and Third) were classified, but had no say in the classification, other than to react or respond. And the time has come.

Geopolitics of knowledge and of knowing was one of the responses from the Third World to the First World. Anchored in the Third rather than in the First World the gaze changed direction. Now the First World, the place of the humanitas, became the object of observation and the unsuspecting subject of critique by the anthropos. There was a difference however. The gazes were not symmetrical. Looking at the First from the Third World implies that you know you are expected to be an informant, not a thinker. Local needs in the Third World have been shaped by both the interference of global designs—exported and imported from the First World—that basically responded to the needs of the First not of the Third World. Humanitas was not interested in the anthropos, but in having an object of investigation to fulfill their own needs and desires. Modernity has its own internal critics (psychoanalysis, Marxism, postmodernism), but in the Third World the problems are not the same as in the First, and therefore to transplant both the problems and methods from the First to the Third World is no less a colonial operation than transplanting armies or factories to satisfy the needs of the First World. What I mean is that Paris and London do not have the same colonial legacy as Mumbai, Algeria, or La Paz. What geopolitics of knowledge is unveiling is the epistemic privilege of the First World. In the three worlds of distribution of scientific labor, the First World had indeed the privilege of inventing the classification and being part of it. In this vein Hountondji contested, "It seems urgent to me that the scientist in Africa, and perhaps more generally in the Third World, question themselves on the meaning of their practices as scientists, its real function in the economy of the entirety of scholarship, its place in the process of production of knowledge on a world-wide basis."[15]

Hountondji touches on several dimensions of the "scientific and scholarly dependency" of African and other Third World countries. While recognizing the "improvements" in material conditions in some countries, such as laboratories, libraries, and buildings, he strongly argues that Third World countries are, in terms of the economy, providing natural resources to industrial countries and, in the sciences, providing data to be processed in the laboratories (literal laboratories in the natural sciences, metaphorical laboratories in the social sciences) of the First World. The bottom line for Hountondji is that in spite of the "material progress" mentioned above, in Third World countries "scientific designs" are not created by Africans but by

Western Europeans or U.S. Americans. Consequently, "scientific designs" respond not to African needs and visions, but to the needs and visions of Western Europeans (mainly those in England, France, and Germany, but also those in the second-order developed countries, like Sweden, Belgium, and Holland). African scholars, furthermore, depend also on the professional magazines and publications created, printed, and distributed in the First World. The situation is not new; it is engrained in the very structure of modernity/coloniality, which Hountondji renders in the language of "trade and colonization": "Thus, it was natural that the annexation of the Third World, its integration in the worldwide capitalist system through trade and colonization, also comprise a 'scientific' window, so that the draining of material resources goes hand in hand with brain drainage and, at another level, with the expropriation of archeological remains or cultural objects that end up enriching metropolitan museums of world cultures."[16]

A counterargument could be thought out by saying that the equation may have been true during the Cold War, but that it no longer holds in the era when "globalization," since the fall of the Soviet Union, overcame the three world division by creating the splendid borderless world that has appeared, is in the process of erasing such differences and refreshing the rhetoric of development enacted during the Cold War years. Development, in the era of globalization, is no longer competing with communism. And in fact, the *Harvard International Review* dedicated an issue to Global Health in which it said, "Ideally, training will be linked to the development of research institutions in developing countries by pairing them with institutions in the developed world. These activities must be adequately funded and researchers from the West must be given time and credit to participate in institution building. A number of first-rate training and research institutions in the developing world, including the International Center for Diarrheal Disease Research in Dhaka, Bangladesh, have come about through years of collaboration."[17]

In the same article just mentioned, we find the following prognosis.

DEVELOPING THE SOUTH

What, then, should be the strategic approaches to promoting health research capacity in developing countries? There are many strategies and goals to be pursued, none of which are sufficient alone. The global health research agenda must be developed by scientists from both the North and the South. Too often, the research agenda of developing countries is set by others outside the country. The golden rule of development—"He who has the gold makes the rules"—usually applies. This is particularly true of health services research wherein local scientists may wish to address questions that seem unimportant to outside donors. These scientists may want to conduct a study similar to one already done elsewhere, a study that is nonetheless essential because it will convince their own medical establishment of the importance of the work. Many countries carried out studies on ORT that added little to the international literature but helped to convince their own pediatricians of the importance of this intervention to treat diarrhea.[18]

Kwasi Wiredu made a call similar to that of Hountondji in his "Formulating Modern Thought in African Languages: Some Theoretical Considerations." But both calls have been lost, forgotten, or ignored by the growing noise of technology, money, laboratories, and global designs drawn in the developed world *for* the underdeveloped world, as Cash's article on global health suggests. Wiredu's call has little chance of making the "front page" of Harvard University publications profiling "experts" on developing the South. The call made by Wiredu was the following: "Conceptually speaking, then, the maxim of the moment should be: 'African, know thyself.'"[19]

If you do not have the time to read Wiredu's argument in its entirety, please do not jump to unwarranted conclusions or think that Wiredu is proposing to do science in the Akan or Luo language. Hold up your smile and your sense that traditionalist, essentialist, out-of-fashion, and out-of-time African philosophers are dreaming of and wanting a world forever gone. Let's pause and pay attention to what Wiredu is saying: it is not a return to anything, in the same way that Evo Morales is not proposing a "return to the Ayllu" before the Spanish arrived and brought with them the seeds of modernity that two centuries earlier England and France had harvested, and that the United States harvested later.

You see, China, India, and Bolivia today, are not "going back in time." They are moving toward the future following different paths. But at the same time, they are not eager to make modernity, according to Western standards, their goal in life. Following up on what is going on in China,

India, and Bolivia (rather than what the Euro-American media said is going on in China, India, and Bolivia), one realizes that there are too many important issues to deal with, and that to be modern, in the Western sense, is becoming less and less of a concern. That is what dewesternizing and decolonial means in the final analysis. Much has been written and said since the Wall Street financial crisis suggesting that the U.S. "model" has collapsed and that history is globally moving toward a polycentric world. Wiredu was calling for an "epistemic awakening" of Africans and Third World scholars and intellectuals, which had already been happening and continues to grow around the world.

These considerations take me to the second example of this section, this time I will focus on an Indian political theorist, Partha Chatterjee. In a landmark article in which geo- and body-politics of knowledge come clearly to the fore, Chatterjee brings—indirectly—the missing chapter in Pletsch's argument. Chatterjee addressed the problem of "modernity in two languages." The article, collected in his book *A Possible India* (1998), is the English version of a lecture he delivered in the Bengali language and in Calcutta.[20] The English version is not just a translation, but a theoretical reflection on geopolitics of knowledge and epistemic and political delinking.

Unapologetically and forcefully, Chatterjee structured his talk on the distinction between "our modernity" and "their modernity." Rather than offer either a single modernity, defended from modern perspectives in the First World (in Pletsch's distinction), or the most dependent "peripheral," "subaltern," "marginal" modernities, Chatterjee plants a solid pillar with which to build the future of an inclusive modernity, one that is not independent from "their modernity" (because Western expansion is a fact) but that is nonetheless unrepentantly, unashamedly, and impenitently "ours."

This is one of the strengths of Chatterjee's argument. Let us remember before exploring his argument that the British entered into India, commercially, toward the end of the eighteenth century and, politically, during the first half of the nineteenth century, when England and France, after Napoleon, extended their tentacles into Asia and Africa. So then, for Chatterjee, in contradistinction with South American and Caribbean intellectuals, "modernity" means Enlightenment, and not Renaissance. Not surprisingly, Chatterjee takes Kant's "What Is Enlightenment" as a pillar of modernity. Enlightenment meant—for Kant—that Man (in the sense of human being) was coming of age, abandoning his immaturity, reaching his freedom. Chatterjee points out Kant's silence (intentionally or not) and Michel Foucault's shortsightedness in his reading of Kant's essays. Missing in Kant's celebration of freedom and maturity and in Foucault's own celebration of the Enlightenment was the fact that Kant's concept of Man and humanity was based on the European concept of Man from the Renaissance to the Enlightenment, and not on the "lesser humans" that populated the world beyond the heart of Europe. So, "enlightenment" was not for everybody. Thus, if you do not embody Kant's and Foucault's local history, memory, language, and "embodied" experience, what shall you do? Buy a pair of Kant's and Foucault's shoes; or, look around you and think about what has to be done in the same way that Kant and Foucault looked around themselves and thought about what had to be done? This is what should be imitated of European thinkers: what they did, not so much what they said.

One point in Chatterjee's insightful interpretation of Kant and Foucault is relevant for the argument I am developing here. Paraphrasing Kant, Chatterjee points out that in the "universal domain of the pursuit of knowledge," which Kant locates in the "public" (not the "private") sphere, where "freedom of thought" has its function, he (Kant) is presupposing and claiming "the right of free speech" advocated only for those who have the requisite qualifications for engaging in the exercise of reason and the pursuit of knowledge, and those "who can use that freedom in a responsible manner."[21] Chatterjee notices that Foucault did not raise this issue, although he could have, given the interest of his own research. I would surmise, following Chatterjee's argument, that what Foucault did not have was the colonial experience and political interest propelled by the colonial wound that allowed Chatterjee to "feel" and "see" beyond both Kant and Foucault. Thus, Chatterjee concludes this argument stating that in both Kant and Foucault, what we encounter is the "theme of the rise of experts and the ubiquitous authority of specialists." And he continues: "In other words, just as we have meant by enlightenment an unrestricted and universal field for the exercise of reason, so have we built up an intricately differentiated structure of authorities which specifies who has the right to say what on which subjects."[22]

Chatterjee acknowledges, like Hountondji and Wiredu in Africa (although independent of each other, since "influence" goes from Europe to United States to Africa and India, but not yet in conversations between

Africa and India), that the Third World (in Pletsch's terms) has been mainly a "consumer" of First World scholarship; and like his African colleagues, Chatterjee bases his argument "in the way the history of our modernity has been intertwined with the history of colonialism. For that reason, 'we' have never quite been able to believe that there exists a universal domain of free discourse, unfettered by differences of race or nationality." Chatterjee closes his argument,

> Somehow, from the very beginning, we had made a shrewd guess that given the close complicity between modern knowledge and modern regimes of power, we would for ever remain consumers of universal modernity; never would we be taken as serious producers. It is for this reason that we have tried, for over a hundred years, to take our eyes away from this chimera of universal modernity and clear up a space where we might become the creators of our own modernity.[23]

I imagine you are getting the point. The argument is similar to arguments advanced by Guaman Poma de Ayala, in the early seventeenth century, and by Ottobah Cugoano, in the second half of the eighteenth century, when they took Christianity in their own hands and instead of submitting to it with the humility of the humiliated, they appropriated it to slap the face of European Christians, using arguments that reflected their unique perspectives—those of an Indian of Tawantinsuyu and of a formerly enslaved African in the Caribbean who reached London—to unveil the inhumanity of European ideals, visions, and self-fulfilling prophecies.[24]

Yes, indeed, Chatterjee is aware that nationalists in the nineteenth century and Hindu nationalism made similar claims. From the recognition of the shortcoming of the ways in which nationalists deal with "our" modernity, it doesn't follow that the solution is to fall into the arms of "their" modernity. The point is this: thanks, Immanuel Kant. Now let us figure out how to pursue "our modernity" now that we have reached maturity, by gaining India's independence, in 1947, and expelling British colonists, their institutions, and their ideals of progress, development, and civilization. We have, so to speak, "our own" ways of being. Independent thought is at stake, as we have seen in the previous chapter, in Lloyd Best's claim. In fact, I would translate Chatterjee into my own vocabulary: we know that we have to decolonize being and to do so we have to start by decolonizing knowledge. Which are the points made by Hountondji and Wiredu.

And this takes me to the third example: Linda Tuhiwai Smith is an anthropologist in New Zealand and a Maori. In other words, individuals of Maori descent live and work beside nationals of European descent; both have coexisted in the same land since the British started their management of New Zealand. James Busby was named "Official British Resident," in May 1833, and instructed to organize the Maori chiefs in a united body to deal with the increasing instability provoked by the grand greed of the French, Americans, and the British themselves. As it is well known, Maoris did not care about "private property," but Europeans did. The "New World" increased their appetite to transform land into private property beginning in the sixteenth century.

In Pletsch's aforementioned article, anthropology (that is, the Western discipline thus named) was assigned Third World status in the scientific distribution of labor that reorganized the politics of knowledge during the Cold War. Now, it is not a secret that quantitatively the majority of anthropologists, men and women, were white and Euro-American. However, anthropology as a discipline found also its niche in the Third World. What, then, would a Third World anthropologist do if he or she were to be part of the "object of study" of a First World anthropologist? This is an uncomfortable situation that has been addressed in Hountondji's articles cited above and by the philosopher Rodolfo Kusch, analyzed in chapter 2. Well, one answer to the question is that a Third World anthropologist would do the same job and ask similar questions as a First World anthropologist, the difference being that he or she would be "studying" people living in his or her own country. After independence in the Americas of the nineteenth century, when anthropology was created, and after decolonization in Asia and Africa after the Second World War, the colonial matrix mutated so as to create the conditions for internal colonialism: that is to say, the same structure of management and control were now in the hands of natives instead of being in the hands of French or British officers. Anthropology-like work in the nineteenth century, as well as anthropologists in the Third World in the second half of the twentieth century, both ran the risk of reproducing in their own regions what anthropologists from the First World were doing. Fortunately, this situation began to be redressed in the mid-1980s, when anthropologists began to focus on the complicities between anthropology and imperialism. There were variations, depending on whether in a given country the nationals were "natives" or "of European descent." It was more commonly accepted that anthropologists in the Third World would be of European descent—for example, in South America, South Africa, or Australia. The end result has been that, in general, anthropological research in former colonial regions would be dependent and secondary to anthropology as taught and practiced in the First World—there is nothing new or remarkable in this. However, Smith pushes the envelope: as ab-original and anthropologist, she embraces the ab-original perspective and uses anthropology to build arguments for the "freedom" of the Maori nation.

The remarkable breakthrough, then, comes when a Maori becomes an anthropologist and practices anthropology as a Maori, rather than studying the Maori as an anthropologist. Epistemic disobedience and delinking are, in this case, two sides of the same coin. Let me explain this idea further by starting with a quotation from Linda T. Smith's *Decolonizing Methodologies: Research and Indigenous Peoples* (1999). One section of the first chapter is subtitled "On Being Human."

> One of the supposed characteristics of primitive peoples was that we could not use our minds or intellects. We could not invent things, we could not create institutions or history, we could not imagine, we could not produce anything of value, we did not know how to use land and other resources from the natural world, we did not practice the "arts" of civilization. By lacking such values we disqualified ourselves, not just from civilization but also from humanity itself. In other words, we were not "fully human"; some of us were not even considered partially human. Ideas about what counted as human in association with the power to define people as human or not human were already encoded in imperial and colonial discourses prior to the period of imperialism covered here.[25]

No, Smith is not still practicing Western anthropology: she is precisely shifting the geography of reasoning and subsuming anthropological tools into Maori (instead of Western) cosmology and ideology. China is a capitalist country, but one couldn't say that China is "practicing Western, neoliberal capitalism, unless we accept the principle that the type of economy that liberals and Marxists describe as capitalism can only be run under neoliberal premises. I suspect it would be a narrow Eurocentered perspective, and an insult for Chinese leaders, that would describe the Chinese economy as neo-liberal. Certainly, there is a self-serving interest in Smith's move, as much as there is a self-serving interest among European anthropologists observing the Maori. The only difference is that the self-interests do not always coincide, and Maoris are no longer amenable to being the objects observed by European anthropologists. Well, you get the idea of the inter-relations between the politics of identity and epistemology, which becomes identity in politics, including academic and disciplinary politics. You could certainly be a Maori and an anthropologist, and, by being an anthropologist, suppress the fact that you are Maori or black Caribbean or Aymara. Or, you can choose the decolonial option: engage in knowledge-making to "advance" the Maori cause, rather than to "advance" the discipline (e.g., anthropology). Why would someone be interested in merely advancing the discipline if not for either alienation or self-interest?

If you engage in decolonial thinking, and therefore engage the decolonial options, and put anthropology "at your service," like Smith does, then you engage in shifting the geography of reason, by unveiling and enacting geopolitics and body-politics of knowledge. You can also say that there are non-Maori anthropologists of Euro-American descent who truly support and are concerned with the mistreatment of Maoris, and that they are really working to remedy the situation. In that case, the anthropologists could follow two different paths. One path will be in line with that of Father Bartolomé de las Casas and with Marxism (Marxism being a European invention responding to European problems). When Marxism encounters "people of color," men or women, the situation becomes parallel to anthropology: being Maori (or Aymara, or Afro-Caribbean like Aimé Césaire and Frantz Fanon) is not necessarily in smooth relation with Marxism, because of the privileged class relations over racial hierarchies and patriarchal and heterosexual normativity. The other path will be to "submit" to the guidance of Maori or Aymara anthropologists and engage, with them, in the decolonial option. Politics of identity is different from identity politics—the former is open to whoever wants to join, while the second tends to be enclosed by the definition of a given identity.

I am not saying that a Maori anthropologist has epistemic privileges over a New Zealand anthropologist of Anglo descent (or a British or U.S. anthropologist). I am saying that a New Zealand anthropologist of Anglo descent has no right to guide the "locals" in what is good or bad for the Maori population. The decolonial and the anthropological are two distinct options. The former puts disciplinary tools at the service of the problem being addressed. The latter tends to put the problem at the service of the discipline. That is precisely the naturalization of modernity that is taken for granted, and that appears as the concept of knowledge in the report of the *Harvard International Review*, wherein a group of U.S. experts expressed the belief that they can really decide what is good and what is bad for "developing countries." Granted, there are many locals in developing countries who, because of imperial and capitalist cosmology, were led to believe (or pretended they believed, or found it convenient to endorse) that what is good for developed countries is good for underdeveloped countries as well, because the former know "how to get there" and can lead the way for underdeveloped countries trying to reach the same level. I am just saying, following Wiredu's dictum ("African, know thyself"), that there is a good chance that Maoris would know better what is good or bad for themselves than would an expert from Harvard or a white anthropologist from New Zealand. And there is also a good chance that an expert from Harvard may "know" what is good for himself or herself and his or her people, even when he or she thinks that he or she is stating what is good for "them," that is, the underdeveloped countries and people.

Returning to the quotation by Smith, it would also be possible to object that the use of the first-person-plural pronoun "we" denounces an essentialist conception of being Maori or that "we" indeed is not a tenable stanza at the time when postmodernist theories really ended with the idea of a coherent and homogenous subject, be it individual or collective. It could, indeed, be said. But . . . remember Chatterjee. It would be fine and comfortable for modern subjects (that is, those who embody the languages, memories, and cosmology of Western modernity, "their" modernity). It would not be convenient for Maori, Aymara, or Ghanian philosophers or for Indians from Calcutta, who are modern/colonial subjects and would rather have "our modernity" than listen to vanguard postmodern critics or Western experts on developing underdeveloped countries. Thus, geopolitics of knowledge comes to the fore. There are many "our modernities" around the globe—Ghanian, Indian from Calcutta, Maori from New Zealand, Afro-Caribbean, North African, Islamic in its extended diversity—while there is one "their" modernity within the "heterogeneity" of France, England, Germany, and the United States.

If you are getting the idea of what shifting the geography of reason and enacting the geopolitics of knowledge means, you will also begin understanding what decolonial option (in general) or decolonial options (in each particular and local history) means. It means, in the first place, to engage in epistemic disobedience, as it is clear in the three examples I offered. Epistemic disobedience is necessary to take on civil disobedience (Gandhi, Martin Luther King) to its point of no return. Civil disobedience, within modern Western epistemology (and remember: Greek and Latin, and six vernacular European modern and imperial languages), could only lead to reforms, not to transformations. For this simple reason, the task of decolonial thinking and the enactment of the decolonial option in the twenty-first century starts from epistemic delinking: from acts of epistemic disobedience.[26]

Geopolitics of Knowing and Sensing: Its Ethical, Theoretical, and Political Consequences

In all three cases (with my own argument here as the fourth case) I have underlined geopolitics of knowledge, which is what comes more forcefully although body-politics of knowledge is obvious in all of them. What do I mean by body-politics of knowledge? Frantz Fanon is again useful to set the stage; and I do so through decolonial interpretations of Fanon such as those of Lewis Gordon (*Fanon and the Crisis of European Man*) and Sylvia Wynter ("Towards the Sociogenic Principle").

First, a disclaimer is necessary. Much has been discussed with regard to and written about Michel Foucault's concept of bio-politics. Bio-politics refers to emerging state technologies (strategies, in a more traditional vocabulary) of population control that went hand in hand with the emergence of the modern nation-state. Foucault devoted his attention mainly to Europe, but such technologies were applied to the colonies as well. In Argentina (and South America in general), for example, the push for eugenics toward the end of the nineteenth century has been studied with certain details lately. The differences between bio-politics in Europe and bio-politics in the colonies lie in the racial distinction between the European population (even when bio-politically managed by the state) and the population of the colonies: less human, subhumans, as Smith pointed out. But it is also important to remember that bio-political techniques enacted on colonial populations returned as a boomerang to Europe in the Holocaust. Many analysts have already pointed out how Hitler re-activated technologies of control and racist ideology that European actors and institutions had applied to the non-European population, to control and exterminate non-ethnic Germans, mostly Jews. This consideration shifts the geography of reason and illuminates the fact that the colonies were not a secondary and marginal event in the history of Europe, but that, on the contrary, the colonial history is the non-acknowledged center in the making of modern Europe. That is why we need coloniality. Bio-politics is half of the story. Coloniality is the missing half, the darker side of modernity and bio-politics, that decolonial arguments unveil. Bio-politics enacts a postmodern critique of modernity. Coloniality enacts a decolonial critique of modernity.

Thus body-politics is the decolonial response to state-managed bio-politics: body-politics describes decolonial technologies ratified by bodies who realized, first, that they were considered less human, and second, that the very act of describing them as less human was a radical un-human consideration. That is what the sociogenic principle is all about. Thus, the lack of humanity was placed in imperial actors, institutions, and knowledges that had the arrogance to decide that certain people they did not like were less human. Body-politics is a fundamental component of decolonial thinking and doing, the sociogenic (together with border thinking) a fundamental concept to engage the decolonial option.

From the Semiotic Apparatus of Enunciation to the Geopolitics of Knowledge

We are now in a position to extend Benveniste's formal apparatus of enunciation to account for knowledge-making and the global power differential described in the previous sections.

Knowledge-making in the modern/colonial world is at once knowledge in which the very concept of "modernity" rests as the judge and warrantor of legitimate and sustainable knowledge. Vandana Shiva suggested the term "monocultures of the mind" to describe Western imperial knowledge and its epistemically un-democratic implementation.[27]

Knowledge-making presupposes a semiotic code (languages, images, sounds, colors, etc.) shared between users in semiotic exchanges. Although knowledge-making is a common human endeavor (and I would say, of any living organism since without "knowing" life cannot be sustained), the racialization of places and people in the formation and transformation of the colonial matrix of power not only established hierarchical ranking between languages and categories of thought, but also built economic and political structures of domination and oppression based on the geopolitical and hierarchical organization of knowledge. Institutions are created that accomplish two functions: training of new (epistemically obedient) members, and controlling who enters and what knowledge-making is allowed, disavowed, devalued, or celebrated. If these conditions apply to all known civilizations, past and present, our focus here is on the modern/colonial world order and in the complicities between politics, economy, and epistemology.

Knowledge-making entrenched with imperial/colonial purposes from the European Renaissance to United States neo-liberalism (that is, political economy as advanced by F. A. Hayek and Milton Friedman), which guided the last stage of globalization (from Ronald Reagan to the Wall Street collapse), was grounded, as mentioned before, in specific languages, institutions, and geo-historical locations. The languages of Western imperial knowledge-making (and the self-definition of the West—the West of Jerusalem—by social actors who saw themselves as Western Christians) were practiced (speaking and writing) by social actors (human beings) dwelling in a specific geo-historical space, with specific memories that said actors constructed and reconstructed in the process of creating their own Christian, Western, and European identity.

Briefly, the formal apparatus of enunciation is the basic apparatus for engaging in institutional and purposive knowledge-making that is geopolitically oriented. At the time, theology was the overarching conceptual and cosmological frame of knowledge-making in which social actors engaged and institutions (monasteries, churches, universities, state, etc.) were created. Secularization, in the eighteenth century, displaced Christian theology, and secular philosophy and sciences took its place. Both frames, theological and secular, bracketed their geo-historical foundation and, instead, made of theology and philosophy/science a frame of knowledge beyond geo-historical and body location. The subject of theological knowledge depended on the dictates of God, while the subject of secular philosophy/science depended on Reason, on the Cartesian ego/mind and Kant's transcendental reason. Thus, Western imperial knowledge, cast in Western imperial languages, was theo-politically and ego-politically founded. Such foundations legitimized the assumptions and claims that knowledge was beyond bodies and places, and that Christian theology and secular philosophy and science were the limits of knowledge-making, beyond and besides which all knowledge was lacking: folklore, myth, traditional knowledge were invented to legitimize imperial epistemology.

Theo- and ego-politics of knowledge bracketed also the body in knowledge-making.[28] By locating knowledge in the mind only, and bracketing "secondary qualities" (affects, emotions, desires, anger, humiliation, etc.), social actors who happened to be white, inhabiting Europe/Western Christendom, and speaking specific modern European languages assumed that what was right for them in that place and fulfilling their affects, emotions, fears, angers was indeed valid for the rest of the planet and consequently that they were the depositors, warrantors, creators, and distributors of universal knowledge.

In the process of globally enacting the European system of belief and structure of knowledge, these actors encountered human beings who were not Christian, did not inhabit the memories of Europe, from Greece through Rome, spoke strange languages and were not familiar with the six modern imperial European languages, and, frankly, did not care much about all of that, until they realized that they were expected and requested to submit to European (and in the twentieth century to the United States) knowledge, belief, lifestyle, and worldview.

Responses to the contrary came, since the sixteenth century, from all over the globe, but imperial theo- and ego-politics of knowledge managed to prevail through economically sustained institutions (universities, museums, delegations, state officers, armies, etc.). Now, the type of responses I am referring to were responses provoked by the making and remaking of the colonial matrix of power: a complex conceptual structure, as explained in chapter 1, that guided actions in the domain of economy (exploitation of labor and appropriation of land and natural resources), authority (government, military forces), gender/sexuality, and knowledge/subjectivity. Since the responses I am referring to were responses to the colonial matrix of power, I would describe such responses as decolonial.[29] The cases and examples I offered in the previous section, "Disciplinary Delinking," also show that in such responses decolonial geopolitics of knowledge confronts—head-on—imperial theo- and ego-politically based assumptions about the universal knowledge-making which happen to be managed in and by institutional, linguistic, and conceptual grounding that defines and is managed by Western civilization.

But there is still another dimension in decolonial politics of knowledge relevant for my argument: the claim that knowledge-making for well-being, rather than for controlling and managing populations for imperial interest, shall come from local experiences and needs, rather than from local imperial experiences and needs projected onto the globe, also invokes the body-politics of knowledge. Why? Because regions and locales in which imperial languages were not ancestrally spoken, and that were alien to the history of Greek and Latin, were disqualified. The disqualification of non-Western languages from the domain of sustainable knowledge was filled up, in the region and domain of those languages, by imperial languages. Notice that Spanish America and British India are not just regions, but regions where imperial languages displaced native languages like Aymara, Quechua, Tzotil, Urdu, Bengali, and Nepali. In Spanish America, Spanish is the only national language. In India, Hindi was established as the national language, alongside English; but the fact remains that Hindi is not a language of international scholarship, and Hindi is not, alongside English, the national language of England. Racism, as we sense it today, was the result of two conceptual inventions of imperial knowledge: that certain bodies were inferior to others, and that inferior bodies carried inferior intelligence and inferior languages. The emergence of body-politics of knowledge is a second strand of decolonial thinking, and a key element of the decolonial option.

You can still argue that there are "bodies" and "regions" in need of guidance from developed "bodies" and "regions" that got there first and know how to do it. As an honest liberal, you would recognize that you do not want to "impose" your knowledge and experience, but to "work with the locals." The problem is, what agenda will be implemented: yours or theirs? Back, then, to Chatterjee and Smith.

Decolonial thinking presupposes delinking (epistemically and politically) from the web of imperial knowledge (theo- and ego-politically grounded), from disciplinary management. Delinking means also epistemic disobedience. A common topic of conversation today, after the financial crisis on Wall Street, centers on "how to save capitalism." A decolonial question would be: "Why would you like to save capitalism and not to save human beings?" "Why would an abstract entity be saved, and not the ecological and human lives that capitalism is constantly destroying?" And you cannot answer those questions by proposing to reform capitalism in order to fulfill those goals and arguing that capitalism, which created poverty, could solve the problem that capitalism created. That is how modernity/coloniality works. In the same vein, geo- and body-politics of knowledge, decolonial thinking and the decolonial option, place human lives and life in general first, rather than advocating for the "transformation of the disciplines." But, still, claiming life and human lives first, decolonial thinking is not joining forces with "the politics of life itself," as Nikolas Rose has it.[30] This is the "politics of life itself," according to Rose, and represents the last development in the "mercantilization of life" and of "bio-power" (as Foucault has it). In the "politics of life itself," political and economic strategies for controlling life join forces with consumerism in a particular way: consumers are seduced to consume not because of the value of having such and such an object (pharmaco) but because consuming such pharmaco will ensure a better and happier life. This allows Rose to elaborate on "biological citizens" the "somatic ethics and the spirit of bio-capital.[31] What is being sold and bought is not merely the commodity but the commodity as the ticket to enter the dream-world of a longer and better life. Bio-politics, in Foucault's conception, was one of the practical consequences of the ego-politics of knowledge that was implemented in the sphere of the state. The politics of life itself extends life to the market. Thus, the politics of life itself describes the enormous potential of biotechnology to generate consumers who invest their earnings in buying artificial-health products in order to maintain the reproduction of technology that will "improve" the control of human beings at the same time as it creates more wealth through the money invested by consumers who buy health-promoting technology. This is the point where decolonial options, grounded in geo- and body-politics of knowledge, engage in both decolonizing knowledge and delinking from the web of imperial/modern knowledge and from the colonial matrix of power.

In the next two chapters, I turn to two basic categories, that of space and that of time, and explore how Western modernity managed to control knowledge by creating an image of the "here and now" (e.g., Europe and modernity) by means of colonizing time (e.g., the invention of the Middle Ages) and the colonization of space (e.g., the invention of the anthropos—pagans, barbarians, etc.), as well as, by the eighteenth century, collapsing space and time by introducing the word *primitive*: primitives existed back in time and out-there in space. Time and space cannot be clearly separated; so you will find analysis of the ideological construction of space in the chapter on time, and the ideological construction of time in the chapter on space. While in the two previous chapters I focused on building genealogies of decolonial thinking and mapping the decolonial option, in the next two chapters I focus on the imperial epistemic construction of space and time. The analysis is carried on from a decolonial perspective. That is to say, my own analysis is an effort to enlist myself in the genealogy of thought that I mapped in the two previous chapters. Now we move to a different landscape to encounter two crucial concepts of the modern imaginary and of Western civilization, time and space, that have been both mapped already by the Treatises of Tordesilla and Saragossa: if both treatises set the foundation for the second nomos of the earth, both treatises were the time-present from which the Middle Ages and Antiquity have been invented.

Part Three

CHAPTER FOUR

(De)Coloniality at Large
Time and the Colonial Difference

The predetermined trajectory of historical dialectic allows no culturally disparate options, at least not cultural options that are decidedly disparate. . . . Whether in its capitalist or socialist guise, then, history and temporality reign supreme in the euro-western episteme. On the other hand, American Indian spirituality, values, social and political structure, and even ethics are rooted not in some temporal notion of history, but in spirituality. This is perhaps the most dramatic, and largely unnoticed, cultural difference between American Indian thought processes and the western intellectual tradition. The western intellectual tradition is firmly rooted in the priority of temporal metaphors and thought processes, while American Indians inherently think spatially.—GEORGE E. TINKER, *Spirit and Resistance*, 106–7.

IN THE EARLY 1950s biologists pulled about a dozen oysters from New Haven harbor and shipped them to Northwestern University, in Illinois, about a thousand miles away from New Haven and in a different time zone, one hour earlier. The oysters were submerged in their original harbor water and kept in total darkness. To explore their feeding patterns, the researchers tied to the shells fine threads that could activate recording pens every time the oysters' muscular movements caused the hinged shells to part or to close. As expected, the oysters continued to open and shut their shells as if they were still snug on the bottom of their home harbor, even though they had been displaced to another time zone, more than a thousand miles to the west. Then, after about two weeks, something strange happened. Gradually the hour of maximal opening of the shells began to shift. Now, anyone who lives near the shore knows that the high- and low-water marks also shift gradually from day to day. Tides are synchronized not with the place of the sun in the sky; rather it is the moon's schedule of appearance that matters, and the moon's cycle runs about fifty minutes behind the sun's cycle. However, the biologists in Illinois were witnessing a daily shift that did not correspond to the one in New Haven. After four weeks of recording and analyzing the data, the biologist determined beyond a doubt that the oysters had restabilized the rhythmic opening and closing of their shells to the tidal cycle that would occur in Evanston, Illinois, if there were an ocean in that location.[1]

The biologists were using the categories of time and space in their experiment. The oysters were not. The oyster did not know about time, but apparently they knew quite a bit about the cycles of the moon. Their living organisms were patterned, so to speak. Not that they internalized time, since time is not an existing entity, but a human concept used to organize repetitions and transformations. First, on the experience of cycles of our own natural body and the bodies of nature—equinoxes, solstices, sunrise and sunset, birth and death, conception and birth, menstrual cycles, moments of harvest and of storage, and so on—repetitions and transformations in the life of the cosmos seem to be a useful descriptive metaphor at this point. And it may not be out of place to surmise that living organisms identified as "human beings" have a biological sense of cosmic repetitions and transformations. However, once the categories of time and space were introduced to organize and describe transformations and repetitions not only in the patterns of the oysters, but also in the memory of human beings, the organization itself took on a life of its own. And whether or not human beings are somehow patterned like oysters, the experience of cosmic changes and repetitions has been increasingly repressed by the very artifice built around concepts such as time and space.

The Making of Modernity and Tradition(s): Experiencing (Living), Reckoning, and Measuring Time

So we could make a distinction between a cosmic or biological way of experiencing repetitions and transformations, like that of oysters, and a way of reckoning repetitions and transformations, like that of the biologists, mediated by a technical and philosophical apparatus to imagine and measure time. "Time," properly, is a category of reckoning, not a category of experiencing; it is a category belonging to culture, not to nature. In the second phase of modernity (in the eighteenth century), it became one of the central categories to distinguish culture from nature. However, this is not the occasion to survey the concept of "time in different cultures," since that would merely mean to reproduce precisely two of the distinctions that "time" contributed to: the distinction between nature and culture; and the distinction between modernity and tradition.

But once we get to this double equation (nature vs. culture; modernity vs. tradition), we can recognize the complicity between culture, time, and modernity and the dependent paradigm in which nature, tradition, and coloniality have been placed.[2] Although this equation became more visible in eighteenth-century Europe, it was already at work in the sixteenth century, with the emerging idea of progress and the distinction between the ancient and the modern. However, I am not interested here in tracing the history of an idea, but in clearing up its formulation, when the concept of time (modernity and tradition) joined, under Newton's influence, the concept of system (system of nature) and was used to imagine the logic of society.[3] As we have already established in the previous chapter, Kant imagined that human societies could be organized following the model provided by the law of nature, and therefore he conceived universal history from a cosmopolitan (e.g., cosmo-polis) point of view. However, we can extend that discussion here by investigating how Western concepts of time also mediated Kant's cosmopolitan ideals (see chapter 5). If you enter the civilizing mission into the equation modernity vs. tradition, you would understand that societies around the planet began to be measured and classified according to their similarity or dissimilarity with the natural order offered by cosmo-polis. But that was not all. History as "time" entered into the picture to place societies in an imaginary chronological line going from nature to culture, from barbarism to civilization following a progressive destination toward some point of arrival. Hegel, as it is known, organized Kant's cosmo-polis on a temporal scale that relocated the spatial distribution of continents (Asia, Africa, America, and Europe) in a chronological order that followed a certain directionality of history, from East to West. The planet was all of a sudden living in different temporalities, with Europe in the present and the rest in the past. The anthropologist Johannes Fabian coined the expression "denial of coevalness" to underline time as a conceptual and colonizing strategy.[4] "Time" became a fundamental concept of coloniality at large. The present was described as modern and civilized, the past as traditional and barbarian. The more you go toward the past, the closer you get to nature, as in Alejo Carpentier's *The Lost Steps* (1953). If geography was translated into chronology by the masters of historical time, and time was transformed into a colonizing device, then the present moment of Europe needed also to be separated from the past—and the concept of the Middle Ages accomplished that function. The second stage of modernity/coloniality established modern Europe as the present by creating the "otherness of the past and the past of the other," as Diana Hugh eloquently puts it.[5] Geopolitically, particularly since the nineteenth century, the translation of geography into chronology was the work of colonization, of the coloniality of knowledge and power. It has served as the justification of the ideology of progress and, in the twentieth century, of development and underdevelopment.

The Fabric of Time in the Modern/Colonial World

The thesis that I'm advancing and that I would like to propose is the following. Whatever the conceptualization of "time" in the social sciences today, the humanities, or the natural sciences, it is caught and woven into the imaginary of the modern/colonial world-system. This is the weak version of my thesis. The strong version is that time itself is a central concept of that imaginary. Let me clarify that I use imaginary to identify the social and geopolitical dimensions of modernity/coloniality; both the coloniality of power (e.g., strategies of colonization implied in modernity) producing the colonial difference and the different forms of adaptation, resistance, subaltern alternatives, forced by coloniality of power. I am thinking, in brief, of the imaginary of the modern/colonial world-system from the perspective of the colonial difference. My understanding of "imaginary" follows the Martinican writer and thinker Edouard Glissant who conceives it as the ways, conflictive and contradictory, a culture has of perceiving and conceiving of the world.[6] Notice, however, that Glissant defines imaginary from the history and experience of people who suffered the consequences of African slavery in the Caribbean, rather than from the history and experience of

those who forced contingents of enslaved Africans to the Americas. Hegel's
and Glissant's engagement with the imaginary of the modern/colonial world
do not come from the same memory: they are at the different ends of the
colonial difference. Hegel contributed to creating the colonial difference by
translating geography into chronology.[7] Glissant is contributing to the undoing of the colonial difference by revealing its structure and that of the
coloniality of power that underlies it.[8] Below I will expand on this definition. Now, I am only interested in rethinking the geopolitical imaginary of
the modern/colonial world-system from the perspectives of coloniality and
colonial difference (instead of modernity).

Let's, first, look at how "barbarians" became an image of modernity to
classify certain people who, subsequently, had no choice but to deal with
the fact that they had been classified as "barbarians." Coloniality of knowledge works here as an epistemic strategy to create the colonial difference.
At the inception of the colonial matrix of power, "barbarians" were located
in space.[9] By the eighteenth century, when "time" came into the picture
and the colonial difference was redefined, "barbarians" were translated into
"primitives" and located in time rather than in space. "Primitives" were in
the lower scale of a chronological order driving toward "civilization."[10]

Second, let's examine how the subalternization of knowledges was implied in the classification of "barbarians" and "primitives" (new categories
in the imaginary of the colonial matrix, added to "pagans," "infidels," and
the like). And third, let's identify the moment in which "natural history"
was transformed from a description of entities and the search for universal
laws (Newton, Kant) into the chronological narrative that starts at the "beginning of time," the secular version of the beginning of the world and of
human beings.[11] I hope that these three episodes will help us to understand
the inter-connections between the conceptualization of time, the colonial
matrix of power in the management of the colonial difference: time was
conceived and naturalized as both the measure of human history (modernity) and the time-scale of human beings (primitives) in their distance with
modernity. The denial of coevalness redefined indeed colonial and imperial
differences (for even Chinese and Russian civilizations were not considered
primitives but back in time) and built them around the notion of time, instead of space. This redefinition contributed to holding together the colonial matrix of power imaginary from its emergence as part of the Atlantic

commercial circuit (in the sixteenth century) to its current consolidation of
the North Atlantic (the United States and the European Union).

Although the linear concept of time was introduced in the Ancient Tes-
tament, or what is also referred to as the "Judeo-Christian tradition," during
the fifteenth and the sixteenth centuries, known and unknown communities
were located not in time, but in space. The famous Christian T-in-O map
imprinted the division of the planet into three continents on the imaginary
of European Christians. The map consisted of a circle with a "T" in its interior, with the horizontal bar of the "T" cutting the circle in two. Asia was
placed at the top of the horizontal line; Europe and Africa to the left and
right of the vertical line of the "T," cutting the bottom half of the circle into
two quarters. Each continent was attributed, in this imaginary, to Noah's
sons: Asia was attributed to Shem, Africa to Ham, and Europe to Japheth.
St. Augustine's description of the Christian cosmo-graphy described in the
T-in-O map is worth being recalled:

> Here by Asia I mean not that region which is a single province of greater Asia
> but the entire area, which is so called. Some regard it as one of two parts,
> but most as a third of the whole world—Asia, Europe and Africa would thus
> comprise the whole. But the divisions are not equal. For the part termed Asia
> goes from the South through the East to the North; Europe, however from
> the North to the West and Africa from the West to the South. So we see that
> half the world contains two parts, Europe and Africa, and the other half only
> one, Asia. These two parts arise because all the water that flows between the
> lands comes in between them from the Ocean, forming the Mediterranean.
> So that if you divide the inhabited world into two, an eastern and a western
> half, Asia will be in the one, Europe and Africa in the other.[12]

Scattered through the chapters devoted to Jewish history, from the Flood to
the time of Abraham, St. Augustine explains the reasons for which a particular continent was attributed to a particular descendent of Noah. Dennis
Hay observes,

> The starting point is a consideration of the meaning of the Hebrew names:
> Shem is interpreted as named, Japheth is "breadth" enlargement; Ham is hot.
> Shem is so named because of his seed was to become the humanity of Christ.
> Japheth is enlarged because as the Genesis anticipates, God shall enlarge

Japheth and he shall dwell in the tents of Shem. Visionaries will say that here was an anticipation of British colonialism. And for Ham he surely signifies the hot brand of heretics, hot not in wisdom but in willfulness.[13]

Up to 1500, Christian cartography left the unknown and the monsters inhabiting its margins. The monsters and the unknown were located in space. The map reproduced in the edition of the *Nuremberg Chronicle*, before 1500, had its margin populated with all kinds of monsters: people with two heads, horse bodies and human heads, several legs, inhabited the confines of the *ecumene*. The emergence of the Atlantic commercial circuits rapidly transformed this imaginary, the monsters were translated into barbarians and cannibals and were no longer located in the unknown space of the planet, but in the New World or Las Indias Occidentales. Waldseemüller's early drawing of what he termed "America," by analogy with the other two continents, Asia and Africa, relocated the barbarians and strange creatures in the Caribbean, insular and continental.[14] Today one would say around Venezuela and northern Brazil!

So "barbarians" then were located in space, not in time. Barbarians were different and lesser humans, but not traditional or primitive back in time. Nor were they conceived as remnants of the past. However, in the foreground of the Christian imaginary being transformed into the imaginary of the modern/colonial world, there was a teleological concept of world history, with an origin (creation) and an end (the final judgment). Hundreds of paintings of the final judgment are dispersed in museums all over the Western world. But time here does not imply "progress" from beginning to end. It does imply, however, a final destination, the end of the world, and the final judgment. If "barbarians," in the New World, were located not in time but in space, this was because their subaltern position was mapped on the "chain of beings" model, a model than ranked the entities of the world from rocks to human beings, and all was subsumed under "nature" as the work of God. The "chain of being" was a "vertical" model complementing the "horizontal" model provided by the T-in-O map.[15] Space was the principle of classification, vertically and horizontally.

By the eighteenth century the translations of barbarians into primitives supplanted the "chain of beings" model with a new one. The new model had two main features. First, primitives were closer to nature and civilized people were at the peak of culture. Second, primitives were traditional, and civilized Europeans were modern. Knowledges beyond the epistemic European imaginary from the Renaissance to the Enlightenment were disqualified as sustainable knowledges, although recognized in their past and traditional values. In the sixteenth century, some knowledges were considered dangerous (Indigenous knowledge, for example), and Spanish missionaries devoted themselves to an extirpation of idolatries that was indeed an epistemic lobotomy. In the eighteenth century, knowledge was not extirpated, but transformed into an object, and in that project "Orientalism" was born.

However, "time" reckoning was already a point of contention between people in Tawantinsuyu and Anáhuac and Spaniards, although not in the conflict between moderns and primitives. The point of contention was the calendar. Why? Because the calendar was, for European Christians as well as for Mayas, Aztecs, and Incas, something more than a system of reckoning dates. It also contained codes of knowing, ways of remembering and of understanding the present by anticipating the future.[16] Looking at the point of contention from a distance, one could say that much like the oysters from New Haven, Incas, Aztecs, and Spaniards had a similar experience of the rhythms of the cosmos—of summer and winter solstices (even if they had it at different times of the year), of the period of the moon, of daylight and night darkness, of the rhythmic movement from hot to cold weather, and so on. In that regard they were all equal. Around these same basic experiences of the rhythm of the universe, Spaniards on the one hand and Aztecs and Incas on the other built different concepts of the moving patterns of the universe (that in the West was conceived as "time") and the place in which people could move and locate other people or objects or just look at the horizon (that in the West was conceived as "space"). But for some reason, the Spaniards managed to impose their concept of time. If the Spaniards paid so much attention to the indigenous calendars, and the Andean dissident Guaman Poma de Ayala, toward the beginning of the seventeenth century, devoted so much attention to comparing the Christian and Inca calendars, it was because something important was at stake.[17] And that could not have been just the differences in the system of time reckoning. One of the direct consequences was the very concept of history that, for Renaissance humanists, was embedded in time. In the European context, "History" had not always been linked to time (like for Herodotus), nor was recording the past necessarily linked to "history." Following the same argument one can say that there is no logical necessity tying together an event that could be dated in the past with its status as an "historical event."[18]

In the New World context, Spanish men of letters as well as those soldiers who attempted the task of writing histories faced people whose manner of recording the past was not grounded in the concept of alphabetic writing and time, that is, of "history." Let me elaborate on this by taking the Aymara word *Pacha* as a case in point. Ludovico Bertonio, who wrote a very important Aymara dictionary in 1612, describes *Pacha* in relation to the sky. As "when the sky is too low" in the expression "laccampu llikhuti" (when the sky is quiet). In both Quechua and Aymara, *Pacha* refers primarily to daylight, rather than to a particular space, the space where birds fly. But, of course, the space where birds fly is where we notice that daylight occurs in space, from sunrise to sunset. Daylight or the space where birds fly is thus also the space of time. The space of time is the best I can do to render the connection between event and movement, which, in Aymara or Quechua, was not rendered with the word *time* as distinct from *space*, but with a word that implied both space and time. And that was precisely *Pacha*.[19] A full description of *Pacha*, as it is known today by the detailed reconstruction from early Spanish chronicles and more recent anthropological work, cannot be pursued here. There is one more aspect, however, that I would like to look at by introducing the notion of *Pachakuti*. Bertonio translated the term as "time of war," which in Aymara philosophy was rather conceived as the "moment in which people cannot be together any longer," or the moment in which dualities become contrary or contradictory, rather than complementary. Apparently Bertonio was collapsing the meaning of *Pachakuti* with the meaning of *Tinku*, generally described as two moieties (say, masculine/feminine; sun/moon) which are complementary and mutually constituted, although tensions and conflicts arise.

In this regard, the word *Tinku* could be interpreted as an instance of space-time in which dualities are complementary. But *Tinku* can also be the ritual that helps dualities to remain complementary rather than becoming contrary or contradictory. *Tinku* as ritual is a performance for the encounter of opposing factions *alasaya* ("of the side of above"; and notice that it is not those from above, but those of the "side of above," or something like that) and *masaya* (those of "the side of below"). Notice that in both cases it is the "side" of above and of below, and not just above and below. *Tinku* is therefore the place of encounter, like in the expression *tinkuthaptatha*, "the place of encounter of those that come and go." *Pachakuti*, then, is a disturbing alteration of the order of things. Any attempt to reduce or subsume *Tinku* under Hegel's dialectics would either fail or end up in another imperial epistemic move of translating the unknown to the known, which started with missionaries and men of letters in the sixteenth century.

Thus, if *Tinku* is the complementary of contrary and contradictories, *Kuti* is the moment in which complementarity becomes non-compatible, that is, at war; and *Pacha Kuti* then becomes the disturbing alteration of the order of things. At its extreme, *Kuti* is "a violent turn around," "a rollover" (like when a "car rolls over"); in Spanish, it is "volcar un auto, hubo un vuelco." The closest I can get to the limit of Pacha Kuti through the imaginary of modern epistemology (which I cannot avoid) is to translate it as "final judgment," akin to that in Christian cosmology, or as "revolution," as in modern and secular cosmology. As in "industrial revolution," "French revolution," or "Russian revolution." However, there is a difficulty: "revolution" is engrained in a linear concept of history and of time, and in an epistemology based on a logic in which dichotomies are always in contrary or contradictory relations; they are never complementary. Pacha Kuti, instead, belongs to an imaginary of cyclical repetitions and regular transformations of the natural/social world. Pacha Kuti is a third element that introduces the colonial difference, the negated knowledge that can no longer be recovered in its "purity," but that allows us to see the limits of "final judgment" and "revolution." The Spanish conquest was perceived and described in Quechua-Aymara as *Pachakuti'*. And it was, from their perspective, an integration of a foreign element into their cosmology that maintained, however, the irreducible difference with "final judgment" and "revolution." With the conquest understood as Pacha Kuti, we can see both sides of the colonial difference and understand why Spanish missionaries saw in Amerindian calendars a dangerous manifestation of the Devil.[20]

Detaching Time Measurement from Cosmological Time

Similar to the cartography of the sixteenth century, which mapped the global and detached the visualization and experience of space, projecting the territory into space measurement and management, so happens with the conceptualization of time in Western societies.[21] Both, the separation of space and time from cosmological experience of time (four seasons, the time of the harvest, the movement and the impact of the rotation of earth and moon around the earth, etc.), explain in part the separation of "nature" from the human body: "natural phenomena" takes place out there, in space and time outside of us.

There are, then, two aspects I would like to stress here that will pave the way toward a reflection on time and "natural history." One is the intersection of the concept of space/time in the organization of memory and society from Indigenous perspectives (either Aymara or Quechua or Native American);[22] the second is the distinction between linear and cyclical time. But let me give you an example provided by the Native American lawyer and activist Vine Deloria Jr., who made a distinction between Western European and Native American people in terms of their approaches to place (space) and time. You can read what follows in tandem with my argument on Linda T. Smith, in the previous chapter. This is not the occasion to go into a detailed commentary on Deloria's position. I am basically interested in stressing the point that "time" is not naturally *the* central category of human experience. Deloria writes,

> Western European peoples have never learned to consider the nature of the world discerned from a spatial point of view. And a singular difficulty faces peoples of Western European heritage in making a transition from thinking in terms of space. The very essence of Western European identity involves the assumption that time proceeds in a linear fashion; further it assumes that at a particular point in the unraveling of this sequence, the peoples of Western Europe became the guardians of the world. The same ideology that sparked the Crusades, the Age of Exploration, the Age of Imperialism, and the recent crusade against Communism all involve the affirmation that *time* is peculiarly related to the destiny of the people of Western Europe. And later, of course, of the United States.[23]

When Indigenous thinkers wrote (at the end of the sixteenth century and beginning of the seventeenth) about their past and addressed their writing to Spanish readers, they had to bargain with two different temporal logics to organize past events.[24] One of them was the "place where the birds fly" (as we saw in the description of *Pacha*). The other will be, like

Muñón Chimalpahín, in the Valley of Mexico, did in his writing of the past of Chalco Amaquemecan, having ancient codices as sources.[25] He dated a period of time as, say, "Year 6 House" (following the Mexican calendar) and next to it he wrote "1472," knowing full well that there is not a one-to-one correspondence between the two dates and that the cosmologies in which these dates are embedded are divided by an irreducible difference—which is not to say that these cosmologies were incommensurable.[26] They were, and they remain, different but inextricably linked to and transforming each other, although with different intensities at each end of the spectrum, in the changing imaginary of the modern/colonial world. They are linked in the colonial matrix of power and the system of knowledge that sustains it, and their differences are constitutive of colonial and imperial differences (e.g., the Chinese, who were not colonized, were considered, by the West, behind in time, just as were the Indian and Andean, who *were* colonized by British and Spaniards). Space and time can be translated into each other, but they cannot be assimilated. It is not a problem of cultural difference or cultural relativism, either. The colonial difference shall remain visible, not as a semantic problem, but as a sign of how coloniality of power works in the imaginary of the modern/colonial world.

But what is the difference between cultural relativism (or cultural differences) and colonial and imperial differences; and why is time so important here? It is because it was through the concept of time that the distinction between modernity and tradition was made. Today when someone claims "tradition" in a non-European history, he or she is critiqued for aiming at an identity that can no longer be retrieved; the vexing question is that tradition was invented in the process of building modernity. The idea of modernity needed its own tradition in order to be distinguished as modernity. Thus while modernity was established by inventing its own tradition (Middle Ages and Antiquity) and colonizing time, it so happens that in the colonization of space the rhetoric of moderniy was used to disavow the legitimacy of the "traditions" (invented in the process of inventing modernity) of civilizations that were colonized. It was by means of the concept of time that cultural differences were classified according to their proximity to modernity or to tradition. The discourse on cultural differences hides the logic of coloniality that the discourse on the colonial and imperial differences displays. The first presupposes that cultures are discrete entities, semantically closed, and that translation is difficult or sometimes impossible when cultures do not share the same language, the same script, or the same religion. The second, instead, tries to conceptualize historically how cultural differences were indeed constructed by the coloniality of power simultaneous with the emergence of the North Atlantic. Colonial and imperial differences raise questions of power and knowledge, of course; but questions concerning the coloniality of knowledge and of complicity in the making of the modern world are better still. Why? Because based on a certain understanding of time and/or space, you may end up believing that you are behind in time; and if you believe so, you are more likely to want to catch up with modernity. If you fall into this trap, you have lost the game before beginning it. The discourse on cultural differences remains within the theo- and ego-political frame of knowledge, meaning, and interpretation. The discourse of colonial and imperial differences is already a departure, a way of delinking, and a form of epistemic disobedience that opens a parallel road to knowing, sensing, believing, and living.

Consequently, my previous narrative about the translation from monsters to barbarians and then to primitives, as well as my underlining the coming into being of the distinction between nature and culture, were prompted by the thrust of my argument: that "time" is a fundamental concept in building the imaginary of the modern/colonial world and an instrument for both controlling knowledge and advancing a vision of society based on progress and development. At the end of the sixteenth century Mathew Ricci suggested that Chinese science was *falling behind* that of the West, since the Chinese had no conceptions of the rule of logic, and because their science of ethics was merely a series of confused maxims and deductions.[27] Ricci's observations were not isolated, but complemented Christian discourses about the Moors and about Incas and Aztecs.

The epistemic colonial and imperial differences did not end with decolonization in Asia and Africa after the Second World War (nor did they end, of course, with revolutions and independences in Americas and the Caribbean from 1776 to 1830). Currently, the transformation of colonial differences is entrenched in what we now call globalization in such a way that it makes sense to think in terms of global coloniality. It continues to be reproduced by global capitalism, and "time" continues to nourish the imaginary that reproduces colonial and imperial difference. However, as we saw in chapter 1, the incomplete project of modernity may never be completed, due to the fact that rewesternization is no longer the only game in town. Differential times and differential memories and histories are delinking from the belief that there is only one line of time; and this is a reasonable conclusion if one follows Christian or secular Hegelian time-linear narratives. All these considerations account for the need to think in terms of coloniality at large, and not only of modernity at large; and by extension—as I do in this book—of decoloniality at large.

Imperial time is translated into the time of a given nation. The emergence of the modern nation-state in Europe, as well as the parallel emergence of the modern/colonial nation-states in the Americas and, subsequently, in Asia and Africa, shows one specific transformation of the colonial matrix of power. The modern nation-state became the imperial tool for the control of authority in the colonies during the process of building (during the nineteenth and twentieth centuries) modern/colonial nation-states. Nation-states (in their modern European or modern/colonial American, Asian, and African versions) are not "outside" the colonial matrix. "Internal colonialism" is a concept that describes the mutation of imperial into national management in the ex-European colonies. What is "internal colonialism" if not the persistence of the coloniality of knowledge (and therefore the control of authority and economy) under nation-building processes after decolonization? This is why coloniality remains as the hidden side of modernity, and why there cannot be modernity without coloniality. The *places* defined by the interaction between modernity and coloniality are the *places* where the colonial difference is being played out in a constant conflict. Imperial narratives were entangled with national narratives after these events, and the emergence of nation-states (modern or modern/colonial) became an exemplar of the linear process and the advancement of global human history.

Again, what does "time" have to do with all of this? As you may have guessed: a lot. Narratives of beginning and end, from the creation to the final judgment, told in the sixteenth century in Christian Europe were imposed beyond the Euro-Christian continent. The possibility of thinking in terms of the sky where birds fly and where daylight is perceived, where the Tinku as ritual maintained the complementarity of the opposites, where Pacha Kuti was the horizon to be avoided—all this was cast out to non-sustainable types of knowledge. The same template (e.g., coloniality of knowledge) will be enacted from the end of the eighteenth on, when British and French imperial designs moved to Asia and Africa. If the sixteenth century was when the global distinction between space and time emerged, including a linear concept of time linked to sacred history, the eighteenth century celebrated the final victory of "time" by opening up the links between time and secular history. Secular history redefined the logic of coloniality, and "time" became a central rhetorical figure in the self-definition and self-fashioning of modernity: modernity is a "time" based concept.

Kant gave the colonial and imperial differences in space its final format when, in *Anthropology from a Pragmatic Point of View*, he coupled race with territories: red people are in America (he was thinking of course in North America), yellow in Asia, black in Africa, and white in Europe (see chapter 5). But Kant also connected time with secular history. Consequently, we (those engage in decolonial thinking) are working to delink and disconnect from Kant's linkages and connections. His theses on the "Idea of Universal History from a Cosmopolitan Point of View" (1784) (see chapter 7) are argued from "progressive" or "developmental" conceptions of the human race. In the first thesis Kant states that "all natural capacities of creatures are destined to *evolve* completely to their natural end" (emphasis added). The second thesis maintains, "In man those natural capacities which are directed to the use of his reason are to be fully *developed* only in the race, not in the individual" (emphasis added). Now, if you put together "anthropology from a pragmatic point of view" and "universal history from a cosmopolitan point of view," what you get is a universal perspective on history based on a racial distribution of the planet.[28] And time has a crucial function in such a distribution. For, according to the thesis argued in "anthropology," civilization can only be defined, implemented, and guided by the white man who is in Europe at the present moment of a linear, historical time. Modernity and tradition, progress and stagnation, city and country, speed and slow motion, and so on were distinctive temporal features of the second stage of the modern/colonial world. Between Kant and the nineteenth century, during the second stage of modernity characterized by the "denial of coevalness," *time* became a central factor in making and recasting colonial differences. Progress, a weapon of the civilizing mission, was the key rhetorical figure in the nineteenth century; development, after the

Second World War, was its successor as the rhetorical figure in a new stage of coloniality of power re-mapping the colonial difference. Modernity, progress, and development cannot be conceived without a linear concept of time defining a point of arrival. To understand what tradition and under-development means, it was necessary to have, first, the concept of moder-nity and progress/development, since they (tradition and development) are non-existing entities outside the discourse of modernity and development. Coloniality is the hidden, logical connection between modernity and tra-dition, and to experience it is also to experience the "magic moment" that makes us believe that modernity and tradition are concepts that name what there is. To be redundant: there is no modernity and tradition beyond the rhetoric of the same modernity that invented itself, by inventing its own tradition and making believe that the concept of tradition is universal. And in order to do that, it was necessary to develop a linear concept of time em-bedded in the very notions of progress and evolution.

The Nature of Time and the Time of Nature

Since I began with a reference to "nature," let's come back to it. How is it, if you remember the narrative I offered at the beginning about oysters and biologists, that biologists became so far removed from oysters? How is it that the biologists became so much taken by time reckoning and oblivious to their own rhythm of life, that rhythm that the oyster sensed and knew but that cannot be reckoned like the biologists did? There may be an incli-nation to say that among the oysters cyclical time is prevalent, while biolo-gists prefer linear time. However, there is still another difference. Oysters do not have a time-reckoning system to describe their own behavior and the behavior of the biologists. Oysters do not have hands and do not engage in scientific observation and philosophical speculations. Time reckoning, however, seems to be an activity that requires the extension of the hands, the inscription of graphic marks on solid surfaces (or of other material de-vices), a semiotic disciplinary frames called science and philosophy.

Stephen Jay Gould, in his book *Time's Arrow, Time's Cycle: Myth and Metaphor in the Discovery of the Geological Time* offers a detailed analysis of linear and cyclical conceptions of time in geology. According to Gould, ge-ologists at the beginning of the nineteenth century "discovered" geological time, the time of nature. And, of course, "natural history" was transformed. "Natural history" was instrumental, in the sixteenth century, and then again in the eighteenth, in the making of colonial and imperial differences. Was it so also in the nineteenth century, through science?

When the Jesuit father José de Acosta wrote and published *Natural and Moral History of the Indies* (1590), he translated Aristotle and Pliny the Elder's legacies in two directions. First, he accounted for the "newness" of what was also conceived, in a metaphorical rather than in a legal and administrative way, as "New World." Now, "new" did not have then the meaning that "progress" imposed on it. "New" in the first case, meant unknown. "New" in the second case is something that comes after, as in "a new model of car." Acosta was in possession of experiences in nature and direct knowledge about nature, that neither Aristotle nor Pliny the Elder could have enjoyed; and, second, he used that new experience as a signifier (nature) of a signified (God).

But, by so doing, Acosta installed the colonial difference in· natural history. He did not pause one single moment to think or to ask what Aymara and Quechua speakers thought about what, for Acosta, was "natural history," a concept with a genealogy of knowledge that he assumed was the only one, or at least the only valid one. Civilizations "were there" but they apparently did not have "knowledge" (experience in and organized knowledge) about nature. If he had asked, and thought about it, perhaps he would have understood that what he, and other Christian missionaries, conceived as "idolatry" was indeed an epistemology in which Pacha was one of the central concepts. Pachamama, whose epistemic function was similar to Greek Gaya, was more than a goddess of earth and fertility; it was also energy manifested in the fertility of earth and of life: a concept in which space, time, and the fertility of the earth (as in "Mother Earth") all came together. Tinku was perhaps not a ritual of idolatry, as missionaries imagined, but perhaps an epistemic expression of the forces that animate the world, the life of nature and the nature of life. In a word was what Spaniards may have considered their own "tinku": theology and philosophy. Acosta, however, was instead working on a double difference: the difference between nature and human beings (that is why he titled his book "Natural and Moral History") and the silenced difference of Quechua and Aymara knowledge, reduced to "idolatry." The extirpation of idolatry was indeed not a religious issue, but an epistemic one. The eradication of other forms of knowledge was the real project at stake in the extirpation of idolatry and the establishment of the limits of the epistemic colonial difference.

In sixteenth-century Europe, "time" brought together encyclopedic knowledge with mercantilism and merchant demands. The Dasypodius clock, built in Strasbourg, in 1570, epitomized the interrelations between time and encyclopedic knowledge.[29] It helps to explain the struggle over the calendar in the New World I referred to above. There was, in Renaissance Europe, a concern with time that did not find its equivalents in China or in the New World. Dasypodius's clock was a consequence of this concern and also a symbol of the implicit complementarity between time and encyclopedic knowledge in the process of building Western civilization and European culture. The clock was an astronomical mechanism that showed

> the motion of the planets around the earth. Another display predicted eclipses, while a perpetual calendar laid out the moveable feasts, leap years, and the twenty-eight-year cycle of the ecclesiastical calendar for the next century. Automata represented the pagan gods for whom the days were named, Time and Death. They both served as an animated almanac and embodied the all-destroying force of time and change. . . . For the clock, like gunpowder and the compass, was one of the first distinctively modern technologies, and late medieval and Renaissance intellectuals loved to cite it when arguing that the ancients had not exhausted all fields of knowledge and invention.[30]

Before then, in the fourteenth and fifteenth centuries, Europeans, Incas, and Aztecs (to limit myself to the New World and Europe) had similar approaches of measuring time. In both cases, time reckoning (in counter distinction to today) was integrated into the flow of nature and the four seasons; to equinoxes and solstices, closer relation was maintained between human beings, as living organisms, and the life of the cosmos. Nature was not yet conceived as something that had to be tamed and dominated, as Francis Bacon would put it at the beginning of the seventeenth century, thus initiating a separation between human beings and nature that would be further developed by the philosophy accompanying industrial capitalism. That is one of the reasons why there were so many striking similarities between the European and the Inca calendar, and why today Native Americans and Western cosmologies seem so distant from each other.[31]

Anthony Aveni provided a sensible narrative to understand time reckoning and spatial organization among the Incas. The system is indeed too complicated to describe here in any detail. What is of interest is to remember and underline the existence of a certain commonality among communities dispersed all over the planet, from the Americas to Europe, to Asia or Africa. Sunrise and sunset, summer and winter solstices, zenith and nadir, menstruation and gestation cycles, the turn of food regeneration, collecting, and storage, and so on are some of the regularities common to living organisms. Now, these regularities are not experienced in the same way near the poles or in the tropics. This is of course common sense, but there are also countless documents from European travelers pointing toward the experiences of the tropics, of the mountains, and correcting ancient speculations about extreme heat and impossible life in certain earth zones. The movements of the sun and the stars, in the tropics, are right above your head. From further north or further south, the sun would circle at a 45-degree angle, approximately. Aveni summarizes this confluence as follows.

> The Incas fixed attention on the zenith sunrise-anti-zenith sunset axis not only because that sector of the celestial environment was so suggestive, but also because they were deeply influenced by the terrestrial half of the environment as well. Imagine a mountainous land in which faraway places are reckoned not by the distance east, west, north or south of the major population centers, but rather by how far above or below them one is situated. The Incas lived in a vertical world, *a space in which the time for human action—* for planting potatoes, burning of the scrub, worshiping the gods—depended critically upon whether a person was positioned in a vertically based ecology, each tier of which was dependent upon every other one.[32]

The Incas invented the horizontal system of *ceques*, a series of lines that emanated from Cuzco, the center of the empire, and organized the city, socially and spatially. They also counted the days of the year lining up the ceques with the movement of the sun. Aveni's evidence suggests that "the Inca had converted the landscape into a natural, self-operating calendrical device powered by the movement of the sun, a system with no need of formal writing to articulate it."[33]

The difference between Andeans and Europeans, in their approach to both Pacha and Pachamama and to time and nature, was not so much in how they "measured" time but in the ways Andean people related to Pachamama, and the ways Europeans related to Nature—which they considered to be outside human beings. For the latter "nature" became an entity to be dominated: "we" and "nature" are two distinct entities. For the former, human/nature were, and still are, one; they are indistinguishable: Pachamama is in us and we are in Pachamama. They were divergent cosmologies that framed the conception of human beings on Earth, and the relationship of Earth to human beings, differently. However, since both Andean and European people were equally intelligent beings, both communities figured out the best way to organize their lives in relation to "time." Nevertheless, since the sixteenth century they have remained irreducible in their difference and inextricably linked through coloniality of power and the colonial difference.

I said before that these differences were and are irreducible. But at the same time, they have been since the sixteenth century inextricably intertwined. Irreducible, and at the same time inextricably entangled, by the rhetoric of modernity and the logic of coloniality (or, what is the same, the colonial matrix of power), which made possible the construction and transformation of colonial and imperial differences, and which defined and used the category of time, the construction of the modern/colonial world-system, and the narrative of Western civilization (I will come back to this issue in chapter 5). The Western concept of "time" became the essential "connector" of colonial and imperial differences throughout the globe. In other words, coloniality at large means that the successive stages of Western expansion predicated on modernity carried with them successive stages in the implementation of its darker side, the logic of coloniality. The zero line of longitude that unites the two poles, vertically, and that crosses the heart of England's Greenwich observatory, reconverted spatial global linear thinking (see chapter 2) into temporal global linear thinking. The zero line of longitude was also a zero point epistemology, controlling time by establishing that "all countries would adopt a universal day," that "the universal day would be a Mean Solar Day, beginning at the Mean Midnight at Greenwich and counted on a 24 hour clock," and that "nautical and astronomical days everywhere would begin at mean midnight."[34]

Now let's go back to time reckoning in the Andes. Two aspects of my previous analysis deserve further comments. One is to provide more contextual information for my previous reflections around Pacha. And the second is to underline how much Acosta suppressed when he interpreted "nature" as God's design and ignored the integrative understanding that Amerindians had of time, space, and nature.[35] Christian cosmology, in the narrative of missionaries or men of letters, suppressed Inca, Aztec, and Maya cosmologies. It was as if an observer outside sixteenth-century Europe had described the Dasypodius clock, stripping it out of the entire cosmology surrounding the mechanism that counted the hours and the minutes.

If Inca and Aztec cosmologies operated at the space/time intersection (e.g., the ceque system, the four divisions of Tawantinsuyu with Cuzco at its center, and the four cycles that preceded the present, the fifth cycle, at the center), Western Christian cosmology operated more on lineal chronology. In Western linear chronology (which means Western discourse on time), events are ordered one after another. In a cyclical chronology, conception of time returns and repeats itself is, so to speak, space/time. In Christian/ Western cyclical time, what returns are the dates—the month of January, or Thanksgiving Day. The events that happened, say, in January or on Thanksgiving Day of 1998 would not necessarily be repeated in January or on Thanksgiving Day of 1999. And finally, Christian cosmology saw nature as a design and a performance of God, and the nature of the New World as an occasion to correct the speculation of the ancients who were not aware that an entire continent and people living in it ever existed. "Natural and moral history" was an interesting concept in the sixteenth century. On the one hand, "time" was not much of an issue in this kind of history. On the other, "the natural and moral history of the Indies" was an anticipation of contemporary museums of "natural history" (mainly in Western Europe and the United States) where indigenous people from America, Asia, and Africa are mixed up with polar bears, terrifying snakes, and colored and exotic fishes. Beyond that there is civilization (and the museums of art history, where time is, indeed, an important component in manufacturing narratives of works, authors, and schools of thought in a chronological order). But, then, when did "time" enter "natural history"? Or, as Gould would have it, when was "time" discovered? Notice also that in running the parallel between Christian and Andean time, I am not opposing them. I am saying that they are different and have been entangled since the sixteenth century. Furthermore, they have been entangled through the epistemic colonial differences that made the timeline of modernity the real time of history, because history was being conceived and written by those who felt themselves riding the horse of "true and objective time," without parenthesis.

In the hundred and fifty years, approximately, that separates Acosta from Kant, significant changes took place in how Western intellectual history conceived of nature and time. Changing conceptions of time and nature went hand in hand with the changing identity of Europe; that is, with its definition of (European) Man, relative to the rest of the planet. Francis Bacon, writing a few decades after Acosta, derailed the Christian hermeneutics practiced by the Spanish Jesuit missionary by interpreting nature as God's design and masterpiece. Bacon was moving away from the theological and rhetorical conception of knowledge that was valid for Acosta. For Bacon, the end of rhetoric was to "overcome an opponent by disputation," while his method had as a final goal "to overcome Nature by action."[36] For Acosta, overcoming nature would have been a heresy, because it would have been like attempting to dominate God. Bacon was concerned not with nature's history, but with nature's system, the vocabulary and concepts later developed in the works of Newton, d'Holbach, and Diderot. So when was "natural time" "discovered"? In the nineteenth century, and, according to Gould's argument, by means of a fascinating intersection of the ideas of time, progress, and science, on the one hand, and of science as capable of measuring the "age" of nature, on the other. Natural history became at this point a question of age: counting the years without anniversaries.

What was "discovered" indeed was "deep time." In eighteenth-century Europe, the age of the planet Earth and the universe was calculated to be a couple of million years. In the sixteenth century, of course, it had been calculated to be much less than that. What matters, however, is that with the discovery of "deep time" European science was able to imagine the age of the universe in a dimension that surpassed the calculus achieved until then by other civilizations. "Deep time" was in a way a confirmation of the superiority of Western knowledges over the rest of the planet and other advanced civilizations. Nature and the universe were subjected to time's arrow, or linear time, and to time's cycle. Stephen Gould believes that these two metaphors are legacies of what he calls the "Judeo-Christian" tradition. This statement is clearly an honest belief that there is no history beyond either ancient Greece or the two major religions of the West. Indeed, linear time and cyclical time could be found everywhere, among the ancient Chinese, ancient Mayas, or ancient Indians. This is another way of saying that the rhythm of the cosmos that told the oysters when to open and shut their mouths also provided human beings around the planet with a pattern they could use to survive and organize their life. Human beings took it on themselves to believe that a certain interpretation of the order of the *cosmos* had to be imposed on other societies to organize the *polis*. The Judeo-Christian metaphor that Gould refers to is, obviously, the theological macro-linear metaphor of creation and end of the world that was translated, in secular time, into the idea of progress, development, and modernization. "Time," cyclical or linear, of nature or of human history, as we know it today, is a result and a consequence of the colonial matrix of power imaginary. The very idea of "time" coupled with "history," progress, and development was so strong that Western modern sciences reached the point in which time was not only the spine of history, but became an entity in itself, with its own history.[37]

Time, the Myth of History, and the Myth of Science

I'm arguing that "time" as it is conceived today is a fundamental piece of the coloniality and Western civilization imaginary that gives support, in part, to both the myth of history and the myth of science. As such, and for these reasons, it was and continues to be a major factor in the making of colonial and imperial differences. When Western history and science were (and still are) contradicted by forms of recording the past and of knowing nature and the universe, in other words when they were confronted with histories and sciences that failed to correspond with their own standards of history and of science, modern historians and scientists had recourse to their own imagined unilinear evolution of humanity, in defense of their claims. Civilizations in which Western expansion did not establish colonies (like China, Japan, or Russia) had to endure the myth of universal history and universal science as a marker of "modernity" with which they were supposed to catch up. Coloniality, remember, is much more than colonialism: it is a colonial matrix of power through which world order has been created and managed. It is precisely the colonial matrix of power that is in dispute today, as I outlined in chapter 2—quite apart from the quarrels within European cosmology that keep both the Left and the Right busy.

The Western notion of time supports "history" and "science" to acquire a hegemonic force and to develop a comparative point of view that allows for the erasure or devaluation of other forms of knowledge. This is a common procedure and strategy in the making of the modern/colonial world as well as in creating colonial/imperial notions of difference. Secular history and science just transformed Christian strategies that, during the sixteenth century, devalued Inca, Aztec, and Maya epistemologies. By this I mean that the Maya were rational beings, and that their logic of knowledge-making manifested the same human capability that in the West was described by the word *epistemology*. Moreover, the word *epistemology* was used to disavow epistemological practices that did not correspond to the Western management of knowledge, and did so by attributing to them devilish designs, and by referring to them as agents of the Devil. To be regarded as being behind the present time of modernity was the secular equivalent of being in the hands of the Devil during the theological moment. I have argued that Western notions of "time" contributed to the distinction between both nature and culture, and modernity and tradition. Because of the illusion this creates, we can easily forget that both the oyster and the biologist who works in the scientific culture of time reckoning belong to the same basic lived time. "Modern man" built his sense of superiority and his pride in the process of cutting the umbilical cord with "nature," while "primitive man" was still too close to it; and being close to nature meant (from the perspective of "modern man") being far from civilization. However, Incas for example, were both, close to Pachamama and civilized. But that idea was destroyed by the rhetoric of modernity in order to build the logic of coloniality justifying actions over the "barbarians" later on translated into "primitives."

Is it possible to think from that silence (the silence created by coloniality of knowledge), to undo the colonial and differences that "time" contributed to make and contributes to maintain? Interestingly enough, this concern arises not only among intellectuals who through childhood exposure and professional training have gained an experience of epistemologies based on principles beyond Greek legacy and beyond Western needs. The Italian philosopher Franco Cassano, in his important book *Il pensiero meridiano*, connects the force of the Sun in Albert Camus's *L'Etranger* (1942) with ancient Greek perception and conception of nature and *Kairos*.[38] He sees in this constellation an aspect of Greek thought that has been suppressed in the construction of Western civilization, an aspect similar to Arabic contributions to Western epistemology that equally went unnoticed in the Renaissance and post-Renaissance readings. Cassano's disclosure allows us to understand the similarities between ancient Greece and Andean cosmologies, the similarities between Kairos and Pacha, as well as the continuity between space, time, nature, and life. Cassano is not concerned with the colonial but with the imperial difference. His claim for a Southern thinking ("un pensiero meridiano") emerged from the imperial (internal) difference, that is, from the European construction of the South as the place of "slow speed." Since the eighteenth century, the European South was simultaneously constructed with the Orient, and the denial of coevalness was at the center of such constructions. Isn't there in Latin America a similar image, and hundreds of jokes, told from the perspective of the (modern) city about the slowness of the (traditional) country? Or in South/Central America and the Caribbean seen from the perspective of the efficient and speedy North? Notice that the imperial internal difference, in Europe, was translated twice, in America, into the colonial difference: first, after 1898 and the Spanish-American War; second, after the end of the Cold War, when the global order moved from West vs. East to North vs. South. Indeed, a powerful double stroke. On the one hand, Orientalism in Europe was reissuing the imperial difference established in the sixteenth-century experiences of the Mediterranean (expulsion of the Moors) and the colonial difference of the Atlantic (contact with Amerindians and African slavery). On the other hand, the making of the South was the imperial difference that paved the way for Hegel's "heart of Europe" (England, France, Germany), and for the current movie-making imaginary, in the United States or in Europe, the South remains the place of sun, love, tourism, good life, and "slow speed." "Time" was and is a fundamental component in such an imaginary. The "East" and the "South" live a slow time, while the North is the location of speed, progress, and of living by the "clock."

Nature (space) and tradition (time) were outcast by the imperial and the colonial differences and constructed as that which is inert and fixed. "Still nature" became a common topic in Western painting late in the seventeenth century. At that point, nature was no longer conceived as a living system (as it was among the Andean and Mesoamerican civilizations), but was transformed into an object external to human life, to be overcome by action, and as the prime resource for the needs created by the Industrial Revolution. Parallel to this narrative of progress and modernity, tradition began to gain ground as the image of a "still" human past. In the Museum of Natural History, in New York or Chicago, you can see "primitives" next to polar bears and Chinese scrolls. But of course there are other places, beyond museums, where nature and tradition are kept under control and are not recognized for the force they have in the present. Or, as the Senegalese singer, musician, performer, and political activist Baaba Maal would have it, tradition is the present, not the past, reminding us that the distinction between modernity/tradition is part of the larger strategy of the denial of coevalness,[39] the creation and reproduction of colonial and imperial differences, and, more generally, of building and maintaining the colonial matrix of power.

Consequently, it seems to me that one of the intellectual tasks for imagining and doing toward communal futures (the conference where this chapter was first presented had in its subtitle "possible futures") is to undo the colonial difference and the contribution of "time" to it. Thinking in terms of "transmodernity," instead of modernity and tradition, and thinking in terms of Pachamama or Gaia as a living system, instead of nature and culture, may open our imaginary to the restitution of suppressed epistemologies—epistemologies inscribed in languages such as Mandarin, Arabic, or Aymara, which were relegated, precisely, to the realm of tradition or almost nature from the perspective of a conception of time and of culture. Certainly, not all is good in non-European traditions, and most certainly not all is good in European tradition. Within the modern/colonial world, epistemology was not so much the "representation or the mirror of nature" as the "domination of nature" (Bacon) and of "traditional" forms of knowledges.[40] "Universality" was a consequence of an overarching concept of space/time and a dominating scientific epistemology that permeated the conception of the social (e.g., the state, democracy). As I have discussed above, decolonial possible futures can no longer be conceived from a universal perspective, anchored in a hegemonic imaginary managed by linear time and final destination. Decolonial possible futures shall be imagined as "diversal" (or pluriversal if you wish), which implies, of course, that philosophies of *time* (as well cosmo-polis, see chapter 7) are anchored in the rhythms of the universe, and are common to all living organisms. Such philosophy would perhaps take us to "times and diversality of being" and to put more effort in reflecting on how the clock, in complicity with capitalism, imposed a conception and a style of life in which time goes together with money. Undoing the colonial difference as was built in the concept of time will involve, among other things, removing "time" from the privileged position it acquires in complicity with science, capitalism, and the mono-culturalism (e.g., uni-versalism) of Western civilization. In sum, undoing the colonial difference means to accept and act on the fact that History is the flat narrative of imperial dominium that pretends to capture the flow of reality, while histories, ancestralities, memories are local, marginal, insignificant narratives from the perspective of History. Sciences, in the same manner, built formulas, invented laws based on the belief in objectivity without parenthesis. Now that colonial and imperial differences are being disclosed, roads to the future are being built, and some are being repaired.

Time and Possible (Communal) Futures

First of all, do not imagine communal futures as the abstract universal that will replace existing abstract universals like liberal capitalism and state socialism, once for all and all at once, and that will reign as the undisputed solution for the humanities (I will come back to this topic in the afterword). The cycle of search for universal models for world order are over. I have been arguing in this book, and in different contexts, that decolonial options are options, not missions of conversions to a universal truth or truth without parenthesis. As such, they are options imagined and acted on by those who find that neither capitalism nor socialism (and these both, yes, with a view of the future in which one or the other should prevail) is the solution, and who find even more so that abstract universals, whether socialist or capitalist, are not the solution. Decolonial options accept the non-pacific coexistence of the diversity of the five trajectories toward the future I outlined in chapter 1. Non-pacific coexistence (which is, therefore, conflictive) doesn't mean that we have to buy our guns before they are sold. Conflict does not necessarily lead to war. War obtains when truth and objectivity without parenthesis reign. Conflicts obtain and are solved without war where and when truth and objectivity in parenthesis reign and there is no enemy to be destroyed and universal truth to be defended and imposed. A world in which truth in parenthesis is accepted as universal is a world guided by pluriversality as a universal principle. In a pluriversal world founded on truth in parenthesis, there is no place for war. It means that the differences between the five trajectories will be negotiated in non-imperial ways, which means that there is no room for an exclusive rewesternization. Western civilization would be merely one among many options, and not the one to guide and rule the many. In other words, there is no one trajectory that has the right to prevail over the other. This is the point at which dewesternizaton, the reorientation of the Left, decoloniality, and the spiritual option all have the common task of reducing Western imperial designs and its desires to their proper and regional place. "Provincializing Europe" acquires a new meaning in this context. That dewesternization, the reorientation of the Left, the spiritual option, and decoloniality all have a common task doesn't mean that one of them has the right to become the "new" hegemon. If that were to become the case, we would remain, *mutatis mutandi*, within the rules of the same games imposed by Western modernity, when secularism appropriated the hegemonic discourse of the church. In such a scenario, the "content" would change and become the cultural biases of the new hegemon. Pluriversality means unlearning, so to speak, modernity, and learning to live with people one does not agree with, or may not even like. Conviviality is not holiday, but a hard and relentless effort toward cosmopolitan localism and pluriversal futures (see chapter 7).

Now, if the goal were to build not only a peaceful world but also a world in which everybody, because of its humanity, is equal to every other body and thus has the basic right to food, shelter, health, and education, and not to be bothered by solicitors (evangelicals, mini-credit saviors, anxious financial agents, military interventions, irresponsible corporations, promoters of socialism, etc.), then pluriversality would be the universal project to which decolonial thinking and doing aspire, and which they promote.

Racing to Death: The Postmodern Recolonization of "Time" and the Decolonial Claim to "Tradition"

"Tradition," like "anthropos" or "space and time," has not ontological but fictional existence, like Don Quixote or Madame Bovary. However, the fact that they do not have ontological existence does not preclude their being taken by many as truth of universal scope. They were inventions of Western imperial modernity, inventions that contribute to consolidate Western modernity. What could anthropos do but remain behind in time, outside the forces of progress and development; because "tradition," in the modernist lexicon, means underdevelopment. But once we accept that tradition does not exist as a transcendental category, who can claim the monopoly of time? Since the Enlightenment, time has assumed the role that natural law had in the sixteenth and seventeenth centuries. Whoever knew what natural law was, and could argue forcefully for it, had the power to rule out all those who did not abide by that (fictional) natural law. Again, this is true because natural law is another entity that does not have ontological existence; rather, it was and is a fiction that was managed to be believed as true—just as with tradition and time. Who would want to be traditional once the rhetoric of modernity put a value on time, progress, and development, and those time-values became accepted by rulers as well as by the governed?

Once you control (the idea of) "time," you can control subjectivity and make the many march to the rhythm of your own time. There are three key moments in the colonization of time and the re-making of the colonial matrix of power. Two were already mentioned: the Renaissance invention of the Middle Ages, and the Enlightenment invention of the primitive and tradition. The third is the postmodern invention of the acceleration of time. When Benjamin Franklin stated his famous dictum "Time is money," time was measured against labor and the outcome of labor. But in the postmodern era, the idea that to *fall behind* is to lose has concomitantly introduced the idea that to go faster is to win (and of course you accept that winning is the name of the game), that you not only have to produce more (of whatever you produce) but that you have to do it first—thus, the "acceleration of time." Success is the companion of moving fast, coming in first, and being the winner. Daniel Innerarity suggested that *chrono-politics* displaces, today, the colonization of space with the colonization of time.[41] That had already happened in the eighteenth century, as I argued above. However, Innerarity's chrono-politics and its companion (bio-politics, and necro-politics) are all diverse spheres of the logic of coloniality;[42] however, while bio- and necro-politics are managed by the state, chrono-politics takes place mainly in the spheres of the market, finances, and media. In this regard, the state—and Innerarity makes this explicit—is "slow": deliberation "takes time," decisions are debated, votes have to go through two or three rounds, and so on. But corporate ideology makes of time an essential component of efficiency and the incremental pace of production; it disregards the possibility of overproduction; it denies that "wasting time" could benefit the many, whose labor is being sold instead of being used for the benefit of the community.

Conceptually, the notion of chrono-politics adds another dimension to our understanding of the colonization of time; it enriches our understanding of the way the European Renaissance colonized by inventing the Middle Ages, and, later, the Enlightenment invented the primitive. While there is a difference between the colonization of time during the Renaissance, the invention of the "primitive" during the Enlightenment, and the corporate politics of time under neoliberalism, all three historical managements of "time" are different instances of the coloniality of time or, in Innerarity's word, chrono-politics. Chrono-politics, in other words, is a specific aspect of theo- and ego-politics of knowledge; it is a *civilizational* principle that serves to ostracize all who do not conform to the modern conventions of time, that devalues "subalterns" for being slow and not racing toward death, which in the rhetoric of modernity is translated as "progress and development." Chrono-politics, in the last analysis, shows how the coloniality of knowledge and being is managed by the Eurocentered system of ideas built around the colonization of time.

While bio-politics or necro-politics are politics of the state as it *regulates* the populations (be it within the imperial state or in the colonies), chrono-politics served (during the Renaissance and the Enlightenment, to detach the Renaissance from its own tradition—the Middle Ages—and during the Enlightenment to detach European modernity from the "primitives") in the era of neoliberal globalization it has become one of the main weapons to *promote competition*, thereby encouraging fast speed and success, consuming the energy of millions of people who live their lives constantly thinking of going faster and getting ahead, to being a winner and to avoiding the shame of being a loser. Take, for example, the "remodeling" of *Newsweek*, which has been amply reported by the media. Jon Meacham, the magazine's editor, has been quoted as saying, "As the number of news outlets expands, it is said, attention spans shrink: only the fast and the pithy will survive." David Carr, who quoted this sentence, comments on it by noting that the statement was made when *Newsweek* was redesigned, in 2007. Carr adds,

"The fact that another redo is at hand in less than two years suggests that there is not a design concept in the world that will serve as a firewall against broader changes in reading and advertising."[43]

Meacham's statement clearly suggests a world in which the faster will survive. Now, when competition and speed are prioritized, the journalistic goal is no longer to inform and educate civil society, but to be *better* (by being faster) than the competition. The naturalized assumption is that by being faster and thus better than your competitors, the more you will fulfill the function of journalism. Whether civil society is informed or not is ir-relevant. What matters is to be fast: quality is another casualty of innova-tion and progress. The goal in the last analysis is not to inform, but to be faster. As in many other instances, institutions come first and society (civil and political) second. It is necessary to win the competition, rather than to have a well-informed and critical audience. The public sphere that reads the news is a "collateral beneficiary," and "good" information is a collateral phenomenon. But how many of the 6.8 billion people on the planet dwell in the acceleration of time and in the survival of the faster? One could say that at least half, the half of the population that live in mega-cities. However, it is not necessarily the entire population of a mega-city who will be trapped in the acceleration of time, which is a feature primarily of the lifestyle of bankers, builders, media figures, politicians, and all of those who strive to make more, to succeed, to get "there" first. The middle class, too, who live to consume (instead of consuming to live), will be trapped in the acceleration of time, in the realm of consumerism: to make more, to buy more, and to buy the newest and the best, to be not only fast, but also first.

In view of the non-sense in which the survival of the faster unfolds, there is good reason to make a case to re-inscribe "tradition" in the present and toward the future (see my discussion of "cosmopolitan localism," in the af-terword). Tradition could hardly be co-opted by chrono-politics; for if tra-dition, which is slow by definition, gets faster, it is no longer tradition, but modern. And if that happens, modernity gets stripped, and the logic of co-loniality is unveiled. That means that next to (conflictively coexisting with) the postmodern acceleration of time and the lifestyle it engenders, decolo-nial thinking shall build arguments for the revival of "the de-acceleration of time," revaluing what modernity devalued with no other reason than to eliminate the difference. There is significant room for maneuver beyond the illusion that if you are not fast, you do not deserve to be in this world. One way to decolonize modernity is to move toward undoing the pair "modernity and tradition." That means that the anthropos, who was also invented in the process of inventing the modern self, would assume delinking from the imperative to be human in the sense that Western modernity conceived humanitas. Once you delink there is no longer modernity and tradition, humanitas and anthropos, but only people who believe in modernity and tradition and in humanitas and anthropos. By delinking you remove yourself from the bases that sustain the edifice. As Groucho Marx used to say, "I do not want to belong to a club that invited me to be one of its members."

The communal, to which I will turn in the afterword, is a starting point and will shed more light on the issue. But before that, let's explore the role of space-politics in the rhetoric of modernity, in the next chapter.

CHAPTER FIVE

The Darker Side of the Enlightenment
A Decolonial Reading of Kant's *Geography*

And lest it be forgotten, nothing that I have said here is particularly new. Friedrich Gentz, who studied with Kant in Königsberg between 1783 and 1786, pointed out that if the goal of Kant's anthropological theories were realized, it would "compact the whole species into one and the same form," a dangerous situation which would destroy diversity and the "free movement of the spirit"—for anyone who disagreed with Kant's compact would be "treated as rebel *against fundamental principles of human nature*."—CHUKWUDI EZE, "The Color of Reason," 13

The question is not whether time or space is missing in one culture of the other, but which metaphoric base functions as the ordinary, and which is subordinate. As noted earlier, American Indians do have a temporal awareness, but it is subordinate to our sense of spatiality and, likewise, the western tradition has a spatial awareness, but that lacks the priority of the temporal. Hence, progress, history, development, evolution and process become key notions that preface all academic discourses in the West, from science and economics to philosophy and theology. GEORGE TINKER, *Spirit and Resistance*, 106

IN THE INTRODUCTION to the volume on Kant's *Geography* edited by Stuart Elden and Eduardo Mendieta, the editors remind us that "in his essay on 'The Conflict of the Faculties,' Kant divides the philosophy faculty into two parts—the one that deals with 'pure rational knowledge' and one that deals with '*historical knowledge*.' The former contains metaphysics of nature and morals, along with pure philosophy and mathematics; the latter includes history, geography, philology, the humanities and the empirical knowledge of the natural sciences."[1]

My interest in Immanuel Kant, beyond reading him as an educated man majoring in philosophy and literature, in Córdoba, Argentina, is indirect. Neither Kant himself nor his *Geography* is the target of this chapter. I am first and foremost preoccupied with certain issues, and, secondarily, to what Kant has to say about them. Or if you wish, Kant himself, through his *Geography*, is part of the problem not of the solution. His work triggers a wealth of issues for someone who is interested, as I am, in the darker side of the Renaissance and, to be oxymoronic, in the darker side of the Enlightenment—which means that I am more interested in what Kant hides than in what he reveals. I will be addressing the links (and complicities), in Kant, between historical and rational knowledges, on the one hand, and the silences that his *Geography* contributes to create on the other. The global totality that Kant searches for in his *Geography*, which parallels other fields of his inquiry, is driven by an anxious will to control knowledge and a blind sensitivity toward what he overrules by means of what he appropriates.

A Geo-historical Detour on the Way to Kant's *Geography*

In chapter 1 I began by remembering and acknowledging what has been forgotten or disguised by overwhelming narratives that started in Greece, persisted in Rome, and ended up in Western Europe, depending on whether the history was told by French, German, or British historians. While those histories are true as far as they go, they tell only half of the story; and, the notion of truth operating in the narratives is a truth in parenthesis. They are not the totality of what transpired historically; and, the version of events told looks even less true from the perspective of truth without parenthesis. Mainstream histories merely express the beliefs of those who told the stories and their supporters. What happened (remember Schmitt's unconscious trick) was that world history, both sacred and secular, was told from the Western perspective, as if there were a single, linear, and ascending history in time and a single center in space. Now we are becoming more aware that when *Western* ideas of history and its narratives started, *world* history did not come to an end. The totalizing scheme operated in the historiography of the discovery of America: when the Spanish arrived, a New History began a New World and previous history stopped. Now, however, we have Evo Morales as the president of Bolivia and robust indigenous movements from the south of Chile to Canada.

The world order around 1500, as I argued in the introduction, was polycentric and noncapitalist. Or, if you wish, the colonial matrix of power was not yet created; imperial and colonial differences were not in place. There were differences traced by the leaders of coexisting civilizations, within their territories and in relation to adjacent ones, of course; but imperial and colonial differences, as described here, appear with sensibilities, discourses, and worldviews entangled with the emergence of a type of economy today called capitalism. That is, imperial and colonial differences are tantamount to racism as we know and sense it today.[2] Before 1500, China and Japan were standing in their millenarian histories. To the south of China were the millennia of India's history, and the wide geographic stretch, intellectual sophistication, and influence of Sanskrit can only be compared to those of Latin under the Roman empire and of Arabic (from seventh century on) under the Islamic caliphate. By 1500, Western Christians were still a marginal society, about a thousand years after the collapse of the Western Roman Empire and about eight hundred years after the Crusades (1095–ca. 2130) and the loss of Jerusalem as the hub of Christianity. By 1500, vernacular languages derived from Latin (Italian, Spanish, Portuguese, French, German, English) were just unfolding, and Latin was still a language of scholarship and theology. Parallel to the origination and unfolding of modern European imperial languages derived from Latin, Hindi (in the area where India is today) and Urdu (in Central Asia and what is today Pakistan) originated and unfolded from Sanskrit, through Hindustani.

Modern European languages embodied, during and after the Renaissance, the "spirit" of epistemology, and emerging capitalism embodied the "spirit" of economy. While it is impossible to describe in two lines how capitalism became confused with economy, I would emphasize (and remind you) of two fundamental aspects relevant to my argument.

First, the massive appropriation of land and resources (gold, silver) made possible by the "discovery and conquest of America," by the massive exploitation of the labor of Indians, and by the trade of enslaved Africans allowed for a qualitative jump in the use of "capital" already accumulated in the banks of Florence, Venice, and Genoa. Genovese lending to the Spanish monarchy facilitated transatlantic explorations and the emergence of a new type of economy: capitalism. The combination of capital, massive appropriation of land and resources, and massive exploitation of labor made it possible, for the first time in the history of the human species, to produce commodities for a global market.

The second condition that made the spread of capitalism possible was the expendability of human lives. For the first time in history, human lives became dispensable and irrelevant to the primary goal of increased production and accumulated benefits. What distinguishes slavery in the Atlantic from all previous forms of slavery is that slavery before the Atlantic was not entrenched with capitalist economy and, therefore, human lives were not a dispensable commodity. Enslaved Africans were not only an exploited labor force; they also came to be treated as a type of commodity—which could be trashed, like any other commodity. Christian ethics condemned slavery, but couldn't stop it. By the second half of the eighteenth century, when Immanuel Kant was delivering his lectures on geography, Adam Smith was providing the theoretical frame for *The Wealth of Nations*, looking toward the future and overlooking the recent past history that allowed him to celebrate free trade and be silenced on the ethical consequences of such an economic breakthrough.

It is from the perspective of Islamic history that the historian Karen Armstrong (as I mention in the introduction) dated the "arrival of the West" in the Islamic world around 1750, as I pointed out in the introduction. In fact, the first "targets" of the second wave of imperial expansion and transformation of the colonial matrix of power, managed at that time by Britain and France, were the Mughal, the Safavid, and the Ottoman Sultanates. What made this expansion possible was, on the one hand, the new type of economy and its associated mentality (e.g., what it takes to control authority and to increase gains), and, on the other hand, the growth of knowledge-making. The Atlantic economy (the historical foundation of capitalism) made it possible, in Armstrong's view, not to rely on "a surplus of agricultural produce (as was the case in the economies of the polycentric world until 1500)." The rising Atlantic economy "was founded on a technology and investment of capital that enabled the West to reproduce its resources indefinitely, so that Western society was no longer subject to the same constraints as an agrarian culture."[3] Armstrong adds that, although it was not planned in advance, the transformation of economic practices resulted in what she calls a second Axial Age, "which demanded a revolution of the established mores on several fronts at the same time: political, social and intellectual."[4] Indeed, there were impressive advances in astronomy, medicine, navigation, industry, and agriculture (these are Armstrong's categories). And she adds,

> None of these was decisive in itself, but their cumulative effect was radical. By 1600 innovations were occurring on such a scale that progress seemed irreversible: a discovery in one field would often lead to fresh insights in another. Instead of seeing the world as governed by immutable laws, Europeans had found that they could alter the course of nature. They were now prepared to invest and reinvest capital in the firm expectation of continuing progress and the continuous improvement of trade.
>
> By the industrial revolution of the nineteenth century, Westerners felt such assurance that they no longer looked *back to the past* for inspiration, as in the agrarian cultures and religions, but *looked forward to the future*.[5]

Economy and knowledge joined forces with navigation through the Atlantic and from there throughout the world. Cartography underwent a radical transformation that culminated with Abraham Ortelius's stamp: *Theatrum Orbis Terrarum*, published in 1570 and steadily reproduced until 1612. While modern European vernacular languages appropriated epistemology, cartography appropriated space in the name of geography.

The historical and theoretical consequences of *Theatrum Orbis Terrarum*, particularly for understanding Kant's lectures on geography, taught about two centuries after Ortelius, are twofold. On the one hand, there is Ortelius's atlas, which maps the world and shows its configuration in land and water masses. Ortelius's depiction of the world overruled all existing territorial conceptions and descriptions prior to 1500. On the other side, we find that polycentric territorialities were subsumed in the *Orbis Universalis*. The end result and its consequences were formidable for European political, economic, and gnoseologic projects. And they were devastating for the rest of the world, as was becoming clear by the end of the eighteenth century: every civilization or culture began to be perceived as stagnant and as falling behind "modernity," receding toward the past. At the time of Ortelius's *Theatrum Orbis Terrarum*, the idea that pagans, infidels, and the "new" barbarians of "America" were in the space beyond Europe was already accepted and humanitas was being defined in contrast to those who were outside the norm, either because of excess or because of lack. Cartography, interestingly enough, was a truly important instrument in the process of defining 80 percent of the world population as out of history. By the end of the eighteenth century, "primitives" in time replaced "barbarians" in space.

On the other hand, the subsumption of all existing territorialities on the world map was derived from a single word chosen by Ortelius: *Theatrum*. "*Theatrum*" belongs, in ancient Greek, to the family of "theorein, theorem, theory." Under "theory" in the Online Etymology Dictionary, we find the following definition.

> 1590s, "conception, mental scheme," from L.L. *theoria* (Jerome), from Gk. *theoria* "contemplation, speculation, a looking at, things looked at," from *theorein* "to consider, speculate, look at," from *theoros* "spectator," from *thea* "a view" + *horan* "to see." Sense of "principles or methods of a science or art (rather than its practice)" is first recorded 1610s. That of "an explanation based on observation and reasoning" is from 1630s.

And for "theatre," we find,

> late 14c., "open air place in ancient times for viewing spectacles," from O.Fr. *theatre* (12c.), from L. *theatrum*, from Gk. *theatron* "theater," lit. "place for viewing," from *theasthai* "to behold" (cf. thea "a view," theater "spectator") + *-tron*, suffix denoting place.[6] Meaning "building where plays are shown" (1570s) was transferred to that of "plays, writing, production, the stage" (1660s). Spelling with *-re* prevailed in Britain after c.1700, but Amer.Eng. retained or revived the older spelling in *-er*. Generic sense of "place of action" is from 1580s; especially "region where war is being fought" (1914).

"Contemplation," "a place of viewing," "spectator (theoros)"—these are some of the key terms. I have argued, in *The Darker Side of the Renaissance*, that the cartographic breakthrough of the sixteenth century was to displace and replace, on the one hand, the ethnic center with the geometric center, by which coexisting territorialities beyond Western intellectual history were relegated to the past. (It appears as if only Western cartography continued its historical march.) On the other hand, the very ethnocentricity of Ortelius himself and of all the Dutch geographers and cartographers around him led them to assume (and I believe that this assumption was honest blindness, not perversity) that their maps did not project their ethnic view of the world, but that they indeed reflected the world as it is and should be for everybody.

When Kant was delivering his lectures on geography, the epistemic foundation of this particular field (mapping and describing the earth) was not only already "mapped" (to be redundant), but it was, above all, epistemologically deeply grounded in the belief that knowledge-making about the world was detached from the knower. Although Kant insisted that knowledge starts from senses and experiences, he assumed that there was a universal formula and therefore that all human senses and experiences would lead to the same reasoning and conception of the world. Kant's philosophy, his lecture on geography and anthropology, as well as the anthropological perspective that infuses his *Observations on the Feeling of the Beautiful and the Sublime* (1764), are all grounded on sixteenth-century theological and cartographic assumptions, according to which not only was knowledge universal, but the knower was equally a universally endowed epistemic subject who embodied the universality of sensing and experiencing—hence, a subject that was beyond the racial and patriarchal hierarchies that the system of knowledge Kant himself was embracing had already been established.

The splendors and miseries in Abraham Ortelius and Immanuel Kant lie both in what they have achieved and in what they have ignored and dismissed. In the internal history of Europe, both contributed to the condition that, from the European Renaissance on, originated the frame of mind we now describe as "modern/modernity." The Middle Ages and Antiquity (Greece, Rome) were invented as both the foundations of Christian and secular European history and as a difference: the past, as different from the present. The European Renaissance founded itself as re-naissance by colonizing time, by inventing the Middle Ages and Antiquity.[7] Western civilization did not start in Greece, but in the Renaissance, with the emergence of stories that Western civilization had started in Greece; these stories became hegemonic through imperial dominance. That was one of their recognized achievements and splendors.

However, Ortelius (born in 1527, at the time that Charles V and Suleiman the Magnificent were establishing themselves in world history) and Kant happened to live at crucial moments of European imperial expansion: Ortelius during the first wave, the Spanish sixteenth century; and Kant during the second wave, when the British empire was taking off in Asia and ready to go to Africa, as was France. Both were able to gather information due to wide-ranging European navigations around the world. Both dismissed the rest of the world to the benefit of their own "universal surface": the map and alphabetically written descriptions allowed them "to eat" the world—metaphorically and epistemically—and to possess it. The accumulation of meaning was an avid enterprise, parallel to the accumulation of money and wealth. In that era of "irrational epistemic exuberance," both Ortelius and Kant were blinded by the excess of information, by the enthusiasm of the *theatrum mundi* filling the eyes, the senses, and the imagination of Europeans, for whom information from around the globe was newly available and enticing. It was a messy and splendid world before them, and they had the pleasure of arranging, organizing, making it "understood." And therefore they missed the fact that while they were "seeing and conceiving the world," the enunciated, they were doing so within the "limits of their own subjectivities and places," the enunciation.

Thus, the modern-imperial epistemic subject was in its infancy with Ortelius, and in its full maturity in Kant.[8] The Colombian philosopher Santiago Castro-Gómez saw the links between cartography and theology-philosophy, and how we find in both an epistemology that assumes and celebrated the "hubris of the zero point."[9] The "hubris of the zero point" is not only what signals European "modernity," but also what legitimizes European imperial/coloniality.

What Questions Could Be Asked about the Knowing Subject?

Stuart Elden and Eduardo Mendieta in the above-mentioned introduction to the volume on Kant's *Geography* (that I have already mentioned in chapter 4) reminded us that in his *Logic*, Kant suggests that there are four fundamental questions.

1 "What can I know?"
2 "What ought I to do?"
3 "What may I hope?"
4 "What is the human being?"

Kant suggests that "*metaphysics* answers the first question, *morals* the second, *religion* the third, and *anthropology* the fourth. Fundamentally, however, we could reckon all of this to anthropology, because the first three questions refer, implicitly, to the last one."[10] It is a very helpful quote to juxtapose with a version of what I would call the "decolonial epistemic platform." From a decolonial viewpoint (and a decolonial sensing, shall I say, not to put all the weight on the eyes), Kant's are not the fundamental questions. The fundamental decolonial perspective would look more like this (here I am taking another tour around being where one thinks, as I did in chapters 2 and 3).

1 Who is the knowing subject, and what is his/her material apparatus of enunciation?
2 What kind of knowledge/understanding is he/she engaged in generating, and why?
3 Who is benefiting or taking advantage of such-and-such knowledge or understanding?
4 What institutions (universities, media, foundations, corporations) are supporting and encouraging such-and-such knowledge and understanding?

These questions (that have been addressed in chapters 2 and 3) cannot be properly answered from the established disciplines, which are themselves part of the problem, and they have been under trial. At the same time, the formulation of the questions, as well as the answers we can provide, cannot avoid what is common to all Western disciplines: a certain way of gathering information, of reasoning, of interpreting. Simultaneously, the questions and the answers have to be epistemically disobedient, that is, teasing out and betraying certain principles of "epistemically correct" reasoning and interpretation. Otherwise, decolonial thinking cannot change the terms of the conversation.

A decolonial platform is trans-disciplinary and originates at the moment that standard conceptions and practices of knowledge (e.g., all disciplinary formations) have been both "advancing" modernity and "contributing" to coloniality of knowledge and of being. Coloniality of knowledge doesn't mean that knowledge was colonized, but that hegemonic ways of knowing and disciplinary world-making, since the European Renaissance, were instruments of colonization and, as a consequence, of colonization of non-European knowledge. By the same token, the modern subject and therefore the modern knowing subject, became the model of all knowing subjects, whether European or not. Coloniality of being refers to imperial enforcement and management of subjectivity, enforcement, and management to which W. E. B. Du Bois responded with his "double consciousness" and

Frantz Fanon with the schism between "black skin/white masks" and with his concept of "sociogenesis." Double consciousness and sociogenesis are two crucial decolonial concepts that at once reveal the forced coloniality behind the benign rhetoric of modernity. Addressing the type of questions formulated above—and starting and following up on Du Bois's and Fanon's epistemic and hermeneutic foundations—allows you to delink or disengage from disciplinary formations, while, of course, addressing them in their imperial complicity. In this precise sense one can say that decolonial thinking is trans-disciplinary, not inter-disciplinary.

Consequently, instead of assuming universal "human nature as a starting point," decolonial thinkers start by assuming, first, that since the European Renaissance, and particularly during and after the Enlightenment, humankind was divided between humanitas, those who controlled knowledge, and anthropos. We are born equal, as the dictum says, but we do not remain equal. Restoration of what the rhetoric of modernity disavowed is the first and basic step to engage in decolonial options toward global equitable futures. Changing the questions being asked with regard to the problems to be solved means changing the terms of the conversation. Therefore, instead of engaging Kant in his own rules in order to question the content, I propose to change the rules of the game, to delink from his presuppositions, and to change the terms of the conversation. The key question is the first one, from which the other three logically follow. We have to return here to the apparatus of enunciation presented in chapter 3. For Benveniste, the formal apparatus of enunciation is structured by the pronominal system of any language and by the spatial/temporal deictic found in any language.[11]

In some languages, the speaker, by assuming the first-person pronoun (generally singular, but it could be also plural), mobilizes the pronominal system and locates the listener (plural or singular) in the second person and the referent (person, event, thing, absent, or present) in the third person (plural or singular). However, not every language has a pronominal system governed by the same logic. In Tojolabal, for example, the third person doesn't exist as such.[12] Temporally, the speaker takes for granted that he is speaking "now" in the present, although he or she can speak about the past, the present itself, or the future. Spatially, the speaker locates him- or herself "here," in the very place where he or she is enunciating. The possibility of registering a conversation and listening to it some place else in the future, doesn't change the basic formal apparatus of enunciation.

Now, thinking decolonially, the formal apparatus is hardly sufficient if we are to change the terms of the conversation and ask the questions I listed above. It is not enough to say that "knowledge is situated" or that "experience is the source of knowledge" if the options and possibilities in which knowledge is situated and experiences experienced are not spelled out. Otherwise, it has to be accepted that there is a universal organization of the world, a universal ontological dimension of "human beings" in which knowledge is situated and experiences are experienced, no matter what they might be. If we start from the premise that there is no universal common ground of experiences and that situated knowledge has to be spelled out in the colonial matrix (rather than in an assumed history of humankind), we shall then spell out in what sense, decolonially speaking, knowledge and experience are marked (situated) through and by colonial and imperial differences. To put it blatantly: Kant's and Fanon's experiences are situated in different departments of the colonial matrix of power. Not just chronologically, but in the epistemic hierarchy of modernity/coloniality. It is the epistemic colonial difference that separates Kant's situatedness from that of Fanon.

The first set of (imperial) assumptions (which I believe are the assumptions by which Kant was able to state that "there are four fundamental questions") presupposes that the rules of the game and the terms of the conversation are those of "objectivity without parenthesis."[13] The second set of (decolonial) assumptions presupposes that the rules of the game and the terms of the conversation are those of "objectivity in parenthesis."

Kant operates under the assumptions that knowledge is objective without parenthesis and that the knower (or observer) can establish objectively that there is a correspondence between the description (in words or in cartography) and the world described. The knower occupies a place, the place of knowing. And—according to the premises of truth without parenthesis—the place of knowing is beyond geopolitical histories and beyond body-political subjectivities: that is again the hubris of the zero point. The knower operates in the domain of the mind, beyond the body and beyond history. Decolonial thinking starts from the assumption that imperial epistemology racialized bodies and places: bodies out of rationality and places out of history.

Take for example the section of *Geography* in which Kant maps the fourth continent. He begins by setting up six fundamental principles that are valid for all the continents:

On dry land, however, we find:

1 Lands whose extent and interior we know.
2 Lands we only partially know.
3 Lands of which we know only the coasts.
4 Lands that we have actually seen, but not relocated.
5 Such of which the Ancients were aware, but are now as lost.
6 Finally, lands whose existence we only suppose.[14]

In the following paragraph Kant observes: "Europe belongs to the first named. To the lands of the second sort, however, belongs Asia."[15] Kant concedes that a better knowledge of Africa is necessary: "The cause, for which the interior of Africa is as unknown to us as the lands of the moon, lies more with Europeans than with the Africans, in that we have let ourselves be made so shy, through the Negro trade."[16] When he gets to America he points toward the North: "whose northern part, situated toward Russia, is still so good as undiscovered, and in whose southern half likewise, particularly on the Brazilian coasts, there still exist many unknown regions."[17]

Kant continues by acknowledging that "on ne connait pas mieux" [we do not know better] and that "la partie nord . . . est encore pratiquement inexploré" [whose northern part . . . is still so good as undiscovered]. He dispatches in less than one line the knowledge that people dwelling "à l'intérieur d'Afrique" [in the interior of Africa] and in "la partie nord" [the northern part] have of those places. Europeans are people who do not know the place because they have not explored it yet. People living there have situated knowledge and knowledge grounded in their experiences, like Kant. Operating under the hubris of the zero point blinds you to the fact that other people, with their own existence and knowledges, do not have the same problems you have and therefore could care less about your knowledge, until the moment that you impose it on them and tell them they do not know about themselves what you know about them. You conclude that they are inferior and ignorant, that their reasoning is defective, that their sense of the beautiful doesn't exist. You do not stop to think that they are as ignorant about your interests and values as you are about theirs. However, you assume that you "know" them because you describe them and include them in your *system of knowledge* and in your epistemic *architectonic*. But when "they" become aware of what you did because they read what you said, the reaction is: "Who are you and who gave you the right to say that about me?" and "To whom are you saying this to and what is your purpose"? The anthropos then began the process of delinking from the ideal and the idea of humanitas, and of decolonizing knowledge and being.

The point here is to underscore the differential of power between—on the one hand—the "institutional" sphere to which Kant belonged and the sphere of the "institute" (e.g., precepts, categories of thoughts) in which he was thinking and, on the other, the "institutional" and the "institute" to which Africa belonged and thought.[18] The power differential between the institutional and the institute was not, of course, a privilege of eighteenth-century enlightened thinkers, but was put in place in the sixteenth century. In Europe, Latinate language and knowledge (theology) set itself up against and above Hebrew and Arabic. From the European Renaissance to the Enlightenment, from theology and theo-politics of knowledge to egology and ego-politics of knowledge, the control and "institutionalization" of meaning makes invisible all non-European histories and knowledges (either by producing the effect that world histories, except Europe, came to an end in 1500 with emergence of the new nomos of the earth, or by watering down knowledge-making in African inlands and in the northern extreme of the Americas).

Operating on the hubris of the zero point resulted in conjoining epistemic and ontological differences.[19] Now, as far as ontological differences (colonial and imperial) in the modern/colonial world are concerned, they are inventions of the narrative of modernity and therefore they are constitutive of the epistemic foundation of racism; then racism is to be looked at not only ontologically, but also epistemically.[20] Mentioning "epistemic racism" is upsetting for many, and not just right-wing thinkers. But if we do not mention epistemic racism, we run the risk of maintaining the terms of the conversation and trying to be "radical thinkers" by operating only at the level of the enunciated.

Kant's *Geography* is one side of its *Anthropology* and both works are inter-connected and provide a hierarchical classification of regions and people.[21] In *Geography* Kant refers to and describes people; in *Anthropology* he talks about places and describes people. In both, the reader is confronted with a sustained argument to disqualify the world and to praise the heart of Europe. What is more important to my argument are the connections between both, as well as his philosophical reflections on the beautiful, the sublime, and pure reason, where geography, anthropology, and philosophy come together. The beautiful, the sublime, and pure reason have their point of origination in the heart of Europe. Kant's cosmopolitanism (see chapter 7) indicates the route of dispersion that the civilizing mission has to follows to bring the world to Europe (and Kant means by that, England, France, and Germany). Kant was a human being, brilliant and committed, but like every brilliant human being, he was just human. It would be a sin to dismiss Kant's contribution to the history of European thought; and it would be a crime to hide or undermine his epistemic racism. Highlighting Kant's racism, and the racism of the humanitas, is the first step of epistemic disobedience and delinking to liberate the/us anthropos and to join decolonizing forces against the persistence of coloniality of knowledge and of being that can no longer be formulated as a project of the humanitas.

Kant's Conceptual Matrix

Beyond what Kant enunciated in different fields of inquiry (philosophy, ethics, religion, anthropology, geography, aesthetics, and education—e.g., *The Contest of the Faculty*), there is a recurrent "matrix" of the enunciation that I will attempt to unveil by looking at his *Geography* in tandem with his *Anthropology* (as many have already remarked) and with his *Philosophy* (e.g., *Critique of Pure Reason*). I claim that Kant's semiotic apparatus of enunciation that I am outlining here is applicable to the Kantian corpus.

Part 3 of Kant's *Geography* is organized—not surprisingly—in four sections and in a very revealing order: Asia, Africa, Europe, and America. Asia is the place of Ancient civilizations, where, a few decades later, Hegel will locate the materialization—to be oxymoronic—of the Spirit. But from where did Kant get the four-partite divisions of the earth masses? Not from the landmasses themselves, unless the Spirit underneath was whispering the landmass names to Kant. Chinese scholars and cartographers could have imagined the world divided in four continents, but for what we know they did not. And, of course, there is nothing wrong with that because the planet was composed of four continents only in the Christian imaginary. The Jesuit father Mathew Ricci introduced Ortelius to the Ming dynasty, in 1582, and since then there have been adaptations and inversions of what continent appeared on the east and the west sides of the map. But this is an unlikely source for Kant's divisions, as the image of the world that for Kant was "natural" was not necessarily meaningful and "natural" in the Arab-Islamic world, which was divided into seven regions, as reported by Ibn Khaldun and other sources.[22] Perhaps at the time Kant was writing the Ortelius type of map was being introduced by the British in South Asia, among the elites of the Mughal Sultanate. The cosmology in the Incanate in Cuzco and the Tlatoanate in the valley was based on a four-partite division of the world, but certainly not in such continental divides.

I have told this story before, both in chapter 5 of *The Darker Side of the Renaissance* (1995) and in *The Idea of Latin America* (2005). The four-partite divisions of the earth prompted by the European invention and appropriation of "America"—and included in the Christian T-in-o map—erased the Incas' "Tawantinsuyu," the Aztecs' "Anáhuac," and the Kuna (Indians) "Abya-Yala" (Panama today). All were subsumed under "Indias Occidental/America," where the "Viceroyalty of Peru" and "New Spain" were included. The Christian tripartite division of the earth into Asia, Africa, and Europe (in the well-known T-in-o maps of Western Christendom, before the Renaissance), became a world of four continents. Kant was living in a period in which the erasures were forgotten, so the four-partite division of the world was what he knew. On that fiction Kant built his *Geography* and his *Anthropology*.[23]

Now, the distribution of the earth into four parts is not merely descriptive. In the T-in-o map, a hierarchy was clearly established. Since Christendom was located in Europe, and Christians were the "enunciators," Europe was attributed to Japheth, Asia to Shem, and Africa to Ham. Whoever knows a little about Noah's three sons will immediately remember that Japheth was the hope for the future and the preferred son; Shem was not bad, after all, and Ham, well, he was willful. When America came into the picture, it was too late for Noah to have a fourth son. In a way, America was first conceived as "Indias Occidentales," that is, Japheth extending to the west, as it was predicted in biblical narratives. On the other hand, this part of Occident was "Indian." When the name "America" began to be accepted, "Indians" were already one of the trademarks of the fourth continent.

But that is not all. As is well known, Kant made a connection between continents and people's skin color. The surfacing of the racist issue in Kant's work was brought about, to my knowledge, in Emmanuel Chukwudi Eze's landmark article, "The Color of Reason: The Idea of Race in Kant's Anthropology" (1997). And it is here where Kant's *Geography* and his *Anthropology* come together, through Carl Linnaeus's classification of "four types of human beings": Homo sapiens *Asiaticus*, Homo sapiens *Africanus*, Homo sapiens *Europeaus*, and Homo sapiens *Americanus*.[24] It is possible, then, to ask the same question about Linnaeus that I have asked about Kant: where did he get the idea that there were four types of Homo sapiens (with variations, of course, and edges), and the idea that each type corresponded to one of the four continents? I am aware that in Kant's *Geography*, parts 1 and 2 precede part 3, where he deals with the four continents. But allow me to push part 3 a little further before attending to parts 1 and 2.

The final section (part 4) of Kant's *Observations on the Feeling of the Beautiful and the Sublime* (1764), is devoted to "national characteristics" and the distinct "feelings" that national characters have of the beautiful and the sublime. He returns to the topic of "national characters" in his *Anthropology*, but it is less developed. In *Observations*, the topic of "national characters" is quite extensive, and it covers the globe. However, the basic structure is the same in both works. In *Observations* Kant opens part 4 with this striking observation (which is geographic, anthropological, and philosophical): "Of the peoples *of our part* of the world, in my opinion those who distinguish themselves among all others by the feeling for the *beautiful* are the Italians and the French, but by the feeling of the *sublime*, the Germans, English and Spanish. Holland can be considered as that land where the *finer taste* becomes largely *unnoticeable*."[25]

Let's parse this paragraph, thinking of the assumed (not analytical) conceptual structure of the *Geography*. "Our part of the world" doesn't need comment: it is the part devoted to Europe in the *Geography*. Second, in this part of the world there are six countries named. The first four—Italy (of the Renaissance), France, England, and Germany (forget about the difference, that is, that the first two excel in the beautiful and the second two in the sublime; instead, think of the European Union now)—are the heart of Europe in Hegel's formulation, a few decades after Kant. That is, they have formed the imperial power since the Enlightenment. Spain is the last of the imperial countries mentioned. Holland barely made it, and Portugal was forgotten. Interestingly enough, Portugal and Holland—unlike the first four countries—were marginal in the imperial epistemic "race," concerned more with commerce than with conversion and civilization. Consequently, the Dutch and the Portuguese are at the margins of the beautiful and the sublime.

Basically, we have here the part of *Anthropology* that deals with the national characteristics of "our part of the world," which will serve as the "standard model" by which to judge all other "national groupings" in other continents. It is not just the beautiful and the sublime that are being tested around the world, but also religion as connected with the beautiful and the sublime: "The religion of our part of the world is not a matter of an arbitrary taste, but is of more estimable origin."[26] "Religion" will allow Kant to ridicule Asian religions (China, Japan, and India): the Japanese, said Kant, could be regarded as the Englishmen of "this part of the world" (here referring to Asia). "Being regarded as the Englishmen" is flattering, but at the same time stamps the racial difference coded in national characters, for "being regarded as" is not like "being the model." The Japanese are like Englishmen in some aspects, said Kant, but "for the rest, they display few signs of finer feeling."[27] Then come the Chinese and Indians. Of the Indians he wrote, "Their religions consist in grotesqueries. The despotic sacrifice of wives in a very small funeral pyre that consumes the corpse of the husband is a hideous excess."[28] And with regard to the Chinese, Kant expressed his surprise at the "verbose and studied compliments of the Chinese" and marveled at the grotesquerie of their painting, as well as the strange and unnatural figures of their sculptures "such as are encountered nowhere in the world."[29]

Kant was writing shortly after the Battle of Plassey (1757), a date that in most histories inaugurates British takeover of the Mughal Sultanate. At that point India was not yet a colony and Kant was looking at its millenarian civilization. Consequently, I would say that Kant here was redrawing the imperial difference that had been inaugurated in the sixteenth century, when Spanish intellectuals (men of letters) established it in relation to the Ottoman Sultanate. But, at the same time, Kant was also remapping the colonial difference. This is how it works: Indians of the Spanish colonies "vanished" from Kant's view, and he instead highlights the "savages of North America" as those who, among all the savages, display the most sublime mental character. Native North Americans (including those in Canada, certainly) won the consolation prize. And with regard to Negros, Kant is famous for his observation quoting Hume, who "challenges to cite a single example in which a Negro has shown talents."[30]

Let me give you one more interesting example of Kant's remapping of both colonial and imperial differences. The section on Europe in *Geography* begins with "European Turkey"—but there is no text under this heading, which is followed immediately by the next title: "Bulgaria." If we now return to *Anthropology*, we find that Kant says, about the Turks: "Since *Russia* has not yet developed definite characteristics from its natural potential; since *Poland* has no longer any characteristics; and since the nationals of *European Turkey* never have had a character, nor will even attain what is necessary for a definite national character, the description of these nations' characters may properly be passed over here."[31]

At the time Kant was writing and lecturing, Catherine the Great was becoming the Empress (no longer the tsarina) of Russia (1762–96). She followed the trend of Peter the Great in extending the Russian domain into the Black Sea of central Europe, and promoted modernization and Westernization. But it was too early for Kant to predict the future. The Poland-Lithuanian Commonwealth, which flourished in the sixteenth century, was falling apart in Kant's time. And the Ottoman Sultanate had already lost its proper name; it became, in Kant's vocabulary, the European Turkey. In this move, Kant reaffirms the imperial difference in relation to Russia, which was still in its formation since the sixteenth century (Ivan the Terrible became tsar in 1558, the same decade in which Philip II of Spain and Elizabeth of England inaugurated their ascensions to the throne). By the same token, Kant contributed to the translation of the imperial difference that was established in the sixteenth century in relation to the Ottoman Sultanate, into the colonial difference that generated Orientalism in eighteenth-century Europe. During that century, the Ottoman Sultanate was beginning the decline that ended up in its collapse after the First World War. Kant was no longer looking at the sultanate but at the Turks. That is, the former imperial difference was translated into the colonial difference that undergirds European Orientalism. The move was not original. It had occurred already, in the sixteenth century. Spaniards not only dismantled the Incas' and Aztecs' domain but also immediately demoted them to "Indians." By so doing, Spaniards had already failed to recognize the Ottoman Sultanate, the Incanate, and the

Aztec Tlatoanate at the same level. But Kant completed the task initiated by the Spaniards: reduce the Ottoman in the terms of colonial difference.

Briefly, it is in the fourth section of Kant's *Geography*, organized around the four-partite continental divide, that we can see the racialization of people and regions: not only Chinese, Japanese, and Indian, but also Asia itself; not only the south of Europe (in what Kant has to say about Spaniards), but also the northeast of Europe (in what he and then Hegel have to say about Poland and Russia); not only Africa, but Africans, that is, Negros. And not only America, but the "savages" and "redskins." Because during Kant's time neither the steamboat nor the railroad were in place (both were technological by-products of the Industrial Revolution, which was in full force from 1850 on), the idea of correlating people and territory was stronger than it is today, though Kant himself acknowledged migrations.

In the second part of Kant's *Geography*, "On Human Beings" (vom Meschen), he most clearly connects his *Geography* to his *Anthropology*. The difference, however, is that *Anthropology* is devoted to cognitive faculty, desires, national characteristics, and races (genus) and species, whereas in *Geography* the section devoted to Man concentrates on skin color. A telling paragraph: "In hot regions, people mature earlier in every sense, but do not reach the perfection of the temperate zones. Humanity is in its greatest perfection in the race of the whites. Yellow Indians have somewhat less talent. Negros are far lower, and at the bottom lies a portion of the American peoples."[32]

In 1590, José de Acosta's widely read *Historia natural y moral de las Indias* was published in Europe and translated into several languages (Latin, French, German).[33] In the mid-nineteenth century, Alexander von Humboldt highly prized Acosta's book, which, apparently, Kant did not know; otherwise he would have not been so dismissive and ignorant of America in his *Geography*. The "white race" that attained such perfection had also its internal hierarchies. The "Black Legend" was, by Kant's time a fait accompli.[34] There is no other explanation for Kant's dismissive description of the Spaniards in his *Anthropology*, or in his *Geography*. Racism, and not just in Kant, is both ontologic (obvious in the previously quoted paragraph) and epistemic. Epistemic racism consists in devaluing ways of thinking, as well as in just ignoring them, not taking them into account.

In retrospect, looking at both Kant's and Acosta's enunciations, and delinking from both, we can see that Kant's *Geography* and *Anthropology*

would not have been possible without the work done by Spanish men of
letters in the sixteenth century. Acosta is a paramount example. Acosta's
book, particularly in the first two chapters, originally written in Latin, set
the record straight and corrected the views that Aristotle, Saint Thomas,
and the Bible had about the antipodes. He also set the record straight vis-
à-vis the natural history of Pliny the Elder and contributed to the debates
about the humanities of the Indians in Europe and among Europeans, since
Indians did not participate in that debate, although it centered on their own
humanity. When Kant and, before him, Carl Linnaeus were in a position
to receive information from around the world and to create a system of
classification and a systemic apparatus (as Kant does in the introduction to
Geography), the foundation had been already established. In other words,
although Kant ignores it, it is not possible to go from Aristotle and Pliny
to the eighteenth century without stumbling across the massive corpus of
Spanish intellectuals who both changed the directions in which natural history was being told and conceived, and placed the debate on human nature
in a different terrain. It is only through Kant and other enlightened philosophers who, through the Black Legend, created the division between the
South of Europe and its Heart (England, France, and Germany) that the
peninsular sixteenth century was obliterated from their own history in a
manner similar to the way Spanish intellectuals obliterated Arabo-Muslim
contributions to their own field of knowledge. As you can imagine, I am not
advocating for a recognition of Spanish contributions but rather highlighting the blindness or intentional dismissal of the very historical foundation
of Western modernity/coloniality. Be this as it may, in order to follow my
argument, it is important to keep in mind that the Spaniards built the external (epistemic and ontological) imperial difference with the Muslim caliphate and Ottoman Sultanate, while Kant initiated the *internal* (epistemic
and ontological) imperial difference in Europe itself. He contributed to the
creation of Orientalism (the remapping of external colonial difference) and
to the establishment of the South of Europe as the foundation of the internal imperial difference.

Linnaeus and Kant were living and acting during the historical period in
which Western thinking was moving from "barbarians in space" to "primitives in time." As we have seen in the previous chapter, Joseph Francois
Lafitau's *Moeurs de sauvages américains* (1724) is a major reference in this

mutation from barbarians into primitives and for starting the primacy of time over space in closing the borders of Western history and civilization. Natural history entered into this frame as it ended up in the present, divided into four continents. The entire debate of the New World, in the eighteenth century, was centered on the idea that even nature was still young in the New World. So, if we take Man, for instance, there would be a linear history of Homo sapiens, from primates to sapiens, that accounts for Man in the present, and Men in the four continents.[35] And when we get to the present, the linear history is translated into the spatial distributions, and Homo sapiens is located in Europe. Homo sapiens could be organized in a hierarchy that, as Kant said, places the "white race" as the one that comes closest to perfection. But, as it happened, the perfection of the "white race" was such because only whites were in the imperial position to classify all the races without being classified themselves. The epistemology of the zero point worked at its best in fusing, so to speak, the enunciated with the imperiality of the enunciation.

The epistemic trick (in the line that will reach Carl Schmitt) to which Kant so much contributed (see the section on "Shifting the Geography of Reason" below) goes as follows: first, in the sphere of the enunciated, it was stated that there are four continents and four races; second, in the enunciation, it was only within the white race that knowledge-making took place and that it was decided that there are four continents and four races. One of the races (white) and one of the continents (Europe) was the house of the enunciation. The rest were enunciated, but were denied enunciation. Epistemic racism was part and parcel of Western epistemology, and modern European languages, embodying the spirit of epistemology, became trumpeters of the known (rhetoric of modernity) and the gatekeepers of the unknown (logic of coloniality).

Consequently, while "the white race" was one among others, it was self-identified as the most accomplished, for which reason it appointed itself to classify and rank all the races, including itself as the prominent race that controlled the enunciation and created the classification. People who belonged and self-identified as such, white and Christian, and lived in the lands of Japhet had the privilege of generating and institutionalizing such knowledge. The privilege of the "white race" consisted in being at the same time one unit of the classification, but the only enunciation in which the classification was made: for all these reasons it can be strongly argued that the hubris of the zero point was, and still is, an imperial epistemology. It is not dialogic, at least in the specific sense of being that which doesn't allow any other type of knowledge to enter into dialogue. And this is one of the key issues of the twenty-first century, as we are already witnessing among Muslim scholars, intellectuals, politicians, and religious leaders, as well as in the wide array of "Indians" from the Americas to Australia and New Zealand,[36] and in the strong arguments being advanced by the advocates of dewesternization.

Shifting the Geography of Reason

Let's close the argument by returning to the basic distinction between Kant's four fundamental questions and the four fundamental questions asked within decolonial projects, by decolonial thinkers. Let's look at Kant, in other words, from the sidewalk across the street from where he is walking.

The term *architectonic* is one of Kant's key concepts and reveals the analogy with edifices and building that orient his oeuvre. The problem with the architectonic is not the term in itself. The problem is that it was stated as *the architectonic*. The concept did not exist among theologians in the sixteenth century. However, the assumption was that a Jesuit, and the Jesuit order, could provide to Europeans the knowledge of what the Indies and the Indians were, naturally and morally, and thus it was possible to totally ignore, dismiss, not even consider the fact that Incas and Aztecs and Mayas had built through centuries sophisticated systems of knowledge; this did not cross theologians' minds.[37]

When it comes to secular philosophy, Kant's architectonic is unthinkable without the apparatus of Western Christian theology.[38] It is the same order of knowledge, based on the same imperial epistemic assumptions. The only difference is that secular knowledge affirmed itself and its right by dismissing theology in the same way Renaissance men of letters created and dismissed the Middle Ages. But all of this refers to families that feud within the same set of assumptions, structures of enunciation, and knowledge-making. And while families have the right to feud, they do not have the right to expect that their problems are everybody's problems. I am proposing, and hopefully enacting, to delink from the system set by the four Kantian questions and to read Kant from the four decolonial questions. Here then, is my last move.

Kant begins the introduction by reminding us that the fountain and origin of all knowledge is pure reason and experience. The introduction to *Geography* is congruent with the four questions asked in his *Logic*: What can I know? What ought I to do? What may I hope? What is the human being? Thus, the introduction lays out the architectonic of systemic knowledge: the system goes from the whole to the parts. Empirical knowledge is a procedural aggregate that from the parts amounts to the whole. Empirical knowledge comes to us through our senses. Sensing would be, then, a parallel activity to reasoning. The first will be developed in the critique of judgment (aesthetics) and will be developed in the critique of pure reason (science). Philosophy, as we know from his work on *The Contest of the Faculties* (1798), stands above all as the vigilant observer of knowledge-making.

For decolonial thinkers, the senses (*aiesthesis*, affects) are also foundational, and Frantz Fanon taught us much about it. The point is not whether Fanon learned from Kant because Kant comes first (which is a naturalized assumptions for modern subjects). The point is that Kant and Fanon, as human and intelligent beings, were reflecting on their own experience, as a white European and as a black Afro-Caribbean. Fanon may have read Kant but he did not need him. Decolonial thinkers would agree with Kant as well as with the Aztec's anonymous *tlamatini* and the Inca's *amauta* ("wise man," in Náhuatl and Quechua-Aymara, respectively), that knowledge starts in and from the heart, and that the mind categorically processes what the heart dictates. They would note further that the heart senses not just the universality of human beings but also that the body feels according to its location in the colonial matrix of power, and according to patriarchal and racial hierarchies. For *amautas* and *tlamatinimes*, knowledge begins with the senses.[39] That is why geo- and body-politics of knowing and sensing is so foundational in decolonoial thinking. In this epistemology you are where you think, thinking makes you, rather than the other way around, while in Cartesian epistemology it is assumed that thinking is beyond body- and above geo-historical constraint; indeed, this is the main principle of zero point epistemology (see chapter 2).

Now, following what I just said, the "senses" are not equally and universally affected in the same way. The colonial matrix of power grounded on a type of economy described by liberals and Marxists as "capitalist" went hand in hand with a type of knowledge mounted on theology and then secularized to philosophy and science. It is not just the modern State that is unthinkable without Political Theology behind it, as Carl Schmitt argued. It is also the entire epistemic secular apparatus of Reason that is mounted on Epistemic and Hermeneutic Theology, to go parallel to Schmitt. Economic practice and epistemic/hermeneutical practices complemented and still complement each other.

So, then, if knowledge starts in and with the senses and in our (human beings) experiences, the senses and experiences of, for example, Quobna Ottobah Cugoano, an enslaved African who was shipped to the Caribbean and then taken by his master to London, where he was liberated, cannot be the same as those of Kant, although they were a generation and a half apart. Both were alive around 1786, when Cugoano published his book, and Kant was fifty-two years old and in his prime. Cugoano was born circa 1757 and published his classical book, *Thoughts and Sentiments on the Evil of Slavery*, in 1786. The date of his death is unknown. Kant was born in 1724 and died in 1804. Kant could have been aware and read *Thoughts and Sentiments on the Evil of Slavery*, which was published in London. Although, it could be that he was not prepared to pay attention to what an ex-enslaved black man had to say. But this is not the point. The point is that what Kant names "sense and experience," which is the most basic body-reaction to the environment (seasons of the years, as well as people and institutions), is connected to the geo-historical configuration of *that world around us*. Cugoano's body was colored black. Kant's was white. Kant was born and raised in the Kingdom of Prussia, at a time when Europe was benefiting from the Caribbean colonies, as well as from the existing commercial routes with regions situated to the east of Europe. Cugoano was born in Africa, captured and detached from his community, and worked as a slave in the Caribbean. The world must look different to each; their worldviews were different because the world-sensing of both responded to specific geo-historical and bio-graphical locations in the colonial matrix of power. So, while Hume and Kant thought that it would be impossible to "cite a single example in which a Negro has shown talents," we (now, here) can say that they were entitled to their own opinion, but that there is no obligation to take their opinion *ad pedem litterae*. Then it is time to delink and to look at Kant from Cugoano's point of view, instead of maintaining Hume's and Kant's perspectives. In other words, it is not sufficient to say, "Oh, well, yes Kant was racist" and then remain within Kant's epistemic dwelling. It is necessary to shift the geography of reason and to start reasoning from the senses and experiences of people like Cugoano. If we can do that, we can begin to think decolonially and to imagine and build possible futures detached from the prison house of Western modernity.

Why decolonially? Because one of the basic hypotheses of decolonial thinking is that knowledge in the modern world was and is a fundamental aspect of coloniality. In other words, knowledge is not just something that accounts for (describes, narrates, explains, interprets) and allows the knower to sit outside the observed domain and, from above, be able to observe imperial domination and colonial societies, ignoring or disguising the fact that *knowledge itself is an integral part of imperial processes of appropriation*. Colonialism has been basically analyzed in terms of economic and political control of territory and population, as if the knowledge being generated was outside Western imperial/colonial history (by which I mean, since 1500). Coloniality (as I and others have argued in the past decade) is constitutive of modernity. There is no modernity without coloniality: hence modernity/coloniality. Modernity is constituted by rhetoric: the rhetoric of salvation by conversion, civilization, progress, and development. But in order to implement what the rhetoric of modernity preaches, it is necessary to drive the juggernaut over every single difference, resistance, or opposition to modernity's salvation projects. Knowledge is of the essence. Thus, coloniality of knowledge means not that modern knowledge is colonized, but that modern knowledge is epistemically imperial and, as we have seen in Kant, devalues and dismisses epistemic differences. Epistemic differences goes hand in hand with ontological ones: "Show me a Negro that has shown talent," or "What trifling grotesqueries do the verbose and studied compliments of Chinese contain!"

Thus, thinking decolonially and reading Kant decolonially means to operate on the basis of geo- and body-politics of knowledge and to shift the geography of reason.[40] And that is, I hope, what I am doing here. I disengaged from Kant's categories of thought and assumptions. Disengaging or delinking doesn't mean that it is possible to "get out" of modern epistemology (or Kant himself, if you wish) as one walks out of the summer resort and goes home, just like that. Delinking means not to operate under the same assumptions even while acknowledging that modern categories of thought are dominant, if not hegemonic, and in many, if not in all of us. This is one of the problems that Muslim thinkers have been dealing with for a long time, and more so recently. Delinking then means to think from the silences and absences produced by imperial modern epistemology and epistemic practices—like Kant's, for example. It means to read Kant from the silences and the *exteriority* that he himself has produced.

The foundational acts of decolonial thinking are, first, delinking and, second, border gnosis (epistemology or hermeneutics). Imperial epistemology rolls over epistemic differences. *Tradition*, *folklore*, and *myth* are some of the terms invented to dismiss differential knowledge. *Reversing* the terms of the conversation will not work, mainly because doing so remains within the same rules of the game and play, yet under inferior conditions. *Changing the terms* of the conversation is, instead, the decolonial project, through border gnosis and border/decolonial thinking. Decolonial thinking consists, then, in deploying in their coevalness forms of knowledge and ways of being that have been pushed aside or buried in the past in order to make room for the triumphal march of modernity. "Pushing aside" and "burying in the past" are two operations of the logic of coloniality, of the invisible, the darker side of modernity—the darker side of Kant's *Geography*, for that matter.

Second, decolonial thinking runs away from the aim of building a system and putting together an architectonic. Indeed, decolonial thinking privileges hermeneutics over epistemology. The expression "border gnosis and border epistemology" already indicates it. In this regard, border gnosis is "critical." You don't need to add the word to distinguish, for example, critical from traditional "theory." For, even if the word *epistemology* is maintained, epistemology proper, in the Western tradition, cannot be in the border between diverse languages and systems of thought (Sanskrit, Latin, and Arabic). Of course, the borders between French and German will not count really as border epistemology, since both are differentials within the sameness of the languages that embodies epistemology. But am I engaging border thinking by writing in English? I believe so. Beyond raising the issues I am raising, my arguments are built on the silence of modernity. And since border gnosis presupposes the disruption of what was dismissed, decolonial thinking and border gnosis are of necessity hermeneutically pluritopic, rather than monotopic.[41]

Kant distinguished between the external and internal dimensions of knowledge. By the external we know the world, and by the internal we know man. Thus, a knowing subject is being formed in Kant's epistemology—a subject that knows "through the experience we have of *nature* and of *man*." What law of enunciation legitimizes this distinction? An assumption of universal nature of man that is none other than the invention of Man and Humanity and that runs from Renaissance humanism to Enlightenment rationalism. In that lineal drive, within a limited geo-historical part of the world—north of the Mediterranean—an idea of Humanity and of Knowledge was created as if it was good for the rest of the world. Kant's geography is, on the one hand, founded on the European system of knowledge and built on the colonial matrix of power (i.e., he was not reasoning within Chinese or Quechua-Aymara logic, worldview, or world sensing) and, on the other hand, deployed in the structure of a *geography*. In such a project, the desire to "totalize" (i.e., to gain and control knowledge) is, from a decolonial point of view, frankly not surprising. Imperial knowing subjects feel anguish in the face of the possibility that there may be something that escapes their totalitarian impulse to "know the world" and to believe that their knowledge corresponds to what the world is. That is what truth and objectivity without parenthesis mean. The epistemology of the zero point (theo- and ego-logy) is predicated on objectivity without parenthesis and is, therefore, unavoidably imperial. However, around the world that Kant totalized are several non-European languages, concepts, epistemologies, and hermeneutics (to use the Western word in the same way the Zapatistas use "democracy"—that is, decolonially already) that have no reason to believe that they are in the past or that they are no longer sustainable, although there is at the time no way to erase Kant's *Geography* in the same way Kant erased all other territorial conceptualizations.

Thus, if Kant's *Geography* aims at the universal, decolonial thinkers aim at the global; that is, they seek to move through the borders drawn by the always-mutating imperial and colonial differences. To the extent that its advocates attempt to spread the ideals of modernity globally, and to the degree that modernity's systems of thought are grounded in Western languages (Greek, Latin, Italian, Spanish, Portuguese, French, English, and German), those advocates and systems disqualify categories of thought not grounded in ancient and modern imperial languages. As an antidote, border thinking aims at pluriversality. Border thinking and border epistemology are the antidotes to the virus of zero point epistemology. These are the anchors that support the shift in the geography of reasoning. Thus, the way to the future is the way toward pluriversality as a universal project.[42] Pluriversality as a universal project is, in Enrique Dussel's words, the route to a transmodern, not a postmodern, world.[43] The plurinational state, a concept that is already in the Constitution of Bolivia and Ecuador, is already a significant step toward global pluriversality. It is important to keep in mind that global pluriversality cannot be managed by reasoning from zero point epistemology, as such a practice would kill and appropriate all pluriversal projects. Once zero point epistemology and Kantian imperial cosmpolitanism are called into question, the next step is to reason on the bases of border epistemology and cosmopolitan localism. The plurinational state in the South American Andes is one decolonial step forward toward pluriversal futures.[44]

Once we are in the borders where imperial Western epistemology meets with its global differences, we face the need for what Raymundo Pannikar described as "imparative method."[45] And once we start thinking decolonially, it is not possible to stand in the borders comparing both sides, because comparative methodology epitomizes the hubris of the zero point. "Comparative methodology," put in place in the nineteenth century, was precisely that: a method to ensure that the observer remained uncontaminated, and guarantee that Western epistemology remained on top, controlling all other forms of knowledge. *Imparative* method, Pannikar stated, is "the effort at learning from the other and the attitude of allowing our own convictions to be fecundated by insight of the other."[46] In contradistinction to the *comparative* method, which privileges dialectics and argumentative reasoning (system and architectonic), the imparative method (for Pannikar, diatopical hermeneutics) focuses on dialogue, praxis, and existential encounters—that is, reasoning from the senses and, in my argument, from the locations of the bodies in the colonial matrix of power. Decolonial thinking, then, is one type of imparative practice that aims to delink from coloniality of knowledge and being (that is, from imperial/colonial subjections of subjectivities through knowledge) and to engage in border decolonial thinking. In reading Kant decolonially, I have aimed at entering into a dialogue with Kant (and modern Western epistemology) by delinking from the rules of the game, and by being epistemically disobedient.[47] I have been trying to show that different kinds of games are possible and, in so arguing, to participate in those games.

It is to these issues that I turn to in the next two chapters and in the afterword. In chapter 6, I take the Zapatistas' theoretical revolution as a radical shift in thinking/doing decolonially, and show what decolonial thinking and decolonial options have to offer. I offer not a model to be exported or applied, but a model of an engagement in doing decolonially what could be followed up in diverse local histories, including those of Europe and the United States. In chapter 7, I take on Kant's cosmopolitan legacies and explore some of the shortcomings of current debates on "cosmopolitanism," suggesting that if cosmopolitanism is possible and desirable, it should be local. The apparent contradiction vanishes if we accept that if a cosmopolitan world order is thinkable and desirable, it could not be universal, but must instead be pluriversal—that is to say, cosmopolitan interconnections of local nodes predicated on truth and objectivity in parenthesis. There is no room for a well-intentioned imperial cosmopolitan order (that is, predicated on truth without parenthesis), be it religious or secular. Cosmopolitan localism will also help end any religious or secular claim to universality and to truth and objectivity without parenthesis. Cosmopolitan localism means working toward a world in which many worlds would coexist; this means working toward pluriversality as a global/universal project. I will explore these ideas in the next two chapters.

Part Four

CHAPTER SIX

The Zapatistas' Theoretical Revolution
Its Historical, Ethical, and Political Consequences

You are rich because you are white, you are white because you are rich. This is why a Marxist analysis should always be slightly stretched when it comes to addressing the colonial issue. It is not just the concept of the precapitalist society, so effectively studied by Marx, which needs to be reexamined here. The serf is essentially different from the knight, but a reference to define right is needed to justify this difference in status. In the colonies the foreigner imposed himself using his cannons and machines. Despite the success of his pacification, in spite of his appropriation, the colonist always remains a foreigner. It is not the factories, the estates, or the bank account which primarily characterize the "ruling class." The ruling species is first and foremost the outsider from elsewhere, different from the indigenous population, "the others."—FRANTZ FANON, *The Wretched of the Earth*

When one says Eurocentrism, *every self-respecting postmodern leftist intellectual has as violent a reaction as Joseph Goebbels had to culture—to reach for a gun, hurling accusations of proto-fascist Eurocentrist cultural imperialism. However, is it possible to imagine a leftist appropriation of the European political legacy?* SLAVOV ŽIŽEK, "A Leftist Plea for Eurocentrism," italics added

When one says Eurocentrism, *every self-respecting decolonial intellectual has NOT as violent a reaction as Joseph Goebbels had to culture—to reach for a gun, hurling accusations of proto-fascist Eurocentrist cultural imperialism.* A self-respecting decolonial intellectual will reach instead to Frantz Fanon: "Now, comrades, now is the time to decide to change sides. We must shake off the great mantle of night which has enveloped us, and reach for the light. The new day which is dawning must find us determined, enlightened and resolute. . . . So, my brothers, how could we fail to understand that we have better things to do than follow in that Europe's footsteps." WALTER MIGNOLO, "Geopolitics of Knowing and Understanding," Keynote address at the conference, "American Studies as a Transnational Practice," Lubbock, Texas, April 2010, quoting from Fanon, *The Wretched of the Earth*

THE ARGUMENT of this chapter was presented for the first time in a lecture at Berkeley (department of ethnic studies) in the spring of 1997. In spite of the series of events that have unfolded since then (e.g., the creation of Los Caracoles, La Otra Campaña [the Other Campaign], the tension between the Zapatistas and the Mexican Left during the presidential campaign of López Obrador, the initiation of the Festival de la Digna Rabia) and the impressive growth and force of indigenous political society in the Andes, mainly in Bolivia and Ecuador, but also in Colombia (Valle del Cauca), I feel that the ideas advanced then are still relevant. My thesis should also help in understanding the differences (as well as the points of connection) between the Left and decolonial options. My original intuition of the "Zapatistas' theoretical revolution" was, in retrospect, what ignited the main argument in this book, chiefly my concerns with geopolitics and body-politics of knowledge. In this case, the uses of the mask and the conceptualization of the "use of the mask to be seen," due to the invisibility of indigenous nations, make it possible to shift the geography of reasoning (which is the core of the Zapatistas' theoretical revolution).[1]

Shortly after the presentation at Berkeley, I delivered the paper as one of the keynote addresses at the conference on "Comparative Colonialism: Pre-Industrial Colonial Intersections in Global Perspective," held at Binghamton University.[2] The title of that presentation was "From 'El Derecho de Gentes' to 'La Dignidad Humana': The Zapatistas' Theoretical Revolution." The original line of argument is maintained here: "rights" are attributed to us by someone who has the right to attribute rights; dignity cannot be attributed, but is taken by the non-person whose rights are being defended. The colonial difference is the main factor that extracts dignity from people: being racialized and seen as inferior by the dominant discourse makes us believe in our own inferiority. That is what taking our dignity away means. "Dignity" is one of the markers of coloniality and therefore one of the engines that moves the decolonial option and the shift from zero point epistemology to border epistemology and decolonial thinking. A non-trivial follow up of the conference shall be mentioned, as it is also relevant to understand that indeed the Zapatismo introduced a theoretical revolution— that shift I have been arguing about.

The conference organizers planned to edit a volume comprising a selection of papers from the conference. Keynote speakers were first on the list of potential contributors, so I began to work on a final version with the organizer-editor. We went through four or five drafts, before we mutually and amicably ended the process: he did not want to publish the paper in his edited collection; I did not want to publish the paper in the collection he was editing. What happened? Well, the editor wanted me to write the article as he would have written it: in a more informative, positivist, and perhaps even explicative way. And I wanted to argue that we were facing a theoretical revolution that could not be analyzed by some other theoretical frame. Today I would say that at that moment I was "seeing" the opening of the decolonial option, although I was not ready to articulate it as such. But that would have not solved the problem: what separated us (the editor and myself) was the Zapatistas' conceptual delinking from a master frame of reference situated in Western ways of thinking, which I was stressing and the editor was unable to see or to accept. Finally, a first version in English was published at Binghamton as well as in *Review*, the journal of the Fernand Braudel Center, directed by Immanuel Wallerstein. In 2008 the essay was translated into Spanish by Ana Gabriela Blanco and Dr. Raymundo Sánchez Barraza, director of CIDECI/Unitierra in San Cristóbal de las Casas and distributed in Mexico. The failure of the paper to appear in the original conference proceeding was indeed a productive one: it highlighted that the theoretical revolution was reinvigorating the decolonial option that had been built through five hundred years of coloniality in the creative responses to the expanding European imperial option and its internal diversity (e.g., dissenting and critical theologians, dissenting and critical liberals and marxists, critical scholars in the canonical disciplinary spectrum). I have added references to events that took place after the essay's publication, updated the bibliography as appropriate, and made links with other chapters in this book. The basic argument, however, remains as it was articulated in the date indicated.

Human Dignity/Decoloniality of Being

There is a story about a young woman who, in a Chiapas market, sometime after January 1994, said "Los Zapatistas nos devolvieron la dignidad" (The Zapatistas returned dignity to us).[3] *Dignity*, from the initial uprising to the recent Festival de la Digna Rabia, is a key word in Zapatistas' doing and thinking. Who took the dignity away from the people of indigenous nations? Certainly, it would be possible to identify collective names, like the Spaniards in the case of the indigenous people of the Yucatan Peninsula, or the Creoles who built the nation-states (Mexico and Guatemala, in this case) after decolonization. However, a similar historical circumstance prevailed in other areas of Latin America and the Caribbean, in Brazil, the United States, in Canada, as well as around the world, in Australia and New Zealand, although the Spaniards did not intervene directly in all of those areas. I would like to propose that the dignity of indigenous people has been taken away by the coloniality of power enacted in the making of the modern/colonial world since 1500.[4] That is, in the world-making process today we identify as modernity/coloniality. Modernity doesn't stand by itself. Without coloniality, its darker side, there is no modernity. The modern/colonial world as I conceive it here goes together with the mercantile, industrial, and technological capitalism centered in the North Atlantic. Coloniality of power, in a nutshell, worked as an epistemic mechanism that classified people around the world (see chapter 5), by color and territories, and managed (and still manages) the distribution of labor and the organization of society.[5]

Thus, the young woman's dictum in the Chiapas market has indeed a larger import than the local history of indigenous people in the Yucatan Peninsula. However, there is also a local history that the Zapatistas put forward in their first declaration from the Lacandon Forest, in January 1994, in which the young girl's dictum makes sense.

> We are the product of five hundred years of struggle. First against slavery; then in the insurgent-led war of Independence against Spain; later in the fight to avoid being absorbed by North American expansion; next to proclaim our Constitution and expel the French from our soil; and finally, after the dictatorship of Porfirio Diaz refused to fairly apply the reform law, in the rebellion where the people created their own leaders. In that rebellion Villa and Septa emerged—poor men like us. (First Declaration from the Lacandon Jungle, 1994)[6]

The Zapatistas' theoretical revolution and its continuity during the decades (from the Lacandon Jungle manifesto to the foundation of Los Caracoles and, more recently the Other Campaign/La Otra Campaña), acquires new dimensions when the events in Bolivia and Ecuador are taken into consideration. In the overall thrust of my argument, here, the Other Campaign is consistent with the Zapatistas' theoretical revolution, as well as advancing and affirming that decolonial options respond to needs that cannot be met by the most talked about "turn to the Left."[7] Decolonial options are roads toward the future. If you follow them you would break away from the legacies of the Renaissance and the Enlightenment, you would begin to shift the geography of reasoning; shaking off your body the enchantments of liquid modernity[8] and the chains of coloniality toward the sear of an-other language, an-other thought, an-other way of being in the world.[9]

"Human dignity" takes its full meaning first within and as a consequence of the local history in which the sentence was pronounced. It is connected to similar colonial experiences, although from different colonial histories (I will develop this idea below in terms of diversality as universal project). In other words, "human dignity" shall not be taken, under any circumstance (even if that circumstance is the French Revolution), as an abstract universal, but as a connector of similar colonial experiences in different colonial histories (in the rest of the Americas, in Asia, in Africa). "Human dignity" on the other hand introduced the ethical dimension in the Zapatista uprising that Subcomandante Marcos underlined as follows.

> All of a sudden the revolution transformed itself into something essentially moral, ethical. More than the distribution of wealth or the expropriation of the means of production, the revolution is becoming the possibility for carving a space of human dignity. Dignity becomes a very strong word. But it is not our contribution, a contribution of the urban component, but a contribution from and by indigenous communities. They want the revolution to be the warranty for the respect of human dignity.[10]

The emphasis on the ethical problem here doesn't mean that the economic question has been forgotten, that land claims, exploitation of labor, and economic marginalization do not count.[11] Remember that for many Native Americans, land and spirituality are two sides of the same coin, while for those living the enchantment of modernity land is private property, a commodity that gives you wealth and prestige. Why should land be universality taken as private property? And why should indigenous people who defend the link between land and spirituality be seen as arcadic, romantic, out of place, and out of time? Who is reproducing coloniality of knowledge and of being when such judgments are pronounced? Really, where do we find the warranty that the first is a modern or postmodern endorsement of truth without parenthesis and that the second is out of history, in the past, superseded? Think about it. Here we can bring ethics to the foreground to remind ourselves that Karl Marx studied the logic of capital to make not an economic but an ethical claim about the adulation of money and commodity at the expense of human life. While we could agree that Marx was right, why should his be the only truth? A non-Christian and a non-Muslim could agree with many aspects of the Bible and the Qur'an. But why should they be taken as the only truth without parenthesis? Or, inversely, why to despise them because they are not secular texts and do not promote the separation of "Church" and the State without considering that "Mosques" are not "Churches" and that the State is not a universal form of government?

Human dignity is something parallel to yet distinct from human rights. Discourse on human rights focuses mostly on the legal question of right while the issue of human dignity shifts to the human individual, and raises the question, "Who speaks for the human in human rights?"[12] There is no institution of "human dignity watch" that can restore the dignity that has been taken away and continues to be taken away from billions of people in the world. While human-rights activists are performing remarkable humanitarian tasks defending the rights of all those who are abused, "dignity" cannot be defended by institutions and regulations and actors who have not suffered or are not suffering the consequences of "indignity," for to feel that our dignity has been taken away is to feel that we are lesser humans. The figure of the damnés is more than that of someone oppressed or exploited—it is the figure of the lesser human. There is the issue of scale. The young girl in the Chiapas market, the Muslim intellectual who rebuts Western classifications, or the East Asian who knows he or she has been classified as "yellow" (whether he or she is peasant or high middle class in Shanghai).[13] (In)dignity is a feeling provoked by he who controls knowledge and is in a position to classify and rank people in the chain of humanity. In the colonial matrix of power such classifications are bestowed on bodies, in a combination of racism and patriarchy. Racial classifications respond to a model of Humanity which is at once modeled on the image of Christian and European Man in relation to non-European. And patriarchal classification is bestowed on bodies ranked in relation to male heterosexuality. As far as such classifications are inscribed in a naturalized order of knowledge, the colonial and patriarchal world is the wound of indignity that engendered decolonial thinking and the decolonial options. The Zapatistas' theoretical revolution is such in relation precisely to the Western imperial order of knowledge that was founded and operated on the coloniality of knowledge and of being. Theoretical revolution means here a potent move toward decoloniality of knowledge and of being, and opening toward the decolonial option—the radical Zapatistas' departure from the reorientation of the Left.

Double Translation and the Zapatistas' Narrative of the Theoretical Revolution

Let us follow Subcomandante Marcos's narrative of his encounter with Old Man Antonio, an encounter in which Rafael Guillén, the Marxist urban intellectual, began the process of becoming Subcomandante Marcos, the double translator. The translator, on the one hand, of local discourses to the Mexican nation and the world beyond Mexico, and, on the other hand, the translator of Marxism to the local population—a double translator that displaced the model implanted by missionaries at the beginning of the colonial world. Missionaries, whether translating from Spanish to Náhuatl or Quechua, or vice versa, never put themselves at risk. It was clear that although translation could go from Spanish to Náhuatl and vice versa, translation was ideologically always uni-directional. Instead, translation as conceived and practiced by Subcomandante Marcos was at risk and bi-directional. Rafael Guillén became Subcomandante Marcos at the moment in which he accepted the fact that Indigenous thinkers and political leaders would use him in the same way he thought he would use them. He realized that his Marxist cosmology needed to be infected by Indigenous cosmology. That Indigenous leaders had their own equivalent of what Marx represented for Rafael Guillén and the urban intellectuals who went to the Lacandon Forest in the 1980s with the hope of propagating the Marxist revolution. The theoretical revolution is here already at work: the role of the missionary (of any missionary, whether Christian, Islamic, liberal, Marxist) who acts in the name of the truth to convert the misguided has been displaced by the role of mediator dwelling in the colonial ontological and epistemic difference.

In contrast to sixteenth-century missionaries who never doubted that conversion to Christianity was the right thing to do, Subcomandante Marcos may have understood that aiming at converting Tzotziles and Tojolabales to Marxism was indeed a reproduction of the same logic of salvation, although with a different content. The self-conversion of Rafael Guillén into Subcomandante Marcos was a change from the Marxist to the decolonial option. One aspect of this transformation comes across in Subcomandante Marcos's reflections on the process of merging Amerindian and Marxist cosmologies in the process of double translation: "The end result was that we were not talking to an indigenous movement waiting for a savior but with an indigenous movement with a long tradition of struggle, with a significant experience, and very intelligent: a movement that was using us as its armed men."[14]

The conceptual transformation emerged in the first encounter between Rafael Guillén and Old Man Antonio. Old Man Antonio died in 1994. Guillén met him in 1984. According to Subcomandante Marcos's narrative told in 1997, a group of urban intellectuals (a Marxist-Leninist group with a profile similar to the guerrilla movements in Central and South America) joined a group of politically oriented indigenous leaders and intellectuals (Tacho, David, Moises, Ana Maria). In the first encounter between Antonio and Guillén, Emiliano Zapata came in as a topic of conversation. Guillén told the story of Mexico from a Marxist perspective and situated Zapata in that history. Then Old Man Antonio told the story of the Indigenous communities from a Mayan perspective and situated Zapata, indeed, Votan/Zapata, in that history. After this exchange of stories, in which Zapata became a connector of two stories embedded in different cosmologies, Old Man Antonio extended a photograph of Votan/Zapata to Guillén. In the picture, Votan/Zapata is standing up, with his right hand grabbing the handle of the sword that is hanging from his right side. While Guillén was looking at the picture, Old Man Antonio asked him whether Zapata was pulling the sword out or pushing it in. Once it is understood that both histories have their reasons, it is only an unconscious structure of power that can decide which one is history and which is myth. And this is not necessarily cultural relativism.

There is a danger here, indeed, of interpreting the encounter between

Guillén and Old Man Antonio in terms of "cultural relativism." I would like, instead, to interpret the event in terms of the political choices and options prompted by the awareness of the colonial difference. *Culture* is a term that acquired the meaning we attribute to it today in the eighteenth century and in a Western secular world that replaced *religion* in a new discourse of colonial expansion.[15] Communities of birth began to be conceptualized as national communities, replacing former religious communities of believers. The notion of "cultural relativism" translated the question of coloniality at large and of coloniality of power into a semantic problem (cultural relativism) that engendered a new discourse of political and ethnic tolerance. If we accept, for instance, that actions, objects, beliefs, languages, ideas, and so on are culture-relative, we hide the power of coloniality from which "different cultures" came into being in the first place. "Cultures" have not been "there" all the time, but have been forced into being what they "are" today by the making of the modern/colonial world. There were no "Indians" in the Americas until the arrival of the Spaniards. Of course, there were people that identified themselves with names, but they were not "Indians."[16] And there was no America either, until Northern European colonialism began to map the world and to include "America" within the Christian trinity of Europe, Asia, and Africa. The world was organized and divided into continents, and the people were identified by their color, their culture, and the continent they inhabited. Coloniality of power emerged in this "original" organization of the modern/colonial world. The issue, then, is not to see Old Man Antonio and Guillén's discourses in the frame of cultural relativism, but to dissolve cultural relativism into the making and reproduction of the colonial difference. That is to say, it was through the exercise of coloniality of power "cultures" in the classification of people by religion, color, and continents (that is, the making of the colonial difference) that created the conditions to conceptualize cultural differences and cultural relativism.

Double translation is then a key component of the Zapatistas' theoretical revolution. Double translation allows one to dissolve cultural relativism into colonial differences and to reveal the colonial structure of power (e.g., the coloniality of power) in the production and reproduction of the colonial difference. From the perspective of double translation there emerges an ethical and political imaginary that opens up the gates for conceiving possible futures beyond the limits imposed by two hegemonic abstract universals, (neo)liberalism and (neo)Marxism. The theoretical revolution of the

Zapatistas shall be located in the double translation (and double infection) that makes possible a double epistemic movement, framed by the colonial difference. That is, forms of knowledge that had been discredited from the very inception of modernity/coloniality enter into a double movement of "getting in/letting in." This movement is allowed by the reversal of the power of coloniality opened up by double translation. The theoretical revolution grounded in double translation makes it possible to imagine epistemic diversality (or pluriversality) and to understand the limits of abstract-universals that dominated the imaginary of the modern/colonial world from Christianity to liberalism and Marxism. The meaning and implications of Zapatistas' theoretical revolution should be clear at this point. For instance, we can understand now that there was not so much of a difference between Shining Path and Alberto Fujimori in terms of the logic of abstract universals. It was the same logic with different content. It was perhaps the tyranny of the logic grounded in the abstract universal that misguided (beyond their noble goals) Che Guevara, in Bolivia, and the Sandinistas, in Nicaragua, in their interaction with the indigenous population and in their blindness to the theoretical, ethical, and political potentials in Amerindian communities.

The epistemic potential of double translation and double infection (e.g., the "getting in/letting in") is indeed the strength of the Zapatistas' discourse and the grounding of their theoretical revolution. Subcomandante Marcos "was born" in and from the process I am here calling the double translation.

> We [the urban intellectuals] went through a process of re-education. As if they [the indigenous intellectuals and indigenous communities] were undoing the tools we had; that is Marxism, Leninism, urban culture, poetry, literature, everything that was part of ourselves. At the same time, they showed us things we did not know we had. . . . They undid us and then remade us again. The EZLN [Ejército Zapatist de Liberación Nacional] was born the very moment in which it was ready to confront a new reality for which some of its members had no answer and to which they [the urban intellectuals] subordinated themselves in order to survive.[17]

Marcos described Old Man Antonio as the translator between the urban and the indigenous intellectuals and communities and described himself as a translator whose audience was the world at large, beyond indigenous communities in Latin America and the Zapatistas and the Mexican government. Thus, the Internet proved to be crucial in the Zapatistas' theoretical "uprising." However, in that translation and in contrast with the model of translation implanted by missionaries in the sixteenth century and around the world in the subsequent centuries, Marcos's translation gave indigenous voices a place similar to that which a translator from Greek into, say, German will give to Aristotle. Indigenous intellectuals were no longer seen as curiosities or objects of anthropology, but as critical thinkers in their own right. One could venture to say that "we, the nothing, not counted in the order, are the people, we are all against others who stand only for their particular privileged interests," as Žižek says to underline the emergence of the "political proper" (his words) in ancient Greece (see below). Such change in the directionality of translation contributed to opening up Marxism to the colonial difference and, consequently, to understanding racism in relation to labor in the planetary order of the modern/colonial world. It also underscored the limits of the Western notion of democracy and showed the way for displacing the concept from its current abstract universal meaning, taking it as a connector for pluriversality as a universal project that can be imagined in the name of democracy. Not all would agree. Those who disagree would be those who defend truth without parenthesis. Let's explore these two points a little bit further.

Marxism and the Colonial Difference

Let's go back once more to Subcomandante Marcos.

> The Zapatismo is and is not Marxist-Leninist. The Zapatismo is not fundamentalist or millenarist indigenous thinking; and it is not indigenous resistance either. It is a mixture of all of that materialized in the EZLN. The regular group, the insurgents, that is Mayor Mario, Capitan Maribel, Major Ana Maria, all of us who lived in the mountains during the late 80's and 90's are a product of that cultural shock.[18]

> Because of all of this, Zapatismo cannot attempt to become a universal doctrine, a doctrine of homogenization, like the (neo)liberal and (neo)socialist goals and ideals. It is important that Zapatismo remains undefined.[19]

> This is why also; the true creators of Zapatismo are the translators such as Mayor Mario, Mayor Moises, Mayor Ana Maria, all of those who also had to be translated from dialects [Marcos is referring here to indigenous

languages] such as Tacho, David, Zevedeo. They are indeed the Zapatistas theoretician . . . they built, they are building a new way for looking at the world.[20]

It should be clear at this point that although I have been referring to Subcomandante Marcos most of the time, I have not been constructing him as a modern subject. The argument I have been advancing should help us understand the French journalist Bertrand de la Grange, who writes for *Le Monde*, and the Spanish journalist Maite Rico, who together interpreted Subcomandante Marcos in the modern (and traditional) frame of biographical narrative.[21] They see him as an "impostura" (imposture) centered on the subject (even though it is condescendingly recognized as "genial"), which means they have missed the point of the theoretical revolution. It means that the Zapatistas' theoretical revolution has not been understood. Even worse, it means that Zapatismo is framed under the very colonial and epistemic model that the Zapatistan revolution has been attempting to overcome; this is a common strategy—intentional by right-wing politicians and journalists, and misguided by presumed progressive postmodern intellectuals and journalists. At stake here is whether the role of Subcomandante Marcos will be interpreted within a philosophy of the modern subject (the hero) and the indigenous community as the silenced and unconscious victims, or whether Marcos will be seen as the mediator/translator that is necessarily implied in the theoretical revolution the Zapatistas initiated. I do not think that Marcos is being modest or—on the contrary—showing off by playing modest when he says that the theoreticians of the Zapatistas movement and the ones who are building a new way of looking at the world are the indigenous intellectuals, not himself. In my interpretation he understood the implications of the decolonial option: to delink, to engage in epistemic disobedience, and to change the terms of the conversation, not just the content. This interpretation could be logically defended if we accept the changes in the directionality of translation. And if we also accept that the ethical and political consequences I have been stressing cannot but come from a theoretical subject no longer located in Western cultures of scholarship. The theoretical revolution shall not be located in a given person or persons, thus celebrating some kind of original indigenous knowledge. It shall be located, instead, in the double process of translation in which

Western (e.g., Marxist) epistemology is appropriated by indigenous nations' epistemology, transformed, and returned. In the process, however, Indigenous subaltern knowledge entered the debate by piggybacking on Marxism and Western epistemology.

Often Subcomandate Marcos has been critiqued for not giving enough room to Indian leaders and thinkers. The fact is that, given the invisible presence of the colonial difference, and at the time of the uprising, a non-Indian mediator was necessary for the media and the urban intellectual elite to listen. At the moment of the uprising, one of the biggest impacts was the Zapatistas' "discourse," and that was Marcos's insights to let Spanish language and cosmology be infiltrated by Mayan languages and cosmologies. In Bolivia and Ecuador history unlocked differently: indigenous leaders and thinkers were able to take the word in their own mouths and hands. The issues, however, are not whether one is preferable to the other, but rather to take them as different signs of a similar phenomenon and different roads to move along, creatively shifting the geopolitics of knowledge, which is necessary to delink from the colonial matrix of power and from racial and patriarchal epistemic chains.

Democracy and Enlightenment Legacies

Based on my last assertion on double translation, the Zapatistas' theoretical revolution is an enactment of border thinking (border gnosis or border epistemology) conceived as the epistemic decolonial thinking and doing, inserting themselves and "breaking the Western code."[22] Let me elaborate on this by quoting the discourse of Mayor Ana María, delivered at the inauguration of the Intercontinental Encounter in the Lacandon Forest in August 1996.

> For power, the one that today is globally dressed with the name of neoliberalism, we neither counted nor produced, did not buy or sell. We were an idle number in the accounts of the Big Capital. Here in the highlands of the Mexican Southeast, our dead ones are alive. Our dead ones who live in the mountains know many things. Their death talked to us and we listened. The mountain talked to us and we listened. The mountain talked to us, the macehualtin, we the common and ordinary people, and we the simple people,

as we are called by the powerful. We were born war [*sic*] with the white year, and we began to trace the path that took us to the heart of yours, the same that today took you to our heart. That's who we are. The EZLN. The voice, which arms itself so that it can make itself heard. The face, which hides itself so it can be shown. The red star that calls to humanity and the world, so that they will listen, so that they will see, so that they will nominate. The tomorrow that is harvested in the yesterday. Behind our black face, behind our armed voice, behind our unspeakable name, behind the we that you see, behind we are (at you) [*detras estamos ustedes*].[23]

There is indeed a strange mixture between the first sentence, which could have been written by a French intellectual in *Le Monde diplomatique*, and the rest of the paragraph. A dialogue with death is invoked; *ser* is confused with *estar* in Spanish. The expression is still more difficult in English, since "to be" is the only possibility. And, finally, a discourse that began with an epistemic (we know the world is such) and political (it shall be done from our perspective) claim ends in a "poetical" note. Perhaps the most distinctive features of Ana María's discourse are the displacement of the epistemic correlation between the knowing subject and the known object, and the semantic effect that this displacement produces. The displacement is obvious, since Ana María is thinking from the structure of her own Maya language, and not from Greek, Latin, or French. It is obvious also in the sense that Ana María is not implementing a discourse "against" an individual thinker recognized by a proper name and located in the pantheon of the "great thinkers" of Western civilization. In Mayan languages (Tojolabal, for example), contrary to European vernacular/colonial languages, there is an intersubjective correlation between first and third persons. "Intersubjective" means here a code devoid of direct and indirect object; a code structured in the correlation between subjects.[24]

If you do not have subject-object correlation in a given language on which your epistemic principles could be built and your knowledge structured, then you do not engage in acts of "representation," for instance, but instead in "intersubjective enactments." Consequently "nature" in Tojolabal language and social consciousness is not an "it." Acts of enunciation in Mayan languages, Tojolabal, for example, not only involve the co-presence of "I" and "you," but also the presence of the "absent" third person, "she" or "they." The sentence in Tojolabal, contrary to that in European modern languages, has two subjects with no identical verbs. This structure could be better understood if we look at a sentence in Spanish or English and then translate it to Tojolabal. For instance, "Les dije (a ustedes o a ellos)," which in English would be "you/them heard it," in Tojolabal would be translated into something like "(lo) dije, ustedes/ellos (lo) escucharon," which in English would be "I said (it), you/them heard (it)."

What is important here is that the indirect object, in Spanish or English, becomes another agency verb with the corresponding subject, in this case "ustedes/you." When, in 1970, the French linguist and philosopher Emile Benveniste convincingly argued that in modern Western languages the pronominal structure has only two persons, "I" and "you," he brought into theoretical light a fact that was presupposed and unknown by speakers of French, for example. Beyond the first and second person there is the horizon of the non-person (she, he, it, them, and they). Benveniste's theory (see chapter 3) of course doesn't apply to Mayan languages. But, better yet, Benveniste's theory cannot be formulated as such thinking in/from Tojolabal, but instead in thinking in/from French. Furthermore still, the "other" can be conceptualized in Western imperial languages, but not in languages of Mayan root. This is what the missionaries who wrote grammars of Indigenous languages never understood, not because they lacked intelligence, but because of blind presuppositions of the universality of Greek and Latin languages. That misunderstanding and the centuries of epistemic damages are being redressed in our time, and the Zapatistas' theoretical revolution is a singular moment of these processes.

But this is not all. From Tojolabal it would have been impossible to come up with a universal principle, such as "the right of the people" (later on, the "rights of man and of the citizen" and, more recently, "human rights"), by which those whose "rights" are "defended" are considered a third person. That is, a non-person. Hence, "dignity" as claimed by the young woman in the Chiapas market was the appropriation of the "rights" attributed to her by a person who considered her a non-person with rights, rather than a person with dignity.

Thinking in/from Tojolabal (or any Mayan language), instead of thinking from German, French, English, or Spanish (or any modern imperial European language), would make it difficult or impossible to conceive people as "other," that "nature" is something outside "us," and to develop an idea of justice and equality by defending the "inclusion of the other."[25] Thinking from Tojolabal there is no "other" that needs to be included, since there is no object but only interacting subjects. And, of course, in Mayan languages there is no concept similar to the European "nation-state" that is presupposed in legal and political theories about "inclusion" and citizenship. Here is where border epistemology comes to the rescue in re-inscribing Mayan categories of thoughts in the present to build pluriversal and decolonial futures. I am not suggesting that Mayan languages will replace European languages, for that would mean doing what Europeans did (if at all possible), but in reverse. I am saying that they have to coexist, in conflictive and tense relations, necessarily, because of five hundred years of power differential. The cycle, during which Mayan languages were taken as inferior to European languages, is coming to an end; and Mayan scholars and intellectuals know it.[26] On the other hand, Spanish and other European languages have been there and they will remain, but no longer as the master's language.

We are now in a position to better understand what the young girl's dictum, "The Zapatistas returned human dignity to us," may mean, and perhaps we could make an effort to understand the dictum from a Mayan perspective. The dictum is, indeed, a decolonial ethical claim that impinges on the Zapatistas' reworking of the idea of "democracy" (e.g., decolonizing democracy).

Sounds strange, doesn't it? It is like bringing back all those beliefs that have been discarded in the name of "reason," of science and knowledge, from Bacon, Descartes, and Kant to Aristotle, until today. Indeed, how can one conceive democracy beyond the foundation of the "political proper" (see below for a discussion of this concept) in Greece, rehearsed and recast by the philosophers of the European Enlightenment, Kant among them? How can one imagine "democracy" from a Tojolabal perspective, a perspective that has been and continues to be enacted by the Zapatistas? But this is precisely what indigenous nations in Bolivia and Ecuador are claiming. Their claims have forced important changes in the constitution of both countries. Certainly, there is no treatise on government written by the Zapatistas, nor are there legal/philosophical speculations about cosmopolitanism and universal peace, as there were in Germany, France, and England after the religious war and the Peace of Westphalia. But there is a principle among the Zapatistas, a principle that comes from Amerindian wisdom and is engrained both in the intersubjective structure of language and the corresponding conception of social relations.[27] This principle reads in Spanish: "Mandar obedeciendo," which could be translated into English as "To rule and obey at the same time." The political principle is also ingrained in the logic of Mayan languages. Last but not least, the question is not to choose whether or not the transformation of the current state in Bolivia and Ecuador (by the re-inscription of indigenous laws and socio-economic organization) is preferable to the Zapatistas' decision to walk the road parallel to the Mexican states. They (Ecuador, Bolivia, Chiapas) are all decolonial options, although different versions of it. Pretending that one is preferable to the other would be too "modern" and would place us on the road to truth without parenthesis, which is not a decolonial option.

There is a letter signed by the EZLN, dated 26 February 1994, that was sent to all Mexicans and journalists in Mexico and across the world. The title of the letter was "Mandar obedeciendo." Let me quote two paragraphs from that letter.

When the EZLN was only a shadow creeping between the fog and darkness of the mountain, when the words justice, freedom and democracy were just words; merely a dream that elders of our communities, the real custodians of the words of our ancestors, had given us at the moment they give way to night, when hatred and death were beginning to grow in our hearts, when there was only despair. When the times turned back over their own selves, with no way out . . . the authentic men talked, the faceless, the ones who walk the night, those who are mountain, so they said:

It is the will of good men and women to search and to find the best way to govern and self-govern, what is good for most is good for all. But not to silence the voices of the few, rather for them to remain in their place, hoping that mind and heart will come together in the will of the most and the inspiration of the few, thus the nations composed of real men and women grown inward and grown big, so that there could be no exterior force capable of breaking them or of deviating their steps toward different roads. . . .

In this way our strength was born in the mountain, where the ruler obeys, when she or he is unquestionable, and the one who obeys command with the common heart of the genuine men and women. Another word came from far away for this government to be named, and this word, called "democracy," this road of us who moved forward before words were able to walk.[28]

Democracy, in this paragraph, as well as *dignity*, as I quoted at the beginning of the chapter, has a double edge: the words are universally used, but they no longer have a universal meaning rooted in one local history. Therefore *democracy*, like *dignity*, is not an empty signifier whose emptiness of meaning doesn't question the logical presupposition and belief in abstract universals. Empty signifiers have been emptied of their meaning, "Democracy," for instance, was taken from its Greek origins and re-inscribed in the European Enlightenment. It was conceived, and is still conceived, as an "abstract universal." But "democracy" conceived, instead, as a *connector across* the colonial difference (e.g., the Zapatistas and the Mexican government) and *within* the colonial difference itself (e.g., the Zapatistas' link with other social movements worldwide that face globalization with shared philosophies and common projects) brings pluriversality as a universal project into the picture. In such a move, there is no need for new, abstract universals. What is necessary is the "universality of the connector" (signs are nodes of connection, rather than empty signifiers being the containers of divers projects)[29] that changes the terms of the conversation and makes it possible to conceive and work toward "pluriversality as a universal project." For if we think in terms of "empty signifiers" instead of "connectors," the question is, Who will control the idea in such a way that it will both accommodate diversity or multiculturalism, and still be controlled by some final agency? If, instead, we regard empty signifiers as equivalent to connectors, the hegemony will be that of the connector/empty signifier, and not of some universal signified that will fill the void. In the conclusion, I will come back to the concept of connector in relation to pluriversality as a universal project, *for it would be difficult to imagine that a singular abstract universal would be universally agreed upon.*

The conditions that engendered the EZLN in Southern Mexico are similar to the conditions that brought Evo Morales to the presidency of Bolivia, although the two trajectories are significantly different. Once again, the point is not to select one over the other, but to understand and support both. Much before the writing of the constitution, a debate had been under way in Bolivia, since the middle 1980s, on "ayllu democracy" and "liberal democracy." *Ayllu* in Aymara is a word similar to the Greek *Oikos*, in the sense that family, economy, social organization, and education are all included. Whether the social organization implied in the ayllu would be similar to "democracy," as elaborated by Western political theorists on the legacy of oikos (*demos*), would have to be explored. The ayllu organization of today is not of course what it was before the conquest. However it remains, today, different from the social organization of the Bolivian state. The Aymara sociologist Félix Patzi Paco explored another dimension, the political-economic organizations that coexist in Bolivia today, the liberal and the communal (ayllu) systems as he named them (I will come back to this in the afterword).[30] The fact that the Bolivian (or the U.S. or French) state is ruled by democratic principles doesn't mean that those principles are not actually violated in everyday life, either within the nation or in international relations. Therefore, it should not be expected that the rules governing the ayllu are not violated in everyday life. We are talking here about "principles" (e.g., institute) of social organization, rather than actual practices in respecting or violating those principles. However, in a personal conversation with the Aymara intellectual Marcelo Fernández-Osco, I came to realize that cases of corruption are registered among people from the ayllu who are "judged" according to the internal-justice system for their conduct outside of the ayllu. One public case has been that of the former vice president Victor Hugo Cardenas (former vice-president of Bolivia), who has been charged, by his ayllu authorities, of failing to comply with communal responsibilities. However, within the ayllu itself, the cases of violations of the rules and of corruptions are minimal. Understandably so: since ayllu organizations are not based on the principles of capitalist economy and the political temptations for gaining positions of power and enjoying the benefits of capitalism, so in the ayllu there are violations of the rules, but not corruptions in the economic and political sense of the term in the culture of capitalism and the democratic state.[31]

Of the essence here is the fact that after five hundred years of external (Spain) and internal (the Bolivian republican state) colonialism, indigenous communities in Bolivia (in significant numbers) based their social organization on principles inherited from ancient Aymaras and Quechuas. The social organization in the ayllu has not been derived from ancient Greece and through the European interpretation of it during the Enlightenment, which is the case for the Creole and (neo)liberal State of Bolivia. Paradoxically, neo-liberal and Marxist intellectuals in Bolivia alike, as well as the NGOs, keep working to "break up" (with bad or good intentions) a social organization that they see leading to a democratic or socialist state. The decolonial option (the legacies of the Bandung Conference) is not seen or considered by either legacies, liberal or Marxist. Only European legacies, democracy and socialism, are present. The "political proper" here shall be identified as the "difference" that the Aymara people were able to maintain for five hundred years—a difference that today is making a move forward with the Zapatistas' uprising, paralleled by indigenous movements in Ecuador, Colombia, Guatemala, and other states of Mexico. The Zapatistas' theoretical revolution is the epistemic frame that indigenous communities were unable to find in either the liberal or the Marxist European legacies grounded in ancient Greece.

Under these circumstances, let's explore "democracy" a little bit further. After the Zapatistas, the "original" meaning of democracy (from its Greek roots to its European Enlightenment rehearsal) is no longer "original" or "authentic"; that is to say, it lost its originality and authenticity. In parallel fashion the ayllu today also lost its originality and authenticity. But they both persist, "the form state" and "the form ayllu."[32] Furthermore, the concept did not travel from Greece to Enlightenment Europe to the Spanish colonies. The word is part of the detour (see chapter 7) that history took in the chronological line from Greece to Europe: the colonial detour. Thus, the idea of democracy in enlightened Europe was introduced looking toward the East (Greece) and with the back toward the West (European colonies in South America and the Caribbean). The word, then, doesn't belong anymore to any community or civilization that owns the right for its imposition or exportation, but is shared by all those people around the world who care for equity and social justice, particularly those who have been and still are victims of injustices and inequities. However, the belief remains that democracy is a Greek invention, rehearsed during the Enlightenment, modified by its socialist version, that Western modernity holds the property rights, and that it shall be exported all over the planet. It is believed and asserted that "democracy" shall be built according to that conceptualization. To question this macro-narrative of "democracy" (written from the perspective of Western civilization and modernity) and to open new avenues to imagine democratic futures is precisely what the Zapatistas' theoretical revolution has achieved. And they have achieved this by postulating another beginning, the beginning of the modern/colonial world and the making of the colonial difference. The Zapatistas' theoretical revolution identified another foundation (like Greece for Western civilization or the Koran for the Islamic world) for building macro-narratives from the perspective of coloniality.

"Mandar obedeciendo" is a principle grounded within an intersubjective structure of the Tojolabal language, a language in which neither "nature" nor the "other" can be conceptualized as objects. Or better yet, a language in which there is not, because it is unthinkable, "nature" and "others" as well as nature as other. Some Tojolabal thinkers or intellectuals, as well as ancient Greeks or eighteenth-century European philosophers, have a sense of social organization for the common good. I do not want to idealize Tojolabal's democratic conception of "to rule and obey at the same time." But I do not want to idealize or romanticize Greek and European concepts of "democracy" and "socialism" either—two notions that became abstract universal and companions of the planetary expansion of capitalism. I do believe, however, that there are people ("non-liberal honest people," as John Rawls would like to say) all over the planet who can entertain a dialogue of equals with liberal notions of democracy and Marxist notions of socialism.[33] Among those people are the Zapatistas—Indians like Mayor Ana María and Comandante Tacho, or mestizos like Subcomandante Marcos—who have been making political and ethical claims grounded in new epistemological principles derived from a double translation. That is, Mayan cosmology into Marxism, and Marxist cosmology into Mayan.

We are back to double translation, which is still difficult to understand, even by an enlightened French scholar like Yvon Le Bot, who was totally supportive of the Zapatistas and completely blind to the colonial difference. Le Bot interviewed the leaders of the Zapatistas' uprising (Mayor Moises, Comandante Tacho, Subcomandante Marcos), but did not feel comfortable with the concept of "democracy" introduced in the letter signed by the EZLN that I quoted at length and commented on. Le Bot offered in the introduction to the series of interviews a definition of "democracy" that Subcomandante Marcos had published in La Jornada (31 December 1994). For Le Bot, this is a "better definition of democracy, less poetic, perhaps more simplistic but more satisfactory" [sic!].[34] And here it is.

Democracy is the situation in which agreements are reached and differences maintained. Not necessarily that everybody thinks in the same way, but that all thoughts or the majority of thoughts look for and reach an agreement which will be good for the majority, without marginalizing or eliminating the minority; that the word of the ruler obeys the word of the majority of the people; that the baton of command be supported by a collective voice rather than by only one will.[35]

Without the previous discourse by the EZLN or of Mayor Ana María, this "satisfactory" definition of democracy by Subcomandante Marcos wouldn't make much sense; or it would be interpreted as a largely common, and because of that, meaningless, description. Consequently, what matters about this definition is not that it is "clearer" and more "satisfactory" for the logic of Spanish and French readers and their corresponding concepts of democracy, but that Subcomandante Marcos's definition follows Tojolabal logic while it is expressed in Spanish syntax and semantics. I described as "border thinking" and "border gnosis" the epistemology that emerges from the subaltern appropriation of mainstream Western epistemology. In the Zapatistas' theoretical revolution, border thinking emerges from the double translation across the colonial difference. The Zapatistas' theoretical revolution can be explained and its political and ethical consequences derived, precisely, from the conceptualization of border thinking.[36]

Ethics of Liberation and Pluriversality: The Theoretical Consequences

It was indeed the liberation theologian Franz Hinkelammert who saw in the Zapatistas' uprising an emerging project with a different logic, a logic that no longer reproduced the need for abstract universals.[37] Pluriversality (or diversality, in the sense of diversity and not in the sense of dichotomy) is not the rejection of universal claims. It rejects universality understood as abstract universal grounded in mono-logic. A universal principle grounded in the idea of the diversal (or pluriversal) is not a contradiction in terms, but rather a displacement of conceptual structures. Diversity as universal project is, according to Hinkelammert, what the Zapatistas are claiming: a world composed of multiple worlds, the *right to be different* because we are all equals (instead of assuming that *since we are all equal* what we have in common is our difference)—to obey and rule at the same time. For a world composed of multiple worlds we need not have abstract universals and empty signifiers, but connectors that will link the Zapatistas' theoretical revolution and its ethical consequences with similar projects around the world emerging from the colonial difference (either as "external" or "internal" national forms of colonialism). A world inter-connected and diversal, in which translation is always at least bi-directional, is very different from a world encapsulated in one abstract universal, even if that abstract universal is the best one can imagine, and whether it could be found in ancient Greece, in the Islamic world, in the Chinese deep past, or among Aymaras, Quechuas, or Náhuatls in South America. A world in which the only past accepted and admitted is the line that goes from Greece to Rome to modern (former) Western Europe will be indeed very sad. And perhaps also very dangerous.

Subcomandante Marcos describes Zapatismo as a phenomenon that increasingly depends on the indigenous question. He also underlines that this particular local problem tends to increasingly find values that are valid for the Japanese, Kurds, Australians, Catalans, Chicanos/as, or Mapuches.[38] He is not talking here, in my understanding, about exporting the content of the Zapatista uprising and theoretical revolution in the way that global designs such as Christianity, civilizing missions, modernity, and development intended to do, but about connecting through the logic of the double translation from the colonial difference. Diversality as universal project emerges, precisely, as a project of inter-connections from the subaltern perspective and beyond the managerial power and monotopic inspiration of any abstract universals, from the Right or from the Left. For it would be difficult to imagine that a singular abstract universal would be universally consensual.

I have been using "diversality" to describe Hinkelammert's position, when, in reality, he did not use this term. Diversality was introduced by the Martinican thinker and writer Edouard Glissant, which is not surprising since his thinking is founded in Creole, as language and Afro-Caribbean consciousness, rather than in Spanish and German, as in the case of Hinkelammert, or in Tojolabal and Spanish, as in the case of the Zapatistas' collective imagination.[39] But, in any event, there is a commonality that binds

Hinkelammert's, Glissant's, and the Zapatistas' experiences of the colonial difference: dwelling in the borders, inhabiting the house of modernity/coloniality—the small "senzala" next to the "casa grande," following Gilberto Freyre's title for his classic book on the history of slavery and Africans in Brazil.[40] It is also in the experience of the colonial difference on which Enrique Dussel based his ethic of liberation (for whom the Zapatistas as well as the Maya-Quiche activist Rigoberta Menchú are paradigmatic examples).

This is a briefing of the decolonial option's theoretical scenario. It opens up new avenues for conceiving decolonial democratic/socialist projects, decolonial subjects that re-appropriate their stolen dignity and relocate human rights as their own decolonial project to relearn dignity, stemming from the interiority of local histories implementing global designs. That is to say, human rights was not a project that emerged in Bolivia or Ethiopia but—from the rights of the people in the sixteenth century to the Universal Declaration of Human Rights, in 1948—it was always an imperial project stemming from the moral imperial sector.

The Zapatistas' Theoretical Revolution: Decolonial Options, Communal Futures

With these cautions in mind, let's explore the Zapatistas' theoretical discourse in relation to what Hannah Arendt (1943) and Giorgio Agamben (1996) identified as the "figure of the refugee" and investigate what help the decolonial option can offer to critical and dissenting European views of a problem that is closer to them (the figure of the refugee) than, say, to China or the Caribbean societies. On the other hand, if the refugee is a global problem, its solution may not be universal. There are so many global problems that they are not, naturally so, on the European (meaning, Western European) radar. The refugee, Agamben states, is "perhaps the only thinkable figure for the people of our time and the only category in which one may see today—at least until the process of dissolution of the nation-state and its sovereignty has achieved full completion—the forms and limits of a *coming political community*."[41] He goes on to suggest, "It is even possible that, if we want to be equal to the absolutely new tasks ahead, we will have to abandon decidedly, without reserve, the fundamental concepts through which we have so far represented the subjects of the political Man, the Citizen and its rights, but also the sovereign, people, the worker, and so forth."[42]

It seems obvious that the crisis of the nation-state brings together the crisis of its major symbols. That is, the complicity between citizen, man, and human rights. One of the consequences of the crisis is that the conditions of citizenship and the concepts of Man and of human rights can no longer be taken for granted. The very concept of "rights of the people" in the sixteenth century, grounded in a "renaissance man" that was still valid in the eighteenth century, brought to light the need for international conviviality. The citizen and the foreigner became central figures of the nation-state (one in, the other out) under which Europe organized itself as Europe, overcoming its past as Western Christendom. The figure of the refugee appears in Europe, indeed, after the first symptom of the breakdown of the nation-state and, of course, of its main figure, the citizen. The first appearance of the refugee as a mass phenomenon, says Agamben, took place at the end of the First World War—the first crisis of European Western countries in great part motivated by their partition and appropriation of the planet, at that point Africa. He further elaborates on the argument introduced by Hannah Arendt in her book on totalitarianism, particularly in the chapter titled "The Decline of Nation-State and the End of the Rights of Man."[43] These historical references allows Agamben to make a strong theoretical move and propose that the refugee should be considered for what he is, namely, nothing less than a limit-concept that at once brings a radical crisis to the principles of the nation-state and clears the way for a renewal of categories that can no longer be delayed.[44]

A new chapter was opened up, shortly after the Zapatista uprising and the North American Free Trade Agreement (1994), by the strong claims in Bolivia and Ecuador that were already inscribed in the new constitutions in both countries, toward the construction of plurinational states. This is a radical change in political theory, a shift in the geopolitics of knowing that unveils the fact that the modern nation-state (created in Europe) translated into the colonies (Bolivia or India) as modern/colonial states. The modern/colonial state in most of the world has this peculiarity: that local elites, representing one nation of the same language, religions, and convictions, take control of the state and marginalize other nations speaking other languages and holding other belief systems. The claim for plurinational states made clear that the modern nation-state is mono-national.[45] Arendt and Agamben are facing crucial issues in Europe, and it is becoming apparent in the United States where it is estimated that by 2050 people of color will outnumber demographically the white population, so that the conditions for a plurinational organization of society will be ripe. In South America and the Caribbean the problems are not the same. Solutions to those problems would be ineffective if they came from the European Union or the World Bank. They should come from the experiences and needs of colonial histories in each part of the world, rather than by "spreading and applying Western political theory" in the same way that "spreading democracy" is argued. My comments are not so much addressed to Arendt and Agamben, since they did what they had to do. What I am saying is that their analysis, critiques, and eventual suggested solutions, if taken as a starting point of political theory in the modern/colonial state, will not go beyond academic exercises and will be without any real consequences.[46]

I placed Agamben's argument in conjunction with the Zapatistas' to push my point that the Zapatistas' theoretical revolution brought a different kind of figure into the political picture. We are facing here two types of political theories, if you wish: one materialized within the local histories of imperial Europe; the other within the local histories in the European colonies. They are facing each other, entangled (not a dichotomy but an entanglement) in the slash of modernity/coloniality; in both cases, they respond to local histories of universal significance. One dwells in the house of modernity; the other in the house of coloniality. They have similar concerns, but a whole lot of differences in languages, categories of thought, skin, affect, concepts, memories, and vision. Can you imagine theorizing the refugee in Europe, taking India as the point of reference?

Like the figure of the refugee that closes the cycle of the nation-state forged since the end of the eighteenth century in Western Europe, the Zapatistas announced the closing of the cycle of the colonial world and the opening of delinking and epistemic disobedience. For that reason it comes as a surprise when reading in Agamben that the refugee is "*the only* thinkable figure for the people of our time and the only category in which one may see today . . . the forms and limits of a coming political community*" (italics added).[47] Let's just put on the table communal futures emerging from the damnés next to the refugee, like the re-inscription of indigenous social organization, in Chiapas as well as in the Andes. And let's insist that at stake here is not so much the question of rights as the question of dignity, of living beyond benevolent management, of building on dignity and the decolonial option. The question, in other words, is who speaks for the "human" in human rights.[48]

The "return of human dignity" that the Zapatistas endowed to the Chiapas population brings to the foreground another figure, the figure of the indigenous, aboriginal, first nation that had been placed on the margin of humanity and beyond the possibilities of producing knowledge, of having ethical principles and political drives—briefly stated, the future of the damnés.[49] The figure of the indigenous, unlike that of the refugee, was supposed to be educated, managed, and either included or totally excluded from the human community. This general perspective, which emerged in the sixteenth century, reproduced itself in the colonial experiences after the nineteenth century in Asia and Africa, and in the internal colonialism of nation-builders in Latin America. Thus, we have the historical context of the Zapatistas' theoretical revolution. There were people whose rights deserved to be discussed seriously, as the intellectuals of the school of Salamanca did, although those people whose rights were being discussed did not have the right to participate in the discussion about their rights. In reversing the modern (sixteenth century) topic of arms and letters, the Zapatistas raised arms in order to reclaim the letter, the voice that had been taken away from them. This is, in my view, the moment an indigenous young girl could feel and say that dignity was returned to indigenous people and nations. As such, the "pueblos originarios" emerges as a figure that was questionable as Man and has never been "citizen"; as such, the figure of the colonized did not qualify for the "right of Man and of the citizen," as the Haitian Revolution of 1804 bears witness. The rights of Man and of the citizen were not meant for black and enslaved people.

I hope it is clear that I am not reaching these conclusions via Agamben (e.g., applying Agamben's figure of the refugee to the Zapatistas) but that I am analyzing Agamben from the perspective of the Zapatistas' theoretical revolution. In other words, I am shifting the geography of reasoning. I am indeed trying to reverse the process, although reversing the process is not simply crossing the street or just switching sides. It means that the side I am crossing to is a side in which modernity/coloniality coexists and frames daily life, while in Europe only modernity is felt, and coloniality is regarded as the darker and distant side, not always remembered as a reality . . . until massive migration comes, and with it the rumor of coloniality—through the colonial external difference that invades the EU. For that reason, European scholars do not have to bother themselves with scholarship and intellectual creativity in the former colonial histories, societies, and histories of thought, while the latter cannot avoid the former: it has to be articulated, always, in relation to European categories of thought, whether conservative or progressive, whether from the Right or from the Left.[50] Hence, the Zapatistas' theoretical revolution strengthened the decolonial option and the possibilities of re-claiming "the epistemic dignity of the damnés." Political and economic debates and ideas toward the ex-colonial world become, in the imaginary of modernity/coloniality, the opportunity to develop the underdeveloped (until China came, and with it the rumor of coloniality through—this time—the imperial external difference that invades the imaginary of the EU and the United States facing the specter of China and East Asia).

Enrique Dussel, in March 1994, and Maurice Najman, in January 1997, clearly understood the theoretical, ethical, and political implications of the Zapatistas' uprising.[51] However, intellectual legitimization of the uprising still depends on the implicit sanction of North Atlantic scholarship. It is for this reason that I am bringing up the figure of the refugee and the figure of the "pueblos originarios" together in the frame of pluriversality as a universal project. Ethical, political, and epistemic pluriversality implies that projects are anchored in local histories (like in Europe after the Second World War and the refugee or indigenous movements in South America). As a consequence it also implies that an abstract universal (be it Christian, liberal, or Marxist) would unite the diverse and bring them together within an abstract universal, or that an empty signifier is no longer desirable. Consequently, the Zapatistas' theoretical revolution is contributing to get us out of Hegelian (temporal) dialectics and the modern sense of lineal progression as well as to reinstating space over time and the geopolitics of knowledge over the universal temporality of dialectics. The conceptualization of "newness" in a temporal rather than in a spatial dimension is part of the abstract universal of modern epistemology and of the denial of coevalness orchestrated by the coloniality of power. The "new" as abstract universal will be either the Hegelian synthesis or the "next" step in an already planned development, progression, modernization, or revolution.

It would be possible to say with Agamben that the political task of our time consists in "selecting in the new planetary humanity those characteristics that allow for its survival, removing the thin diaphragm that separated bad mediatized advertising from the perfect exteriority that communicates only itself."[52] But it would also be necessary to start from someplace else. By recognizing, for instance, that the selection will be made by social actors in singular local histories and that the theorization would also be grounded in experiences similar to, but different from, those of the refugees. Such claims and actions would be made neither expecting a universal design nor pretending to install a "new," singular one. The only singularity would be the connectors (not empty signifiers) that would anchor pluriversality as a universal project.

There are several places to start, not only in the future of the refugee. Ali Shari'ati devoted one of his famous lectures (in English translation) to "Modern Man and His Prison," the concept of "man." He clarifies from the outset that in the Qur'an there are two words, *Bashar* and *Ensan*, instead of one "man" as human being. The first refers to the biological configuration of certain types of animals, spread all over the planet, who stand on two extremities and use the others to perform a number of operations not seen in other types of living organisms generally translated from Greek into Western languages as "animal." Ensan refers to the self-awareness and self-consciousness that that kind of animal uses to describe itself in another dimension: that of seeing "itself" (Bashar and Ensan do not carry gender marks, like "man" in modern Western languages) as a particular kind of living organism that creates options and makes choices. Shari'ati, deeply familiar with Western philosophy, described Ensan as the sphere of "becoming" rather than being. Thus "I am where I think" *takes Ensan* rather than the Cartesian subject as anchor, without, of course, denying the Cartesian subject that has its right of existence; however, it is not universal. You cannot expect that "I am, therefore I think" could be meaningful for someone in Uzbekistan or Senegal, unless that person in Senegal or Uzbekistan was educated in the Alliance Française or in an equivalent Western institution. Also, I can surmise that the Quechuan concept *of Runa* has much more in common with Islamic *Ensan* than with Western *Man*, for *Runa Simi* means the language of the *Runa*, that is of living organisms that, like Man and Ensan, not only speak but also describe and name their actions of speaking.

In the Andean regions, *Runa* and *Jaque* are Quechua and Aymara words used to refer to experiences similar to those in the West or described by the concepts of man and humanity, and in the Muslim world by the words *Bashar* and *Ensan*. However, the organizations of the world and of society based on these concepts manifest significant differences. If we add, still, the long discussion on "the human and humanity" in the Caribbean philosophical tradition, from C. L. R. James to Frantz Fanon and Sylvia Wynter, we have still another factor to add to the selection "in the new planetary humanity (of) those characteristics that allow for its survival, removing the thin diaphragm that separated bad mediatized advertising from the perfect exteriority that communicates only itself." Agamben's claim is important, but it is only one among several: we need to move from universality to pluriversality; to decolonize the imperial concept of the Human and to build decolonial notions of Humanity.

Here we recall Sylvia Wynter's claim (from chapter 2) in the formula "After Man, toward the Human." Her confrontation with the imperial notion of Humanity stems from—as mentioned—Frantz Fanon's decolonial concept of sociogenesis. Beyond Darwin's philogenesis to explain the evolution of the species, and Freud's ontogenesis to account for the singularity of the individual, sociogenesis is the necessary decolonial concept to account for the fact that "being a Negro" is ontogenetically and philogenetically irrelevant: "being a Negro" is an epistemic sociogenetic construction of imperial discourse—the creation of the colonial ontological and epistemic difference. "Having black skin" is not the same as "being a Negro." The first is just a biological configuration. The second is a disqualifying operation from the perspective of a universal and imperial concept of Humanity.[53]

This is the context in which the Zapatistas' theoretical revolution acquires its decolonial meaning. Why? Because the question is not to compete among different concepts of "humanity," but to start from the fact that non-Western notions more or less equivalent to what in the West were constructed as man, human, humanity have to be redefined in conflictive interaction: while Western concepts of humanity didn't need to take into account similar concepts in other languages and categories of thought, non-Western categories of thought had to redefine themselves in dialogue with Western categories. The end result of such decolonial work is border gnosis or border epistemology: decolonial ways of knowing and becoming which, at the same time, work on the decolonization of Western imperial knowledge—hence, another aspect of the Zapatistas' theoretical revolution.

There is one claim in Dussel's argument that connects with an early quotation by Subcomandante Marcos, as transcribed above, and with the statement I just made.[54] In the paragraph in question Subcomandante Marcos underlined the ethical option advanced by the Zapatistas' uprising. While Hinkelammert capitalized on the Zapatistas to formulate the need for pluriversality as a universal project instead of looking for new abstract universals, Dussel relied on his own distinction between "ethics of discourse" and "ethics of liberation." In a nutshell, ethics of discourse has been arguing for the "recognition of difference" and for the "inclusion of the other." But benevolent recognition and inclusion presupposes that those to be included have not much say in the way they are recognized or included. Ethics of discourse assumes an abstract universal space from which to recognize and where to include. That is the standard version of multiculturalism, from Charles Taylor to Jürgen Habermas, in spite of the differences between both. Ethics of liberation instead underlines and thinks from the thinking of the excluded, like Rigoberta Menchú or the Zapatistas. There is no place for pluriversality as a universal project in ethics of discourse. There is room, of course, for tolerance of diversity within a refashioning of existing and hegemonic abstract universals. Ethics of liberation à la Hinkelammert and Dussel, proposes instead, pluriversality as a universal project. Such a project can only be pursued as far as double translations and the theoretical revolution would continue to create the conditions for new ways of thinking at the borders structured by the coloniality of power in the making of the modern/colonial world. In this way, ethics, politics, and epistemology come together next to an already existing one that will continue to exist and that has been the legacy of the modern/colonial world.

In the same way that the figure of Indian nations and Indian people is complementary to the refugee (and vice versa), each of them with their own local histories and their entrenchment with (the logic of coloniality), the Zapatistas' (decolonial) conception of democracy is complementary (and vice versa) to democracy as conceived and enacted within a hegemonic tradition, that is, from the Greco-Enlightenment legacy. Slavoj Žižek has recently made a plea for a "Eurocentrism from the left" and extended an invitation to recover the "political proper" in its Greek legacy.[55] Displeased with identity politics, mainly in the United States, which he considers the end of the political proper, Žižek makes a new claim in favor of a universal (instead of the particular implied in identity politics) concept of democracy rooted in the Greco-European legacy. He needs such re-conceptualization to get out of the impasse in which both the Left and the Right find themselves in the fight against globalization and in the emergence of identity politics that announces the end of the political proper. There are two main lines in Žižek's argument. One is the diagnosis of the loss of what he calls "the political proper," and the other is how he proposes to move out of the impasse in which both the Right and Left find themselves today. Žižek's diagnosis is not so much the question of his conceptualization as it is the location of what he calls the "political proper." What is in the first place the "political proper"?

From a decolonial perspective, something similar to what Žižek calls "the political proper" shall not be found in ancient Greece, but in the Atlantic from the sixteenth century to the eighteenth: this is where indigenous leaders and runaway slaves initiated a series of actions and thoughts in which "the decolonial political proper" was historically founded. This is the historical detour, about which I will discuss in the next chapter, that lead us to parallel histories, one visibly celebrated by the rhetoric of modernity, the other invisible, the logic of coloniality hidden under the rhetoric of modernity. The Zapatistas' revolution is nothing but a continuation in the history of the invisible aspect of the historical detour in the living tradition of such genealogy of doing and thinking. But let's see what Žižek has to say about "the political proper." Žižek clarifies,

> It is a phenomenon that appeared for the first time in ancient Greece when the members of the demos (those with no firmly determined place in the hierarchical social edifice) presented themselves as the representatives, the stand-ins, for the whole of society, for the true universality ("we—the 'nothing,' not counted in the order—are the people, we are all, against others who stand only for their particular privileged interest"). Political conflict proper thus involves the tension between the structured social body, where each part has its place, and the part of no-part, which unsettles this order on account of the empty principle of universality, of the principled equality of all men, all speaking beings, what Etienne Balibar calls ega-liberté.[56]

There are two claims here; although the structure of the paragraph gives the impression that there is only one. One claim is the definition of "the political proper." The other is the location of its origin in ancient Greece. The first is a logical move, while the second is geopolitical. That is, the second move introduces the geopolitics of knowledge disguised as the universality of the political proper. This disguise becomes crucial in Žižek's argument when he distinguishes globalization from universalism and calls for the "fundamental European legacy."[57] What is, for Žižek, the distinction between them? With the term *globalization* Žižek refers to the "emerging global market (new world order), and with *universalism* he refers to the "properly political domain of universalizing one's particular fate as representative of global injustice."[58] Why is this important? Because "this difference between globalization and universalism becomes more and more palpable today, when capital, in the name of penetrating new markets, quickly renounces requests for democracy in order not to lose access to new trade partners. This shameful retreat is then, of course, legitimized as respect for cultural difference, as the right of the (ethnic/religious/cultural) Other to choose the way of life that suits it best—as long as it does not disturb the free circulation of capital."[59]

Žižek provides several examples to substantiate the distinction. One of them is Singapore's "wise" (the quotation marks are Žižek's) ruler Lee Kuan Yew. It is true that Lee has been playing the game of differences between East and West in order to justify capitalism in the Asian way.[60] It is coherent to say, then, following Žižek's argument, that this is a case of globalization without universalism. That is, it is an example of globalization in which the political proper has been suspended—or not. Today (May 2009), I have a different interpretation of Lee's statement as argued in chapter 1, under the heading of "Dewesternization." He was initiating, curiously enough in the same year of the Zapatista uprising, the project of "dewesternization" that is today very much under way as one of the trajectories, and options, toward the future, by confronting rewesternization (including rewesternization of the Left, as Žižek is proposing in this article). Rather than being suspended, the political is being enacted in the dispute for the control of the sphere of authority in the colonial matrix of power. Lee was enacting a "dewesternization of the political proper," which continues with force today and was very much present in the debates over the "future of capitalism." Thus, here we have two emerging options toward the future: on the one hand, the decolonial options, of which the Zapatistas' theoretical revolution is one; on the other, the dewesternizing options, which Lee was already announcing in the early 1990s. The third option is the rewesternization of the Left, of which Žižek is a case in point. It is unlikely that one of these options—including rewesternization, which is President's Obama project—will prevail over the other in the future. Indeed, the future seems to be pluralized. Forecasts about "how to run the world"—based on the past five hundred years of Western civilization and its local history traced back to the Holy Roman Empire and Byzantium—seem already déjà-vu.[61] In this case, history is no longer repeating itself.

So, then, one could say, even in disagreement with Lee's opposition between East and West capitalism (an opposition, after all, created from the West), that the alternative would have been to accept capitalism in the Western way. That is, to accept, at once, means of production and (neo)liberal ideology. Lee is not operating at the level of the Zapatistas: the former project is dewesternization and the latter decolonization (see chapter 1). His position was defined from the neo-colonial state, similar to Mexican government. Consequently, I am not sure that in the case of Lee the political was *suspended*, although from the U.S. perspective, as well as from Žižek's, his position was very much *suspected*.[62] Lee's political move was "conservative" in the sense of conserving a certain sense of Singapore's past. It is true that Lee may not qualify to be the equivalent of the "demos" as in ancient Greece, as redefined by enlightened philosophers. But it is also true that the slaves, in ancient Greece, were not part of the demos. However, Lee is in an imperial/colonial subaltern position: imperial because of his endorsement of capitalism, colonial because he is "yellow." His was already a dewesternizing stance. As I said in chapter 1, I am not saying that dewesternization is to be promoted. I say that it just is. In a world order managed now by the G8, it could be said of him that "we the nothing . . . we are all, against others who stand only for their particular privileged interest."[63]

Žižek makes a similar move when he insists "on the potential of democratic politization as the true European legacy from ancient Greece onwards."[64] But there is a remarkable difference between Žižek and Lee, of course. Žižek proposes a return to "his" past in view of a transformative future, while Lee puts the accent on preserving "his" past and to re-inscribing it into the future in a "dewesternizing" fashion. In sum, Žižek is proposing rewesternization from the Left while Lee is proposing dewesternization from the Right. The difference is that Žižek is operating on the *diverse homogeneity* of Western cosmology (which fits with the diverse projects of re-Westernization), while Lee has to deal with the re-inscription of a non-western past into a future that carries the traces of the Western present. Lee has to deal with racism inscribed in both imperial and colonial differences; Žižek has not (and perhaps he is not even aware of them), for he is "on this side" of the fence, on the side of the humanitas. However, wouldn't it be possible to imagine a transformative future from the very past that Lee proposes to preserve? According to Žižek's argument, this would not be possible because the political proper has been geopolitically linked to Greece and appropriated as "European legacy." And the only progressive possible re-inscription would be that of the tradition of modernity extended to the re-inscription of Vladimir Lenin. Now, Lenin and Lee may be closer to each other than one would imagine at first sight. Lenin took in his hands the project of Westernization initiated by Peter and Catherine the Greats, certainly with a different content (socialism), but with a similar logic. What Lee has introduced, and I here call dewesternization, is to break out with the monocultures of the mind according to which the future of the world rests on Greek legacies (the "true European legacy" for Žižek) appropriated either by the Right or the Left.

As the astute reader may have imagined, it is not my intention to advocate for Lee's position over Žižek's. Rather, I am trying to show how much Žižek's and Lee's positions are entangled. Žižek has his own local histories (his past, his tradition) and references to anchor his argument (ancient Greek thought, and later Lenin). For Lee, neither Greek philosophy nor Lenin is of much relevance; one does not see why they should be. Confucius is close to Lee's home. The reorientation of the Left doesn't throw away Marxism because, on the way, Marxism encountered Stalin. So, one should not dismiss the legitimacy of dewesternizing options when rewesternization and the reorientation of the Left are competing for their right to rule the world based on Greek legacies.

The Zapatistas' dictum "Because we are all equal, we have the right to the difference" opens another venue to think about the ethical and the political proper in imagining possible futures; and it brings us back to decolonizing the imperial human (defined by commonalities with the imperial Human rather than by differences with colonial anthropos). The right to be different the Zapatistas are claiming is the difference claimed by the political society, while in Ecuador and Bolivia similar claims have been articulated in the indigenous efforts to reorient the mono-national into a plurinational state. To move "difference" at the level of the state means also to introduce the distinction between civil and political society.[65] At the level of the civil society we encounter reform and dialogic negotiation, as Žižek himself will have it.[66] At the level of the political society we encounter struggle and demands for participation in managerial transformation, as the Zapatistas' and Indians political project have it. The Zapatistas' goal is not to take control of the state (like in the Cuban Revolution), not even to contend for elections (hence, the divergence between Zapatismo and the Movimiento al Socialismo, lead by Evo Morales in Bolivia), but to participate in opening up the space for the political society. And we can certainly agree with Žižek's definition of the political, although not necessarily in its geopolitics. That is, ancient Greece and the European legacy! It is precisely at the level of the political society that the second Zapatistas' dictum, "To rule and to obey at the same time," is the necessary corollary of the first ("The right to be different because we are all equal").

There are, then, two issues that need to be clarified. The first issue is the conception of the "political proper" in local histories where imperial differences predominate. That means, states like Russia or China[67] in the sphere of international relations and of the consequences of global racism. The imperial difference is the connector of "differences" between imperial countries in the West where the conception of the political proper originated and civilizations that couldn't be colonized (like the Russian Tzarate converted into Russian Empire and then Soviet Union) or the Chinese Dynasties. These civilizations were not colonized like Africa or America, but they became inferior in the eyes of the West—the first for having a Cyrillic alphabet, Orthodox Christianity, and Slavic ethnicity; the second for being yellow and dwelling in a millenarian memory older than Greece and independent of it. It is basically a "North Atlantic legacy," parallel to the history of capitalism until the end of the twentieth century (i.e., before capitalism began to locate itself in Asia, and no longer using Asia as a source of natural resources and a place to colonize from afar). It is in this particular local history that Žižek's argument shall be understood. Dewesternization operates in the sphere of imperial differences (where international relations matter most and the economy and the state have central roles).

The second issue is the conception of the political in the local histories of the colonial differences. The "political proper" in the conflictive making of the colonial difference doesn't have its origin in Greece. Or if it does, it is in the discourse of the colonizers who grounded themselves in the Greco-Roman tradition to justify colonization. The "political proper" in the colonial difference appears "for the first time" (I am using Žižek's expressions in quotation marks) in the Caribbean, in Anáhuac, and in Tawantinsuyu. At that moment, "we-the nothing" were those left out of the frame of Greek and Christian-European legacy, and those who had to figure out how to deal with a political order that was being imposed on their own conception of the organization of the social. Naturally, for "we-the nothing," Greece may very well be the cradle of European legacy, but that "we" does not have much to do with it. Briefly, "we-the nothing" were those who were spoken of by "good" Spanish humanists (like Bartolomé de Las Casas and Francisco de Vitoria), but whose voices were suppressed by the colonial difference built on the Greek and Christian-European traditions. For example, Guaman Poma de Ayala, in Tawantinsuyu, who wrote a political treatise titled *Nueva corónica y buen gobierno* (New Chronicle and Good Government), which was written between the end of the sixteenth century and the beginning of the seventeenth, but printed for the first time in 1936.[68] For Aymara's and Quechua's intellectuals and political figures, Greek thinkers do not have much to offer to the constitution building of a plurinational state. But Guaman Poma does. The "political proper" for a decolonial thinker has its fountain not in Greece but in the anti-colonial and decolonial (in this case Guaman Poma) responses to the imperial designs of Greek legacies in the pens and minds of Spanish men of letters.

There is, then, for decolonial thinkers in America a legacy similar to the legacies that European thinkers find in Greece. Obviously, Central or Eastern Asian intellectuals will find their own legacies to engage the "political proper." Unless, however, we assume that only the Greeks are the sources of the political proper. It is also within the legacy of political struggles framed by the colonial difference that Enrique Dussel was able to postulate a distinction between ethics of discourse and ethics of liberation. The project of ethics of discourse (Apple, Habermas) means inclusion and reform, in Dussel's words. It is dialogic negotiation and depoliticization, in Žižek's words. Ethics of liberation is transformation grounded in a philosophical discourse that questions the fact that in the politics of inclusion and recognition that is left unquestioned is the very place in and from which inclusion is being proposed. Those who propose inclusion do not reflect critically on the fact that those who are welcomed to be included may not necessarily want to play the game generously offered by those who open their arms to the inclusion of the difference. This is the issue at stake, in my understanding, in Lee Kwan Yew's insistence on the Eastern and Western way of doing things. We may not agree with the way in which Lee frames the issue, but we should not overlook that there is an issue in which the imperial differences (e.g., today differences within capitalist states; yesterday differences between Western civilizations and civilizations that couldn't be colonized) and colonial differences (e.g., created in relation to civilizations and people that were colonized) come together in very interesting ways. The Zapatistas' theoretical revolution may prove to be of the essence to get out of the vicious circle steaming from the local history of Europe, either by reaching back to Greek legacies or to the short history of the European post-Enlightenment (e.g., Protestant ethics, whiteness, and secularization).

Closing Remarks

The Zapatistas' theoretical revolution and its ethical and political consequences suggest that the time has come to look around, beyond European legacies (Greece or the Enlightenment), as Fanon suggested in the epigraph to this chapter. Beyond rewesternization and the reorientation of the European Left, there is an entire world to look for "the political proper" when the political requires us to deal with the long-lasting presence of Eurocentrism, in its European and U.S. guise. Furthermore, it is not only the figures of European refugees and the Holocaust that concern us. The non-European damnés, responding to Westernization and rewesternization, are also of concern. They are contesting dewesternizing and decolonial projects, the re-inscription of the spiritual into land claims, and the process of decolonizing aesthetics and religion by liberating spirituality and subjectivity.

In between these trajectories and options, decolonial democracy/socialism becomes a connector and no longer the liberal model of democracy/socialism managed by rewesternizing agencies or socialist futures managed by the reorientation of the Left. Decolonial democracy/socialism is the site of struggle for control and domination, on the one hand, and for liberation on the other. The figure of the colonized (indigenous people, black slaves in the Atlantic in the sixteenth century, Indians under British rule); the logic of coloniality operating without colonies (China under British and U.S. regulations after the Opium War, in 1848); and the figure of the immigrant from local colonial histories moving toward local metropolitan histories shall be added to the spatial scenario of planetary transformations, where dewesternization and decoloniality emerge as options to rewesternization that, for their mere existence, transform rewesternization into another option and no longer seen as the only road to the future.

I am not saying of course that the "end" of European legacy has arrived. On the contrary, rewesternization consists in the effort to re-inscribe European modernity's own tradition into the future. To frame the issue in terms of "end" and "new beginning" would imply remaining within Western modernity's frame of mind and maintaining the uni-linear conception of historical changes and human progress(ion). No, it is not the "end of Western democracy" that has arrived, but the time of its regionalization. The frame in which "democracy" has been introduced by the Zapatistas has opened up the need to look at the multiplication of interlocking histories and their corresponding legacies, linked by the coloniality of power and the colonial difference. Those who are imagining democratic futures in Latin America (the Zapatistas, the constitutions of Bolivia and Ecuador) or in India (Chatterjee) can hardly take seriously the invitation to "insist on the potential of democratic politization as the true European legacy from ancient Greece onwards."[69] These kinds of claims have been made by right-wing politicians who felt the discomfort of rapid demographic transformations when industrial "development" began to emerge in the first half of the twentieth century. However, such claims could only be legitimated within the "proper history" of the North Atlantic, from ancient Greece to the modern United States, and the "silence" of the rest.

The recently initiated Festival de la Digna Rabia continues the work of the Zapatistas' theoretical revolution and is the constant reminder that theories are where you can find them; and now you can find them all over the world, not just in Europe or the United States.[70] The difference is that theories all over the world, or emerging from "minorities" in Western Europe and the United States, imply border thinking, and for border thinkers the reference point is no longer Greece or Rome; or if it is, like in the case of Muslims, it is only half of the story.

CHAPTER SEVEN

Cosmopolitan Localisms
Overcoming Colonial and Imperial Differences

Existentialism in our country is an immature Western imitation in need of being enriched with our 3000-year-old theosophic experience in order to be eligible to be called philosophy. . . .

   This is what I mean by originality and free-thinking, rather than our Iranian free-thinker's hundred years of regurgitation of Marx's ideas which are of not use to anyone. Those individuals who have been successful in Africa and Asia have been able to teach European philosophies and forget them. They were able to get to know their societies, find and propose new solutions, based upon their existing cultural, historical and social resources, and create a new foundation. We see that they have become successful too.
ALI SHARI'ATI, "The Mission of the Free-Thinker for Building Up the Society"

COSMOPOLITANISM IS A CONCERN of Western scholarship whether or not scholars who engage in cosmopolitan issues are natives of the Western (epistemic) world. The point of origination of "cosmopolitanism"—in other words—is the West, although its routes of dispersion encountered partisans beyond Western history of ideas and political debates. By this I mean that it is not a concern—at least not to the degree which it is in the Western world—of Chinese intellectuals and scholars in China, Iran, Zimbabwe, Bolivia, or Uzbekistan, for example. And when they are, they are taken up by local intellectuals looking toward the West rather than to the issues of their own local histories, of which Western interventions are part. Cosmopolitanism is a concern of Western scholarship, though not necessarily of Western scholars. There is no one-to-one relationship between both. In the global distribution of scholarly and intellectual labor, the geopolitics of knowing, understanding, and knowledge run parallel to other geopolitical spheres, say, in the management and control of authority, economy, and information.

Cosmopolitanism and (De)Coloniality

I approach the issue as something that fell upon me when dealing with the question of coloniality, and how to get out of it. So that unless one accepts that Western scholarship is global (or universal) and therefore that cosmopolitanism is truly a global (or universal) concern independent of the institutional and individual *loci enunciationis*, a one-to-one relationship between cosmopolitan projects (or visions) and the global (or universal) does not (and cannot) obtain. And this means that indeed there are places, locations, nodes, projects of short and long reach in which cosmopolitanism is not at all a concern. Chiefly among them are those who engage in decolonial and dewesternizing projects. For, if one is where one does and one does by engaging in dewesternizing and decolonial projects, what would one gain by jumping onto the Western cosmopolitan bandwagon? Quite the opposite, one may feel that cosmopolitan projects run indeed counter to dewesternizing and decolonial ones and that cosmopolitanism aims to erase the differences that dewesternization and decolonialism need to overcome that cosmopolitan razor trying to mold the planet according to the subjectivity, desires, comfort, satisfaction, and security of those who embrace, theorize, and push cosmopolitanism. But the razor now has to confront and to cross two enormous mountains: the imperial and colonial differences on which dewesternizing and decolonial projects are based and from where they nourish. There is a question of dignity in the eyes of those who, at the top of the mountain, look at the cosmopolitan army marching down the valley. Only that this time, the end of the movie may no longer be the classical ending of Hollywood "Westerns" of the golden age, the triumphal march to the frontier.

Now, it is important to set the terms in which dewesternization and decolonialization should be understood in my argument. I am not proposing a competition from which a winner will emerge as the global leader. That scenario is a modern one, perhaps postmodern; perhaps this aim could be attributed to dewesternization, although it is not clear to me whether this option's claims are for global leadership or for a balanced distribution of decision-making in the future. That is, I would like to think instead that dewesternization is moving toward a polycentric world order. In other words, to the extent that dewesternization is by definition a non-Kantian project, and based on the fact that in the past five hundred years Western imperial building and management changed hands from time to time (Spain, Holland, England and France, the United States), it doesn't follow necessarily that this trend will continue and that the next turn will be China's. The difference is that while in the successions of Western imperial hegemony and domination a changing of hands took place "within the white family" of Euro-America; Chinese are "yellow" (see chapter 1) and do not belong to the family. There is a divide here mapped by the imperial epistemic and colonial difference; that is, the line of global racism that divides Western Christians and white from Eastern mostly non-Christians and yellow. That is the boundary that may be diffusing the play of forces into a polycentric and capitalist world, rather than into the same kind of world order we had for five hundred years, with the only difference that the new hegemon will be in "yellow hands" instead of "white hands."

Furthermore, where is the knowing subject who brings about cosmopolitan issues located? Does he or she belong to three continents? Is this a necessary condition of cosmopolitanism and for being cosmopolitan? Who is concerned with cosmopolitanism, where and why? Is cosmopolitanism an individual business or a global project? Is she observing and describing cosmopolitan issues from a non-cosmopolitan perspective, or is she a cosmopolitan herself who attempts to advance the project or intervene in the debate toward cosmopolitan futures? Since I announced in the title that my arguments promote communal futures, the question is: Would then communal futures be compatible, and if so, to what extent, with current cosmopolitan ideals?; or not. Briefly, how would cosmopolitanism and communalism (in the sense I will describe in the afterword, based on indigenous concepts of the communal) interact?

In fact, the geopolitical imaginary nourished by the terms and processes of globalization lays claim to the homogeneity of the planet from above—economically, politically, and culturally. In this sense globalism sounds very similar to cosmopolitan ideals. The only difference is that the former is brutally capitalist and monocentric, while the latter is, as Costas Douzinas puts it, "globalization (or globalism) with a good face." I would add that while *globalism* is the term to designate the neo-liberal project, *cosmopolitanism* is the term that names honest liberal projects.[1] So that decolonial cosmopolitanism shifts the geography of reasoning and asks, within the principles of the decolonial option, whether cosmopolitanism can be preserved or abandoned? Is pluriversal cosmopolitanism possible? Yes, if we are all engaged in that project, accept that cosmopolitanism can be local. Cosmopolitan localism is an oxymoron, indeed; an oxymoron that unveils the universal pretenses of universal cosmopolitanism in a single story. Now we have a pleonasm: *universum* is a Latin equivalent to Greek *cosmopolis*.

Cosmopolitanism and Globalism

The term *cosmopolitanism* is, instead, employed more often than not as a counter to globalization, although not necessarily in the sense of globalization from below. Globalization from below invokes, rather, the reactions to globalization from those populations and geo-historical areas of the planet that suffer the consequences of the global economy. There are, then, local histories that plan and project global designs and others that have to live with them. Cosmopolitanism is not easily aligned to either side of globalization, although the term implies a global project. What options does cosmopolitanism offer vis-à-vis globalism and globalization from below?

Let's assume that globalism is a set of neo-liberal designs (now in the process of rewesternization) to manage the world, while cosmopolitanism is a set of projects that work toward planetary conviviality. In the Andes, they will prefer the general expression "vivir bien" (a common translation of kichwa "sumak kawsay" or Aymara "sumak kamaña" that etymologically would mean something like "to live in plenitude" or, paraphrasing the expressions, "living in fullness and harmony with Pachamama").[2] Such a horizon of life is alien to capitalist societies, in which competition and personal success—economically and politically as well as in the world of entertainment and sport is encouraged, celebrated, and rewarded. In the Andean culture, "to live in harmony" is a project delinking from competition and success. It is indeed a convivial project toward noncapitalist-based societies. In other words, these projects work to eliminate forms of competition that promote getting ahead of or outdoing one's neighbors.[3] And such principles only promote cosmopolitanism of the fittest. The fittest are those who fit capitalist and neo-liberal designs, which of course are not universal, but, postulated as such, leave out of the cosmo-polis all those who are not interested in "fitting." Today, in the United States the idea that the survival of the fittest is "naturally" connected with competition is being contested. One can think of survival of communities, rather than of the fittest. The idea of the "common good" is returning to liberal thinking. However, there is still a barrier that prevents the detachment of "economy" from "capitalism," and while the idea of the "survival of the fittest" is contested, "capitalism" is seen as necessary. By so doing, the link between capitalism and survival of the fittest is being erased.

The first global design of the modern/colonial world was Christianity, a cause and a consequence of the incorporation of the Americas into the global vision of an Orbis Christianus. It preceded the civilizing mission, the intent to civilize the world under the model of the modern European nation-states. Christian global designs were part of the European Renaissance, and they were constitutive of modernity and of its darker side, coloniality. The global design of the secular civilizing mission was part of the European Enlightenment and of a new configuration of modernity/coloniality. The cosmopolitan project corresponding to Christianity's global design was mainly articulated by Francisco de Vitoria, at the University of Salamanca, while the civilizing global design was mainly articulated by Immanuel Kant, at the University of Königsberg.

In other words, cosmopolitan projects, albeit with significant differences, have been at work during both moments of modernity/coloniality. The first was a religious project; the second was secular. The colonization of the Americas in the sixteenth and the seventeenth centuries, and of Africa and Asia in the nineteenth and the early twentieth centuries, consolidated an idea of the West: a geopolitical image that exhibits chronological periodization. Three overlapping macronarratives emerge from this image. In the first narrative, the West originates temporally in Greece and moves northwest of the Mediterranean to the North Atlantic. In the second narrative, the West (in the specific sense I have given to the word in my argument) is defined by the modern world that originated with the Renaissance and with the expansion of capitalism through the Atlantic commercial circuit. In the third narrative, Western modernity is located in Northern Europe, where it bears the distinctive trademark of the Enlightenment and the French Revolution. While the first narrative emphasizes the geographical marker "West" as the keyword of its ideological formation, the second and third link the West more strongly with modernity. Coloniality as the constitutive (and darker) side of modernity emerges from these latter two narratives, which cosmopolitanism and coloniality are entangled: cosmpolitanism becomes a key concept of modernity to hide coloniality. By this I do not mean that it is improper to conceive and analyze cosmopolitan projects beyond these parameters. My point is to make explicit the goals and conditions under which "cosmopolitan" projects could be said to have been in place before 1500. Was the expansion of the Islamic caliphate of the Abbassid dynasty a cosmopolitan or global project? Or were intellectuals advancing these goals? Or is cosmopolitanism an invention of Western modernity and therefore the brighter side that obscures coloniality?

I'm therefore situating modern cosmopolitan projects temporally since 1500 within the scope of the modern/colonial world—and spatially in the northwest Mediterranean and the North Atlantic: in other words, within the Christian/Secular West. While it is possible to imagine a historical narrative that, like Hegel's, begins with the origins of the spirit, it is also possible to tell stories with different beginnings, which is no less arbitrary than to proclaim the beginning with the origin of humanity or of Western civilization. The crucial point is not when the beginning is located, but why and from where and for whom a beginning is such? That is: what are the geo-historical and ideological formations that shape the frame of such macronarratives? Narratives of cosmopolitan orientation could be either managerial (what I call global designs—as in Christianity, nineteenth-century imperialism, or late-twentieth-century neo-liberal globalization) or emancipatory (what I call cosmopolitanism—as in de Vitoria, Kant, or Marx, leaving aside the differences in each of these projects), even if they are oblivious to the saying of the people that are supposed to be emancipated. The need for a critical cosmopolitanism arises from the shortcomings of both. Yet "critical" is not enough. It should be decolonial.

Within the five major trajectories of global futures that I describe in the introduction, all of the existing cosmopolitan projects are inscribed squarely in the trajectory of renewed Westernization and in the reorientation of the

Left. There is no cosmopolitan project (as yet) stemming from dewesternizing or decolonizing trajectories. The question is, would cosmopolitanism be a project that dewesternizers and decolonials would engage in and promote? What would be the gains to join a project that in its imperiality aims at eliminating or absorbing differences? So then, we are entering into the fuzzy terrain where cosmopolitanism without parenthesis and cosmopolitanisms in plural and in parenthesis meet. In other words, cosmopolitanism is either a Western project, and as such part of rewesternization, or a project in which all will participate, in which every cosmo-polis (local histories) will join as a project in which the pluriversal will be the universally agreed-upon goal; that is cosmopolitan localism.

Cosmopolitanism, International Law, and Rights

In 2000 I published an article in *Public Culture* titled "The Many-Faces of Cosmopolis: Border Thinking and Critical Cosmopolitanism." The starting point was to brazen out "cosmopolitanism" with "globalization." For, indeed, is not globalization cosmopolitan? And, in reverse, is not cosmopolitanism global by definition? It appears then, and in retrospect, that *globalization* was a term introduced in the vocabulary of political theory and political economy when markets were deregulated and profit was equated with growth. In the 1980s "globalization" replaced "development," which had invaded the field of political theory and political economies from 1950 to 1975, approximately. But once the theories of Milton Friedman began to take hold, in the late 1970s, and were institutionalized by Ronald Reagan and Margaret Thatcher in the 1980s, *globalization* came to be the rhetorical term used to describe imperial designs in the remaking of global coloniality. Global coloniality, the darker side of globalization, explains the frequent concern that during the last quarter of the twentieth century, globalization meant also the expansion of the poverty line and the growing divide between the haves and have-nots.

Thus, I was asking myself, what is the place of cosmopolitanism in the dreary scenario at the end of the twentieth century? My response, at the time of writing the article (late 1990s) and its publication (mid-2000), started from Francisco de Vitoria's foundation of international law and from Immanuel Kant's cosmopolitan ideals (and by extension with Enlightenment, clear cosmopolitan ambitions) coexisting with his notorious racist underpinning; racist principles were already at work in de Vitoria's subterfuges to manipulate the rights of the Indians in international law and the rights of the nations (ius gentium, see below and chapter 2). So, the question was, how could cosmopolitanism be possible when the designer of the project had a hierarchical view of humanity around the planet? It so happened that cosmopolitanism was, willingly or not, a project of Western expansionism (that today has been updated as globalism), whose implementation was carried on through the "civilizing mission" rather than by the free market in economics and democracy in politics. In that regard, Kant's cosmopolitan ideals were as imperial as late twentieth century's march through free-trade, military bases, and "spreading democracy."

Once I reached this conclusion, I set myself to explore the issue in two directions: one historical and the other coeval with particular "faces" of cosmopolitan projects. Historically, I realized that Kant's cosmopolitanism was coeval with the Declaration of the Rights of Man and of the Citizen (the Declaration). While cosmopolitanism was a world (or global) project, the Declaration was a concern with what would be the modern (and European) nation-states. It doesn't take too much effort to conclude that the Declaration in France, and by extension the formation of the modern nation-state in England and Germany, would become—directly or indirectly—naturally bonded to cosmopolitan projects. How come? If the Declaration in Europe were to warranty the civil security of Man (let's say, of human beings) and that the civil security of Man was tied to citizenship, then the Declaration worked in two complementary directions. One was chronological, as the Declaration was necessary to secure the life of the citizens under the secular rule of governmentality within the history of Europe itself. The other was geographical, as the Declaration would become the measuring stick by which to judge social behavior that, according to Western standards, was uncivilized and, therefore, violated the rights of Man outside Europe. The silent assumption was that there was no violation of the rights of citizens, because there was no such social role outside Europe. Thus, the civilizing mission and cosmopolitanism appeared to be the underlying project of secular Western expansion.

September 11, 2001, was a wake-up call not only for globalism, but for cosmopolitanism as well. It was perhaps the first global event that put a halt to the dreams of Kantian cosmopolitanism, but it also revealed the imperial underpinning of the Kantian vision and legacy.

Why Did Cosmopolitanism Become a Buzzword in the 1990s?: Four Motivations and a Detour

Cosmopolitanism was a buzzword in the late 1990s and continued to be in the first decade of the twenty-first century. Why such widespread interest in cosmopolitanism? I see four main motivations.

The first motivation was the widespread limits of "national thinking." Nationalism was what cosmopolitanism was trying to overcome. Cross-cultural and planetary dialogues were argued as ways toward the future, instead of leaping to defend and enclose the borders of the nations. Immigration contributed to the surge of cosmopolitanism. Nationalists saw immigration as a problem; cosmopolitans saw it as an opening toward global futures.

The second motivation was the need to build arguments that, moving away from nationalism, did not fall in the hands of neo-liberal and economic globalization. That global world was not what cosmopolitans liked to support at the end of the twentieth century. Thus, one of the strands of cosmopolitan thinking, confronting globalization, was caught in between honest liberalism opposed to neo-liberal globalization and a renovated Marxism that saw new global players invited to think cosmopolitanism beyond the international proletarian revolution.

A third motivation, related to the first two, was to move away from closed and monocultural conceptions of identity supporting state designs to control the population by celebrating multiculturalism. At this level, cosmopolitanism focused on the individual: the person was invited to see herself as an open citizen of the world, embodying several "identities." In a word, it was a liberal conception of cosmopolitanism, born in the nineteenth century, and now translated into an ideal of flexible and open cultural citizenship.

The fourth motivation, compatible with but also distinct from the second, was the legal proposal putting on the agenda "cosmopolitanism from below," which was eventually connected with the agenda of the World Social Forum.

I see behind those motivations a story that has not been told. In that untold story there is one stop and one detour that have not been accounted for. And when you think about it, the story of the idea in Greece has been restricted to Athens and Sparta. Not much is said about Macedonia. The standard historical trajectory of the word *cosmo-polis* goes from Greece to Königsberg: the Greeks introduced the word into their vocabulary; Kant revamped it and put it to good use in the eighteenth century.[4] However, the cosmopolitan line doesn't go directly from Greece to Königsberg. The trajectory took a detour through the Atlantic, in the sixteenth century, and it is through this detour that it got to Kant: from the Atlantic, not from Greece. Let's see.

Orbis was the Latin word equivalent to the Greek word *cosmos*. Whether the meaning was strictly equivalent, I leave the research for another opportunity. What is important to notice, however, is that *orbis* was a word in the vocabulary of imperial Rome. Thus, perhaps *orbis* did not translate the arcadian *cosmos* conceived when Greece was in the idealized period of democratic organization of the *polis*. Perhaps *orbis*, in Latin, translated *cosmo-polis*, which better describes the emergence of Macedonia (the barbarians to the north of Athens and Sparta) of Alexander the Great (356–323 B.C.) at the moment he ruled over Persian civilization and its dominium and extended his control into a vast portion of the known world. Thus, *cosmopolis* under Alexander the Great doesn't describe the pacific democratic Greece of Athens and Sparta, but that of Macedonia and the conquering and military administration. The fact is, then, that in Roman Latin *orbis* and *urbe* were the equivalents of *cosmos* and *polis*.[5] So *cosmos* and *orbis* are therefore concepts related to Alexander's dominium and to the Roman Empire: *imperium* is a Latin word, not a Persian or Greek one.

This is not yet the detour, but a shortcut. There is an intellectual and scholarly tradition in Germany of tracing German roots to Greece. Rome is in the tradition embraced by Latin countries and also by England. Rome has been claimed by imperial Western countries like Spain, France, and England. Germany was not one of them. These assertions are understandable. Rome is the city claimed by Catholic Christians, who see their roots in Rome and in Latin languages, rather than in Athens and the Greek language. The detour comes, as I mentioned, through the Atlantic. To start with, Pietro Martire d'Anghiera (1457–1526), an Italian man of letters at the royal court of Isabella and Ferdinand of Castille, wrote a famous report, *De Orbe Novo* (On the New World), on the early process of explorations, from 1492 to 1520 approximately. By the time of Kant's revamped cosmopolis, he was also engaged in lecturing on geography (see chapter 5). Although he used the word *cosmo-polis* he was certainly familiar with the *Orbis Universalis* of Petro Apiano, circa 1524 (see fig. 4).

If Kant did not know this version, he certainly was familiar with the well-known *Theatrum Orbis Terrarum*, by Abraham Ortelius, printed in 1570. Notice the use of the word *theatrum*. "Theatrum" is the translation of the Greek word *theatron* (a place of viewing), in the same family as *theoria* (contemplation, speculation, looking at), from which is derived *theorein* (to consider, speculate, look at) and *theoros* (spectator) and *theorem* (speculation, proposition to be proved). All are *theo-* words and were concentrated in Latin *theo-logy*, and *theo-logy* set the stage for the *hubris* of the zero point (see chapter 3). Border gnosis or border epistemology emerged precisely in confrontation with the epistemology of the zero point. Now, all existing cosmopolitan projects seem to rest on the *hubris* of the zero point and to debate without questioning the very imperial epistemic foundations of cosmopolitan claims.

So, then, we have three moments to take into consideration: the Greek, the Roman, and the Atlantic. It was basically the emergence of the *Theatrum Orbis Terrarum* that really shaped the courts' visions of and ambitions for a cosmopolitan world. The word was Greek, but the world was "possessed" by the Europe of linear global thinking, in Carl Schmitt's account (see chapters 1 and 2). It was also at the moment in which the Renaissance period of imperial expansion, led by Spain and Portugal, was closing that imperial modernity and world leadership was changing hands. Changing hands in two senses: from Spain and Portugal to England, France, and Germany. And internally, in Europe, monarchies and the papacy were giving way to the emerging bourgeoisie and a brave new world, which Kant was conceptualizing through many of his writings, including *The Contest of the Faculties.*

However, Kant's notion of cosmopolis comes to the fore more clearly in his lectures on *Anthropology from a Pragmatic Point of View* (published toward the end of his life) and in his *Geography* (see chapter 5). In *Anthropology from a Pragmatic Point of View* Kant introduced cosmopolitanism

in the section devoted to the "characters of the species." The characters of
the species, in relation to his cosmopolitan ideas and ideals, should be understood in relation to two preceding sections: "the character of the nations" and the "characters of races." The characters of the nations are limited
to six European nations: France, England, and Germany in the first round;
Italy, Spain, and Portugal in the second round. Kant arrives at the frontier of
"nations" and closes this section by stressing its limits: "Since Russia has not
yet developed definite characteristics from its natural potential; since Poland has no longer any characteristics; and since the nationals of European
Turkey never have had a character, nor will ever attain what is necessary
for a definite national character, the description of these nations' characters
may properly be passed over here."[6]

Now you begin to see that a cosmopolitan vision based on his geography
and on racist underpinnings is indeed a problematic, risky, and dangerous
proposition. For that reason, dewesternizing and decolonial projects immediately put on the table the question of imperial and colonial differences.
Overcoming imperial and colonial differences, as I argued in chapter 1, is
indeed a burden for current cosmopolitan projects. At stake is the question
of human rights. As far as human-rights operations in a world in which
the population is racially ranked, human rights will necessarily and naturally focus on the "most valuable sector of the population." Thus, Western
cosmopolitan proposals, from the Left and from the Right, will be always
confronted with the racial classification in which the very enunciation of
cosmopolitan projects is embedded. It is in this sense that the decolonial
and dewesternizing perspective (can Asians think?) begins from the very
structure of racism on which international law was founded (e.g., de Vitoria, Grotius).

But colonial and imperial differences (epistemic and ontological, as I argued previously) are only part of the problem cosmopolitanism would face
today. Another aspect is that in the same way that much of the world stopped
following the directive of the World Bank, the World Trade Organization's
Doha Development Rounds register the increase of Western failures. In
the Seventh Doha Round, China and India joined forces and refused to be
told what to do with cosmopolitan "free trade." What, indeed, would be the
advantages of cosmopolitanism if you are engaged, for example, in working toward "our modernity," as Chatterjee has argued, or in decolonizing

4 Petro Apiano's world map of 1520, most likely based on Martin Waldseemüller's world map of 1507, which was the first to include "America" (to honor Amerigo Vespucci).

"Apianus World Map," 1520 / Accession # 07832. Courtesy of the John Carter Brown Library at Brown University.

knowledge, as argued by Linda T. Smith or Hountondji, as I explored in chapter 3? From this perspective, cosmopolitanism once again looks very much like a Western, intellectually geared project, an internal debate, with not too many followers in 80 percent of the non-European cosmos.

Let's get back to Kant to further elucidate these issues. Taking one more step, Kant moves to the "characters of races," in a short section in which "nature" takes the place of "nations" held in the previous section. Kant delimits the question of races by focusing instead on "the character of species." And in this section the character of the species "human" (of the race animals) deserves close scrutiny. Cosmopolitanism comes into the picture in the section "Main Features of the Description of the Human Species' Character." And here is how Kant envisions cosmopolitanism.

> The human race taken collectively (as the entire human species) is a great number of people living successively and simultaneously. They cannot be without peaceful co-existence, and yet they cannot avoid continuous disagreement with one another. Consequently, they feel destined by nature to develop, through mutual compulsion and laws written by them, into a cosmopolitan society (cosmopolitanismus) which is constantly threatened by dissension but generally progressing toward a coalition. *The cosmopolitan society is in itself an unreachable idea*, but it is not a constitutive principle (which is expectant of peace amidst the most vigorous actions and reactions of men). *It is only a regulative principle demanding that we yield generously to the cosmopolitan society as the destiny of the human race*; and this not without reasonable ground for supposition that there is a natural inclination in this direction.[7]

Both the idea and the horizon of a cosmopolitan society are predicated, by Kant, on considerations (explored in my previous analysis of his *Geography*) that he established between freedom and law, the two pivots or pillars of any civil legislation: "If authority is combined with freedom and law, the principles of freedom and law are ensured with success."[8] Now, cosmopolitanism, as a regulative principle, is acceptable, as long as it is being imposed as a universal principle of regulation. Unless we believe that the majority of people enjoy killing each other and do not care for yielding "generously to the cosmopolitan society" (until European cosmopolitans get there to teach them), there is no excuse for establishing a regulative and imperial principle.

Kant considers four conceivable combinations of authority with free-dom and law.

1 Law and freedom without authority (anarchy).
2 Law and authority without freedom (despotism).
3 Authority without freedom and law (barbarism).
4 Authority, with freedom and law (republic).[9]

Needless to say, Kant prefers the last one. And, therefore, cosmopolitan ideals presuppose the republican organization of society in which author-ity goes hand in hand with freedom and law. As Kant himself recognizes it, cosmopolitanism is an idea which may become despotic and anarchic if authority with freedom and law in place A is considered the ideal of social organization for B, C, D, E, F, G. And this was precisely the presupposition underlying Kant's ideal envisaging of a global order he conceived as cos-mopolitan. De Vitoria was contributing to shape the colonial matrix in the sphere of international law; Kant to the principles of social organization. Both were working out cosmopolitanism in the management of the sphere of authority.

Toulmin's Hidden Agenda of Modernity

There is still another aspect in this scenario we shall bring to the foreground to understand the implications of a cosmopolitan social order that was put forward in the eighteenth century.

Now we come back to Stephen Toulmin (see introduction) from a differ-ent angle. In his landmark book *Cosmopolis: The Hidden Agenda of Moder-nity*, Toulmin brought the idea of a cosmo-polis into new light—*cosmo-polis* as a significant aspect of the hidden agenda of modernity. Why the hidden agenda? What motivated Toulmin to write this book was the moment when he understood that the image of modernity he had learned in England in the 1930s and 1940s was faulty, partial, and overtly celebratory. Toulmin un-covers two dimensions of the idealistic and triumphal image of modernity ingrained mainly in Protestant Europe. One is that the seventeenth century, far from being a European golden age that prompted the advent of science and philosophy, was a moment of economic crisis marked by the decay of the Spanish empire and the absence of a new imperial era. Holland was en-joying a moment of commercial glory, but Western Christians were killing each other in the Thirty Years' War. The second aspect underlined by Toulmin, prompted by his early reading of Michel de Montaigne's *Essais*, is the humanistic strand of the Renaissance that followed and ran parallel to the advent of modern science and the secular philosophies of Galileo, Bacon, and Descartes. The humanistic tradition, initiated during the European Renaissance, broke away from the theological and epistemological control of the church and the papacy, and prepared the ground for the secular philosophy of the Enlightenment. That, in a nutshell, is the hidden agenda of modernity and the context in which cosmopolis appears. Toulmin argues that the humanist creativity of conceiving *the polis* followed the pattern of *the cosmos* through the mediation of science. Precisely, *cosmo-polis* or the *polis* (society) was organized following the model of the cosmos that physics and astronomy were making available at the time; this is the hidden agenda of modernity. Toulmin adumbrates the issue in the following manner: "We are here concerned, not with 'science' as the modern positivists understand it, but with a cosmopolis that gives a comprehensive account of the world, so as to bind things together in 'politico-theological,' as much as in scientific or explanatory, terms."[10] The Western conception of science was the only novelty of the hidden agenda of modernity. Of the millenarian civilizations in the Andes, the Incas were the latest and the last: theirs was modeled on the Tawantinsuyu, starting from the pattern of the Southern Cross, while the Maya, who were north of the equator and could not see the Southern Cross, used instead the Milky Way as their source of inspiration. Thus the hidden agenda of modernity, interestingly enough, was a consequence of the ground gained by the philosophical-scientific strand from the Renaissance to the Enlightenment. It was in this scenario that Kant introduced his own idea of *cosmopolis*.

Toulmin explains that the reconstruction of European society after the Thirty Years' War was based on two pillars or principles: stability and hierarchy. Stability applied to inter-relations among sovereign nations. Sovereign nations were a conception in the mind of European thinkers (like Kant, for example), and it applied to the society in which they were dwelling and thinking. Thus, beyond the realm of sovereign nations (which were basically the six modern and imperial European nations: Germany, England, France, Spain, Italy, and Portugal, with Holland interregnum), the imperial question was not in the picture of stable relations among sovereign nations in the process of becoming states.[11] Hierarchy applied to the internal organization of society or within the internal organization of each individual state. But, again, the presupposed totality was that of the six or seven Western European countries.

He further explains that by 1700 social relations (hierarchy) within nation-states were defined horizontally based on super-ordination and subordination of class relations: "Social stability depended on all the parties in society 'knowing their place' relative to the others, and knowing what reciprocal modes of behavior were appropriate and rational."[12] The planetary model of society was based on the hierarchical relations within nation-states, which was, Toulmin observes, "explicitly cosmopolitical." How come? Without such a justification, he adds, the imposition of hierarchy on "the lower orders" by "the better sort" of people would be arbitrary and self-serving. To the extent that this hierarchy mirrored the structure of nature, its authority was self-explanatory, self-justifying, and seemingly rational.[13]

Here we encounter authority and law (posited by Kant), but not yet freedom. Let's take it one step further and see how the polis can be organized following the model of the cosmos to grant freedom to its citizens. In this light we understand that the undisclosed assumption was, first, that the hierarchical organization of each nation-state (*polis*) shall follow the model provided by the law of the cosmos; and, second, that the stability of relations among nation-states shall also be modeled on the law of nature (cosmos) that serves the model for the organization of each state within itself (polis).

Thus, Toulmin puts it this way: "The philosophical belief that nature obeys mathematical 'laws' which will ensure its stability for so long as it pleases God to maintain it, was a socially revolutionary idea: both cosmos and polis (it appeared) were self-contained, and their joint 'rationality' guaranteed their stability. As recently as 1650, people worried that the World was grinding to its End: by 1720, their grandchildren were confident that a rational and omniscient Creator had made a world that ran perfectly."[14]

Shortly after that (by 1776), the idea was applied to the economy, and the belief took, and God was replaced by the State: the "invisible hand" manipulated by the state, was supposed to secure free and private initiatives. Thus it was not the role of the state to rule the economy, but to make sure that the economy ruled itself. The invisible hand was the invisible hand of the state, as Arrighi has recently and convincingly argued.[15] This idea lasted until the fall of 2008, when Wall Street exploded, blowing off the fingers of the invisible hands and depriving them of playing the strings and guiding the marionettes.

Introducing Decolonial Cosmopolitan Ideals

If cosmopolitan ideals are maintained in and for the twenty-first century, cosmopolitanism shall be accountable for its crimes: the very foundation of cosmopolitanism, as envisioned by Kant and explained by Toulmin, was complicitous with the formation of European imperial powers and of European expansion in America, Africa, and Asia, as well as with the continuation of Europe in the United States, as Hegel was anticipating.[16] To maintain cosmopolitan ideals, we (all those who engage in this project) need to decolonize cosmopolitanism, which means moving toward a decolonial cosmopolitan order no longer modeled on the law of nature discovered by science, but from various models of conviviality that Western cosmopolitanism suppressed. Cosmopolitanism cannot be a top-down global order, nor can it be the privilege of "frequent travelers" and tri-continental subjects. Cosmopolitanism shall be thought out in relation to a heterogenous historico-structural conception of history and society (as we saw in chapter 1) and world order, rather than in a unilinear narrative of history and a hierarchical organization of society. Decolonial cosmopolitanism shall be "the becoming of a pluriversal world order" built on and dwelling in the global borders of modernity/coloniality. In what follows I explain this idea. I will proceed by taking a step back from the seventeenth century, where Toulmin learned that "modernity" planted its seed during the Renaissance and where he discovered humanism as modernity's hidden agenda beyond the celebration of science and secular philosophy. And I will take a step forward, toward the formation of the United States and the transformation of European cosmopolitan ideals, in the early twentieth century, when massive immigration from Europe agitated the quiet waters of two centuries of pilgrim's pro-creation, Native American repression, and enslaved African exploitation.

About one hundred and thirty years before Immanuel Kant pronounced his lecture on anthropology from a pragmatic point of view (1772–73), the need of international law emerged in the consciousness of Western Christians. While in Europe the Council of Trent was setting the stage for a bloody scenario that would consume Western Christian Europe until the Peace of Westphalia (1648), ending the Thirty Years' War, which had piggybacked on the eighty-year war between Spain and the Netherlands, legal theologians at the University of Salamanca were starting their long journey to solve two interrelated problems: to what extent Indians in the New World were Human, and to what extent, as a consequence, they had property rights. For Castilians land was a matter of property rights, while for the Inca and Aztec civilizations, as well as other existing communities in the Caribbean, neither property nor right was a known concept. This was even less germane to land: land was for them and still is the source of life, and not a commodity. Francisco de Vitoria and his followers were confronting, during the second half of the sixteenth century, issues of a history parallel to and intertwined with the internal history of Europe that Kant framed in terms of nation-state and national characters. This double history, its imperial and colonial side, were certainly at work in the seventeenth century, but as Toulmin has elegantly narrated in the first chapter of his book, only the bright side of imperial European history was transmitted to his generation, in England, in the 1930s and 1940s.

In retrospect, another aspect of the story that has not been told deserves to be brought to light. Greek *cosmopolis* has many more similarities to Quechua-Aymara words like *Pacha* or even *Tawantinsuyu* than to Kant's *cosmo-polis*. Tawantinsuyu was not only the organization of the Incanate, but—as I just mentioned—it was modeled on their knowledge of *Pacha* (which, translated into Greek, would be "cosmos" and into Latin would be "orbis"), a malleable word that collapses space and time, energy and life. And that is a problem, really. Imagine, as a thought experiment, that Kant relied on Tawantinsuyu to imagine a global and social organization of the human species, much like Guaman Poma de Ayala did exactly 250 years before Kant, when he laid out his *Nueva corónica y buen gobierno* and proposed to Philip III an organization of "The Indies of the New World." The organization of the first imperial/colonial society since the sixteenth century was meant to solve a cosmo-political problem of a particular kind: the formation of modern/colonial inter-state relations and inner-state social organization (stability and hierarchy). The fact that Europeans managed and controlled knowledge doesn't mean that in terms of the future and well-being of the humanity a global order based on Tawantinsuyu would have been less effective than a cosmopolitan global order imagined after the Greeks. Indeed, Kant was missing the transformation during his own time whose consequences we are witnessing today. What, indeed, could have gone wrong?

Toward the end of sixteenth century, merely fifty years from the moment Spaniards were able to gain control of Tawantinsuyu (1548) and began to build the Viceroyalty of Peru, there was plenty of time to figure out what to do in a new situation in the history of humankind. Guaman Poma knew both his own history and the history of the world that he read in Spanish authors, mainly those writing on the New World. He solved the problem of internal organization for the Tawantinsuyu by giving one *suyu* to each of the existing ethnicities at this time: Spaniards, Indians, moors, and blacks. Tawantinsuyu, the domain of the Incas, meant "the world divided in four." Each part of Tawantin-suyu was called a "suyu." Each "suyu" was assigned, through complex internal rules, to particular family lineages. Once the Incas vacated Tawantinsuyu and moved to Vilcabamba, north of Cuzco, Guaman Poma filled the void with the current demography of his time. Furthermore, the world was remapped according to Tawantinsuyu: he drew a map dividing it into two parts. On the upper part he located Tawantinsuyu, and in the lower part Spain. However, Spaniards did not see themselves "below" Tawantinsuyu, and they prevailed. Prevailing, however, did not mean that the forces of history were killed forever. The current process of re-writing the constitutions of Bolivia and Ecuador, and the entire discussion of the plurinational state, is nothing more than the continuation of the problem Guaman Poma saw emerging five hundred years ago, when the territory of Incas and Aymaras became a mix of ethnicities. His decolonial political treatise was and remains exemplary, in that he did not propose to coexist with the enemy. On the contrary, the very idea of "the enemy" was not in his mind. Thus, one of the first steps of decolonial cosmopolitanism was to get rid of the idea of friends and enemies in which the political finds its raison d'être. Carl Schmitt's proposal only makes sense with European "political theology," that is, in the secularization of Christian theology in which the world is already divided between Christianity and "those barbarians who hate it and want to destroy it."

The problem is not minor, and the whole idea of decolonial cosmopolitanism is at stake. I should also add to the previous description of the *suyu* the point that each *suyu* was composed by association of units called *ayllu* (organizations with many similarities with the Greek *oykos*). Ayllus were grouped into *markas* and the compound of ayllus and markas formed a suyu. In this case Tawantinsuyu was at once the city and also the extension of the city, to the territorial domains of Inca rulers. Thus, the argument has moved from *Cosmo-polis* to *Urbis-orbe* to *Pacha-suyu*. The first two belong to the same family, although Orbe was overruled by Cosmos. And Pacha never entered the conversation. By bringing it up now I am stressing why any cosmopolitan project today cannot be a project from one local history and particular locus of enunciation, as if all people in the world should be happy to be "included" in such a generous universal cosmopolitan project. Indeed, why would Pacha-suyu be ruled out and its contribution to global communal futures dismissed in favor of cosmo-polis or urbis-orbe? (See the afterword to this book.) What, indeed, are the privileges of the Greco-Roman models over all other possible ones? Now, when I argue for communal futures, and introduce the model of Pacha-suyu, I am not proposing a "new" and "better" (two key concepts of imperial modernity) model to replace the old and bad ideas of "cosmos" and "orbis." That would be to do the same, and with little change to move forward. For if you define cosmopolitanism as a world in which the citizens belong to the cosmos rather than to the nation, then why not Pacha-suyu, where, from its very inception, *runa* (what Westerners call " humans") belonged to and were crossed, ingrained, and sunk in the cosmos; it includes the cosmological rotations of each individual life, as well as incorporating the life of each member of the community in the cycles of days and nights, of the seasons that bring the harvest and the food, and the hundreds of plants and roots used to keep the body in synchrony with the cosmos (e.g., what Westerners called medicine).

The Zapatistas, aware of that long genealogy of thought, mapped a decolonial cosmopolitan vision in the formula "a world in which many worlds would coexist" ("un mundo en el que co-existan muchos mundos"), and in doing so shifted from the universe of imperial cosmopolis to the pluriverse of decolonial cosmopolitanism. The Zapatistas' dictum is not pointing toward a "multicultural cosmopolitanism" where the G7 will govern and the rest will dance and eat ethnic food.[17] To get there, to a world in which many worlds will coexist, all parties involved have to engage in the politics of decolonial cosmopolitanism, and, today, such a project could begin by confronting the imperial and colonial differences that divide and rank the world, among people and regions, as well as natural and cultural resources. As I have been arguing in this book, we are living in a polycentric and capitalist world in which three major trajectories are contending: Westernization, dewesternization, and decoloniality.

The next question is, how are rewesternization projects and Western critical cosmopolitanism related? By critical, I mean cosmopolitan projects from liberal or Marxist persuasions that are confronting neo-liberal globalism. I am asking this question because my argument is built on premises that are not part of Western mainstream debates on cosmopolitanism. I work and live in the United States, but as far as I know, the collective modernity/coloniality/decoloniality is not part of those debates. The collective project dwells in the history of South America and the Caribbean, the histories of indigenous diversity, African-descent diversity, and European-descent diversity. And my personal trajectory as the son of an Italian immigrant in Argentina who studied in France and migrated to the United States is tainted by the Latino/as cultures in the country where I am writing this book. It is imaginable that similar positions are being taken in different parts of the world among those who do not want to become cosmopolitan according to Euro-American designs. What would responses to Western cosmopolitanism look like from the various histories of South America and the Caribbean (European, African, Indigenous) or, for that matter, from any part of the Islamic world, China or Africa, North and sub-Saharan? If you shift the gaze and look from the margin toward the center, cosmopolitanism changes color; or may become blurred.

However, fruitful connections could be made between "us," meaning those who are not working within the European cosmopolitan tradition, and thinkers like Bruno Latour. Latour's responses to Ulrich Beck's cosmopolitanism are telling of how critical cosmopolitanism can work within the current Euro-American project of rewesternization. Needless to say, I see Latour's position as akin to decolonial cosmopolitan ideals. One could even think of Latour as a decolonial European thinker and, as such, see his horizon as the imperial rather than the colonial side of coloniality. For, if it is not clear yet, coloniality is the darker side of modernity and therefore is what connects and entangles both the imperial and the colonial ends of the modern colonial/world.[18] Let me be clear: I do not think that Latour is endorsing the G20 (although Beck may), that is, the new organization created after Wall Street began limping. I sympathize with Latour's critique, which, interestingly enough, he qualifies as his "Western Burgundian point of view." From my "Italo-Argentinian point of view" (which means, of European immigrant descent), and thinking decolonially, Isabelle Stengers and Peter Sloterdijk are quite interesting, but their conceptualization comes from dwelling in a different world: hence, literally, the future shall be a world in which many worlds would coexist. I am advocating for worlds guided by communal principles, and of course if we aim for a world in which many worlds will coexist, we cannot have an imperial (Right or Left, progressive or conservative) blueprint of how that world would be, nor can we mount an army to force everybody to acquiesce: this simply is the stronger claim of the decolonial option among the options of a noncapitalist world (that is to say, capitalism will no longer be an option, because the very principle of capitalism is that if there are many worlds, they can only coexist under capitalism). If you have a blueprint and not an open horizon of pluriversality, you would be forced to destroy and kill in order to implement the blueprint.

Cosmopolitanism in a decolonial vein shall aim at *the communal* not as a *universal model* but as a *universal connector* among different noncapitalist socio-economic organizations around the world. Thus, communalism is not a model of society, but a principle of organization. Many models will emerge, based on local histories, memories, embodiments, practices, languages, religions, categories of thought. The communal as a connector, rather than as a universal model, means, in the first place, to delink from both capitalism and communism (or socialism in its softer version), brothers of the same parents, the European Enlightenment. What comes after delinking will depend on what has been at work in different local histories. It could be a remapping of *the three principles of the people* (1926) of Sun Yat-sen;[19] it could be the Andean legacies and history of the Ayllu; it could be the philosophy of freedom and re-existence (not just resistance and survival, but an active project of re-existence that overcomes the social death that coloniality—during the colonial as well as the republic period—imposed on black communities in South America); it could be the remaking of South Africa;[20] or, it could be the possibilities at work in noncapitalist social organizations that could unfold from current debates, explorations, and creativity in the Islamic world.[21] Consequently, it would make sense for cosmopolitanism, in order for it to be meaningful from a decolonial perspective, as it is not imperial. Therefore, the Western cosmopolitan vision could exist among other visions, but would not function as the guiding light and the blueprint for global futures. If that were the case, then globalism and cosmopolitanism would be two sides of the same coin: the first being brutal and imperial, the second gentle, friendly, and convivial, but both taking place within the project of continuing rewesternization. The communal and the decolonial envision cosmopolitan localisms breaking away, delinking, building, and being in the world otherwise than the liberal or Marxist cosmopolitan.

Cosmopolitanism, International Law, and Coloniality

The concept of "good governance" recently entered the vocabulary of international relations and international law. Paradoxically the term is not used in the sense proposed by Guaman Poma ("Buen Gobierno"), and even less in the sense used by the Zapatistas in Southern Mexico ("Juntas de Buen Gobierno," "Council of Good Governance"), but in the implied version elaborated by legal theologians of Salamanca. Thus, there is a direct line connecting the emergence of international law in the sixteenth century (there was no such conceptualization and practice before that time) with cosmopolitan ideals in the eighteenth century and with good governance and development in the twentieth century, as promoted by the United Nations and the World Bank. Not by chance, the Universal Declaration of Human Rights, in 1948, came at the time when such institutions were being created, and, therefore, human rights, good governance, and development began to work in tandem toward the new version of "cosmopolitanism" that came to be baptized as "globalism." "Globalism," like "cosmopolitanism," names a vision rather than a process (e.g., globalization).

Francisco de Vitoria was celebrated mainly among Spanish and other European scholars as being one of the founders of international law. His treatise *Relectio de Indis* is considered foundational. The idea of the Orbis Christianus (or the Christian cosmos) was not new. It was the legacy of the Roman empire, particularly from the moment Constantine brought Christianity together with imperium (e.g., dominium), to which later on England and, more recently, the United States would claim their own inheritance. The novelty of the sixteenth century was the emergence of a part of humanity (named Indians by Christians) and lands (named Indias Occidentales, New World, and later on America). The historical and colonial foundation of international law was at the same time the foundation of rights and racism as we know them today. Let's see how.

Central in de Vitoria's argument is the question of *ius gentium* (rights of the people or rights of nations). In de Vitoria's time a distinction was made between divine, human, and natural law. According to divine law, the pope was the ultimate sovereign, stationed above even the monarch—more precisely, stationed between God and the monarch. De Vitoria was a humanist, and he rejected divine law. Nations, that is, communities of people, were bound by natural law and therefore had the rights of the people. Thus, there was no difference for de Vitoria between Spaniards and Indians in regard to ius gentium. The problem appeared when he had to find a reason to legally authorize Spaniards to take possessions of Indian lands. De Vitoria found his way out by recognizing the Indians as human, but suggesting that they "lacked" something. Lack and excess were two features persistently assigned to Indians, as well as non-Christians, in order to locate their correspondence with the standard model of humanity. Thus, although bound and equal to Spaniards in the domain of ius gentium, Indians were in a sense childish and thus needed the guidance and protection of Spaniards.

At that moment de Vitoria inserted the colonial difference into international law. Orbis Christianus encountered its limits, limits that would remain when secular cosmopolitanism recast the imperial project and set the stage for the civilizing mission. Anthony Anghie has provided an insightful analysis of the historical foundational moment of the colonial difference.[22] In a nutshell, the argument is that Indians and Spaniards are equal in the face of natural law, as both, by natural law, are endowed with ius gentium. In making this move, de Vitoria prevented the pope and divine law from legislating on human issues. That is, it deprived the pope of sovereignty. Natural law endows the monarch and the state as sovereign. The question, then, is whether Indians, who, like Spaniards, are endowed with ius gentium by natural (and not divine) law, are sovereign. If they are sovereign, then war with Indians would be ruled by international law legislating between two sovereign states. De Vitoria's foundational move consisted of the following.

By bracketing divine law and denying the pope legislation of human affairs, de Vitoria established natural law as the ultimate sovereign. According to this perspective, society would be governed according to natural law, and, at the time, when science (astronomy and physics) was in its inception and not on good terms with theology, the interpretation of natural law was in the hands of legal theologians, like de Vitoria himself. Now, by natural law all human beings are born equal—a principle to which no one will object—and thus endowed with ius gentium, with the rights of people or nations. De Vitoria devoted the first two of the three sections of *Relectio de Indis* to defending the rights of Indians (to whom he consistently refers to as "los bárbaros" [the barbarians]), to their rights not to be dispossessed or invaded, and he thereby undermined Spaniards' will to invade and dispossess.

However, de Vitoria established the distinction between "principes Christianos" (and Castilian in general) and "los bárbaros" (the barbarians)—and he made his best effort to balance his arguments based on the equality he attributed to both people by natural law and ius gentium—he based his entire discussion on what rights and limits the Spaniards had with regard to "the barbarians": whether to expropriate or not; whether to declare war or not; whether to govern or not. De Vitoria frequently offers counter or parallel examples, imagining what would happen if instead of being between Christians and barbarians, the situation were between French and Castilians, without calling attention to the difference. The communication and interactions between French and Castilians were established on the assumption of two sovereign nations or peoples, in which case in any litigation both parties would have a say. On the contrary, communication and interactions between Christians and barbarians were one-sided—the barbarians, for example, having no say in whatever de Vitoria said, because they were deprived of sovereignty, even when they were recognized as equal per natural law and ius gentium.

The move is foundational in the legal and philosophical constitution of the modern/colonial world and was maintained through the centuries, modified in the vocabulary from barbarians to primitives, from primitives to communists, from communists to terrorists. Thus Orbis Christianius, secular cosmopolitanism, and economic globalism are names corresponding to different moments of the colonial matrix of power and distinct imperial leaderships (from Spain to England to the United States). These are the many-faces of cosmo-polis, as I have outlined in an article in *Public Culture*, taking the question of rights (of people, of man, and of the citizen and of human) to flag the limits of imperial cosmopolitan projects.[23]

Anghie made two decisive points about de Vitoria and the historical origins of international law.

> My argument, then, is that Vitoria is concerned, not so much with the problem of order among sovereign states but the problem of order among societies belonging to two different cultural systems. Vitoria resolves this problem by focusing on the cultural practices of each society and assessing them in terms of universal law of ius gentium. Once this framework is established, he demonstrates that the Indians (e.g., barbarians in Vitoria's vocabulary) are in violation of universal natural law. *Indians are included within a system only to be disciplined.*[24]

I see three limits to cosmopolitan ideals in the trajectory from Orbis Christianus to globalism. The first limit is that the distinction between two cultural systems was not proposed by Indians (or barbarians), but by de Vitoria, unilaterally. Unilateralism in this particular case means that the colonial difference was inscribed in the apparent equality between two cultures or nations endowed by natural law with ius gentium. The colonial difference was mainly and foremost epistemological. That is, by recognizing equality by birth and by natural law, de Vitoria established Spaniards and barbarians as ontological equals. However, epistemically, he deemed barbarians not yet ready to govern themselves according to the standards established by human law. And here is where de Vitoria's distinction between divine, natural, and human law pays its dividends. Epistemic colonial differences are built on the presupposition that epistemic deficiencies indicate ontological inferiority.

The second limit is that the framework was put in place to regulate its violation. And when a violation occurred, then the creator and enforcers of the framework had a justification for invading and for using force to punish and expropriate the violator. John Locke perfected that strategy, which remains a familiar procedure to this day.[25] This logic was wonderfully rehearsed by Locke in his *Second Treatise on Government* (1681). One can say that "coloniality" (the darker side of Western modernity) shows up in de Vitoria as he carefully works toward setting the stage not only for international law but also for "modern and European" conceptions of governmentality. It seems obvious that Locke did not get as much from Machiavelli as from the emergence of international law in the sixteenth century and from de Vitoria and his followers, who were already discussing the question of both "property" and "governance" in the interaction between Christians and the barbarians. Here we are at the crossroads when someone like Locke has the Platonic and Aristotelian tradition in political theory on his European back, and the most recent Atlantic history that de Vitoria in Castile and Grotius in Holland were confronting. At the beginning of the sixteenth century Machiavelli was living in and thinking about the conflicted situation of Italian city-states. His concern was to advise the prince as to how to obtain or maintain power and how to regulate conflict—in Italy, not between Spaniards and the barbarians! So, for Machiavelli, there was no "thief," as there was for Locke, nor were there violators of natural law, as there were for de Vitoria.

The third limit is that the "framework" is not dictated by divine or natural law, but by human interests; in this case, the interests of Christian Castilian males. Thus, the "framework" presupposes a well-located and singular locus of enunciation (created, of course, in the process of stabilizing the regulations for punishing violators) that, guarded by divine and natural law, is presumed to be universal. And the universal and unilateral frame "includes" the barbarians or Indians (a principle that is valid for all politics of inclusion that we hear today) in their difference, thus justifying any action Christians will take to tame them. The construction of the colonial difference goes hand in hand with the establishment of exteriority: the place outside the frame (barbarians) that is brought into the frame.

Anghie made a second observation that coincides with one of the basic principles on which decolonial thinking and the analytic of modernity/coloniality has been built: "Clearly, then, *Vitoria's work suggests that the conventional view that sovereignty doctrine was developed in the West and then transferred to the non-European world is, in important respects, misleading. Sovereignty doctrine acquired its character through the colonial encounter.* This is *the darker history of sovereignty*, which cannot be understood by any account of the doctrine that assumes the existence of sovereign states."[26]

Anghie points toward a radical epistemic shift necessary to decolonize the inherited view of Eurocentered modernity. That is, that international relations based on the concept of sovereignty emerged in Europe, after the Peace of Westphalia, to regulate an emerging inter-state system, within which European states were considered sovereign. This is the local and regional situation in which Kant was thinking of cosmopolitanism.

But beyond the heart of Europe, as we saw above, when Kant faced Russia, Turkey, and Poland, what he faced was indeed the colonial/imperial differences. And these differences, at the time of Kant, were refashioned in two complementary directions: first, Orientalism, as analyzed by Edward Said, was nothing other than applying to secular Europe and the Orient the colonial difference that de Vitoria had already established with regard to Christian Europe and the barbarians; second, the invention of the South of Europe (clear in Kant and Hegel) recast the colonial difference into internal imperial difference, and the emerging imperial countries (England, Germany, France, which now lead the European Union) separated themselves from Christian and Latin countries (France occupying an intermediary position, but also taking the leadership of the southern Latin countries—Italy, Spain, and Portugal).

Kant's cosmopolitanism was cast under the implicit assumptions that beyond the heart of Europe was the land of those who had to be brought into civilization and, in the South of Europe, was the land of the Latin and Catholic countries, some of them—like Spain and Portugal—too close to North Africa because of the long presence of the Moors in the Iberian Peninsula, Iberians were also of mixed blood.

Now, if we jump from the era of European "cosmopolitan" modernity and the civilizing mission (with England and France leading the way) to a postmodern world guided by "globalism," we have a sketch of the continuity and diachronic accumulation of the rhetoric of modernity (salvation, conviviality, prosperity, and freedom) and its darker side, the logic of coloniality (discrimination, racism, domination, unilateralism, exploitation). What is "globalism"? Manfred Steger suggests that globalism is "an Anglo-American market ideology that reached its zenith in the 1990s and was inextricably linked to the rising fortunes of neo-liberal political forces in the world's sole remaining superpower."[27] Of extreme interest with regard to globalism, in relation to the previous periods of theological international law and secular state and inter-state regulations after Westphalia (Locke, Kant), is that while the first period (Orbis Christianus) had Christian theology (divine, natural, and human law) as the overarching frame and the second period (secular cosmopolitanism) had secular philosophy and science (the physical law of the cosmos unveiled by from Copernicus and Galileo to Newton) to regulate society and imagine a cosmopolitan world, the third period (globalism) had an "invisible hand" regulating economy. The "invisible hand," introduced by Adam Smith—during the same years that Kant was imagining cosmopolitanism and conviviality—as the regulator of economic transactions, always had for me a hidden complicity with de Vitoria's (and Christian) divine and natural laws.

Thus, when we moved from "good governance" in the sense de Vitoria and Locke imagined it (the first through international law, the second through the regulation of the nation-state) to globalism, we put *Homo economicus* in the front row (instead of Christians and the civilized confronting the barbarians) and the underdeveloped in the back. At that point, "barbarians" of all kinds lost their appeal and their force: globalism was not so much concerned with taming the barbarians and with the legality of international relations, but with reducing costs and increasing gains under the rhetoric of developing the underdeveloped. And when "barbarians" in the global scenario questioned the rhetoric of development and acted on it, they became, first, "communists" and later, "terrorists": the forces that prevent *Homo economicus* became global. These labels not only targeted specific sectors of the population, but served to identify whoever disputed global designs, whether he or she was a "communist" or a "terrorist" according to official discourse. Honestly working toward democratic futures could be labeled as communist or terrorist if the vision of the future you hold doesn't correspond with imperial global designs. Cosmopolitanism becomes difficult in this scenario.

Questions related to the nature of humanity, of who is human, of who is less or more human, lose their relevance. What counts are people who can work and consume, disregarding their religious beliefs, their skin color, or their sexuality. "Globalism" is the global sharing of a particular type of economy, disregarding, once again, whether the leader of that economy is Saudi Arabian, Indonesian Muslim, Hindu Indian, Orthodox or Slavic Russian, or white and Christian French, British, or Anglo-American. Globalism and cosmopolitanism could be different versions of Western civilization's imperial impulses: globalism being its brutal version and cosmopolitanism its benign face. The illusion that Western civilization could create the problem and solve it is facing its limits. It was possible to maintain that illusion while the colonial matrix of power was in the hands of Western actors and institutions and the Right, the Left, and the center disputed within the family, so to speak, the rights and the wrongs, while the entire world watched and waited for the civilized—the winners and the saviors. No longer. All that was possible when the anthropos was not struggling over knowledge, like today with Twitter and Facebook, web pages, independent graphic media, radio, and independent publishing houses, but also in established publishing houses that open their catalogues to promote the decentralizaton and decolonization of knowledge and being. Decoloniality and dewesternization are making a statement; they are making evident that the road(s) to the future can no longer be controlled and marked by Western gatekeepers and road-helpers. Gatekeepers are losing their function, saviors and missionaries are being looked at with suspicion, and road-helpers are no longer needed.

Toward Decolonial Cosmopolitanism or Cosmopolitan Localism

If we are to think in terms of decolonial cosmopolitanism (which means to turn Kant's legacy inside out, and thinking of pluriversal connections emerging from border action and border thinking, as I have been arguing throughout this book), then the cosmo-polis of the future would be composed of "communal nodes" around the planet cooperating rather than competing with each other, and there will be no node that, like the one inhabited by Kant, envisions itself extending all over the planet in a grand cosmopolitan salvation mission. In other words, decolonial cosmopolitanism is not the actualization of Kant's cosmo-polis, but its subsumption in what Kant's cosmopolitan project denied: the cosmopolitanism of the planetary anthropos, including European humanitas. Thus, decolonial cosmopolitanism proposes a double departure, a radical shift in the geopolitics of knowing and being. There are two scenarios in which decolonial cosmopolitanism could be thought out and acted on.

The first scenario begins with the transformation of the monocentric (and unilateral) Western world from sixteenth-century establishment of the colonial matrix of power to 2000. In that period emerged the colonial matrix of power that was created, consolidated, augmented, and controlled by Western imperialism (Spain, England, and the United States, basically). Since 2000, approximately, the colonial matrix of power has been under dispute (chapter 1). We have been witnessing the transformation of a mono-centric world into a poly-centric one that shares the same type of economy, a capitalist economy. However, poly-centricity appears at the level of control of political authority, control of knowledge, and control of subjectivity (e.g., gender, sexuality, religiosity, etc.). At the moment in which I wrote this, the G20 were meeting in Washington to fix the Wall Street disaster. However, while the G20 agreed on many points regarding the economy, there was no question that China and the United States, India and Brazil, Saudi Arabia and Germany, and other nations facing off across colonial lines would have contentions in other arenas, from political to epistemic and religious. Fur-thermore, countries like Iran and Venezuela, economically powerful and capitalist, were not part of the G20 precisely because contentions are played out in the domain of controlling authority, subjectivity, and knowledge.

Second, a polycentric capitalist world is not, of course, a decolonial world: a world that has dispensed with the colonial matrix of power and with the colonial and imperial differences regulating the field of forces in the modern/colonial world. I am not saying that a polycentric capitalist world is better than a monocentric one. I am just describing the polycentric capitalist world that exists today, like it or not. Decolonial cosmopolitanism is not so much (yet) thought out and activated in the sphere of the state (perhaps with exceptions like Evo Morales in Bolivia), but in the domain of what Partha Chatterjee identifies as "political society."[28] That is, the sphere of the "civil society," conceived by Hegel in the framework of liberal cos-mopolitanism and the secular order of society, has been expanded, mainly in the twentieth century, by the irruption and disruption of the "political society," part of which is described as "social movements." Decolonial cos-mopolitanism shall be placed in the sphere of political society, although not necessarily the entire sphere of political society would endorse decolo-nial options. Once again, we are dealing with the domain of the pluriversal and truth in parenthesis. Decolonial cosmopolitan projects, as I am argu-ing here, are contending with the sphere of coloniality; that is, within the formation and transformation of the colonial matrix of power as described above.

In any event, whatever the genealogy of thoughts and feelings, decolonial cosmopolitanism emerges from the borders, in exteriority, in the realm of colonial difference, while cosmopolitanism, in its different versions (Orbis

Christianus, globalism) was concocted and enacted in and from the metropolitan centers. Actors imagining, enacting, and advancing decolonial projects would most likely come from either the "damnés de la terre," the wretched of the earth, in Fanon's expression, or from actors who, not belonging to the damnés, have joined the cause and shifted their geography of reasoning from imperiality to decoloniality. The margins are places, histories, and people who, not being at once Christians and secular Europeans, were forced to deal with the encroachment of their modernity.

Some Decolonial Orientations

If cosmopolitanism is a Western concern with two faces—the imperial face of globalism and the Westernization of the world (de Vitoria, Grotius, Kant) and the internal critique of Westernization in the past two decades (Ulrich Beck, Anthony Appiah)—and if, in spite of it, we would like to maintain cosmopolitan ideals, then decolonial cosmopolitianism shall be a concern of all parties involved, each local history and interest, and shall shift or move beyond those two Western faces.

What could be "beyond the two Western faces of the cosmopolis"? Is there any real possibility of thinking and projecting futures without following the blueprint of globalism or of Western critical cosmopolitanism? "Human" interests do not stem from the Big Bang or from God's creation of the world, but from the imperial and modern/colonial world order, on the axis of colonial and imperial differences. Thus, scholars, intellectuals, and activists in the non-European world have their own concerns, and their own concerns have been expressed (although none of them has made the "breaking news") around "independent thought," rather than around cosmopolitanism. So, then, responding to the question of cosmopolitan localism and decolonial futures would involve, first, following up on the demands and needs being expressed around the world, rather than projecting Eurocentered demands and needs around the world. Let's take the following three cases as examples, to flesh out and to better understand the point of my argument.

The first case comes from "Extractions and Refinement of Cultural Resources," one of the finest and most revealing lectures Ali Shari'ati ever delivered. (It was first delivered in the 1970s; however, it was not published until 1981, in the volume *Man and Islam*.) In that lecture, which is a combination of scholarship, intellectual gaze, and political direction, he stated,

> It is impossible to achieve economic independence without having achieved
> spiritual independence, and vice versa. These two are interdependent as well
> as complimentary conditions. In order to have an independent character in
> the material, social, and economic sphere, we must develop an independent
> consciousness before the West and vice versa. What should we do, and in
> what way? We must know that the best teacher for regaining and wresting
> one's independence and national character [remember Kant on national
> characters] is the enemy (or enemies) who robbed us of our independence
> and national character. Therefore, we must develop consciousness of how
> the West has deprived us of our cultural and spiritual resources and con-
> sequently trained a generation of Easterners who have lost the capability of
> utilizing their rich treasure of thought, ethics, spirit, and culture. In reality we
> have become estranged from these resources. We must search for the steps
> that the West has taken, as well as the methods, and the stratagems it has
> used to succeed and reach its goals in the East, to such an extent that she has
> accused the grand East, the origin, cradle, and the fountain of Western man's
> civilization and culture, of savagery, backwardness, and corruptions. Once
> we study and find the tracks through which the West has entered our lands,
> we can then retrace them and return to the origin.[29]

Well, this seems to be a provocation to cosmopolitan projects. Are not
cosmopolitans against this kind of vision? And does not cosmopolitanism seek to get out of precisely this kind of "national" and "local thinking"
about origins, when the origin is not Greece? But notice two aspects of this
paragraph. The first one is the decolonial concept of the political. For Carl
Schmitt the political was defined in terms of foe-friend relations. But Schmitt
was mainly thinking with Western Europe in mind at that time. He was not
yet into *The* Nomos *of the Earth* (see chapter 2) and tracing the history of
imperial international relations. And when he did, the European scene in
which he formulated the concept of the political had vanished. Global linear thinking and doing created a different scenario, wherein the political
was defined in the struggle between imperial designs and local histories.
Shari'ati's work is a case in point. He does not define the political in terms of
foes and friends, following Schmitt's formula, but takes the decolonial arena

into account. The political is no longer defined between foes and friends within Eurocentrism itself, but rather in the terrain where Eurocentric ideals move toward *it*, uninvited. The political is located in another realm, in another space of the geopolitics of knowledge: the political becomes decolonial, for it has to deal with the decolonization of the political as defined by the confrontation between foes and friends in the territory of Western imperial Europe. It cannot be subsumed under Schmitt's concept of the political; it stretches it; and, because it is more capacious, applies to any situation around the globe—beyond the local history of Germany. Therefore, Schmitt and Shari'ati both provide local definitions of the political, under dissimilar conditions, to solve dissimilar local problems. Schmitt was facing the confrontation between Western European empires and his struggle with liberalism. Shari'ati was facing the confrontation of the Western imperial powers (whose problems Schmitt was trying to solve) in Iran and trying to solve the problem of European interference (e.g., Occidentalism). There is no reason for one to be universal and the other not, for imperial modernity goes together with coloniality. The problem for Schmitt was Western Europe; the problem for Shari'ati was coloniality in Iran. There is no reason to give the priority to Schmitt to be universal (unless one defends imperial European ideals) and Shari'ati to be local. That distinction is one of the basic pillars of the coloniality of knowledge that ends up, more often than not, in epistemic racism. Schmitt was dealing with the political in Germany, while Shari'ati was dealing with the political at the junction of Iranian history and Western European interventions. Thus, critical Western cosmopolitanism may not bow to projects of cosmopolitan localism; their representatives bring to the table sensibilities, conceptual tools, demands, and needs that can no longer be satisfied with recognition and concessions that would merely maintain the one-sided cosmopolitan vision. In other words, a one-way cosmopolitanism is a local concern of Western scholarship, as I said; and it is out of place if the pretense is to update Kant to the imperial needs of the West in the twenty-first century. If cosmopolitan ideals shall be maintained, they shall be decolonial. Therefore, decolonial cosmopolitanism would be a central issue in either the dispute over control of or delinking from the colonial matrix of power that I described in chapter 1.

The second example I would put forward is that of Lloyd Best, introduced in chapter 2 from a different angle. Although one of the towering figures of Caribbean thought, naturally, little is known of him in mainstream scholarship.[30] Imagine a question-and-answer session after a talk in which the names of Shari'ati and Best have been invoked, or that some of their work was explained; imagine too that someone in the audience brought Nietzsche into the picture. One can assume that bringing Nietzsche into the picture may have been provoked by the intellectual profile of both Shari'ati and Best; both are, like Nietzsche, irreverent and provocative. It is safe to assume that the imaginary interlocutor does not know who Shari'ati and Best are; so someone must fill the gap in his knowledge and familiarize himself with the work of men who quite legitimately fall within the category of "irreverent and provocative thinkers." Naturally, there are some connections between Shar'iati and Best, and Nietzsche—chiefly, that they were deeply ingrained in and concerned with their time and situation. But that is not the point of the question. The point is that of the three, only Nietzsche's name is likely to be known. I would wonder, while responding to the question in a polite way, what Nietzsche would have said if he had visited Iran and the Caribbean and had a good long conversation with Shari'ati and Best. I imagine that if the three of them had learned from each other and then returned to deal with their own situations and continued working together, it would have been a successful cosmopolitical summit. However, that is not what I would suspect was presupposed in any questions I was asked about Nietzsche. (Keep in mind that in this imagined talk I had not mentioned Nietzsche.) I would guess that the person asking the question was thoroughly unfamiliar with Shari'ati and Best; furthermore, I would suspect that Nietzsche was a security blanket for this person, who had also, perhaps, asked with the secret hope that I would endorse Nietzsche as someone who was first, or ahead of these other thinkers regarding the issues that Shari'ati and Best were dealing with.

But now you may wonder what Shari'ati, an Iranian, and Best, a Trinidadian from the Caribbean, have to do with each other? Much, indeed, but this commonality does not tend to make the "breaking news." In the publisher's preface to *Man and Islam* this story is told.

> Dr. Shari'ati gained significant experiences as a result of his interactions with Dr. Frantz Fanon, the Algerian spokesman, while he was residing in Paris. So impressed was Shari'ati with this young psychiatrist, for both his reveal-

ing analysis of the racist character of French imperialism and his unwavering sacrifices in helping shape the dynamics of the Algerian struggle, that he is inspired to translate into Persian several of Fanon's works, including highlights of one of his most memorable achievements, *The Wretched of the Earth*.[31]

Connections between Shari'ati and Fanon abound. What they have in common is the darker side of Western modernity that they perceived and felt in their skin from their respective local histories. Commonalities that have not been perceived by imperial narratives that tell stories from above and ethno-national histories told from inside. The job of decolonial thinkers and doers is precisely to bring those relations (most generally ignored as the anecdote about Nietzsche indicates) to the foreground, which is crucial to imagine and plan the future. First of all, both share the colonial wound, at different times and in different spaces. When you read Kant, for example, you will understand that even if Africans were placed at the bottom of the chain of human beings and "national Arabs" were taken as the ethnicity of what is today the Middle East, both ethnic groups were considered below standards.

It is not by chance that one of Best's classic articles is titled "Independent Thought and Caribbean Freedom."[32] Notice that Shari'ati's first sentence of that article, "It is impossible to achieve economic independence without having achieved spiritual independence, and vice versa." Best's titles are almost identical. There is no influence to be anxious about here. It is just the commonality of decolonial thought, prompted by the colonial wound; it doesn't matter whether one is writing about Iran, the Caribbean, Algeria, or the young girl in the Chiapas market, stating that the Zapatistas returned dignity to the Indians. And notice also that both link "independent thought with freedom." Freedom, however, is not always and naturally connected with independent thought. This is the decolonial view. A liberal ideal of freedom would be related to economic growth. Indeed, the Nobel Laureate Amartya Sen would see a natural connection between "development with freedom" (I will return to this topic in the afterword). The parallel here between benevolent development à la Amartya Sen and Western cosmopolitanism, on the one hand, and independent thought and decolonial freedom, on the other, as the major claim to engage in cosmopolitan localism shows two of the conflicting horizons in the quest toward convivial futures.

Let's pursue this argument further (and connect it with chapter 2) by returning to Lloyd Best's unfolding of "independent thoughts":

> It is being proposed here, that being who we are, what we are and where, the kind of action to which we must be committed is determinate. Action in the field, if it is not to be blind, presupposes theory. To acknowledge this is to set ourselves three tasks. The first is to fashion theory on which may be based the clear intellectual leadership for which the nation calls and which it has never had. The second is to conduct the enquiry on which theory can be soundly based. This is what may be called, in the jargon of my original trade, the creation of intellectual capital goods. Thirdly, we are to establish media by which these goods may be transmitted to the rest of us who are otherwise engaged. As one of our statements in the New World has put it: we may wish to create a media of direct democratic expression suitable to the native Caribbean imagination.[33]

The quote above tells clearly what "being when one does and thinks" means, and how doing and independent thought are the starting point of this particular decolonial project and, by extension, of any engagement with cosmopolitan localisms not as one design, but as the place where decolonial pluriversality takes place, where, again, Nietzsche's, Shari'ati's, and Best's legacies could coexist in guiding our thinking about how to coexist and work through differences without anxiety about any sort of imposition, be it forcing democracy, cosmopolitanism, the free market, or a given religion.

Now bring dewesternization into the picture. Still another horizon opens, one that further complicates the future of cosmopolitan scenarios; in this situation, development and freedom, independent thought, and decolonial freedom contend with one another. Kishore Mahbubani quotes at length a paragraph by Professor Wu Zengding, who, according to Mahbubani, gives us a hint of debates taking place (not well known in the West) in China that parallel the daily debates about international and economic relations that the Western press reports on profusely. As one may suspect, there is more going on in China beyond the economic and political strength than is highlighted in the European Union and U.S. mainstream media. There is also the question of humiliation and dignity that I pointed out in chapter 1, when I introduced dewesternization. Cosmopolitan projects, in other words, cannot obviate the history of Western racism; the colonial wound is not limited to the subalterns or the damnés; it cuts across social strata. Dignity (the key word of the young girl in the Chiapas market) and humiliation endured during centuries of control and management of knowledge that implanted the idea—and the Chinese themselves at some point bought into it—that Asians cannot think and that China is a glory of the past. Development and freedom are not enough to deal with long-lasting humiliation, and apologies are not enough to heal colonial/imperial wounds. Professor Wu Zengding comments,

> The construction of new China, the great achievement in reform and opening up for over twenty years, is a further manifestation of the vitality of Chinese civilization. Thus the success of over twenty years of reform and opening up firstly affirms the great revolution and the construction of China, it then also affirms the strength of the Chinese nation, but mostly it affirms the authenticity of the Chinese civilization and tradition. It is this strength rather than some song and dance in praise of globalization and international practices that has brought China through. This is not a form of narrow-minded xenophobia, but it is the great faith and hope one can place in the ancient Chinese civilization.[34]

Most cosmopolitans would object to this statement, too, since it is precisely what cosmopolitanism would like to overcome. One of the common objections is that statements such as the one just quoted are hypocritical justifications of capitalist economy. Sure they are; but in that regard there is not much difference in justifying capitalism by celebrating neo-liberal globalism—as opposed to justifying it by appealing to Chinese tradition and Confucianism. Take your pick, globalism or nationalism? But such an objection would not be fair. Why not? Because it doesn't recognize the colonial/imperial wound, or the fact that Chinese nationalism is a response to Western neo-liberalism, that the first engendered the second in the same way that state terrorism engenders terrorism in the political society. That these are not roads to cosmopolitan futures seems obvious. But it also makes obvious the fact that cosmopolitan futures cannot be realized with a master plan and a one-way street.

Concluding Remarks

Bruno Latour explained that the misunderstanding between himself and Ulrich Beck on the idea of "cosmopolitanism" lay in their differing interpretations of the historical present, which, of course, is understandable. More explicitly,

> The "first modernization," to use his [Beck's] favorite expression, came with a certain definition of cosmopolitanism, which corresponded to the great idea that the whole earth could actually fit snugly inside what Sloterdijk has called the "metaphysical Globe" (as imagined by Mercator, Galileo, Descartes, Leibniz and of course Hegel). *The problem is that when this version of the global was invented the world was just beginning to be globalized. The Globe on which Hegel could rely to house every event "in it" was a purely conceptual one; it was for this reason perfect, with neither shadow nor gap.*[35]

But that situation no longer holds, in the sense that globalism ended with the metaphysical globe. The end of the metaphysical Globe is being replaced—in my view and as I explained in chapter 1—by a polycentric capitalist world. Decolonial cosmopolitanism, instead, looks and works toward pluriversal futures that are only possible if the reign of economic capitalism ends. In this regard, and as Elena Yehia has convincingly argued, there are many compatibilities between Latour's position in Europe and the project modernity/coloniality/decoloniality in the Americas and the Caribbean.[36]

Therefore, concludes Latour, another definition of *cosmopolitics* is called for, one that does not rely on the "first modernity" dream of an already existing common sphere. It would be a tragic mistake to pursue peace by dragging in the defunct "Globe" as a locus for the common world of cosmopolitanism. Since Ulrich Beck does not wish to be Munich's Hegel, he knows fairly well that the parliament in which a common world could be assembled has got to start from scratch.[37]

Looking at this European exchange on cosmopolitanism, between a French philosopher and anthropologist and a German sociologist, is indeed very interesting. I imagine that it would also be interesting to look at it from the perspective of Islam.[38] After all, *Umma* is, in my understanding, a word whose meaning captures what Western cosmopolitans have been concerned with since Kant. *Umma* was reduced to a religious concept by

Western secular interpretations, though it connotes social solidarity and cultural identification beyond ethnic and regional boundaries. Is that not a cosmopolitan ideal? Another complication emerges here in cosmopolitan debates—the cosmopolitanism of a community. "Muslim cosmopolitanism" reminds us that there cannot be "cosmopolitanism" as such; that when "cosmopolitanism" is being invoked without a modifier, it is either "liberal cosmopolitanism," "Marxist cosmopolitanism," or perhaps "postmodern cosmopolitanism" (all three post-Kantian cosmopolitanisms).[39] I wonder, also, how much interest Western debates on cosmopolitanism will awaken among all of those in East Asia who are working hard on de-westernization instead of on cosmopolitanism, or among the Ecuadorians and Bolivians who are very much involved in debating and solving problems about future plurinational states—efforts, which, in the last analysis, have cosmopolitan seeds in them. In fact, debates are taking place in both countries on how inter-culturality (indeed inter-epistemology) could help in building global and decolonial cosmopolitan futures.[40] Doesn't cosmopolitan localism presuppose inter-cultural and inter-epistemic relations? And are we not witnessing in Bolivia and Ecuador that the very concept of a plurinational state is already a local way of dealing with cosmopolitan issues? If we fail to understand that it is, it would be because we are still thinking cosmopolitanism in the same way we think about globalism: as a master plan concocted and executed from above. If not, how could liberal and Muslim cosmopolitanism coexist? Decolonial cosmopolitanism is not one more among others, but a project that promotes the shift in the terms of the conversation: from imperial cosmopolitanism (or cosmopolitanism without modifiers and without parenthesis) to cosmopolitan localisms (coexistence of cosmopolitanism with modifiers and with parenthesis). That is to say, inter-culturality and inter-epistemology should prevent the phenomenon in which one culture and one epistemology come to be considered good enough for the entire "metaphysical Globe."

Your location in the colonial matrix of power shapes the way you look at the world. A related question concerns your location in the colonial matrix of power. Notwithstanding either "location," cosmopolitanism may be invigorating, or depressing, or not really a concern. For those of us for whom it is a concern, it is invigorating. Latour's pluriveral cosmopolis and decolonial cosmopolitan localism could join forces in promoting the coexistence of cosmopolitanism, with modifiers and in parenthesis. To what extent cosmopolitan localism may lead to a polycentric and noncapitalist world is still a question. And to what extent cosmopolitanism of any sort is viable and sustainable under global capitalism is still another, more pressing one. What is certain is that cosmopolitan localism has of necessity to operate on truth in parenthesis and border thinking—cosmopolitan localism means decolonial cosmopolitanism. I will explore these questions further in the afterword.

"Freedom to Choose" and the Decolonial Option
Notes toward Communal Futures

THE IDEAS, MANY of which will unfold through years of engaged political work, need not be perfect, for in the end, it will be the hard, creative work of the communities that take them on. That work is the concrete manifestation of political imagination. Fanon described this goal as setting afoot a new humanity. He knew how terrifying such an effort is; for we do live in times for which such a radical break appears as no less than the end of the world. In the meantime, the task of building infrastructures for something new must be planned, and where there is some room, attempted. As we all no doubt already know, given the sociogenic dimension of the problem, we have no other option than to build the options on which the future of our species rest.[1]

Take, for instance, the Plan of the Millennium. The UN appoints committees to work with other committees that are appointed by the ten or so industrialized countries; they involve prestigious universities and include distinguished scholars; they all produce reports that are used to raise funds to fight poverty; ironically, they solicit this money from the same people whose wealth is founded on the system that produces poverty, and whose policies keep it in place. The same vicious circle informs the fight against pollution and global warming—commissions spend money on committees; they host summits and hold conferences in luxurious places; then they write reports that they use, likewise, to solicit support (in this case for environmental protection) from those who make money polluting the environment.[2]

Closing Down

If building options appears today as the unavoidable option (which is tanta-mount to pluriversality as a universal project and to decolonial cosmopoli-tanism), it is because Western modernity, in all its diversity (from theologi-cal to secular frames, from the common code of all the disciplines in the social sciences and humanities, the professional schools, performance, art and visual studies), with all the implied consequences of imperial diver-sity (quite different from the decolonial pluriversality I am advocating), has been built since the sixteenth century, and increasingly it is being viewed as the only and best option for the entire planet. A set of key concepts has been advanced such as Christian God, Humanitas, Democracy, Socialism, Sciences, Reason, Beauty, Faith, Freedom, Progress, Development, and so on. While there have been internal debates on the politics of knowledge, within Western civilization around each of these concepts, the internal "differences" and debates have been carried on under the presupposition that Western civilization has it and that the rest of the world, all coexisting civilizations, languages, and epistemologies had nothing to contribute. It is in confrontation with the *diversity of the only option* (the Western way) that dewesternization and decolonialization arise. Both trajectories are contributing to multiply the options and to limit the Western option (re-westernization) to one among several.

Dewesternizing "Freedom"

I return here to Kishore Mahbubani. Needless to say, I am interpreting dewesternization from the perspective of decoloniality. Mine is not a dis-ciplinary (sociological, historical, political theory, philosophy, etc.), but a decolonial perspective that has drawn from, when necessary, existing disci-plinary formations. One of the key points in the dewesternizing argument is the concept of "freedom." The same concept is also a key in an influential book titled *Development as Freedom* (1999) by Amartya Sen, a Nobel Prize-winner in economics. Sen's book was written at the closing moment of the cycle of Westernization (1500–2000) but doesn't contradict the process of rewesternization initiated by President Obama. I bring Sen's argument into the conversation here for two reasons. One is that Sen's argument may be confused with dewesternization, when in reality what he proposes falls in line with rewesternization. Not that Sen was supporting neo-liberal projects at that time. His argument, parallel to those advanced by the philosopher and entrepreneur George Soros, looks for a form of capitalism with a good heart, which, of course, is a logical dead end. If modernity cannot be detached from coloniality, it is because modernity and capitalism show the pretty face of progress and hide the ugly face of the costs and consequences. Contrary to the lack of concern in neo-liberal thought, Sen was well aware, and clearly reminds us through the book, of the increasing gaps between have and have-not. He believes in development and that development is the road to freedom. I will come back below to the question of "development." Now I want to concentrate on "freedom."

Let me start by juxtaposing Sen's position with a controversial statement by Mahbubani, in which he claims that the concept of freedom was invented and used in the process of Westernization and would most likely continue to be used in what I describe here as the process of rewesternization: "The Western incapacity to see how happy most Chinese are with their current condition reveals how ideologically biased Western observers have become. The Western mind cannot conceive of the possibility that the 'unfree' people of China could possibly be happy. The Western mind has a rigid, one-dimensional, and ideological understanding of the term 'freedom.'"[3]

Mahbubani continues to characterize the Western concept of freedom as being presented as an absolute virtue in such a way that it has to be total, a totality. Therefore, the idea that freedom can be "relative" and can take many forms is, according to Mahbubani, alien to the Western mind. From the perspective of China and the Chinese, at least a sector of the population, comparing "their lives today with their lives a few decades ago," Mahbubani concludes, feel they have achieved much greater "freedom." Therefore, he argues, instead of assuming a unified condition for the notion of human freedom, it is necessary to work with concepts and conditions that were con-natural to Western history, not in absolute terms, but in terms of imperial/colonial conditions: China, for example, has to deal with a concept (freedom) that did not emerge from its own history. Which doesn't mean that the Chinese were "lacking" something—"freedom" is not a universal concept coming from God, but a regional concept invented in certain places, at certain times, and by certain "men." Nor does it suggest that Chinese are totalitarian by nature because they did not come up with such a word.[4] It is at this point that border thinking and border epistemology is unavoidable for dewesternization: "freedom" has to be engaged, but it cannot be engaged from the very history of the West. It has to be engaged from the history of the non-Western world upon which the concept of freedom was impinged. From this argument Mahbubani comes up with a series of issues related to "dewesternizing freedom." Going through some of the issues will help in understanding the connections and differences between the five trajectories: rewesternization, reorientation of the Left, dewesternization, decoloniality, and the spiritual option. This will help clarify the relevance of multiplying options and avoiding reduction to one abstract universal—it doesn't matter which one—since any and all abstract universals struggle to reduce options to one: to a totalitarian one.

The first postulate of human freedom is, for Mahbubani, freedom from want, for the simple reason that "a human being who cannot feed himself or his family cannot possibly be free. Famine is more damaging to human freedom than a politically closed society." Therefore, as a consequence of China's economic growth, "Chinese people had never enjoyed greater human freedom."[5]

We can certainly argue that there is still poverty and exploitation in China; but at the same time, it has been recognized internationally that indeed China's economic growth has lifted many out of poverty and created a consumerist middle class. The success of China's efforts confront Western liberal and neo-liberal criticisms, as China is doing what Western modernity has advocated for a long time. China's success cuts the wings of Western aspirations and poses a serious challenge to liberal and neo-liberal possibilities of dominance. Mahbubani's argument shows, in a nutshell, that rewesternization is not the only option. On the other hand, if proponents of Westernization want to export democracy, why not "export" the well-being of what was the U.S. middle class until recently? What is wrong with China doing the "bad" things that Western imperial states and corporations did and continue to do? And why hide the many problems associated with Katrina's cleanup, while critiquing the way Chinese capitalism is moving? I am not defending China. I am trying to understand and explain Mahbubani's argument, which does not pit China against the West. Instead, the significance of Mahbubani's argument is that it, above all, shows that the (re)westerning option is no longer the only game in town. We may like it or not; but that is the way the world order is moving. I am not trying to defend or promote Mahbubani's analysis either, but just trying to understand the logic of dewesternization in historical context, rather than in terms of a utopian future, however paradiselike it may be. There is a limit, however, in Mahbubani's "freedom to choose"; that is, his belief that a capitalist economy allows for the freedom to choose your work. There are two fallacies in his argument. The first one, as we frequently see and saw again after the collapse of Wall Street, is that you may not have the freedom to choose your job because there may be no job to choose. Second, even if you are fortunate enough to belong to the less than 5 percent for whom it is possible to choose a preferred job, still "you have to choose" from among offerings or selections that you did not contribute to creating. And by so doing you blind yourself to the fact that there are many other options that have been successfully silenced and erased as options. When, for instance, La Via Campesina opts for and chooses the freedom of their own sense of economy and their own destiny by working for themselves, we find out that corporations like Monsanto and Syngenta as well as the governments supporting these companies move to disallow that kind of choice: "freedom to choose" in a capitalist economy is the freedom to choose only among the capitalist economic options. Since La Via Campesina is putting forward a decolonial option, that is not what rewesternization would support. The situation would be more ambiguous for the dewesternizing option, for the issues are not economic decisions that have to go through the political sphere in which de- and rewesternization compete for the control of the colonial matrix of power. Because Western governments and corporations are still controlling the rules of the game, rewesternization is less restricted than the possibilities that the dewesternizing option has. In a nutshell: in the dispute for the management of the colonial matrix, China is still in a subaltern position, if you wish. Freedom to choose within a capitalist economy is reminiscent of democracy, wherein the freedom to vote means that you elect the government that will use your vote against you. Here is where dewesternization and decoloniality find a common ground in their efforts to underline and reveal the limits of the "development and freedom" formula. This common ground doesn't mean that dewesternization and decoloniality have one and the same goals.

The second postulate of human freedom is freedom of security: "The only way to enjoy freedom is to stay alive. Dead people do not enjoy Freedom. Any society that creates higher conditions of security improves the real and practical freedoms that people can enjoy, while a society that diminishes personal security also diminishes human freedom."[6] Well, you can object, what about Tiananmen? The Tiananmen example shows a situation in which security and safety were at odds. And you would be right if you thought that such an event could not be forgotten. At the same time, it doesn't disqualify the argument Mahbubani is making: many people living in Iraq have a hard time believing that they now have greater freedom than they had under Hussein. Mahbubani topped the argument by assuming that many Iraqis would like to go to Beijing, while it would be hard to find many people in Beijing who would like to go to Baghdad.

A third postulate of human freedom could apparently run parallel to Sen's "development and freedom." Mahbubani underlines the fact that because of the Industrial Revolution and because China joined a market economy, millions of Chinese have the freedom to choose their own jobs. His argument is that, except during the past thirty years (since Deng Xiaoping opened up China to capitalist economy), the Chinese were restricted in their freedom to choose their jobs because simply the options were not there. From a decolonial perspective, the problem with this argument is the lack of distinction between work and labor, and the fact that the Industrial Revolution allowed for the rhetoric of modernity to make waged labor premium labor while living labor was left behind and conceptualized as traditional labor; that is, non-modern. The Industrial Revolution indeed expanded labor options, but at the same time it shut down the options for living beyond waged labor. It also reduced people's ability to choose their own lifestyles—as farmers, for example, or in communal organizations organized around living labor. What the Industrial Revolution apparently created were *options within the same option* (that is, opportunities): waged labor, rather than being an option, became an obligation and the illusion was the possibility to choose among different kinds of waged labor. Within the fluctuation of the labor market, the millions of people who lost their jobs because of the Wall Street crisis are not only unemployed, but have been deprived of the possibility of thinking and acting, of organizing their lives and their communities, on the basis of living labor and not waged labor.

Waged labor is indeed a form of colonizing being; it exemplifies the hidden logic of coloniality. Under the illusion that they have the freedom to choose your labor (rhetoric of modernity), the unemployed have been reduced to human beings whose best hope is to wait for the economy to recover and to make waged labor again possible. What I am trying to rescue from Mahbubani is that he does not make universal claims, as Sen does; instead, he pushes the argument of dewesternization. And dewesternizing arguments allow us to better understand the logic of coloniality underlining Sen's argument. Mahbuabani's goal is to show that "freedom of choice" in labor is another way of thinking about freedom, while in Sen's argument, freedom is not associated with labor, but with development.

A fourth postulate of human freedom is freedom of expression, and I will quote here at length.

> The growing conviction among Muslims of the malevolent intentions of the West toward the Islamic world has been strongly reinforced by several Western actions since the end of the Cold War. Many Muslims now believe that the West, for all of its respect for the sanctity of human life (which is reflected in the abolition of the death penalty by the European Union), shows scant concern when innocent Muslim civilians are killed. The United States launched a huge global furor in 1983, when the Soviet Union downed a Korean civilian airliner, yet it showed little remorse when the US Navy guided missile cruisers of USS *Vincennes* downed an Iranian civilian airliner in 1988 in the Gulf. Muslims will also mention the initial silence of the West when Muslim citizens were slaughtered in Bosnia (and Dutch soldiers actually handed over young Muslim men to be immediately killed by Serbian warlords). They remember too the launch of cruise missiles into Afghanistan in 1998 in retaliations for the bombings of US embassies in Kenya and Tanzania. The US attack did not kill Osama bin Laden but twenty-one Afghan civilians.[7]

If the previous statement was closer to Amartya Sen's concept of development as freedom, this fourth postulate gets closer to decolonial claims about the dispensability of human life based on racial classification. Mahbubani is not making this argument. He is pointing out Western double standards. Thus, while the double standard argument made from a dewesternizing perspective could be supported, it should also be pushed further to show the connections between double standards and the colonial matrix of power.

By this I mean that double standard arguments show to the public the rhetoric of modernity in its many forms (human rights, freedom, democracy) condemning the lack thereof among non-Western countries while hiding, at the same time the logic of coloniality (violation of human rights, freedom, democracy) by actors and institutions that present themselves as defenders of the values that they themselves transgress. Is the charge of double standard applicable to China? Perhaps. But what cannot be charged to China is control of mainstream global media. And here is where the ethical and political side of the argument joins the control of popular knowledge manipulated by mainstream imperial media.

One more example: this one about the Western idea that the Chinese—like the Russians—do not have the freedom to leave their country. The argument is based on an anecdote about when Deng Xiaoping visited the United States and was received by President Jimmy Carter. According to the anecdote, Carter told Xiaoping that Congress had passed a law, in 1974, permitting normal trade relations with countries that allowed free emigration. (One of the goals of the law, according to Carter, was to put pressure on the Soviet Union to allow free emigration of Jews. Apparently, Carter was not interested in the emigration of non-Jews from the Soviet Union.) Xiaoping, who had listened carefully, responded: "How many Chinese would you like me to allow to emigrate to the United States? One million? Ten million? A hundred million? You can have as many as you want."[8] Mahbubani argues that China "saved" the United States from a massive Chinese migration. By adopting and adapting a free-market economy, China could create conditions in which people would not want to emigrate. The punch line of the argument was that "America had effectively 'liberated' hundreds of millions of Chinese, even though they were still perceived to be technically held captive by the CCP [Communist Party of China]."[9]

Let's now turn to the decolonial option.

Decolonizing Development

In "Population, Food and Freedom" (chapter 9 in *Development as Freedom*), Amartya Sen focuses on freedom in relation to food and argues that the problem cannot be properly addressed by concentrating on food output only. He recognizes this as only *one* of the variables, albeit an important one, since the price consumers have to pay is affected by the size of the food output. In this context, the issue raised by Sen that I would like to concentrate on is the following: "Furthermore, when we consider food problems at the global level (rather than at the national or local level), there is obviously no opportunity of *getting food from 'outside' the economy*. For these reasons, the often-aired fear that food production per head is falling in the world cannot be dismissed out of hand."[10]

On the other hand, another Indian scholar (based in New Delhi, not in Cambridge) has a different view of development. Ashis Nandy opened his essay "The Beautiful Future of Poverty: Popular Economics as Psychological Defense" with the following words: "The undying myth of development, that it will remove all poverty forever from all corners of he world, now lies shattered. It is surprising that so many people believed it for so many years with such admirable innocence. After all, even societies that have witnessed unprecedented prosperity during the last five decades, such as the United States of America, have not been able to exile either poverty or destitution from within their borders."[11]

The key expression in Sen's statement is "there is obviously no opportunity of getting food from 'outside' the economy." What economy? Sen is not questioning "capitalist" economy. By "capitalism" I mean that which many have been desperate to save by re-imagining its future after the debacle of the Wall Street collapse and its global consequences. Along these lines, the *Financial Times* compiled articles in a newspaper supplement, published on 12 May 2009, titled "The Future of Capitalism: The Big Debate." The issue is revealing on many counts. Nothing equivalent was published about the "food crisis," since the food crisis did not endanger the life of capitalism (only the lives of billions of people living under or just above the poverty line). Thus, "saving capitalism" means the preservation of the institution by those who benefit from the institution and who believe or pretend that saving capitalism will be beneficial for all, by resulting, among other things, in the end of poverty, of corruption and immorality to get ahead, of the will to accumulate and be competitive in order to succeed, disregarding the consequences. Furthermore, on 13 May, the *Financial Times* published—in the same series, "The Future of Capitalism"—an op-ed by Lezek Balcerowicz, a former Polish deputy prime minister and governor of the National Bank of Poland. The op-ed has a great opening: "Only the rulers of Cuba,

Venezuela, Iran and some ideologies in the west condemn capitalism. Empirically minded people know that there is no good alternative. However, capitalism takes forms and evolves over time. The questions to ask, then, are 'What capitalism?' and 'Does the present crisis shed new light on this issue?'"[12] And Balcerowicz concludes, after pondering these two questions, and confirming his own intuition, that there is no alternative to capitalism: "Dynamic, entrepreneurial capitalism has nowadays no serious external enemies. It can only be weakened from within. This should be regarded as a call to action—for those who believe that individual's prosperity and dignity are best ensured under limited government."[13] Capitalism, in a nutshell, is the hegemonic structure, philosophy, and value of economy in the past five hundred years; this doesn't mean that it is the only option or the best. It is only the best or the only option for those who have built it, benefit from it, and therefore are interested in maintaining it. But, as I have been arguing, there are many choices for managing capitalist economy beyond the U.S. and the EU. Today we are witnessing dewesternization (China, Singapore, Indonesia, Brazil); or "socialism of the twenty-first century" (Venezuela); "capitalismo andino-amazónico" (Bolivia). On the other hand there are growing claims of working decolonially toward noncapitalist economic future.

Nandy's words are a call for "dignity" and "prosperity" rather than for development and growth. What if you do not want the economy of growth, or do not want the technology that modernity and capitalism brought to us? This is a common question when these arguments are advanced. The counter questions are: Why should "growth and development" be the goals of the economy if "success and domination" were not two of its main drivers? The world needs a well-organized economy, not one based on gains (which brings corruption), or that puts personal and institutional interests (and the person managing those institutions) ahead of people. Why do we need "growth and development" if we know that the beauties that the rhetoric of modernity promotes hide and dismiss the "growth and development of poverty?" As for the second question, yes, I am for "technological innovations," but not at the expense of Third World regions that pay the costs of transnational mining (which provide natural resources for the technological industry) that are poisoning the rivers and exhausting the soil that are the "sources of life" for entire populations?[14] However you look at it, "development" is a capitalist mission; as such, it would undermine whatever population and whatever region that is useless for such a mission. The challenge is to think in economic terms that are satisfactory for living, rather than in economic terms that increase control over management and that satisfy personal needs through the accumulation of wealth by any means. The means to the end of accumulation change, but accumulation remains the horizon of development; and not for distribution, of course. Growth, as we know it, benefits perhaps one billion of the almost seven billion people on the planet (as of 2009). The beneficiaries, however, do not benefit equally. They are organized in concentric circles. The smallest circle, in the privileged center, comprises perhaps 1 percent of the total population, and the outermost circle, of workers and consumers, consists of perhaps 10 percent of the total population.

I am not equating Sen's observation squarely with that of Balcerowicz. There are differences, certainly. Balcerowicz is concerned with prosperity, while Sen is concerned with solving problems of hunger, injustice, and inequality. Sen believes that capitalist development is the way to freedom. Development, for Sen, doesn't mean prosperity in the way it does for Balcerowicz. Balcerowicz is also an interesting example of the persuasive force of conversion: capitalism has to find not only converts in Eastern Europe and other parts of the world, but converts who take an active role in defending capitalism. The politics of conversion applies as well to millions of workers (employees) in the financial and technological sector (and, of course, university professors) who defend the creed of "innovation" and maintain that capitalism promotes "innovation." This is another argument that colonizes the human bent toward creativity, and casts it in terms of "capitalism and innovation," that is, in a formula that parallels "development and freedom."

In Latin America and the Caribbean and other parts of the world, "development" has been a kind of crucifixion since projects of modernization and development began after the Second World War. "Dependency theory" emerged precisely as a contestation of the impossibility of the fiction of developing underdeveloped countries to close the gaps between First World and Third.[15] From the perspective of those who are at the receiving end of capitalism, there are two stages to focus on in the past sixty years. The first stage, that of modernization and development, wound down in the global crisis of 1968, ushering in the end of the welfare state and the beginning of the neo-liberal projects that started in Chile after the fall of Salvador Allende, in 1973. The second stage, neo-liberal development as globalism, started in the 1980s and ended with the collapse of Wall Street, of General Motors, of Lehman Brothers, and of the "triumph" of the capitalist market economy.

However, a turning point—a conceptual Pachakuti—took place with the affirmation of indigenous political society and its reshaping of Western political theory and political economy. There are various examples of this in the past thirty years that have been expressed by different indigenous organizations, including the Indigenous Leaders Summit of the Americas, the Confederation of Indigenous Nationalities of Ecuador (CONAIE), Amawtay Wasi University, also in Ecuador, etc.; however, the impact has been achieved primarily through various declarations, discourses, open letters, and interviews with Evo Morales. More recently, the impact of indigenous concepts of "to live in fullness, to live in plenitude" (*sumak kawsay, suma kamaña*) has the virtue of re-directing a previously Marxist/socialist/theology of liberation, and critiquing development and turning it into a radical decolonial option.[16] The revolution is not announced for next week. However, it is an undeniable and unstoppable decolonial epistemic, political, economic, and ethical march to the future. And remember, it is not an abstract universal destiny to overcome all existing ones. It is one option, the decolonial option, with many avenues.

I just mentioned what is called *sumak kawasy* in Quichua or *suma kamaña* in Aymara. This is a category of thought in Andean philosophy that has had a stellar career in the last decade, one that accelerated when it was included in the last Constitution of Ecuador. It has been taken out of context by the NGOs and by the Left, not only in Latin America but also in the United States and Europe. NGOs see it as a new catchy word to replace development, and the Left sees it as a useful word to continue the critiques of development. In the meantime, indigenous voices are most of the time left out of the debate. In the pages that follow, I intend to articulate a decolonial take that on the one hand distances itself from NGOs and the Left, and on the other to address non-indigenous readers (since indigenous people do not need to read about Sumak Kawsay to know what it is). And let me be clear: I do not intend to be "representing" indigenous activists and thinkers, first of all because they do not need to be represented, and second, because for that reason I avoid as much as I can the concept of "representation," which is always already a concept of the rhetoric of modernity.[17]

Sumak kawsay could be better translated as "to live in harmony." Such a translation doesn't include the idea of "nature," while Sumak Kawsay implies live in harmony with Pachamama. In Western cosmology, "nature" is outside "human." In Andean civilizations such separation doesn't obtain. To "live in fullness" (vivir en plenitud) could be another translation. To live well (buen vivir) is an approximate translation that has the advantage of being understood by non-Aymara, Quechua, or Quichua speakers, although it has the disadvantage of being appropriated by projects of rewesternization (specifically, by the Inter-American Development Bank and the World Bank) as a new face for development—in the vocabulary of the "happiness economy."[18] Simon Yampara, an Aymara sociologist, countered such appropriations and uncouples suma kamaña (in the Aymara language) from "development." He argues that sumak kamaña doesn't make a distinction between different kinds of living (as a capitalist society does), to live well or not well, but means "vivir en armonía y complementariedad integral de los diversos mundos de la comunidad eco-biótica natural, que está en el Tayyip-centro, entre la jaka-vida y jiwa-muerte, allí está la kama-(ña)/vivencia con-vivencia de los diversos mundos en armonía" (to live in harmony, in the complementation of the diverse worlds of the eco-biotic natural community. This community occupies the Tayyip-center, between jaka-life and jiwa-dead. In that center dwells kama-(ña)/existentia-experiencia and in the armonious co-existence of the diverse worlds).[19] A translation of the Spanish version of Aymaran philosophy risks flattening and eliminating the difference, which is the case when the concept is translated as "development." It could be rendered as "to live in plenitud," which is counterproductive for all projects of development and growth. Imagine that you have to translate "development" into Aymara. If you translate it as suma kamaña, you intensify the connotation of economic growth, which is one of the consequences of using the word *development*. In that sense, *development* cannot be translated into Aymara without losing its substance, because Aymara language and cosmology don't have room for a concept that belongs to Western cosmology and capitalist economy.

The epistemic and political dimension at stake here has been aptly summarized by another Aymara intellectual, sociologist, and cultural critic, Marcelo Fernández Osco:

> indigenous protests and mobilizations are not merely about opposition or resistance to specific policies or political leaders. Rather, they express an indigenous episteme, a system of understanding the world that has a completely different basis for thinking about socio-political relations and practices, based on a model of horizontal solidarity that extends not only to all humans but also to non-humans in the natural and cosmological world. In contrast, mainstream knowledge, rooted in European colonial understandings of the world, is structured along vertical, hierarchical lines. That is, certain groups of people and certain ways of acting and thinking are deemed to be superior to others. This difference is the key to understanding Andean politics, because it is in the indigenous episteme that the concept of (an)other autonomy is located. The versions of autonomy currently understood in mainstream politics (and promoted by nation-states) provide indigenous groups limited opportunities for decision making but only within the same body of laws that existed before. This notion of autonomy for Indigenous peoples places them under the same subjugation that they have been experiencing since colonization.[20]

Since the Andean philosophy—where the heart of the debate is taking place—doesn't make a distinction between the nature of the (human) body and the body of nature, "to live in harmony" means to live in harmony not only among *runas* (a Quechua word that can be approximated by the Western concept of *human*), but also with all living organisms, of which the human body is one kind. And I say that the Western idea of *human* can only approximate *runa* because the latter doesn't imply the hierarchy between humanitas and anthropos that the former implies. Recently incorporated in the political debate, the concept of sumak kawsay has been crucial in the wisdom of *Kallawaya* (loosely translated as "indigenous medicine").[21] Thus, to understand sumak kawsay, in Quichua (or suma kamaña in Aymara), and Pachamama, would presuppose a reorientation such that the horizon of life emerges from the history of indigenous societies, rather than from the history of European societies. What is wrong with that? Would you say that thinking from the history and experience of indigenous people is fundamentalist, while thinking from the history and memories of Europe (and the United States) is not essentialist, but reflects modern development? Probably you would prefer "modernity and development," instead of modern development, because, after all, development promises improvements, while the concepts of sumak kawsay or suma kamaña, or other ideas of harmony and plenitude, look archaic from the perspective of the rhetoric of development that promises, precisely, to move away from living in plenitude and harmony in order to live better. You may be one who does not want to live like that, and that is fine. But there are many who do not like to live in a developed and capitalist society. And what is wrong with that? Which city dwellers who believe in development would have a problem with people who do not believe in development? Why should development be the only option? Why can't people who believe in sumak kawsay live according to their option? Why would someone who believes in development argue (and fear) that he doesn't want to live according to sumak kawsay, while at the same time the same person or institution will endorse development policies that are forcing believers in sumak kawsay to accept developmental policies and philosophy? To shift this oneway of thinking and doing is the task of border epistemology and the decolonial option.

On several occasions Evo Morales addressed the United Nations, advocating for the future of Pachamama. On 22 April 2009, the United Nations approved President Morales's initiative to declare an International Mother Earth Day. For Andean people, "Mother Earth" is Pachamama; for Westerners, it is Gaia. There is indeed an interesting paradox in Western people's turn to the term *Gaia*, which began when James Lovelock and Lynn Margulis used the Greek term *Gaia* in advancing the scientific hypothesis of the earth and its biosphere as a "living organism." By doing so, Lovelock and Margulis countered the idea that "Nature" is outside of us and is thus to be exploited and conquered; in this, they defied four hundred years of Western mythology whose earlier reference was Francis Bacon, at the beginning of the seventeenth century. The paradox is that the implementation of Bacon's thesis was increasingly executed in the European colonies, where Nature provided the economic reach of England via its Caribbean and Atlantic plantations of sugar, tobacco, cotton, coffee, and so on. And after the Industrial Revolution, Nature provided "natural resources" that nourished machines (charcoal, oil) and that could be processed and converted into "artificial commodities." In this process, Indian's conceptions of Pachamama were neglected, disregarded, taken to be pure credulity, and viewed as Indian myth. In other words, after four hundred years of disregard for Indian cosmology that defined Pachamama as a living organism, Western scientists themselves discovered earth to be a living organism. Lovelock and Margulis should not necessarily be charged with ignoring Pachamama, along with many other equivalent terms in all non-Western cultures and civilization. But, yes, Gaia should not be taken as the universal name around which we imagine the future. Today, *Gaia* is the term around which a community of European scientists, journalists, and activists join forces to counter the idea, taken for granted by developers and corporations, that Nature should remain at the service of development and profit.

In the Andes, the same struggle is being conducted in the name of Pachamama. However, the *connector*, in the UN declaration, is "Mother Earth" under which Pachamama, Gaia, and other equivalent names will find their place and be assured (although as we saw above, Simon Yampara specifies "Pachamama" is more than "Mother Earth" for it invokes the living energies of the universe and not only the planet earth). Why is this important? Actors and institutions that understand Nature as "natural resources" are to be confronted globally, but by the coordination of many local histories, through what should become a series of "integrative decolonial projects." I am not sure if European scientists and activists taking Gaia as their banner will replace it with Pachamama. At the same time, I am not persuaded that Andean people will be interested in adopting Gaia instead of Pachamama. Within each name are subjectivities, memories, ways of life, vocabularies, concepts, and, in brief, cosmologies. Andean indigenous leaders seem less interested in "resisting" than in advancing in a noncapitalist direction, toward the "communal" (I will explain below).[22]

In his address to the UN, in 2009, Evo Morales made four proposals.[23]

1 The first one is the right to life, the right according to which no ecosystem, no species of animal or plant, no snow-capped mountain, river, or lake would be exterminated or eliminated or polluted by the irresponsible attitude of human beings.

2 The second principle is that Pachamama (Mother Earth) has to be able to regenerate her bio capacity. The key term here is *re-generation*, which of-

fers an option to *production* and *recycling*, which are the terms in economic theory to describe the transformation of "natural resources" into "artificial commodities."

3   The third is the right to clean life, that is, the elimination of pollution, which means the regulation of how much production is needed to ensure "el bien vivir", instead of production without limitations to ensure "good profit."

4   The fourth is the right to harmony with all and among all. This is the right to be recognized as part of a system in which we are all interdependent: first, among human beings, and, second, among human beings and Pachamama.

At this point, development is no longer an option for freedom, but a global design that disrupts harmony, pollutes, transforms natural regeneration into artificial regeneration through the use of herbicides and genetically modified seeds, and, as a consequence, prevents "living in harmony and fullness. "Development" promotes the competitive dimension and a philosophy of happiness based on economy, and artistic, and sportive success. Sumak kawsay promotes living in harmony and complementing each other with Maturana's truth and objectivity in parenthesis. Success here is not the goal; to "live in harmony and plenitude" is the goal of sumak kawsay.[24] In this sense, indigenous leaders would agree with Amartya Sen, provided that the economy that ensures sumak kawsay is not capitalist and that the project is not "development," but "enhancement" of communal horizons of life. "Communal," once again, points toward a non-capitalist horizon of society, and in that sense it differs from both the liberal notion of "common good" and the Marxist notion of "the common." The communal is the overall horizon of decolonial options. For indigenous thinkers, development is the economic project for "living better than my neighbor." In this sense, too, we can understand the claim that has been made recently on the future of capitalism and the lack of alternative to it.[25]

You can ask: yes, but can this be done? One answer is that it is being done although not in the same way that the G8 operates. The expectations that this should be a revolution like the American, the French, the Haitian, or the Russian revolutions is no longer an adequate model for imagining the future. It is simply unimaginable at this moment to think "revolution" when the nation-states created by processes of "revolution" are undermined by globalization. The economic structures that maintain "capitalism," from the banks, the corporations, the state, the media, will be undermined by delinking from the rules that these institutions establish for the convenience of the global economic and political elites. But it is imaginable and possible to create institutions and to modify existing ones, turning them in a different direction. That is precisely what the current government of Bolivia is trying to do with the state and with the economy. Evo Morales speaks of socialism, which he distinguishes from communism and from capitalism. His conception of socialism is not derived from Marx, but from the communal organizations of the Ayllus, which are noncapitalist organizations that coexisted with the colonial Viceroyalty of Peru, during three centuries, and with the República de Bolivia in the past two centuries. Sumak kawsay/suma kamaña is the principle he submitted to the Cumbre Sudamericana de Naciones that met in Cochabamba in December 2006.[26] On that occasion President Evo Morales encouraged the formation of a true South American Community of Nations whose future would be guided by the philosophy derived from sumak kawsay/sumak kamaña and Pachamama. Since then, the debate in Bolivia has increased to the point in which radical critics from the white Left engendered a polemical debate with the participation of white progressive scholars and intellectuals and, fortunately, of indigenous intellectuals. Thus, the complexity of the situation is such that while the World Bank and the state tend to appropriate expressions such as sumak kawsay and Pachamama and to use them to put some fresh make up on the concept of "development," sectors of the Marxist Left see the indigenous advance of their philosophy and politics as a romantic return to the past.[27]

Coming back to the question of how it can be done, the answer is, again, it is being done. It is an irreversible process of delinking. Delinking doesn't mean—let's repeat—to abandon, but instead to invent decolonial visions and horizons, concepts and discourses, which is what Evo Morales as well as the Zapatistas and other indigenous movements are doing in the Americas.

A Glimpse at a Communal Vision

In General: Delinking and Independent Thought

As I mentioned earlier, controversies about "development" have a long tradition in Latin American critical thinking. Recently, the independent media outlet Agencia Latinoamericana de Información dedicated a special issue of *America Latina en Movimiento* to "La agonía de un mito: ¿Cómo reformular el desarrollo'?"[28] All contributors to the issue had substantial experience, dedication, thinking, and acting in showing that the logic of coloniality remains embedded in the rhetoric of development, adapting and transforming itself to the circumstance. What was new in the issue was that the contributors, Latin Americans of European descent (mestizos and immigrants), endorsed the indigenous concept and philosophy. Gustavo Esteva argues that "buena vida" is the horizon beyond "development." José María Tortosa shows the underside of development (the logic of coloniality in my terminology), arguing that at the receiving end the consequences are "mal desarrollo" (bad development) and "mal vivir" (bad life), while at the loci of enunciation, where "development" is planned, argued, projected, and executed, it appears (or is presented) as the solution for all. Libia Grueso, a lawyer and activist Afro-Colombian, shows how in the Colombian Pacific development means land expropriation. Arturo Escobar and Eduardo Gudynas take seriously indigenous options elaborated around Pachamama and "buen vivir" as options *to* development—an argument that has been pressed by Andean indigenous leaders at several opportunities.[29]

"To live in harmony" has been undermined by a different philosophy of life, "living to work and to develop," wherein "development" becomes the goal and life is at the service of development. "To live in harmony" means that the goal is *crianza* (nurturing), rather than development, and re-generation of life, rather than re-cycling of industrial product. Of course re-cycling would continue to be needed on a planet with seven billion people, but not on the scale that a capitalist economy requires. If the goal is crianza and re-generation, then re-cycling becomes secondary, and "development" would be translated into "improving the means of nurturing and re-generating," rather than increasing wealth and the gross national product for nurturing.

> el proceso de la crianza recíproca, fundamento de la cosmovisión andina, se realiza en el *ayllu* andino, cuyo significado va más allá del grupo humano emparentado, porque incluye también a la *Pachamama* y todas sus divini-dades y la naturaleza silvestre circundante, donde la comunidad andina vive, trabaja, celebra y donde además convergen las tres comunidades de seres

vivos: la *Sallqa* (comunidad de los seres vivientes que pertenecen a la naturaleza silvestre), la *Runa* (comunidad humana) y la *Waka* (comunidad de
los seres espirituales o divinidades). Estas tres comunidades convergen en la
chacra andina (*uywa chakra, mikhuy chakra*), que es el centro y el escenario
de la vida, el templo del culto andino a la vida.[30]

The procès of reciprocal nurturing, which is one of the foundations of Andean cosmology, takes place in the Andean *ayllu*. The meaning of ayllu is
more than a human group of relatives. And this is because Pachamama is
included in the ayllu as well as all sacred entities and silvester nature. That
is the space where Andean communnities live, work, and celebrate. It is also
the place of convergence of the three communities of living beings: *Sallqa*
(communities of living organism in the domain of silverter nature), *Runa*
(human community), and *Waka* (community of spiritual beings or sacred
entities). These three communities converge in the "chacra andina" (*uywa,
chakra, mikkuy chakra)*, which is the center and the scenario of life, the
temple of the Andean cult **to** life. (boldface added)

This quote implicitly distinguishes between schooling (the republican
state education) and nurturing (in the ayllus). They are not opposed: they
coexist. Sometimes an Indian child could be nurtured and schooled, sometimes just nurtured, while a non-Indian child would be, almost 100 percent of the time, nurtured and schooled among urban and white or mestizo
families. The danger of development has been perceived not only in Latin
America, but also in Africa, the Caribbean, as well as in the Islamic Middle
East, during the Cold War. And the way out has been also suggested on
several occasions. I remind you of two of them, whose force emanates from
their coincidence across local histories and from the fact that their proponents did not know each other. One comes from Ali Shari'ati, in Iran: "It
is impossible to achieve economic independence without having achieved
spiritual independence, and vice-versa. These two are interdependent as
well as complementary conditions. In order to have an independent character in the material, social and economic sphere, we must develop an independent consciousness before the West and vice-versa."[31]

The second example comes from Black Caribbean activists and intellectuals. Although critiques to development coexisted in Latin America
and in the Afro-Caribbean, there was not much commerce between them.

Each project unfolded from its respective local history. What is remarkable, however, is the coincidence between Shari'ati and Lloyd Best, whom I mentioned before. One of the axes of Best's intellectual and political pursuits was his early manifesto "Independent Thought and Caribbean Freedom."[32] His argument mirrors Shari'ati's, and, like many Muslim intellectuals and state officers (as well as in the project on dewesternization) Best's charges are not much or not only "against the West" but about failure of the Caribbean intelligentsia for being unable "to think" (as Mahbubani will have it), to raise up and to engage in independent thinking, which is another way to claim for epistemic delinking. In 1996, Best revisited his earlier ideas in the article "Independence and Responsibility: Self-Knowledge as an Imperative."[33] He depicted the situation in two broad and insightful strokes.

> Since 1962, two visions of the future have been offered to Caribbean peoples. Both have been aborted. The first proved to be an illusion; the second turned into a nightmare. The first vision, that of a self-reliant Caribbean, was inspired by a brilliant group of West Indian economists, known as *The New World Group*. The New World Group focused on the dependence of the Caribbean states on their former colonial masters and argued that only by delinking from the metropolitan economies could the Caribbean reverse the syndrome of persistent poverty in the region. They recommended policies such as ownership and control of our national resources, occupation of the commanding heights of the economy, the use of indigenous technologies and urged us to produce what we consume and consume what we produce. This strategy involved a sharp increase in government ownership and operation of economic enterprises and hastened the emergence of the omni-competent state.[34]

Delinking economically without independent thought is what proved to be an illusion. In independent countries in Africa after decolonization, for example, independence was an illusion of the surface, while the colonial matrix of power continued its work. Independent thought means, in this context, decolonial thought, and delinking shall take place at the epistemic level before confronting authority (e.g., state) and the economy. Thus, "independent thought and Caribbean freedom" pledge epistemic delinking. Best's second vision was that of the socialist state, with the means of production predominantly owned and controlled by a paramount Leninist party. The vast majority of economic operations would be centrally planned and the private sector would be "miniaturized" to use the term coined by Forbes Burhman. The Guyanese economist, Clive Thomas, was the most eloquent proponent of this Marxist approach and Bernard Coard its most fanatical exponent. Since 1975, I have been perhaps the most vehement Caribbean critic of the New World and Marxist schools.[35]

So then, what? We shall now come back to chapter 2 of this book ("I am where I do") and repeat a paragraph I quoted there for the reader's convenience and to see the continuity of that argument here, in the afterword.

> It is being proposed here, that being who we are, what we are and where, the kind of action to which we must be committed is determinate. Action in the field, if it is not to be blind, presupposes theory. To acknowledge this is to set ourselves three tasks. The first is to fashion theory on which may be based the clear intellectual leadership for which the nation calls and which it has never had. The second is to conduct the inquiry on which theory can be soundly based. This is what may be called, in the jargon of my original trade, the creation of intellectual capital goods. Thirdly, we are to establish media by which these goods may be transmitted to the rest of us who are otherwise engaged. As one of our statements in the New World Group has put it: we may wish to create a media of direct democratic expression suitable to the native Caribbean imagination.[36]

Let's go back now to "Independence and Responsibility," and how Best follows up on the critique of two Caribbean visions since 1962. The focus is what Best calls "context," which means what is generally framed as history and events. First, instead of thinking about "Black Dispossession in the Diaspora" (the title of the conference in which he presented the paper), he suggested amending the expression to "Possession, Dispossession and Repossession in Black Diaspora," because he wanted to focus on "possession as process, as recurring phenomenon," repossession not simply as product. The "context" in this case remains Afro-America and America. He is not referring obviously to the United States, or to the United States only, since his concern is the Caribbean. Once he had established the question of context, his argument addressed the following aims.

We will begin with the context to the theory of knowledge, the epistemology. Once the theory of knowledge is clear—and we shall again be detained for some time by the requirements of clarifying how knowledge intervenes in the universe, to what ends and with what modalities—we will clarify how the other modalities, those of intervention in the field of actions are largely determined. . . . *Finally we can turn to the future to play with some of the projections, an exercise which is imperative since nothing is more eloquent concerning what we might have learnt about ourselves. And the projections that we make can only start from the point of departure. My title then is "Independence and Responsibility: Self-Knowledge as an imperative."*[37]

We have here in a condensed formula what I am attempting to argue: being where one thinks and does (pluriversal localism); self-knowledge as imperative, in a word; the analytic of decolonial thinking as the point of departure for decolonial visions of and actions toward the future. All of this was perfectly done by the agents of European modernity; the problem was that in doing so the architects of modernity either prevented others from doing it, or "others" did not realize what was going on. The second half of the twentieth century was the moment of global awakening and the realization that the struggle is for knowledge and at the level of "mediations" of several local histories in which self-knowledge is imperative (as with Shari'ati, but also in the case of dewesternization). The awakening is not just the economic growth of China and other East and South East Asian countries, but also the project of dewesternization that accompanied it and the responsibility of self-knowledge and independent thought as imperative. It is, after all, what Quijano also claimed when he called for the need to disengage, to delink from Eurocentered epistemology.

Lloyd Best would have agreed. Referring to the New World Group, he mentions that in 1964, the group approached the modeling of "contemporary Caribbean economy by a method of successive approximation inferred from historical experience. We identified the slave plantation as the original and generic economic institution of Caribbean economy."[38] In his preface to the volume (co-edited with Levitt), Best pushes further, and makes more specific, the reason independent thought is a must for Caribbean freedom. Admiring what Michelet did in France, in his understanding of the role of the people in the French revolution, and Marx's explanation of how capital works in the European industrial economy, he shifts his attention to a different type of economy, the plantation economy of the Caribbean. What Best calls for is a re-structuring of the social sciences that takes all the world's populations as social actors. And the experiential bases for such re-structuring are world histories in the past five hundred years. The Caribbean has one such history.

Levitt laid out four stages of plantation economy: the garrison economy, between the period of British settlement and the initiation of sugar plantations; the pure plantation economy (sugar and slavery); the modified plantation economy (sugar and free labor with domestic agriculture); and, the plantation economy further modified (organized labor with industrialization). This last state was regarded as, in their words, the anti-model that breaks away from the three previous states of the colonial model. It was conceived as a decolonial economy. However, the initial work did not take off as planned. One of the reasons, Levitt surmised forty years later, was the beginning of the neo-liberal counter-revolution: "an ideological counter-revolution in economics has trivialized academic economics by elevating market-driven behavior over all other aspects of human and social motivations" (191). But Levitt was already acknowledging, in 2002, that "the rising perception of the failure of policies based on neo-liberal market fundamentalism . . . is creating a backlash against 'globalization' in the intellectual arena" (191). Now the time has arrived, Levitt suggested in 2002, to re-inscribe the reflections on plantation economy into the present and toward the future. The new starting point was phrased in this question: "Are we on the cusp of a renewal of independent thought and Caribbean freedom, or are we merely indulging in a self-congratulatory ritual concerning the originality of work done thirty years ago, which has given rise neither to serious critique nor innovative intellectual development?"[39]

Although rewesternization is very attentive to each and every project that would undermine its continuing march, decolonial options are opening up at a remarkable rate. Let's move now from the Caribbean plantation economy and independent thought to the Andean communal decolonial projects. But first, it is helpful to remember Best's and Levitt's distinction of three types of economies in the Americas: "Hinterlands of conquest correspond to the case of Andean America. Hinterlands of settlement correspond to the English and French colonies of North America. Hinterlands of exploitation are most clearly exemplified by the Caribbean plantation economy."[40] This is a useful distinction for future explorations of the complexity of the colonial matrix of power, as well as for imagining directions that decolonial options may follow. I turn now to decolonial thinking in the Andes.

In Particular: The Communal and the Decolonial

IT IS HALF OF THE STORY, BUT IT SEEMS LIKE THE FULL ONE

When Evo Morales was elected president of Bolivia, in December 2005, Maurice Lemoine, an editorial chief (*rédacteur en chef*) at *Le Monde diplomatique*, wrote an enthusiastic article in which he celebrated that "la Bolivie Indiene rejoins la gauche Latine" (the Indian Bolivian is joining the Latin Left).[41] The situation was indeed not only the contrary, but it was also idly formulated: it was, instead, the "Latin Left" that was joining a movement lead by Bolivian Indians. The "gauche Latine" (lead by Creoles and mestizos, that is, by Bolivian whites) and the "Indian decolonial" were two totally different projects with a common enemy: the local pro-neoliberal elite that had been ruling the country since the mid-1980s, when Gonzálo Sánchez de Losada was secretary of economy and Jeffrey Sachs one of his advisors.

What Maurice Lemoine called the "Latin gauche," which by now is the most visible in Latin America, is grounded in a genealogy of thought of European provenance, roughly, Marxism-Leninism (see chapter 1). Their "recognition" of and alliances with the indigenous struggles head in the same direction; however, they follow different paths and come from different experiences and genealogies of thought, with regard to their societal visions. The commons—either in the imperial sense of the British Commonwealth, or in the liberal dilemma formulated by Garret Hardin in his influential article, "The Tragedy of the Commons" (1968), or yet in the Marxist-oriented version that was debated in a recent workshop at Birkbeck College on "The Idea of Communism" (March 2009)—are all based on Euro-American history, experiences, and modes of existence.[42] The communal is something else. It comes not only from social organizations before high civilizations in Tawantinsuyu and Anáhuac (baptized Indias Occidentales by the Spaniards, and later dubbed America by non-Spanish Europeans), but from five hundred years of experience coexisting under Spanish colonial rule and under nation-states after independence, during the nineteenth century. Like "democracy," "common good," if you would like to use such an expression, does not belong to anyone; furthermore there are horizons for "living in harmony," and living in harmony means that the Latin Left, the European Left, the Christian Left, and the Islamic Left, along with the decolonial option and the global political society, would all have their share in building the common good, but no one would have the privilege of pretending to be universal. Pluriversality means that "common good" and "democracy" are not empty signifiers to be filled with meaning, but *connectors* that make possible pluriversality as a universal/global project. The "communal" contribution to the "common good," simply asks for the right to be part of *building* global futures and *avoiding* totalitarian projects of "liberation."

THE OTHER HALF OF THE STORY

The communal refers to a type of social organization that was disrupted by European invasion, but that nonetheless subsisted for five hundred years. The Zapatistas are re-activating it in the organization of Los Caracoles or the Juntas de Buen Gobierno.[43] Los Caracoles adopted and adapted indigenous ways of life and social organization. It puts into practice one of the basic principles of the Zapatistas' political theory: "To govern while obeying at the same time." There is no supreme position in such a governing structure, and "the state of exception" would not emerge as a political problem because, simply, it is pre-empted by the very structure of governance. Now, the immediate question is, can this be extended to all of Mexico or even to be a form of global governance? To ask the question in this form is to fall into the trap of thinking that the political theory behind Los Caracoles is a "new" theory that would replace the liberal-based, constitutional platform of the Mexican state. Once thinking in terms of pluriversality takes hold, rather than of universality (which is still not yet acceptable by many thinkers from the Left), the illusion that there is only one type of economy (now cast in terms of development) that the Right would prefer to be independent of the state, and the Left would like to have the state managing a just distribution of wealth, loses its totalizing and totalitarian effects (e.g., there is no life outside of capitalism). The very existence of Los Caracoles contributes to an understanding of what the Zapatistas meant when they pronounced the second fundamental political principle: "a world in which many worlds would coexist."

Thus, Los Caracoles should not be interpreted as a "new" abstract universal to replace existing ones, either from the Right (market democracy) or from the Left (socialism), for it is something else. That something else is the communal, and the way to get to it is through decolonial thinking and doing. For, if Los Caracoles follows the rhetoric of neo-liberal globalization and the logic of coloniality that is necessary to make globalization work, the project won't be decolonial, but an imperial project of the Left. The "global communal" is not a happy cosmopolitanism, but rather a pluriversal and global nativism, if we can put it in this way. In such a structure there would be no need for the G8 or G20. Instead of offering itself as a new benevolent socialist *mission*, the decolonial horizon presents itself as an *option* (a pluriversal and global option).

Certainly, to move in such a direction is not easy. But neither is rethinking communism or revamping—from the Left—the idea of the common. When the noted French philosopher Alain Badiou talks about "the common," he refers to Jean-Jacques Rousseau, the Jacobins, and the Chinese Cultural Revolution spirited by Mao Zedong. He doesn't mention what is behind Mao's Cultural Revolution that is alive, and transformed, in China today.

China is not only an economic powerhouse. It has already given ample evidence (e.g., the Seventh Doha Round, the positions adopted by China in the meeting of the G20 in London, in July 2009, to deal with problems of the global financial crisis) that it has been taking decisive positions questioning the monopoly of Western authority in global decisions and positioning itself at a distance from Western capitalism and Western versions of socialist futures. Beyond that is a clear struggle for the control of knowledge that informs and grounds decisions. And behind that is a Chinese nationalism that is questioned by the Western media, which pretends that the West is global and is not grounded in national memories and national interests.

Thus, when Alain Badiou places the Chinese Cultural Revolution next to Rousseau and the Jacobins, he is making two moves: advocating the reorientation of the European Left and noting the importance of the Cultural Revolution, which is meaningful to Badiou. Despite this, one can imagine that Rousseau and the Jacobins will have less or no meaning outside their own local histories. As we have briefly seen above, when referring to the dewesternizing option, dewesternization brings to the forefront issues that are alien to Western ideological discourses that support capitalism and that, in consequence, make the question of the "common" more a concern of the European Left than an East Asian issue. Beyond dewesternization, there is the Chinese Left whose vocabulary, at the moment, doesn't include the commons. It seems rather that the reorientation of the Left goes in the direction of putting pressure on the state "to secure the institutional bases for guaranteeing free competition and fair exchange, and the means employed here must include the power of the society, the states, and the localities to further the democratization of the international economic order itself." Additionally, "Chinese intellectuals are now engaged in discussions of the question of globalization in contrast to Western media's discussion of Chinese nationalism."[44] There are also other trajectories that are looking for transformative roads to the future, through deimperialization and decolonization, for whom "the common" is, paradoxically, quite uncommon.[45]

One can surmise that similar conclusions could be applied to Maurice Lemoine's dictum that the Indians of Bolivia joined the Latin Left. This was obviously a dictum that made sense to the European Left. Nonetheless, I would further surmise that even the Bolivian Left knew (although it may have remained silent) that that was not the case, either in Bolivia or for the Indians. You can imagine that belonging to the population of European descent in Bolivia, and thus likely being of "the Latin Left," is not the same as being Aymara or Quechua or Chiquitano, for whom the idea and experiences of the communal are meaningful, while those of the commons or the French *comune* are alien. Thus, if the idea of the commons is meaningful for the European Left, as well as for the Bolivian Left, the idea of the communal is meaningful for decolonial Indian projects. So what do we do?

I see two ways to start undoing the logical puzzle.

The first would be a Hegelian solution, a synthesis. The critical media theorist, Douglas Kellner, proposed a synthesis between the Frankfurt School's legacy in critical theory and the philosophy of liberation.[46] He noted that they provide complementary perspectives on liberation. For the philosophy of liberation, racial and patriarchal oppression was a crucial issue, while it was neglected by critical theory. He noted that critical theory tends to be ethnocentric, and that it focuses on liberation within Western capitalist societies.

Second, and consequently, Kellner goes on to suggest, one obvious way to articulate the difference would be to indicate that critical theory projects a "First World" perspective, while philosophy of liberation projects a "Third World" perspective. But he is not happy with pursuing this avenue, because such a generalization obscures the fact, he says, that there are differences within the First World and within the Third World that may occlude "internal" forms of domination. Moreover, he states, since we all live in one world, we do not want to just underline differences, but need also to point out commonalities.

What are the problems with this argument? Certainly, commonalities should be kept in focus, and the fact that there are internal forms of domination within the First World and within the Third World is also clear. However, what should be kept in mind also is that neither critical theory nor philosophy of liberation "represent," or stand for, the First World and the Third World respectively. What is crucial and undeniable is that each theory emerged in critical response to a particular form of domination, local histories, sensibilities, and genealogies of thought in the First World and the Third World. Two forms of nativism, if you wish, one an internal critic to Eurocentrism and the other emerging from the exteriority: the margins that Eurocentrism needed in order to set Europe at the center. In that regard, they have much in common, but they cannot be subsumed into each other, nor should they be.

Why—after all—aim for a synthesis and not for a world in which many worlds (in this case, theoretical worlds) would coexist and work together in their respective milieus? Is it necessary to make one out of two? Furthermore, given the historical power differential in the structure of knowledge, a synthesis would prioritize critical theory, with philosophy of liberation as a runner up in the Third World. If racism was of the essence for philosophy of liberation, it was because philosophy of liberation realized that racism operates also in the domain of knowledge, not only down there in society. Philosophy of liberation, in other words, made an early statement about the fact that knowledge is geopolitical and that knowledge has been ranked, hierarchically, in relation to regions of the world (from developed to underdeveloped) and to imperial languages (Greek and Latin behind the six main modern and imperial European languages: Italian, Spanish, and Portuguese, from the Renaissance; German, English, and French, after the Enlightenment). Philosophy of liberation was not only a Third World philosophical intervention, but from its inception was written in Spanish, while critical theory was not only in the First World, but was expressed in the German language.

AND NOW WHAT?

Now we are in a better position to return to the communal. What is the communal? Let's start with a simplified description offered by the Aymara sociologist Félix Patzi Paco.[47] By "communal" we understand that Patzi Paco refers to the collective management of resources and at the same time to the rights that families, for example, have to use and benefit from what is collectively produced and shared. He makes clear that while the communal has its millenarian foundation in agrarian societies in the Andes, it currently applies to urban centers as well. Thus, in contradistinction to modernity, in which the fields of knowledge, the political field, the economic field, and the subjective field are distinguished from each other and understood as separate, in the communal system all forms of knowing and doing interact.

The notion of "property" is meaningless in a vision of society in which the goal is working to live, and not living to work. It is in this context that indigenous thinkers has been promoting the concept of sumak kawsay/ suma kamaña that was also included in the constitution of Ecuador.[48] There is a horizon of life behind the communal—as I explained above—that cannot be subsumed under some abstract universal ideal of the commons endorsed by the Latin Left. And once again, while the European Left could sympathize with the directions Bolivia and Ecuador have taken, it is also the case that what is going on in Ecuador and Bolivia has not much to do with the reorientation of the European Left.[49] So the "Indian Left" is not really joining the "Latin Left" for, above all, there is no such thing; but, if we need to name it, it would be rather the "Indian decolonial." There is no Indian Left in the first place, but rather decolonial thinking and doing. This is the point that Maurice Lemoine misunderstood in *Le Monde diplomatique*, when he celebrated the election of Evo Morales as the turn of the Indian Left toward the Latin Left. The election of Evo Morales was the culmination of a long process in which Indians were coming into their own, sometimes welcoming the Left, but subsuming it in their own decolonial projects.

What are the memories behind the idea of the communal, and why is the communal linked to the decolonial? We have to have some basic understanding of the organization of Tawantinsuyu, the organization of the Incanate, improperly and Eurocentrically called the "Inca empire." Knowledge of Ancient Greece and Rome won't do. And I would say that it is here where the divide between the Left (and obviously the Right) and the decolonial begins.

Tawantinsuyu means—as explained above—the world divided into four "suyus," or sections, if you prefer. Imagine the two diagonals of a square without the square. The spatial shape of Tawantinsuyu was derived from the Southern Cross constellation, which cannot be seen from the northern hemisphere (it was one of the constellations that alerted Amerigo Vespucci to the fact that he was not in the Indies imagined by Columbus). At the center, where the two diagonals cross each other, we find Cuzco, the city, which means "the belly of the world," similar to Jerusalem for Jews and Christians or to Mecca and Medina for Islam. Each suyu was organized around a group of ayllus, and each group of ayllus were organized in a larger structure called a *marka*. Each ayllu in each suyu belongs to a marka, and each marka is administered by a Malku, who in turn reports to the Apu-Malku, who is the ruler in each suyu.

Now imagine the same structure in each of the four suyus. How are they interrelated? Each ayllu of a given suyu is defined by a territory that includes not just a piece of land but the ecosystem of which the land is one component. The territory is not private property; it is not property at all, but the *home* for all of those living in and from that territoriality. Remember, we are not, in this case, in a capitalist economic organization, nor am I saying that this arrangement is ideal. I am saying that it was, and still is, more and more difficult today to ignore that the decolonial is an option, and even more difficult still to discredit this line of reflection and genealogy of thought as non-modern, whether your arguments are inspired by liberal capitalism or by state socialism.[50]

The fact is that from Indian decolonial perspectives, the problem is not capitalism only, but also Occidentalism, which includes both capitalism and Marxism. An Indian leader like Fausto Reinaga (1906–94) made clear the distinction between what he called "la revolución India" and the "Communist Manifesto." Marx, according to Reinaga, confronted the bourgeoisie from the perspectives and interests of the working class and proposed a class struggle within Occidental civilization, while the Indian revolution was a revolution against Western civilization, including the Left, which originated in the West.[51]

In a nutshell: Marxism defines itself as an option in the struggle against capitalism; the decolonial option defines itself as an option for delinking from Westernization, in the past, and from rewesternization both in the present and toward the future. It would have been difficult for Marx, Labriola, or Gramsci to confront and delink from Westernization, for they were in the midst of it. Or at least, their project would not have had the same motivations as delinking from non-European histories entangled with Western domination. For European thinkers the need to decolonize or dewesternize was not their priority. But for Gandhi in India, Shari'ati in Iran, Fanon in Martinique-France-Algeria, and Reinaga in Bolivia, it was obvious that the proletarian revolution was a far cry from what was intended and that there were other urgent needs beyond the central issues addressed by the struggle of the European Left confronting liberalism, industrial capitalism, and a huge working class. The point is not that the former shall supplant the latter. The point is that there is no reason for the latter to subsume the former. Marxism focused on class struggle, decolonialism on the racism that justified the exploitation of labor in European colonies. Marxism and decoloniality are two different agendas that could nevertheless work in collaboration if both were to understand their own limits and potentials. But if the issues are cast by the Left in such a way that "the Bolivian Indians joined the Latin Left," the collaboration may not work; and indeed, it is not working. If the situation is described as that "under Evo Morales, the Latin Left joined Indianism," we may be closer to a significant shift in the geography of understanding what decoloniality means.

Now suppose that on a given morning you pick up a newspaper in England, France, Italy, or Spain, for example, and you read something like this headline: "The Process of Political Territorial Reconstitution at the Conjunction of the Asamblea Constituyente in Bolivia." Then you start reading, and the article states,

> In May and June of 2002 indigenous authorities from *ayllus* and *markas* organized a march that lasted more than thirty days in order to press Bolivian

society on the need for a Bolivian Constitutional Assembly to rewrite the existing constitution. . . . From the perspective of indigenous leaders and communities, this was part of a long struggle that in its present form started in 1980, when a new form of politics, identity *in* politics, made it possible for indigenous organizations to organize themselves, to make claims, and to re-inscribe the *ayllu* in the present and future organization of Bolivia. For Indian people, the *ayllu* forms of life, experiences, political and territorial organization, and the hope of projecting a future of collective and communal organization.[52]

Certainly, the probability of reading something like that in a European newspaper is minimal. *Le Monde diplomatique* may not be eager to publish it. But imagining that someone in Europe would make this article accessible to the audience of progressive intellectuals, the reaction could be either a dismissive smile or engaging the article and seriously asking: If what Mamani Condori (the Aymara intellectual who wrote the article) is arguing appears to be a nice idea, can it be implemented, and how? I do not have the answers for such complex questions, but I do have some ideas on how to start thinking about them. Let's start with three.

First, Patzi Paco made an important disclaimer in his proposal toward a communal system as an alternative to the liberal system. First of all, the reconstitution of ayllus and markas, is a task that is also being pursued by the national organization Consejo Nacional de Ayllus y Markas del Qullasuyu (CONAMAQ).[53] Having already defined *ayllu* and *marka*, we can add now the meaning of *Qullasuyu* (Bolivia is the territory of the people of European descent, Qullasuyu the territory of Aymara and Quechua population). As you remember, Tawantinsuyu was divided into four suyus (Chinchaysuyu, Qullasuyu, Kuntisuyu, and Antisuyu). The area that is today Bolivia was built as a nation-state on top of the territory of Inca's Qullasuyu and on top of the Spanish colonial organization of the Viceroyalty of Peru that first erased the Qullasuyu. From a modern chronological perspective, Tawantinsuyu was relegated to the past, to a history that stopped with the arrival of the Spaniards; the advent of the Republic of Bolivia, in the nineteenth century, superseded colonialism and, of course, the organization of Tawantinsuyu. But from the Indian experience and perspective, that was never the case. The reconstitution of the ayllus and markas of Qullasuyu is fundamental to understanding what a plurinational state may mean. And the idea of a plurinational state is already inscribed in the new constitution of Bolivia and Ecuador. The idea is not coming from the Jacobins, Rousseau, or Mao. It is coming from the simple existence and memories of millions of Indians who are not convinced that they can live the existence and memories of millions of Europeans and their descendants in the Andes, whether from the Left or from the Right. To be sure, you can find Indians who join the Left or the Right, but that doesn't deny the fact that the reorganization of the Qullasuyu is an Indian project and not a leftist one. Therefore, the reconstitution of ayllus and markas is not just for Indians, but for all Bolivians.

Second, does it mean that the communal is a proposal simply to replace the Bolivian liberal-(neo)colonial state founded after the independence from Spain and that lasted until today? Such a route would not lead to a plurinational state. It would result in an Indian national state, instead of a Creole-mestizo national state, forcing Indian leaders and community to rewrite the constitution. There are indeed other organizations claiming the right to intervene in the constitution of a plurinational state, but the point I am trying to make is that the Indian communal system and the idea of decolonizing the actual state, education, and economy are not grounded in the genealogy of thought and memories of the European Left and its expansion or adoption in non-European regions.

Third, the idea of a communal system as an alternative to the (neo)liberal system that emerged from the memories and lived experiences, today, of Indian communities should not be reduced to Bolivia only, but should have a global scope. Global scope doesn't mean that the "ayllu system" should be exported like other previous models (Christian, liberal, Marxist), but that it is an invitation to organize and re-inscribe communal systems, all over the world, that have been erased and dismantled by the increasing expansion of capitalist economy, which the European Left was unable to stop. If ayllus and markas form the singular memory and organization of communities in the Andes, the memories of communal organizations all around the globe that predate and survived the advent of capitalism are what make possible the idea of a communal system that is not mapped in advance by a totalitarian ideology, of any kind or color. Once again, that Zapatistas' dictum "A world in which many worlds coexist" may be a world of communal systems in a pluriversal and not universal world order.

Pluriversality, Border Thinking, and Cosmopolitan Localism

In his book on Iranian intellectuals, Mehrzad Boroujerdi distinguished between "Orientalism in reverse" and "Nativism."[54] In the first case, subjects who became Oriental objects in Western knowledge responded by making the West the other. By so doing, Orientalism in reverse accepts the rules of the game and attempts to change the content—not the terms—of the conversation. Nativism, in Boroujerdi's conceptualization, is something different. The term *nativism* here may surprise members of the cosmopolitan club. Let's first read, and then comment.

> Nativism stands in the same relation to Orientalism in reverse as Eurocentrism does to Orientalism proper. Both Nativism and Eurocentrism provide an ontological and epistemological umbrella under which it becomes possible to develop a theory of history and a political platform. Whereas Eurocentrism does advocate such ideas as the uniqueness and superiority of the West and its unequivocal manifest destiny, Nativism champions the cause of abandoning, subverting, and reversing these same meta-narratives and master codes. *Nativism was born of the lamentable circumstance of colonialism and the agonizing milieu of the post–World War II period of decolonization.* It represents a cultural reflex on the part of many Third World intellectuals from Southeast Asia to the Caribbean eager to assert their newly found identities.[55]

The reader may suspect that we are here confronting another essentialist proposal. The interesting aspect of the proposal is that Frantz Fanon appears, for an Iranian intellectual, as a paradigm of nativism. Boroujerdi doesn't offer any specific reference or quotation as to why Fanon would exemplify nativism, but I suspect that he has in mind statements like this one.

> I am ready to concede that on the plane of factual being the past existence of an Aztec civilization does not change anything very much in the diet of the Mexican peasant of today. . . . But it has been remarked several times that this passionate search for a national culture which existed before the colonial era finds its legitimate reason in the anxiety shared by native intellectuals to shrink away from that Western culture in which they all risk being swamped. Because they realize they are in danger of losing their lives and thus becoming lost to their people, these men, hotheaded and with anger in their hearts,

relentlessly determine to renew contact once more with the oldest and most pre-colonial springs of life of their people.[56]

Let's then translate "nativism" into "localism" and be clear that locals have been con-formed by the formation and transformation of the colonial matrix of power. Locals are not necessarily natives, although natives can be local, too. Some natives, though, prefer to be cosmopolitan. Immigrants are locals in the place to which they have migrated, and they were also locals in the place from which they emigrated. Natives where migrants arrive are as local as immigrants themselves. The point is, then, that localism—in the sense described by Boroujerdi—emerges because of the advent of a powerful intellectual and political elite in the colonies, linked to Europe though education. Localism is thus a historical phenomenon of the Third World, which in cases like those of Shari'ati and Bennabi, discussed in previous chapters, brings in conversation with both Islam and Third World decolonization. Localism, crossed and con-formed by historical forces (in this case, Persia, Islam, the Western creation of the Middle East as a region, which then became part of the Third World), then emerges as a pluriversal response and confrontation with universal Eurocentrism.

Eurocentrism, in the last analysis, is Western localism (or perhaps "nativism" is a good name for Eurocentrism) with a global design that became synonymous with universalism. Thus, Kant's cosmopolitanism and its legacy propose the universalization of Western nativism/localism. And the Marxist Left, for better or worse, belongs to that world. This is a challenge for cosmopolitanism. On the other hand, non-Western localism is plural, since there are many multiple memories and colonial wounds inflicted by racism, ways of life, languages, beliefs, experiences connected to the West, but at the same time not subsumable to it. Localism (which should not be confused with "national fundamentalisms" or "nativism from the Right") should be pluriversal and therefore decolonial. Since localism originated "from the lamentable circumstance of colonialism"—or, better yet, from the logic of coloniality common to different Western imperial/colonial expansions (by Spain, France, England) and its imperial surrogates after the sixteenth century (imperial Russia, Soviet Union, Japan)—a trademark of localism is the decolonial thread that connects and makes of pluriversality a global project. Why, because Western imperial surrogates became surrogates by reproducing the logic of coloniality and, by the same token (of being second-hand imperial states) became second-class empires. Their destiny varied: Russia mutated into the Soviet Union that finally collapsed. And Japan by now is turning toward dewesternization and is ending its second-class status in relation to Western empires. Decolonial localism—therefore—is global, or, if you wish, cosmopolitical. Thus we arrive at the paradoxical conclusion that if cosmopolitanism is to be preserved in humanity's goals toward the future, it should be in the form of "cosmopolitan localism"—an oxymoron, no doubt, but the Kantian project of one localism becoming the universal is untenable today. Cosmopolitan localism (which is decolonially critical cosmopolitanism) is another expression for pluriversality as a global project. The Kantian legacy should be reduced to its proper localism and stripped of its imperial/global pretensions. Recognizing the "idea" doesn't mean accepting its implementation. Cosmopolitanism can only work if there is no master-global design, but a global agreement in which no one will rule without being ruled. This constitutes a tough call for those who believe that their party, religion, or ideology is in the best interest of all and has to be imposed to achieve universal peace and well-being. It's a tough but realistic call now that the global political society is growing and on its feet; it is aware that the era of being ruled and obeying, or being repressed for disobeying, is reaching its limits.

Opening Up

I turn now to Anibal Quijano, who inspired the epistemic and political project modernity/coloniality/decoloniality, specifically to a powerful op-ed he published in *America Latina en Movimiento*, in February 2009. Quijano argues that the global financial crisis, which coincides with global warming and the march toward death, is not just another crisis of capitalist cyclical self-adjustment. There is something radically different, Quijano argues, in this crisis; there is a new and important element that emerged from all of this: hope. The title of his opening contribution to the special issue is titled "An Other Historical Horizon" (Otro horizonte de sentido histórico).

> Después de 500 años probablemente es la primera vez en la historia de este patrón de poder en el cual comenzamos no solamente a esperar un futuro,

a trabajar por ese futuro, pues estamos de cierta manera comenzando ese futuro, estamos conviviendo con el futuro que necesitamos, porque lo estamos comenzando a hacer ahora. Esta idea no es una mera imagen . . . no es en ese sentido clásico una utopía, algo que no tiene lugar en el universo. Esto tiene lugar en el universo, para que esto tenga sentido no sólo como imagen sino como fenómeno, como una tendencia real y necesaria de esta realidad.[57]

It is probably the first time in the history of the "patrón colonial de poder" (colonial matrix of power) that we all are not only hopeful toward the future, we are also working toward that future, and we are beginning to build that future, we are at this very moment building it. This is not a simple image . . . neither is an utopia, in the classical sense of the word. This is happening in the planet and in that sense it is not an image but a phenomenon that manifests itself as a real tendency of a historical necessity.

"An other historical horizon" is at work, because the growing decolonial awareness emerges from the fact that for many, for 70 percent of the world's population, there is a question of survival. They no longer hope that God or the State or the Corporations will help them to live their lives, for they realize not only that God is absent, but that the State and the Corporations are not on their side, that "development" (a particular form of the rhetoric of modernity), rather than leading to freedom, leads to coloniality: poverty, enslavement, the killing of "nature" in favor of "commodities." For Quijano, the historical horizon that we are living in now, that we (all "we") are part of, is constituted not only of discourses and theories, but of the organization and re-organization of communities, of global networks that generate structures of governance, and of economic management. This is another way of describing the emerging global political society and the materialization of decolonial options leading the way to noncapitalist global futures. It won't be an easy ride, but it is a ride full of hope and creativity—creativity motivated not by competition, but by love and the will to live in search of the *communal*.

But the last word shall go to Nina Pacari, a prominent lawyer, politician, and activist from an indigenous community in Ecuador.[58] Her words come from a weeklong seminar in the summer school organized by the Universidad Complutense de Madrid in July 2006.[59] Pacari, who was the only Indian and woman at the seminar, began her presentation by confronting non-Indian understanding of Indian nations.

> En estos últimos tiempos se habla de la "emergencia indígena." De unos seres anclados en los museos para el gusto colonial de muchos, hemos pasado a ser unos actores que les provocamos miedo, incertidumbres o desconfianza. *Y es que no se acaba de procesar y asumir la presencia "visible" de los indios (en el sentido individual) y la de sus pueblos (en el sentido colectivo) para compartir la construcción y ejecución de un proyecto común relacionado con países pluri-étnicos que los pueblos originarios seamos reconocidos como portadores de un pensamiento, de una filosofía, de unos valores de una cultura política diferenciada.*[60]

> In the past years the "indigenous emergence" has become a topic of many conversations. In those conversations we have moved from people anchored in the museums (according to the colonial preferences of many) to being social actors who provoke fear, uncertainty, and mistrust. The problem is that the presence of the Indians (in the individual sense of the word) and the people (in the collective sense) has not been yet entirely processed and assumed. Therefore, Indians are not yet accepted in building common [state] projects in pluri-ethnic countries. It is not yet accepted that "pueblos originarios" be recognized as carriers of a different system of thought, philosophy, values, and political culture.

Pacari's opening statement resonates, loudly, with the philosophical perspective of the Maori anthropologist Linda Tuhiwai Smith, in New Zealand (see chapter 3), and certainly with that of Patzi Paco, who thinks politically from the history and experiences of indigenous nations subordinated to Spanish colonialism and then to the Creole-mestizo idea of one nation–one state, instead of thinking politically from the history and experiences of European nations that subordinated many people around the globe. The initiatives and the necessary work to dispense with the logic of coloniality can hardly only come from actors embedded in European history, as Frantz Fanon made clear in his debate with Jean-Paul Sartre: Fanon thanked Sartre for setting an agenda for black people, for telling them what to do in order to liberate themselves. Here is where the Left comes together with the Right: while the Right (white, liberal, and conservative) undertakes a mission to civilize and develop, the Left (white also) is assuming the savior's mission of how to liberate from the oppression of capitalism.[61] At the moment when the entire world is participating, there is no longer room for saviors of the other, since the others themselves are doing the work that in the last analysis will be beneficial for the saviors of all kinds, secular (political and economic) and religious.

Nina Pacari goes on to add that in such circumstances (the resistance of the Creole-mestizo population), "indigenous political participation . . . is a fundamental tool for epistemic decolonization which is nothing other than the re-inscription of ancestral knowledges and its inclusion in the dynamic of civilizational co-existence in their execution of public management [gestión pública]."[62] Pacari then explains the "cultural codes of indigenous nations," that is, the political and economic philosophies that guide their living, their thoughts, and their aims in the construction of plurinational states in the Andes in an irreversible process of decolonizing political economies that sustain capitalist practices and political theories that support the (neo)liberal state. The philosophical (epistemic and political), categorical apparatus that suspends the claims, needs, and aims of indigenous nations, is summarized by Pacari as follows:

1 *Yachai*, which means the *wisdom* to orient people by means of programs and proposals. (Notice that she is not calling for expertise, but for wisdom.)

2 *Ricsina*, which means *to know* (*conocer*), is necessary to understand the complexity of human geography and with that knowledge to promote and support harmony and conviviality.

3 *Ushai*, which means *to know and be able to execute* (*saber o poder ejecutar*) in order to avoid improvisation.

4 *Pacta-Pacta*, which means to *enact democracy*, relationships built among equals, and collective participation in social administration.

5 *Muskui*, which means *utopia* in the sense of a historical horizon, rather than a fiction or imagination. It is a vision conceived in short and long terms in order to avoid immediacy and acting guided by reactions and improvisation.

Thus, power understood in these terms and in this codification is not a model to be executed, but the signpost of processes in permanent construction. What is at stake, Nina Pacari observes, "is the reformulation of the political culture, the reformulation of the very political doing. Thus the contribution *of identity* (collective entities) *in politics is necessary and innovative.*[63] Identity in politics is a necessary corrective also of the idea that traditional political parties (in Ecuador, the United States, France, etc.) represent *politics without identity* because they belong to the universal and neutral modern theory of the state. But it so happened that theories of the state, whether in imperial countries or in their former colonies, and the political parties formed around the principles of Western political theories, were not invented, debated, or defended by Indians, or Africans, or Chinese, or Iranians. In other words, the belief and the illusion that political parties are empty of identity corresponds with the general Western principle of objectivity without parenthesis, that is, objectivity without identity (see figure 2, page 35).

Finally, indigenous empowerment through identity in politics rests in four general philosophical principles.

1 *Proportionality-Solidarity.* This principle proposes and motivates political actions and thinking in favor of those who have less.

2 *Complementarity.* This principle points toward the right of all to participate in the making of what society needs, not just as waged labor or being left out because there aren't jobs. It is the principle of convergence and conviviality in the harmony of two contradictory terms.

3 *Reciprocity.* Another expression for reciprocity is *la minga*: rights and responsibilities from which no one is exempt; it implies to receive and to give.[64]

4 *Correspondence.* This principle points to the need to share responsibilities.

During the days in which I was finishing the afterword, several listserves were distributing news about, and petitions for, condemning the killing of Indians in the Peruvian Amazon, in the north of the country. The events started in the early morning of 5 June 2009, when the state Direccion Nacional de Operaciones Especiales attacked without warning a group of four thousand Peruvian indigenous citizens of Awanjun origin. The function of the "forces of order" was to unblock the highway that the Awanjun Peruvian citizens had blocked to avoid being dispossessed of their lands by the government of Alan García, which proposed to allow on those lands "el desarollo de industrias extractivas" (the development of industry extracting natural resources, such as oil, minerals, and biofuel). The Amazonian movement was a peaceful and massive event defending human rights and the participants' territory, which had for centuries provided their way of life and subsistence.[65]

Events of this kind have been common, particularly in the past sixty years. I am sure that when Amartya Sen wrote *Development as Freedom*, he did not think of development as going hand in hand with expropriation and killing, if necessary, rather than with freedom. The attitude of President Alan García is consistent with the kind of subjectivity that characterizes capitalist culture: a state politics that privileges "development" at the cost of the lives of citizens, who are just guilty of existing. In spite of the massacre, the historical process initiated by the political society is irreversible; or as Quijano states, instances of the global process could be and are defeated here and there, or perhaps life on the planet is extinguished before, but the decolonial march of the global political society has reached the point of no return.[66]

NOTES

Preface

1 An initial exploration of this issue can be found in "Globalization and the Relocation of Languages and Cultures", in *Local Histories/Global Designs: Coloniality, Subaltern Knowledge and Border Thinking* (Princeton: Princeton University Press, 2000), chapter 7.

2 Trouillot, "Pour l'évidence des subjectivités."

3 A chronicle of the work done has been laid out in the documented collection by Houston, Mazariegos, and Stuart, *The Decipherment of Ancient Maya Writing.*

4 Coe, *Breaking the Maya Code.*

5 Mangabeira Unger, *Knowledge and Politics,* 110.

6 Mignolo, "Semiosis y universos de sentido"; Mignolo, "La semiosis colonial."

7 Mignolo, "Cartas, crónicas y relaciones del descubrimiento y la conquista"; Mignolo, "El metatexto historiográfico y la historiografía indiana." Other articles from this period can be found also at the *Dialnet* website, http://dialnet.unirioja.es.

8 Quijano, "Colonialidad y modernidad-racionalidad." An English translation can be found in *Cultural Studies* 21, nos. 2–3 (2007): 168–78.

9 Anzaldúa, *Borderland/La Frontera.*

10 Mignolo, "Geopolitics of Knowledge and the Colonial Difference." The article contributed to shape an installation in the Centro Andaluz de Arte Contemporáneo, *Geopolíticas de la Animación/Geopolitics of the Animation.* It was translated and printed in the catalogue of the same title (Seville: Centro Andaluz de Arte Contemporáneo and Consejería de Cultura, 2007), 13–39.

11 Escobar and Mignolo, *Globalization and the Decolonial.*

12 There are exceptions, always. See for instance Latouche, *The Westernization of the World.*

13　See Mignolo and Tlostanova, "The Logic of Coloniality and the Limits of Postcoloniality"; Mignolo, "Introduction: Coloniality of Power and De-colonial Thinking."

14　Gordon, *Existentia Africana*.

15　The term was introduced by the Colombian decolonial thinker Adolfo Albán Achinte to capture Afro-Colombian communities in Colombia from the eighteenth to the twentieth centuries. Albán Achinte argued that their thinking and doing were not ways of resistance but of reexistances. See Albán Achinte, *Tiempos de Zango y Guampin*.

16　On Guaman Poma de Ayala's and Ottobah Cugoano's decolonial thinking see Mignolo, "La opción de-colonial: Desprendimiento y apertura: Un manifiesto y un caso," *Tabula Rasa* (2008): 243–81.

17　See chapter 2, "I Am Where I Do," in this book for my comments on Malek Banabib and Ali Shari'ati, and my comments on Adhelkebir Khatibi in Mignolo, *Local Histories/Global Designs*.

18　Dussel, "World System and Transmodernity."

19　On how and when Marx acquired that nickname (being himself a Jew), see Seigel, *Marx's Fate*, 79. Interestingly enough, the nickname picked up both African Arabic and Black African identifications (e.g., *blackamoors*, an adjective used by Shakespeare, of whom Marx was an avid reader).

20　Reinaga, *La revolución India*, 382.

21　For a historical and critical summary of the divide between Indianismo and Marxismo in Bolivia, see Lineras, "El desencuentro de dos razones revolucianarias."

22　Rahnema, "Shari'ati's Audience and Discourse at the University of Mashhad."

23　Boroujerdi, "Ali Shari'ati."

24　Mignolo, "Geopolitics of Knowledge and the Colonial Difference"; Mignolo, *The Idea of Latin America*.

25　See the website for the Latin American Center, University of Aarhus, http://www.lacua.au.dk, and Lalibreriadelau.com, http://www.lalibreriadelau.com.

26　Mignolo, *The Idea of Latin America*; Mignolo, "Delinking: The Rhetoric of Modernity, the Logic of Coloniality, and the Grammar of Decoloniality."

27　Of more recent vintage is Fernández-Osco's very important article "Ayllu: Decolonial Critical Thinking and an (Other) Autonomy."

28　Translated as Dussel, *Twenty Theses on Politics*. This manifesto, in my view, follows up on the line of Guaman Poma de Ayala and Ottobah Cugoano, which I discuss here and elsewhere. See also Mignolo, "El pensamiento descolonial."

29　See the program description for the Doctorado en Estudios Culturales Latinoamericanos, available at the Universidad Andina Simón Bolívar website, http://www.uasb.edu.ec.

30　Escobar's "Worlds and Knowledges Otherwise" was originally published in 2003.

31　One of the collaborative articles was Walter D. Mignolo and Madina Tlostanova, "Theorizing from the Borders: Shifting to Geo- and Body-Politics of Knowledge," *European Journal of Social Theory* 9, no. 2 (2006): 205–22.

32   For general information about the Académie de la Latinité, see its website at http://
     www.alati.com.br. The pre-publication of "texts of reference," also available at the
     website, contains all the papers presented in a given conference.

Introduction

1   The first publication in English of the work done by the collective since 1998 ap-
    pears in *Cultural Studies* 21, no. 2 (2007), a special issue on "Globalization and the
    De-colonial Option."

2   When I use the word *capitalism*, I mean it in Max Weber's sense: "The spirit of
    capitalism is here used in this specific sense, it is the *spirit of modern capitalism* . . .
    Western European and American capitalism" (*The Protestant Ethic and the Spirit of
    Capitalism*, 51–52).

3   Mignolo, "Cosmopolitanism and the De-Colonial Option."

4   Armstrong, *Islam*, 142, emphasis added.

5   Ibid.

6   Williams, *Capitalism and Slavery*, 32.

7   Dagenais, "The Postcolonial Laura."

8   "Ayiti," the indigenous names for the islands where Arawaks and Tainos dwelled,
    was respectfully reinvested by Jean-Jacques Dessalines when he rebaptized "His-
    paniola" with the name of "Ayiti."

9   Ottobah Cugoano, *Thoughts and Sentiments on the Evil of Slavery*, 72.

10   See Greer, Mignolo, and Quilligan, *Rereading the Black Legend*.

11   See my commentary in Acosta, *Natural and Moral History of the Indies*, 451–518.

12   For example, see Castells, *The Rise of the Network Society*.

13   Mignolo, "*(Post) Occidentalism, (Post) Coloniality, and (Post) Subalternity*"; Mi-
    gnolo, *Local Histories/Global Designs*; Mignolo, "*Delinking Epistemology*." The
    last appeared in *Reartikulacija*, an art project of the group Reartikulacija (Marina
    Gržinić, Staš Kleindienst, Sebastjan Leban, and Tanja Passoni).

14   Rose, *The Politics of Life Itself*.

15   Schmitt, *Political Theology*.

16   At the moment of going over the copyedited version of this manuscript the Ley
    Educativa Avelino Siñani y Elizardo Pérez was approved in Bolivia. It is clearly
    stated and clarified on several occasions that this is a decolonial law for a plurina-
    tional state, iicyt.fcyt.umss.edu.bo/download/ariel/boletin/nueva_ley_ASEP.pdf.

17   Contrary to the purpose of the Ley Educativa mentioned above (note 16), Davos
    University and in general the corporate university are the clear example of rewest-
    ernization of education and the reproduction of the cmp. See, Mignolo, "The end
    of the University . . . ," http://publicuniversity.org.uk/2010/11/23/the-end-of-the-
    university-as-we-know-it.

18   Grosfóguel, "Transmodernity, Border Thinking and Global Coloniality."

19   Ibid.

20 Greer, Mignolo, and Quilligan, *Rereading the Black Legend*.

21 Wallerstein, *The Modern World-System*.

22 Anghie, *Imperialism, Sovereignty and the Making of International Law*.

23 Wallerstein, *The Capitalist World-Economy*.

24 Quijano, "'Raza,' 'Etnia' y 'Nación' en Mariátegui"; Quijano, "Coloniality of Power, Ethnocentrism, and Latin America."

25 Anghie, *Imperialism, Sovereignty and the Making of International Law*.

26 Garza Carvajal, *Butterflies Will Burn*, 2003; Trexler, *Sex and Conquest*; Segal, *From Moon Goddesses*; Enloe, *Bananas, Beaches and Bases*; Tlostanova, *Gender Episemologies*; Oyesumi, *Gender Epistemologies*; Oyesumi, *The Invention of Women*.

27 Lugones, "The Coloniality of Gender"; Lugones, "Toward a Decolonial Feminism"; Tlostanova, "The Janus Faced Empire Distorting Orientalist Discourses"; Suárez Navaz and Hernández, *Descolonizando el feminismo*.

28 Sigal, *Infamous Desire*; Sylvia Marcos, *Taken from the Lips*.

29 Masuzawa, *The Invention of World Religions*.

30 Kant, *Observations on the Feeling of the Beautiful and the Sublime*; Mignolo, *Learning to Unlearn*; Mignolo, *Aesthesis Decolonial*; Tlostanova, *Contemporary Art as Decolonial Knowledge*.

31 Mignolo, *The Darker Side of the Renaissance*; Mignolo, "(Post) Occidentalism, (Post) Coloniality, and (Post) Subalternity"; Quijano, "Coloniality and Modernity/ Rationality."

32 Mignolo, "(Post) Occidentalism, (Post) Coloniality, and (Post) Subalternity."

33 Quijano, "Coloniality of Power, Ethnocentrism, and Latin America"; Wynter, "Towards the Sociogenic Principle."

34 Mignolo, "(Post) Occidentalism, (Post) Coloniality, and (Post) Subalternity."

35 On this see Catherine Walsh, *Interculturalidad, estado, sociedad*.

36 A Google search on "decolonial, decoloniality, decolonization of knowledge," shows an increasing number of entries in the past five years. Before this period, not much could be found on "decoloniality." The scholarly tendency was toward "postcoloniality," particularly in the United States. In the former Third World, with the exception of India, postcoloniality doesn't have much currency—even less so in the Arabo-Islamic world, in Central Asia and the Caucasus, or even in Southeast Asia, South and Central America, and the Caribbean.

Chapter One | The Roads to the Future

1 Schmitt, *The* Nomos *of the Earth*, 351.

2 See "Mercator World Map in 16th Century," at the Mapsorama.com website, http://www.mapsorama.com.

3 Schmitt, *The* Nomos *of the Earth*, 352.

4 Mignolo, *The Idea of Latin America*.

5 Schmitt, *The* Nomos *of the Earth*, 352–53, emphasis added.

6   Césaire, *Discourse on Colonialism*, 36.

7   Schmitt, *The* Nomos *of the Earth*, 355.

8   Ibid.

9   To be clear: I am not endorsing Schmitt's argument or using him to support my ideas. I am confronting his arguments, which tell only half of the story. The other half has been told and has become increasingly visible in the past two or three decades. My own argument is based on that other half of the story, and it intends to contribute to it. See for instance Blaut, *The Colonizer's Model of the World*; Grovogui, *Sovereigns, Quasi Sovereigns and Africans*; Grovogui, *Beyond Eurocentrism and Anarchy*; Mignolo, *The Darker Side of the Renaissance*.

10 The polycentricity of the world order was already envisioned from a Marxist perspective by the Egyptian sociologist Samir Amin in *Delinking: Towards a Polycentric World*; and it was later anticipated by the liberal political theorist Samuel Huntington in *The Clash of Civilizations? The Debate*.

11 Pukara, *Historia, Coyuntura y descolonización*; Walsh, *Interculturalidad, estado, sociedad*; Walsh, *Interview*; Medina, "Forma Estado y Forma Ayllus."

12 Brooks, "Tradition versus Innovation"; Pérez, *Chicana Art*; Matory, *Black Atlantic Religion*.

13 Chuji, "Modernidad, desarollo . . ."; Walsh, "Development . . ."

14 Mignolo, "The End of the University as We Know It."

15 On Ireland, see Prior, *Bible and Colonialism*. On Central America, see Hinkelammert, *El Grito*. On the Muslim world of North Africa, see Qutb, *The Islamic Concept and Its Characteristics*. On Qutb and Western political theory, see Euben, *Enemy in the Mirror*.

16 Hinkelammert, *El asalto al poder . . .* and *El huracán . . .*

17 Buck-Morss, "Can There Be a Global Left?"

18 A gathering of this re-orientation of the Left took place at Birkbeck College, London, in March 2009. See Keenan, "Communism."

19 Hardin, "The Tragedy of the Commons."

20 Horowitz, *Unholy Alliance*.

21 Buck-Morss, *Thinking Past Terror*.

22 Hunter, "Islamic Reformist Discourses in Iran"; Rahnema, *An Islamic Utopian*.

23 Shari'ati, *Man and Islam*.

24 De Sousa Santos, "The World Social Forum and the Global Left." For De Sousa Santos's conceptualization of the political option that the WSF put on the table, see his celebrated monograph, *The World Social Forum: A User's Manual*.

25 De Sousa Santos, "O China o Sumak Kawsay."

26 Linda Tuhiwai Smith, *Decolonizing Methodologies*, 33.

27 Bello, "The Past, Present and Future of the World Social Forum." http://www .thestrategycenter.org/radio/2009/03/09/walden-bello-past-present-and-future-world-social-forum; Bello, *Deglobalization* (especially the last chapter, "The Alternative: Deglobalization"); Bello, *The Food War* (especially the last chapter, "Resistance and

the Road to the Future"; Bello, "The World Social Forum at the Crossroad." http://
www.zcommunications.org/the-world-social-forum-at-the-crossroads-by-walden-
bello.

28 For an overview of current debates on the turn to the Left and the decolonial turn,
see Escobar, "Latin America at the Crossroad"; for the specific issue of the Left and
the decolonial, see Mignolo, "Evo Morales: Giro a la izquierda of giro descolonial"
and "The Communal and the Decolonial"; Espejo, "La izquierda Latino americana."

29 Gresh, "Iran, vers une "communauté internationale." http://blog.mondediplo.net/
2010-05-21-Iran-vers-une-communaute-internationale-post.

30 García Linera and Stefanoni, *La potencia plebeya*.

31 On the Sur-Sur project, see the program description available at the CLACSO website, http://www.clacso.org.ar.

32 Huntington, *The Clash of Civilizations and the Remaking of the World Order*.

33 Mahbubani, "Peeling Away the Western Veneer," http://www.digitalnpq.org/archive/
2008_spring/02_mahbubani.html.

34 For accounts on anti-Western manifestations, see Buruma and Margalit, *Occidentalism*; Aydin, *The Politics of Anti-Westernism in Asia*.

35 Mahbubani, "Peeling Away the Western Veneer."

36 Ian Bremmer's *The End of the Free Market* provides a good description for the current and future scenarios of dewesternization, although without naming and conceiving it as such. He sees that the conflict of the Cold War has been translated now
into one between capitalist countries who promote free markets (you know which)
and countries who promote strong state regulations of the economy (China, India,
Rusia, Saudi Arabia, the United Arab Emirates). We are all in a capitalist world
now; the dispute for the colonial matrix of power appears, in this scenario, in the
conflicts between Western countries that would like to maintain the control of the
colonial matrix and non-Western countries that are clearly moving in a different
direction and asserting their authority in the global world order. While this, of
course, doesn't make a world better, it makes the current world quite different than
the one we have seen over the past five hundred years.

37 This story is detailed in Spence, *The Chan's Great Continent*.

38 Issues discussed in Heinze and Steele, *Ethics, Authority and War: Non-State Actors
and the Just War Tradition*.

39 Safi, *Progressive Muslims on Justice, Gender and Pluralism*; Bell, *The New Confucianism*.

40 Hui, *The End of the Revolution*; Chen, *Asia as Method*.

41 See, for instance, Curran and Park, *De-Westernizing Media Studies*.

42 Mihesua and Wilson, *Indigenizing the Academy*. On the stand taken by Prime Minister Mohamad, see "Malaysia ex-P.M. Sparks U.K. Walkout," BBC News, 9 September 2005. For Attas's persective, see, for instance, Naquib al-Attas, *Prolegomena to
the Metaphysics of Islam*. Strong and influential arguments could be found between
trajectories of dewesternizing and decolonial options. Sharing much with dewest-

ernization in the thinking of the state and with decoloniality in the belief in the need to reinscribe Islamic civilization in the present and toward the future, these arguments emerge from the local need to find solutions for the consequences of the invasion and occupation of Iraq. See, for instance, the recent arguments by the former minister of defense (2003–4) and minister of finance (2005–6) Ali-Abdul-Amir Allawi, in *The Crisis of Islamic Civilization*. See also his interview in *Guernica*, "Incoherence of Power."

43 Linda Tuhiwai Smith, *Decolonizing Methodologies*.

44 Quijano, " 'Raza,' 'Etnia' y 'Nación' en Maríategui," 177.

45 Gordon, "Fanon and Development," 71–93.

46 Castro-Kláren, "Posting Letters," 131.

47 For an account of these conceptualizations, back in the late 1990s, see Mignolo, "Post-Occidental Reason."

48 Young, *Postcolonialism: A Very Short Introduction*; and for a counter-balanced account, see Gabilondo, Introduction, *The Hispanic Atlantic*, 91–113.

49 See also on this topic Mignolo and Tlostanova, "The Logic of Coloniality and the Limits of Postcoloniality." This debate goes back to the early 1990s. See Mignolo, "Colonial and Postcolonial Discourse."

50 For an analysis of parallel histories leading to subaltern studies in British India and (de) coloniality in Ibero-America, see my own "Coloniality of Power and Subalternity."

51 Chen, *Asia as Method*.

52 Pannikar, *Myth, Faith and Hermeneutics*, 9. My interest in Pannikar is not new. I have engaged in his philosophy in an article I published in 1991, "Canon a(nd)Cross-Cultural Boundaries," as well as in the introduction to *The Darker Side of the Renaissance*. Pannikar rejected comparative method. Clearly, comparative method assumes the detached role of the observer in relation to what he or she is comparing. I rejected this method, too, in both cases. Pannikar instead talks about *imparative method* and defines it as "the effort at learning from the other and the attitude of allowing our own convictions to be fecundated by the insights of the other" (*Myth, Faith, and Hermeneutics*, 9). See also his "Aporias in the Contemporary Philosophy of Religion."

53 Mignolo and Tlostanova, "On Pluritopic Hermeneutics, Trans-modern Thinking and Decolonial Philosophy."

54 See, for instance, Efrem Smith and Jackson, *The Hip-Hop Church*; Watkins et al., *The Gospel Remix*; Péres, *Chicana Art*.

55 Andrea Smith, "Walking in Balance," 62.

56 Charleston, "From Medicine Man to Marx." For the conflict with the FBI, see Murray, *Matter, Magic and Spirit*, 136.

57 Ibid. See also the writings of Charles Eastman, in *The Essential Charles Eastman (Ohiyesa)*.

58 Deloria, *For this Land*; Tinker, *Spirit of Resistance*; Cajete, *Look to the Maounain*.

59 Chuji, "Modernidad, desarrollo, interculaturalidad y Sumak Kawsay."

60 See Yavuz and Esposito, *Turkish Islam*; and Ebaugh, *The Gülen Movement*. Parallel to this movement one could think also of the increasing intervention of women in shaping the future of Islam. See Mahmood, *Politics of Piety*. I shall also mention a tendency among progressive Jews to delink from the turn that Judaism took with the creation of the State of Israel and to reorient Judaism toward a spiritual and decolonial option. See Slabodsky "De-colonial Jewish Thought and the Americas."

61 The first incursion into this argument exploring actors, institutions, projects, and identities can be found in Mignolo, "Los estudios culturales"; and in "The Decolonial Option and the Meaning of Identity in Politics."

62 Maturana and Poerksen, *From Being to Doing*, 42.

63 Ibid. Humberto Maturana elaborated these ideas in several places. An introduction to them can be found in Fell and Russell, "An Introduction to 'Maturana's' Biology." Notice that in many cases Maturana's epistemology has been turned around. For example, in Niklas Luhman's *Social Systems* "objectivity in parenthesis" has been erased and the concept of autopoiesis, which in Maturana moves toward epistemology in parenthesis, has been subsumed in epistemology without parenthesis. For Luhman the objective truth of the social sciences account for the truth of the social systems. I will come back to this in the afterword, when I elaborate on the Aymara sociologist, intellectual, and activist Félix Patzi-Paco and his "use" of Luhman to put forward "the communal system as an alternative to the (neo) liberal system," in a brilliant enactment of border thinking and decolonial thoughts.

64 For specifics on the topic, see the landmark discussion in Catherine Walsh, *Interculturalidad, estado, sociedad*.

65 Maldonado-Torres, *Against War*.

66 There are various other cases of intellectuals and activists "dwelling" in the South and moving in similar directions, for instance Franco Cassano in Italy; see his *Il pensiero meridiano* and *Homo civicus*. Also the cultural critic and philosopher Roberto Dainotto, *Europe (in Theory)*. For more details, Levander and Mignolo, eds., *The Global South*.

Chapter Two | I Am Where I Do

1 Schmitt, *The Nomos of the Earth*.

2 Ortelius, *Theatrum Orbis Terrarum*.

3 Castro-Gómez, *La hubris del punto cero*.

4 Castro-Gómez, "The Missing Chapter of Empire," 301.

5 Ibid.

6 Osamu, "Anthropos and Humanitas."

7 All these concepts are explained in Mignolo, *Delinking*.

8 Mignolo, "On the Colonization of Amerindian Languages and Memories"; Mignolo, "Nebrija in the New World"; Mignolo, "The Darker Side of the Renaissance: Colonization and the Discontinuity of the Classical Tradition."

 9 Mignolo, *Delinking*.

10 Huntington, *The Clash of Civilizations and the Remaking of the World Order*.

11 Mignolo, *Delinking*.

12 "Les indigènes de la république" in France is a clear case of what I am talking about; in the United States, Latino/a engagement with decolonial thinking and doing is another.

13 Anghie, "Francisco de Vitoria and the Colonial Origins of International Law," 13–32, 89–108; Keene, *Beyond the Anarchical Society*, 101–19.

14 I will come back to Guaman Poma in chapter 6, "The Zapatistas' Theoretical Revolution."

15 For the concept of "epistemic colonial difference," see Mignolo, "Dussel's Philosophy of Liberation." For the "ontological colonial difference" in tandem with the epistemic, see Maldonado-Torres, "On the Coloniality of Being."

16 Brague, *La voie Romaine*.

17 The distinction between humanitas and anthropos could be further expanded and explored through the double coloniality of being; that is, both epistemic and ontological. See Maldonado-Torres, "On the Coloniality of Being."

18 Kusch's *Pensamiento indígenas y pensamiento popular en América* was translated into English, by María Lugones and Joshua Price, as *Indigenous and Popular Thinking in America*.

19 Wynter, "Towards the Sociogenic Principle."

20 Badrane Benlahcene, "A Metatheoretical Study of Malek Bennabi's Approach to Civilization"; Barium, "Malik Bennabi and the Intellectual Problems of the Muslim Ummah." Rodolfo Kusch's works, written between 1952 and 1978, were recently collected in the three-volume *Obras Completas* (2000). An English translation, by María Lugones, of one of Kusch's fundamental books, *Pensamiento indígena y pensamiento popular*, was published in 2010.

21 For an updated summary of Bennabi's work, life, and influence, see Sebastian J. Walsh, "'Killing Post-Almohad Man'" and El-Messawi, "Religion, Society, and Culture in Malik Bennabi Thought." I am thankful to Ebrahim Moosa for calling my attention to the work of this Algerian thinker.

22 Bennabi, *The Question of Ideas in the Muslim World*, 111.

23 Descartes, *Discours de la méthode*; Descartes, *Meditationes de prima philosophia*.

24 Bennabi, *The Question of Ideas in the Muslim World*, 105.

25 I am referring here to two of Best's essays on the topic: "Independent Thought and Caribbean Freedom" and "Independence and Responsibility: Self Knowledge as an Imperative."

26 Best, "Independence and Responsibility," 3.

27 Best, "Independent Thought," 29.

28 Bennabi, *The Question of Ideas in the Muslim World*, 45.

29 Giddens, *Beyond Left and Right*; Ferguson, *Empire*.

30 Bennabi, *The Question of Ideas in the Muslim World*, 81.

31 Ibid.

32 Sabet, *Islam and the Political*, 4.

33 Ibid.

34 Ibid., 5.

35 Gordon, *Existentia Africana*.

36 Du Bois, *The Souls of Black Folk*.

37 Anzaldúa, *Borderland/La Frontera*.

38 Menchú, *Me llamo Rigoberta Menchú*.

39 Kusch, *América profunda*.

40 Dussel, "World System and 'Transmodernity.'"

41 Fanon, *Black Skin, White Masks*, 11.

42 For the concept of languaging, see Mignolo, *Local Histories/Global Designs*.

43 Fanon, *Black Skin, White Masks*, 17.

44 Ibid., 18.

45 Wynter, "Towards the Sociogenic Principle," 13.

46 Ibid., 17.

47 See Boroujerdi, *Iranian Intellectuals and the West*; and Euben, *Enemy in the Mirror*. For an expression of the dewesternizing position in Islamic perspective that is akin to Mahbubani's Asian perspective, see Allawi, *The Crisis of Islamic Civilization*.

48 For a strong argument, with historical depth, that shifts the geopolitics of capitalist reason, see Mahbubani, *The New Asian Hemisphere*. There is an intellectual genealogy of this line of thought. One reference point is Lee Kuan Yew and Zakaria, "Culture Is Destiny." Needless to say, Bennabi was intuiting the path unfolding in East Asia, which he contrasted with Muslim societies. Certainly, he was probably unaware of the future of Muslim Indonesia.

49 Sara Rimer, "Gatsby's Green Light Beckons a New Set of Strivers," *New York Times*, 17 February 2008.

Chapter Three | It Is "Our" Modernity

1 The issue was raised by Horkheimer, "Traditional and Critical Theory," but he posited a universal subject for both traditional and critical theory. The difference that Horkheimer introduced was that traditional theory separates the known from the knower, while critical theory asserts that the known is the creation of the knower. Decolonial critical theory introduces a knower who is crossed by imperial and colonal differences. Horkheimer, "Critical and Traditional Theory." Also Eze, "The Color of Reason"; and Mignolo, "The Darker Side of the Enlightenment: A Decolonial Reading of Kant's *Geography*."

2 I am here building on Ahmad, *Occidentosis*.

3 Speech by Prime Minister Mahathir Mohamad, presented at the Tenth Islamic Summit Conference, Putrajaya, Malaysia, 16 October 2003, available at the website for the Anti-Defamation League, http://www.adl.org.

4   To avoid misunderstanding, I am going back here to my semiotic training in France and to earlier publications on the topic. See chapter 5 of this book. See also Mignolo, "Colonial and Postcolonial Discourse."

5   On "languaging" see Mignolo, *Local Histories/Global Designs.*

6   Benveniste, "L'appareil formel de l'énonciation"; Todorov, "Problèmes de l'énonciation."

7   Mignolo, "Semiosis, Coherence and Universes of Meaning."

8   On the Kantian-Humboldtian paradigm, see the classical argument advanced by Bill Readings in *The University in Ruins.* Readings looks mainly at the history of Euro-American universities. Starting from Readings, I explored the consequences of the colonial university (Santo Domingo, Mexico, Lima, Cordoba, founded all during the sixteenth century) and Harvard University (founded in 1636, when Descartes was publishing *Discours de la méthode*). See Mignolo, "Globalization and the Geopolitics of Knowledge." On resistance to Christian theology, see Kant, *The Contest of Faculties.*

9   For a historical account, see Heilbron, *The Rise of Social Theory*; Foucault, *Les mots et les choses*; Wallerstein et al., *Open the Social Sciences.* And, if there is any doubt that "les sciences humaines" (social sciences and the humanities in the United States) are one and the same with "la pensée occidentale," see Gusdorf, *Les origines des sciences humaines et la pensée occidentale.*

10 Dilthey, *Introduction to the Human Sciences.* Secondary bibliographies abound. I have dealt with a specific aspect of the distinction between nomothetic and ideographic sciences, and between epistemology and explanation (the former) and hermeneutics and interpretation (the latter). See Mignolo, "Comprensión hermenéutica y comprensión teórica"; and Mignolo, "Teorías literarias o de la literatura / Qué son y para qué sirven?"

11 See the entry for "Education," particularly the discussions on "Ancient China" and "The New World Civilizations of the Maya, Aztecs, and Incas," at *Encyclopedia Britannica Online*, http://www.britannica.com.

12 Fanon, *Black Skin, White Masks*, translated from the French by Charles Lam Markmann (New York: Grove, 1967), 11. See in this respect the groundbreaking study by Lewis Gordon, *Fanon and the Crisis of European Man.*

13 Mignolo, "Geopolitics of Knowledge and the Colonial Difference."

14 *Pletsch*, "The Three Worlds, or the Division of Social Scientific Labor, circa 1950–1975"; Agnew, "Know-Where."

15 Hountondji, "Recapturing," 238. The article was based on a previous lecture, delivered in 1983.

16 Ibid., 242.

17 Cash, "Research Imbalances," 33.

18 Ibid.

19 Wiredu, "Formulating Modern Thoughts in African Languages," 308.

20 Chatterjee, "Talking about our Modernity in Two Languages."

21 Ibid., 271.

22   Ibid., 273–74.

23   Ibid., 275.

24   Galfarsoro and Mignolo, "Critical Stew: Epistemic Disobedience and the Decolonial Option." http://criticalstew.org/?p=193.

25   Linda Tuhiwai Smith, *De-colonizing Methodologies*, 25.

26   Gandhi's philosophical and political positions are complex and sometimes contradictory. On the one hand, he has been critiqued by Ranahit Guha in *Dominance without Hegemony* for his intolerance toward the subalterns. On the other hand, he continues to be considered a leading decolonial thinker by Ashis Nandy in "Looking in the Mirror of the East," and in Parta Chatterjee's "Modernity and Indian Nationalism." Finally, during my week as visiting scholar at Warwick University (November 2010), Raza Saeed, from the law school, urged me to think more about Gandhi's concept of *Satyagraha*, a concept that Saeed thought was already a proposal for epistemic disobedience. I will think more about it, although I already have the intuition that he is right.

27   Shiva, *The Monocultures of the Mind*. An interview on the topic can be found in Shiva, "Monocultures of the Mind."

28   Mignolo, "Delinking: The Rhetoric of Modernity, the Logic of Coloniality and the Grammar of Decoloniality."

29   Mignolo, "The Decolonial Option and the Meaning of Identity in Politics."

30   Rose, *The Politics of Life Itself*.

31   Ibid., 131, 252.

Chapter Four | (De)Coloniality at Large

1   See Brown, "Life's Mysterious Clocks." See also Brown, Hastings, and Palmer, *The Biological Clock*; and the wonderful critical summary offered by Anthony Aveni, *Empires of Time*.

2   I assume coloniality as a constitutive component of modernity, and not as a derivative one. Thus, the expressions "modernity/coloniality" and "modern/colonial world-system" you will find throughout the chapter. The historical point of reference is the emergence of the Atlantic commercial circuit, in the sixteenth century, that connected the Mediterranean with the Atlantic, on the one hand, and created the conditions for the transformation of Europe from a marginal to a hegemonic place. On Europe before the sixteenth century see Abu-Lughod, *Before European Hegemony*; on the emergence of the Atlantic circuit, see Quijano and Wallerstein, "Americanity as a Concept, or the Americas in the Modern World-System." For the concept of coloniality or power, see Quijano, "Colonialidad del poder, cultura y conocimiento en America Latina." For modernity/coloniality and modern/colonial world-system, see Mignolo, *Local Histories/Global Designs*.

3   Kant, "Idea of a Universal History from a Cosmopolitan Point of View"; Thiry, "*Nature, and Her Laws as Applicable to the Happiness of Man*."

4   Fabian, *Time and the Other*.

5   Owen Hughes, Introduction.

6   "Thinking thought usually amounts to withdrawing into a dimensionless place in which the idea of thought alone persists. But thought in reality spaces itself out into the world. It informs the imaginary of peoples, their varied poetics, which it then transforms, meaning, in them its risk becomes realized" (Glissant, *Poetics of Relation*, 1). Think of the coloniality of power and the colonial difference when you read "thought in reality spaces itself out into the world," and you will have a description of the "imaginary of the modern/colonial world."

7   Hegel, *The Philosophy of History*.

8   "History is a highly functional fantasy of the West, originating at precisely the time when it alone 'made' the history of the World. If Hegel relegated African peoples to the ahistorical, Amerindian peoples to the prehistorical, in order to reserve History for European people exclusively, it is not because these African or American people 'have entered History' that we can conclude today that such a hierarchical conception of the 'march of history' is no longer relevant" (Glissant, *Caribbean Discourse*, 64).

9   See Mignolo, *The Darker Side of the Renaissance*.

10   Lafitau, *Moeurs des sauvages américains, comparées aux moeurs des premiers temps*.

11   Lyell, *Principles of Geology*.

12   Augustine, *Confessiones*.

13   Hay, *Europe*, 11–12.

14   Mignolo, *The Darker Side of the Renaissance*, 269–81.

15   Lovejoy, *The Great Chain of Being*.

16   Farriss, "Remembering the Future, Anticipating the Past."

17   MacCormack, "Time, Space, and Ritual Action."

18   Mignolo, *The Darker Side*, chapters 4 and 5.

19   Bouysse-Cassagne and Harris, "Pacha." See also Yampara Huarachi, "La sociedad Aymara."

20   On Pachakuti as theory of abrupt changes ("teoria del vuelco"), see Kusch, *Pensamiento indígena y pensamiento popular*. On "Tinku," see Bouysse-Cassagne and Harris, "Pacha."

21   See Mignolo, *The Darker Side of the Renaissance*, chapter 5, "The Moveable Center."

22   Deloria, "Thinking in Time and Space."

23   Ibid., 63.

24   Florescano, *Memory, Myth, and Time in Mexico*.

25   Chimalpahín, *Relaciones originales de Chalco Amaquemecan*.

26   For the intricacies and interrelations of "space/time" in the double-side of the colonial difference, see Miller, "Transformations of Time and Space."

27 Spence, *The Chan's Great Continent.*

28 Kant, "Idea of a Universal History from a Cosmopolitan Point of View"; and Kant, *Anthropology from a Pragmatic Point of View.*

29 On the construction and significance of the Dasypodius clock in the European Renaissance, see Grafton, "Chronology and Its Discontents in Renaissance Europe."

30 Ibid., 140.

31 MacCormack, "Time, Space and Ritual Action." For an overview, see the classical work of Zuidema, for instance his *Inca Civilization in Cuzco.* And for an overview of Andean cosmology focusing on Aymara instead of Quechua, see the introduction by the Aymara intellectual Domingo Llanque Chana, in *La cultura Aymara.*

32 Aveni, *Empires of Time*, 297, emphasis added.

33 Ibid., 289.

34 See the description of the International Meridian Conference of 1884, available at the Millenium Dome website, http://wwp.millennium-dome.com.

35 I explore in more detail Acosta's lack of attention to Indigenous thinking (as Kusch will have it) in Mignolo, *Commentary.*

36 Bacon, *Novum Organum: With Other Parts of the Great Instauration*, 19.

37 In his classic *A Brief History of Time: From the Big Bang to Black Holes* (1988), Stephen Hawking locates his narrative in a well-known genealogy: Ptolemy, Newton, Kant, and so on, as if there were only one genealogy to tell the "history of time." And perhaps there is only one genealogy that is leading to the homogenization of the planet. Perhaps there is a "historical universal" that will end up winning over the differences. That will be the final victory of coloniality at large.

38 Cassano, *Il pensiero meridiano*, 81–108. Now translated into English. See Cassano, *Southern Thoughts.*

39 Sugnet and Maal, "I Sing All the Space."

40 Rorty, *Philosophy and the Mirror of Nature.*

41 Innerarity, "Cronopolítica."

42 Hinkelammert, *The Ideological Weapons of Death*; Williams, *Capitalism and Slavery*, 3–29; Mignolo, "Bare and Dispensable Lives."

43 The quote and the comments by David Carr come from "Newsweek's Journalism of Fourth and Long," *New York Times: Week in Review*, 23 May 2009.

Chapter Five | The Darker Side of the Enlightenment

1 Elden and Mendieta, *Reading Kant's Geography.*

2 Mignolo, "Racism as We Are Sensing It Today."

3 Armstrong, *Islam*, 142.

4 Ibid.

5 Ibid., emphasis added.

6 Dagenais, introduction, *Decolonizing the Middle Ages.*

7 Ibid.

8   Mignolo, "De-linking: Globalization, Don Quixote and the Colonies."

9   Ibid.; Santiago Castro-Gómez makes this argument in the introduction of his book *La hubris del punto cero*. A short version in English can be found in his article "The Missing Chapter of Empire."

10 Kant, *Lectures on Logic*, 538.

11 Benveniste, "L'appareil formel de l'énonciation."

12 Lenkersdorf, *Los hombres verdaderos*.

13 Maturana, "Reality."

14 *Physische Geographie*, cited according to the Akademie edition of *Kants gesammelte Schriften* (hereafter AK, with volume and page number), AK 9: 228.

15 "L'Europe fait partie du premier type; L'Asie, en revanche, appartient au second." *Physische Geographie*, AK 9: 228.

16 "La raison pour laquelle on ne connait pas mieux l'intérieur de l'Afrique que les pays de la lune tient davantage a nous, Européens, qu'aux Africains, car la traite des Nègres nous a rendu effrayants." Ibid., 229.

17 "Dont la partie nord, proche de la Russie, est encore pratiquement inexplorée, et dont la moitié sud contient encore de nombreuses régions inconnues, en particulier sur les côtes du Brésil." Ibid.

18 Grovogui, "Mind, Body and Gut!"

19 Mignolo, "Dussel's Philosophy of Liberation"; Mignolo, "Geopolitics of Knowledge and the Colonial Difference"; Maldonado-Torres, "On the Coloniality of Being."

20 Eze, "The Color of Reason."

21 For the interconnections between Kant's teaching and the editing of both works, see the introduction to the volume edited by Stuart Elden and Eduardo Mendieta, *Reading Kant's Geography*.

22 Khaldun, *The Muqaddimah*; Zaid Ahmad, *The Epistemology of Ibn Khaldun*.

23 Hodgson, *Rethinking World History*, 29–35.

24 See the entry for "Philosophical Anthropology" at *Encyclopedia Britannica Online*, http://www.britannica.com.

25 Kant, *Observations on the Feeling of the Beautiful and the Sublime*, 97, emphasis mine.

26 Kant, *Anthropology from a Pragmatic Point of View*, 107.

27 Ibid., 110.

28 Ibid.

29 Ibid.

30 Ibid., 111.

31 Ibid., 245.

32 *Physical Geography*, AK 9:316. (G, 223).

33 A relevant article for the argument developed here is Rod, "Stranger in Foreign Land." See also my "Commentary" to the edition of Acosta's *Natural and Moral History of the Indies* translated by Frances López-Morillas and edited by Jane E. Mangan.

34   Dagenais, "Introduction," *Decolonizing the Middle Ages.*

35   See the entry for "Homo Sapiens" at *Encyclopedia Britannica Online,* http://www
.britannica.com.

36   For example, the Maori anthropologist Linda Tuhiwai Smith assumes both identities; she uses anthropologist as a disciplinary identity, and Maori as an imperial/
colonial identity attributed by European indigenous actors to non-European indi-
genes. See her *Decolonizing Methodologies.*

37   I analyze this issue in my "Commentary" to Acosta's *Natural and Moral History of
the Indies.* I also address it in *The Darker Side of the Renaissance.*

38   The myth that secularism was a racial break with theology lasted for a while, perhaps a century or so. But it is clear today that theology provided the sword with
which the secular intellectual cut the Gordian knot with God. For an early argument, see Carl Schmitt's *Théologie politique.* Schmitt, like Kant, operates in a pure,
secularized frame of reference, wherein the sacred, in the domain of religion, or the
metaphysical, in the domain of philosophy, is out of consideration. For Schmitt,
"political theology" refers to the juridical rationality of the Catholic Church, translated into the *ius publicum Europaeum,* a distinction still accepted as Christian in
Thomas Hobbes's political system. Schmitt, *Théologie politique,* 168.

39   At this point, neuro-philosophy, for example (which operates under Cartesian
principles from which Kant was not exempt), becomes questionable. Of course,
given the ideological and economic weight today of "science," the argument cannot be refuted in an end note. But this remark should serve as a record of things to
come. I am thinking here of neuro-philosophical arguments advanced by Patricia
Smith Churchland in *Brain-Wise* and by Paul Churchland in *Neurophilosophy at
Work.*

40   On the geo- and body-politics of knowledge, see Mignolo, "Geopolitics of Knowledge and the Colonial Difference." On the geography of reason, see Gordon, *Disciplinary Decadence,* particularly chapter 6, "Próspero's Words, Caliban's Reason,"
107–32.

41   Mignolo, *The Darker Side of the Renaissance.*

42   I develop this argument in the next chapter, "The Zapatistas' Theoretical Revolution," and in "Geopolitics of Knowledge and the Colonial Difference."

43   Quijano, "Coloniality of Power, Ethnocentrism, and Latin America," 546.

44   Medina, "Forma Estado y forma Ayllus." Medina has outlined the major difficulties
to overcome in the process of building a plurinational state in Bolivia and harmonizing two forms of government embedded in two cosmologies. In spite of the
difficulties, the very awareness that "forma Estado" by itself doesn't work anymore
reached the point of non-return.

45   Pannikar, "Aporias in the Contemporary Philosophy of Religion," 370; Pannikar,
"What Is Comparative Philosophy Comparing?" A preliminary version of these
ideas, following Pannikar's work, is in my introduction to *The Darker Side of the
Renaissance.*

46 Panikkar develops this notion of *imparative method*, elsewhere called *dialogical philosophy*, in "Aporias in the Contemporary Philosophy of Religion," 370, and "What Is Comparative Philosophy Comparing?," 127. See also Hall, "Intercultural and Interreligious Hermeneutics."

47 Galfarsoro and Mignolo "Epistemic Disobedience and the Decolonial Option." See also chapter 3 above, "It Is 'Our' Modernity."

Chapter Six | The Zapatistas' Theoretical Revolution

1 For a well-informed and sensible narrative of the Zapatistas' projects until 2003, see Muñoz Ramírez, EZLN, also published in English as *The Fire and the Word*.

2 Mignolo, "From 'El Derecho de Gentes' to 'La Dignidad Humana': The Zapatistas' Theoretical Revolution," paper presented at "Comparative Colonialism: Pre-Industrial Colonial Intersections in Global Perspective," thirty-first annual conference at the Center for Medieval and Renaissance Studies, Binghamton University, State University of New York, 31 October–1 November 1997.

3 For a better understanding of the meaning of this statement, in terms of gender issues in Mexico, see Sylvia Marcos, "The Borders Within." And for its understanding in the history of Mayan nations, see Sylvia Marcos, *Taken from the Lips*. Also, see *Chiapas*, http://www.revistachiapas.org/No1/ch1.html.

4 Mignolo, *Local Histories/Global Designs*.

5 Quijano, "Colonialidad del poder, cultura y conocimiento en America Latina"; Mignolo, *Local Histories/Global Designs*.

6 See EZLN, "First Declaration of the Lacandon Jungle."

7 Mignolo, "Turn to the Left or Decolonial Turn?"; Mignolo, "The Communal and the Decolonial"; Escobar, "Latin America at a Crossroads."

8 Bawman, *Liquid Modernity*.

9 I summarized this process in the post-face of *Local Histories/Global Designs*. Thus, to briefly review the recent events in Bolivia before moving into the logic of the theoretical decolonial revolution (or Pachacuti), see EZLN, "Sixth Declaration of the Selva Lacandona."

10 Quoted in Le Bot, *El sueño Zapatista*, 146.

11 Subcomandante Insurgente Marcos, "The Fourth World War"; and Subcomandante Insurgente Marcos, "Siete piezas sueltas del rompecabezas mundial." For some of the implications of "Siete piezas," see Coronil, "Naturaleza del postcolonialismo."

12 Mignolo, "Who Speaks for the 'Human' in Human Rights?"

13 That Ali Shari'ati admired Frantz Fanon is not surprising: an Iranian Muslim and an Afro-Martinican have in common the colonial wound, the loss of dignity in front of Western eyes. Reflecting back on his years in France, Shari'ati laments, "I wish we knew Kateb Yassini instead of Breatch, Omar Mawloud, Omar Ozgan, Frantz Fanon and Aimé Césaire instead of Jean-Paul Sartre and Camus" (Shari'ati, "Extraction and Refinement of Cultural Resources," 34).

14 Quoted in Le Bot, *El sueño Zapatista*, 147.
15 Dirks, Introduction.
16 Silverblatt, *"Becoming Indian in the Central Andes of Seventeenth Century Peru."*
17 Quoted in Le Bot, *El sueño Zapatista*, 149–51.
18 Ibid., 99.
19 Ibid., 261.
20 Ibid., 338–39.
21 De la Grange and Rico, *Subcomandante Marcos*.
22 Mignolo, *Local Histories/Global Designs*.
23 Quoted in Le Bot, *El sueño Zapatista*, 263.
24 Lenkersdorf, *Los hombres verdaderos*.
25 Habermas, "The Inclusion of the Other."
26 Montejo, *Maya Intellectual Renaissance*.
27 Lenkersdorf, *Los hombres verdaderos*.
28 Quoted in Le Bot, *El sueño Zapatista*, 176–77.
29 I am alluding here to Ernesto Laclau's notion of "empty signifier." See Laclau *Emancipation(s)*.
30 Paco, *Sistema comunal*.
31 On the ayllu justice system, see Fernández Osco, *La ley del Ayllu*.
32 Medina, "Forma Estado y forma Ayllus."
33 Rawls, *The Law of Peoples*, 1–54.
34 Le Bot, *El sueño Zapatista*, 83.
35 Ibid.
36 Mignolo, *Local Histories/Global Designs*, 49–90; Mignolo, "Stocks to Watch."
37 Hinkelammert, *El mapa del emperador*, 238–40.
38 Le Bot, *El sueño Zapatista*, 259–60.
39 Glissant, *Poetics of Relation*.
40 Freyre, *Casa-grande e Senzala*.
41 Agamben, "Beyond Human Rights," 162.
42 Ibid., 160.
43 Arendt, *The Origins of Totalitarianism*.
44 Agamben, "Beyond Human Rights," 162.
45 For an extended discussion of this topic, see Mignolo, "Citizenship, Knowledge and the Limits of Humanity."
46 For a detailed update, analysis, and consequences of building plurinational states in Bolivia and Ecuador, see Catherine Walsh, *Interculturalidad, estado, sociedad*.
47 Agamben, "Beyond Human Rights," 159.
48 Mignolo, "Who Speaks for the 'Human.'"
49 For a full exploration of the figure of the damnés and its consequences in philosophy, politics, history, and (de)coloniality see Maldonado-Torres, *Against War*.
50 This point was made by Dipesh Chakrabarty a while ago, but it needs to be repeated and not forgotten. Chakrabarty, *Provincializing Europe*.

51 Dussel, "Ethical Sense of the 1994 Maya Rebellion in Chiapas"; Le Bot, *El sueño Zapatista*, 83.

52 Agamben, *The Becoming Community*, 64–65.

53 Fanon, *Peau Noires, Masques Blanches*, esp. the introduction.

54 An important theoretical continuity of the events that have been taking place in South America in the past two decades, in which series of events the Zapatistas have played an important role, is the publication of Enrique Dussel's *Twenty Theses on Politics*. Dussel brings together, in these twenty theses, the decolonial trajectory of his own philosophy of liberation, now thinking politically from the combination of Left-oriented and decolonial-oriented governments that have been elected in South America and the Caribbean in the first decade of the twenty-first century.

55 Žižek, "A Leftist Plea for 'Eurocentrism'"; Žižek, *The Ticklish Subject*, 171–244.

56 Žižek, "A Leftist Plea for 'Eurocentrism,'" 988.

57 Ibid., 1006.

58 Ibid., 1007.

59 Ibid.

60 Lee Kuan Yew and Zakaria, "Culture Is Destiny."

61 The argument advanced by Khana in *How to Run the World*—an analogy with the disputes between the Western Roman Empire (today the EU) and Byzantium, the Eastern Roman Empire (today the United States)—seems to be an attractive but backward-looking metaphor. There will not be a "next Renaissance" because everybody is watching and more than just the EU and the United States are ready to play. Those are the trajectories and options I underlined in chapter 1.

62 Ibid.

63 Žižek, "A Leftist Plea for 'Eurocentrism,'" 988.

64 Ibid., 1009.

65 Chatterjee, "On Civil and Political Society in Post-colonial Democracies."

66 Žižek, "A Leftist Plea for 'Eurocentrism,'" 1008.

67 For Russia, see Tlostanova, *Gender Epistemologies*. For China and East Asia, see Ching, *Becoming Japanese*, and Chen, *Asia as Method*.

68 Adorno, *Guaman Poma de Ayala*; Mignolo, "The Decolonial Option: Detachment and Opening."

69 Žižek, "A Leftist Plea for 'Eurocentrism,'" 1008.

70 Celebration of the fifteenth year of the Zapatistas' uprising took place between the end of December 2008, in Mexico City, and the beginning of January 2009, in San Cristobal de las Casas. The "comunicaciones" were reported in *Rebeldía* 65 (August 2009): 18–23, under an editorial, "La digna rabia con la que otro mundo se está construyendo." In the same issue, a communication by Melina Plata and Patricia Caldera was subtitled "La rabia nos mueve, la dignidad nos guía." See Lascano and Muñoz, *Rebeldía* 65, pp. 1 and 2, http://revistarebeldia.org/?cat=160. The celebration of the sixteenth anniversary took place the following year (December 2009–January

2010) under the title "Seminario internacional de reflexión y análisis" and was reported in *Rebeldia* 68 (February 2010): 18–23, http://revistarebeldia.org/?cat=163.

Chapter Seven | Cosmopolitan Localisms

The first version of this chapter was presented as a lecture: Walter D. Mignolo, "De-colonial Cosmopolitanism between Theology and the Spirit of Global Capitalism," for the project "Multiple Trajectories, Critical Interrogations," led by Kamari Clarke, Ariana Hernández-Reguant, and Moira Fradinger, Yale University, 2 November 2008.

1 Appiah's *Cosmopolitanism* is a paradigmatic example. His cosmopolitan individual has all the good qualities you might find in a well-meaning Christian with a vision of a friendly world, though Kwame uses secular terms. Kwame Anthony Appiah, *Cosmopolitanism*, 152–76.

2 Yampara ("Debate sobre el Pachamamismo") explains: "Del suma–kamaña si, del 'vivir bien' is a forced translation with certain limitations 'Suma kamaña' doesn't draw the distinction 'to live well,' as it implies that there is a zone of 'not living well.' The expression means to live in harmony and complementarity, integrating the diversity of the eco-biotic that is at the center (tayip) and looms between life and death (jaka and jiwa) (es vivir/con-vivir en armonía y complementariedad integral de los diversos mundos de la comunidad eco-biótica natural, que esta en el taypi/centro, entre la jaka/vida y jiwa/muerte). That is kama-(ña)/vivencia (vivir-to live) con-vivencia (and to live with) de los diversos mundos en armonía (harmonizing the diversity of worlds)." Of Pachamama, he explains, "'Pacha-mama,' is a generalization of pacha-tayka, which means the duplex, force-energy of Mother Nature is not restricted to Mother Earth." See Yampara, "Debate sobre el Pachamamismo."

3 In the past three or four years, more specifically since Evo Morales was elected president and the constitutions of Bolivia and Ecuador (under Correa) entered the process of being rewritten, the expressions *buen vivir*, Sumak Kawsay, and Suma Kamaña have proliferated on Google. Although the concept is indigenous, it is mostly mestizo and mestiza intellectuals as well as Europeans who write about it. Indigenous intellectuals and activists are enacting it, but not much writing from them is being posted or published. I select one example akin to my own argument, by the Colombian ambientalist Roa Avendaño, "El Sumak Kawsay como expresión de la descolonialidad del poder," http://totumasymaracas.wordpress.com/2010/01/18/el-sumak-kawsay-como-expresion-de-la-descolonialidad-del-poder. The same author has written a useful pedagogical article, http://totumasymaracas.wordpress.com/2010/01/18/el-sumak-kawsay-en-ecuador-y-bolivia-vivir-bien-identidad-alternativa. The indigenous interpretation of their own concept could be consulted in the Ecuadorian activist and politician Monica Chuji; in her explanation of Sumak Kawsay, she underlines the meaning of "to live in harmony and in fullness," http://www.miradoriu.org/spip.php?article168.

4 Douzinas, "Empire or Cosmopolitanism?"

5 For instance Titus Livius's *Ab Urbe Condita* ("from the city have been founded") tells the story of the city of Rome.

6 Ibid., 235.

7 Ibid., 249, emphasis added.

8 Ibid., 248.

9 Ibid.

10 Toulmin, *Cosmopolis*, 128.

11 Holland had a flourishing commercial interregnum in the seventeenth century, but Dutch is not among the top ten languages in terms of number of speakers. Portuguese is in seventh place, above Italian and French, and below Arabic and Bengali.

12 Toulmin, *Cosmopolis*, 133.

13 Ibid.

14 Ibid.

15 Arrighi, *Adam Smith in Beijing*.

16 The logic of coloniality is unthinkable in the beautifully written and well-advertised essay by Kwame Anthony Appiah, "Cosmopolitanism."

17 In 1976 Canada joined the G6: France, Germany, Italy, Japan, the United Kingdom, and the United States. Japan may be an anomaly today, but it was not then, when it was the U.S. signpost in East Asia and China was still under Mao. Japan, "the yellow empire," and Israel, the Jewish State, functioned as two signposts of U.S. international politics. Israel still does, but Japan has taking significant steps toward dewesternization.

18 It is not by chance that Elena Yeah perceived the commonalities between Latour's Actor Network Theory and the Modernity/(De)Coloniality project. Her analysis clearly shows that there are two projects walking in the same direction and dwelling in different, although entangled, local histories: the European imperial local histories and the South, Central American, and Caribbean local histories. It shows also that although the point of origination of coloniality was the Third World, its routes of dispersion can move to the First World. See Yeah, "Towards Decolonizing Encounters."

19 "Three Principles of the People," available at the Absolute Astronomy website, http://www.absoluteastronomy.com; Cantlie and Jones, *Sun Yat Sen and the Awakening of China*.

20 Adolfo Alban Achinte, Colombian artist, activist, intellectual, and scholar, introduced the concept in a doctoral dissertation presented at the Universidad Andina Simón Bolívar, Quito, Ecuador: "Tiempos de zango y de guampin: transformaciones gastronómicas, territorialidad y re-existencia socio-cultural en comunidades afro-descendientes de los valles interandinos del Patia (sur de Colombia) y Chota (norte del Ecuador), siglo XX." For more information about Albán Achinte, see http://www.mibugalagrande.net/nuestra-gente/alban-adolfo-achinte/prologo.

21 See for instance Ernst and Martin, *Rethinking Islamic Studies*. The book announces that there was already a shift—when the "Orientals" built their arguments; in such cases, there is no room for the "Occidental" to pretend that knowledge is here and the object is there. Cosmopolitan localism takes up from breaking away and shifting of this kind.

22 Anghie, "Francisco de Vitoria and the Colonial Origins of International Law." My own take on de Vitoria can be found in "The Many-Faces of Cosmopolis."

23 Mignolo, "The Many-Faces of Cosmpolis."

24 Anghie, "Francisco de Vitoria and the Colonial Origins of International Law," 102, emphasis added.

25 Hinkelammert, "The Hidden Agenda of Modernity."

26 Ibid., 103, emphasis added.

27 Steger, *Globalism*, 12.

28 Chatterjee, *The Politics of the Governed*, 53–80.

29 Shari'ati, "Exchange and Refinement of Cultural Resources," 33. For a biography of Shari'ati, see Rahnema, *An Islamic Utopian*. Although the debate today is much "advanced" (see An-Na'im, *Islam and the Secular State*), it is still formulated in institutional and legal terms. The question of "Human" is bypassed in the debates about rights and law. And it was the "Human" that was the core of Shari'ati's reflections and concerns, and that is still missing in most current debates about Islam, democracy, shari'a, religion, and the state. I was recently told by Zahra Maranlou (Warwick University, 23 November 2010) that Shari'ati is despised by the new generation in Iran. It is not surprising that most of the young generation should tend to be "modern" (that is, to think according to a hegemonic, mass media–produced idea of modernity). The same phenomenon can be found in China, and among Native Americans and Central Asian youth. That is the way it is. Rewesternization is the most visible of all available options.

30 Norman Givan offers this profile in his semblance, "Lloyd Best: The Great Conceptualizer," http://www.normangirvan.info/lloyd-best-a-great-conceptualiser.

31 Shari'ati, *Man and Islam*, Preface.

32 See also Best, "Independence and Responsibility."

33 Best, "Independent Thought and Caribbean Freedom," 29. "New World" refers to a Caribbean intellectual think tank, of which Best was a key figure.

34 Mahbubani, *The New Asian Hemisphere*, 133.

35 See Latour, "Whose Cosmos, Which Cosmopolitics?," emphasis added.

36 See Yehia, "Decolonizing Knowledges and Practices."

37 Latour, "Whose Cosmos, Which Cosmopolitics?," 462.

38 Bruce Lawrence, "Competing Genealogies of Muslim Cosmopolitanism," an intervention at the workshop "(De)Colonial Cosmopolitanism (Political Economy, Religion and International Relations)," held at the Center for Global Studies and the Humanities, Duke University, 26–28 February 2009.

39 Lawrence and Cook, *Muslim Networks*; Ernst and Martin, *Rethinking Muslim Studies*.

40 Walsh, *Interculturalidad, estado, sociedad*. See also the interview with Walsh by Mignolo, "Decolonial Thinking and Doing in the Andes."

Afterword

1 Gordon, "Fanon and Development."

2 José Avendaño, leader and activist of indigenous communities, personal conversation, 23 April 2009, my own translation from Spanish.

3 Mahbubani, *The New Asian Hemisphere*, 134. There is however a slow awakening of the "Western mind" reviewing the pre-judgment about China and Asia. See, for example, the reference I made to Philip Stephens's op-ed in chapter 1. It was reproduced under a slightly different title elsewhere, "An Encounter with History That Hangs over the Present," *Financial Times*, 13 December 2007. Also see the recent article by James Kynge, "West Still Miscasts 1989 Protestors," *Financial Times*, 4 June 2009, 9. Acknowledging that he was one of the confused journalist during the events, and without justifying the violent state reactions against protesters, Kynge dispels the Western myth that the protesters were demanding "democracy." Kynge argues that the youth of the time had no sense of Western democracy and that if they were demanding something specific, it was closer to Mao's socialism than to Western democracy.

4 Mahbubani, *The New Asian Hemisphere*, 134.

5 Ibid.

6 Ibid.

7 Ibid., 157.

8 Ibid., 137.

9 Ibid.

10 Sen, *Development as Freedom*, 205, emphasis added.

11 Nandy, "The Beautiful Future of Poverty," 482–83.

12 Balcerowicz, "This Has Not Been a Pure Failure of Markets," *Financial Times*, 13 May 2009, 9.

13 Ibid.

14 One example, among many, is open-sky mining in Argentina. See "Argentina: La Rioja se mobiliza."

15 See the classic account by Escobar, *Encountering Development*.

16 The concept was incorporated in the new constitution of Ecuador. If you Google "Sumak Kawsay," you will find that many entries have appeared in the past year or so, mostly written by mestizos and mestizas in Latin America and by intellectuals of the European Left. I select two pieces closer to my argument: "El Sumak Kawsay como expresión de la descolonialidad del poder," by the Colombian journalist and activist Tatiana Roa Avendaño; and "Modernidad, desarrollo, interculturalidad y

Sumak Kawsay o Buen Vivir," presented by Monica Chuji, a Kichua activist from the Ecuadorian Amazon, at the International Forum on Interculturality and Development, Uribia, Colombia, 23 May 2009. This article was available on the web until mid-2010. The original meaning of the term radically differs from the principles underlying the Western idea of development.

17 For NGOS' use of Sumak Kawasy, see the United Nations webpage http://www .unv.org/en/what-we-do/thematic-areas/culture-sports/doc/caminando-al-sumak-kawsay.html; for the Left there are plenty of examples on the web, but one starting point would be the World Social Forum, http://blogs.oxfam.org/en/blog/09-01-29-sumak-kawsay-and-what-got-lost-translation-development; for an indigenous take on it, see the Ecuadorian politician and activist Monica Chuji, "Modernidad, desarrollo, interculturalidad y Sumak Kawsay," http://www.inredh.org/index .php?option=com_content&view=article&id=216%3Amodernidad-desarrollo-interculturalidad-y-sumak-kawsay-o-buen-vivir&Itemid=86.

18 The web is already full of references, descriptions, and interpretations of Sumak Kawsay, which has become a point of debate between the (white) Right and the Left, http://mundomicrofinanzas.blogspot.com/2009/03/sumak-kawsay-y-el-debate-sobre-economia.html. For authoritative indigenous voices in the debate, see Simon Yamapra, in Bolivia, "Sobre el Pachamamismo," http://mundomicrofinanzas .blogspot.com/2009/03/sumak-kawsay-y-el-debate-sobre-economia.html; and Monica Chunji, in Ecuador, http://www.web.ca/%7Ebthomson/degrowth/Monica_Chuji_espanol.htm.

19 Yampara, "Debate sobre el pachamamismo," http://www.alminuto.com.bo/content/debate-sobre-el-pachamamismo-habla-simon-yampara.

20 Fernández Osco, "Ayllu: Decolonial Critical Thinking," http://www.globalautonomy .ca/global1/summary.jsp?index=RS_FernandezOsco_Ayllu.xml.

21 Enriquez Salas, "Pachamama-Runa-Sallqa." A useful description of the meaning of *runa* can be found in Rengifo Vázquez, "The *Ayllu*."

22 See the impassioned argument in Stengers, *Au temps des catastrophes*, 51.

23 Evo Morales's discourse can be found at www.un.org/en/ga/64/generaldebate/pdf/BO_en.pdf.

24 See Yampara Huarachi, *El Ayllu y la territorialidad en los Andes*, for another explanation of the meaning of Sumak Kawsay which was derived from and integrated into the re-inscription of Tawantinsuyu in the present of Bolivia (that is, equivalent to the re-inscription of Greece and Rome in the present of Western European countries).

25 Evo Morales explains at length the concept of "bien vivir": "Vivir bien es vivir en igualdad y justicia," in an interview with Fernando Bossi. See Bossi and Morales, "Entrevista a Evo Morales."

26 See the report and evaluation by Eduardo Gudynas, "Evo Morales renueva las propuestas de integración regional orientándolas al 'buen vivir'"; and more recently, Catherine Walsh, "Interculturalidad, de-colonialidad y el buen vivir."

27 For an overall view of the debate see "Debate 'Pachamamismo,'" http://www.amigo-latino.de/indigena/noticias/newsletter_5/329_pachamama_PS.html. It would be interesting to follow up on this debate now that vast deposits of lithium have been discovered in Bolivian state territory, http://boliviarising.blogspot.com/2010/08/lithium-gift-of-pachamama.html.

28 "La agonía de un mito: ¿Cómo reformular el 'desarrollo'?," *America Latina en Movimiento* 445 (June 2009).

29 Bossi and Morales, "Entrevista a Evo Morales."

30 Enriquez Salas, "La concepción andina de la crianza de animales y plantas."

31 Shari'ati, "Extraction and Refinement of Cultural Resources."

32 Best, "Independent Thought and Caribbean Freedom."

33 Best, "Independence and Responsibility."

34 Ibid., 3.

35 Ibid., 4.

36 Best, "Independent Thought and Caribbean Freedom," 29. This statement is from 1966. He broke relations with the New World Group by 1975.

37 Best, "Independence and Responsibility," 5, emphasis added.

38 Best and Levitt, Preface to *The Theory of Plantation Economy*, xi.

39 Levitt, "In Search of Model IV." The legacies that Levitt reviewed in 2002 were revamped in 2010 with the publication of *The Thought of New World: The Search for Decolonization*. See Garvin, "Long Live Independent Thought," http://www.normangirvan.info/wp-content/uploads/2010/10/new-world-book-launch2.pdf.

40 Best and Levitt, *The Theory of Plantation Economy*, 41.

41 Maurice Lemoine, "Coup de tonnerre à La Paz: La Bolivie indienne rejoint la gauche Latine," *Le Monde diplomatique*, 22 December 2005.

42 Hardin, "The Tragedy of the Commons"; video clips of the conference "On the Idea of Communism" at the Birbeck Institute are available on YouTube.com and Sciencestage.com.

43 Gonzalez Casanova, "Las razones del Zapatismo y la Otra Campaña."

44 Hui, *China's New Order*, 124, 183.

45 Chen, *Asia as Method*.

46 Kellner, "Critical Theory, Poststructuralism and the Philosophy of Liberation."

47 Patzi Paco, *Sistema comunal*. For a detailed description of Ayllus and Markas, where the communal system operates, see Yampara Huarachi, *El Ayllu y la territorialidad en los Andes*; and on the arrival of capitalism and on "haciendas" coexisting with but displacing the sovereignty of the ayllu, see Nadine Sebill, *Ayllus y haciendas*.

48 To be more precise, in Aymara the expression is *suma jaqaña*, which means to live in harmony with all living organisms; it is a philosophical vision. *Suma Kamaña*, which is the more popular term today, is used in a more restrictive sense, although it is compatible with the original expression (personal communication with Marcelo Fernández-Osco). In addition to the proliferation of writings on the concept

of buen vivir, there is a documentary that was made in Bolivia by indigenous video and filmmakers: *Suma Qamaña, Sumak Kausay, Teko Kavi/For a Better Life* (2008). The documentary was directed collectively and produced by the Cinematography Education and Production Center, Bolivian Indigenous Peoples' Audiovisual Council.

49 In fact, Rafael Correa is adopting more and more a dewesternizing position.

50 See the debate referred to in note 26.

51 Reinaga, *La revolución India*, 382.

52 This is a free translation of an article published by the Aymara intellectual Carlos Mamani Condori (Presidente del foro permanente de las Naciones Unidas sobre cuestiones Indígenas), http://www.scribd.com/doc/4093276/mamani.

53 Consejo Nacional de Ayllus y Markas del Qullasuyu, "Constituido el 22 de Marzo de 1997," http://www.conamaq.org.

54 Boroujerdi, "Ali Shari'ati."

55 Ibid., 14, emphasis added.

56 Fanon, *The Wretched of the Earth*, 209–10.

57 Quijano, "Otro horizonte de sentido historico," 441.

58 See "Nina Pacari," a short biography by Marc Becker and Judy Hinojosa.

59 Papers from this seminar has been collected in Cairo Carou and Mignolo, *Las vertientes Americanas del pensamiento y el proyecto des-colonial*. See also Cairo Carou, "Palestra."

60 Pacari, "La incidencia de la participación política de los pueblos indígenas," 47, emphasis added.

61 A sensible narrative can be found in Diawara, "Pan-Africanism and Pedagogy." Diawara summarizes this conundrum (the salvationist white Left telling black people what to do): "Ironically, this awareness of common struggle, of the worldwide demand for human rights from White supremacists and capitalists, seems to take away Negritude's first claim to authenticity and singularity. As some students in the class pointed out, it may not be possible to take everyone in the direction that Sartre is taking Negritude. The desire to appear universal may cause Negritude to forget or ignore some of its constituent elements, and therefore to disintegrate. The students were concerned about Sartre setting the agenda for the Negritude poets, a white man telling them what to do and how to do it and therefore diluting the radical ideas in the movement" (ibid.).

62 Nina Pacari, "La incidencia de la participación política de los pueblos indígenas," 56.

63 Ibid., 57. For a distinction between identity politics and identity *in* politics, very much in line with Pacari's pronouncement, see Mignolo, "The Decolonial Option and the Meaning of Identity in Politics."

64 *Minga* is a Quechua word that expresses a sense of community and cooperation in "bar raising." Bar raising was common in the rural United States in the late eighteenth century and the nineteenth, but *minga* carries the weight of the Indian lifestyle and way of being in the world.

65 See Equipo Nizkor, "Perú." In October 2003, the president of Bolivia, Gonzálo Sánchez de Losada, left the country after ordering a military repression of citizens, the
majority being Indians, who were defending their territories against government
threats to expropriate their land in order to support extraction of natural resources
by private and international corporations. See Clavero, "¿Genocidios Afines?"

66 While this book was in production, I received a copy of *Descolonización en Bolivia.
Cuatro ejes para comprender el cambio*, edited by Vicepresidencia del Estado Pluri-
nacional de Bolivia y la Fundación Boliviana para la Democracia Multipartidaria
(La Paz: December 2010). Aymara and Quecha leaders and thinkers involved and
engaged in making Bolivia a plurinational state participated in creating the book,
which is the most detailed examination to date of the possibilities and difficulties of
advancing processes of decolonization within the State.

BIBLIOGRAPHY

Abu-Lughod, Janet L. *Before European Hegemony: The World System, A.D. 1250–1350*. New York: Oxford University Press, 1989.

Acosta, José de. *Natural and Moral History of the Indies*, ed. Jane Mangan, trans. Frances L. Morilla, introduction and commentary by Walter D. Mignolo. Durham: Duke University Press, 2002 [1590].

Adorno, Rolena. *Guaman Poma de Ayala: Writing and Resistance in Colonial Peru*. Austin: University of Texas Press, 1986.

Agamben, Giorgio. "Beyond Human Rights." *Radical Thought in Italy: A Potential Politics*, ed. Michael Hardt and Paolo Virno, 159–66. Minneapolis: University of Minnesota Press, 1996.

———. *The Coming Community*, trans. Michael Hardt. Minneapolis: University of Minnesota Press, 1993.

Agnew, John. "Know-Where: Geographies of Knowledge of World Politics." *International Political Sociology* 1 (2007): 138–48.

Ahmad, Jalal Al-i. *Occidentosis: A Plague from the West*. Berkeley: Mizan, 1984.

Ahmad, Zaid. *The Epistemology of Ibn Khaldun*. London: Routledge-Curzon, 2003.

Albán Achinte, Adolfo. *Tiempos de zango y de guampín: Transformaciones gastronómicas, territorialidad y re-existencia socio-cultural en comunidades Afro-descendientes de los valles interandinos del Patía (sur de Colombia) y Chota (norte del Ecuador), siglo xx*. Ph.D. diss., Universidad Andina Simón Bolívar, Quito, 2007.

Allawi, Ali-Abdul-Amir. *The Crisis of Islamic Civilization*. New Haven: Yale University Press, 2009.

———. "Incoherence of Power: An Interview with Ali Allawi." *Guernica* (April 2007). http://www.guernicamag.com/interviews/323/incoherence_of_power_1.

America Latina en Movimiento (June 2009): 445. Special issue: "La agonía

de un mito? Cómo formular el desarrollo." http://www.alainet.org/publica/445
.phtml.

Amin, Samir. *Delinking: Towards a Polycentric World*. London: Zed, 1990 [1985].

Anghie, Antony. "Francisco de Vitoria and the Colonial Origins of International Law."
Laws of the Postcolonial, ed. Eve Darian-Smith and Peter Fitzpatrick, 89–108. Ann
Arbor: University of Michigan Press, 1999.

———. *Imperialism, Sovereignty and the Making of International Law*. Cambridge:
Cambridge University Press, 2008.

An-Na'im, Abdullahi Ahmed. *Islam and the Secular State: Negotiating the Future of
Shari'a*. Cambridge: Harvard University Press, 2008.

Anzaldúa, Gloria. *Borderland/La Frontera: The New Mestiza*. San Francisco: Aunt Lute,
1987.

Appiah, Kwame Anthony. *Cosmopolitianism: Ethics in a World of Strangers*. New York:
W. W. Norton, 2006.

Arendt, Hannah. *The Origins of Totalitarianism*. New York: Harcourt Brace, 1976 [1948].

Armstrong, Karen. *Islam: A Short History*. New York: Modern Library Chronicles,
2002.

Arrighi, Giovanni. *Adam Smith in Beijing: Lineages of the Twenty-First Century*. London: Verso, 2007.

Augustine, Saint, Bishop of Hippo. *Confessiones*, trans. E. M. Blaiklock. Nashville: T.
Nelson, 1983.

Aveni, Anthony. *Empires of Time: Calendars, Clocks, and Cultures*. New York: Basic
Books, 1989.

Aydin, Cemil. *The Politics of Anti-Westernism in Asia: Visions of World Order in Pan-
Islamic and Pan Asian Thought*. New York: Columbia University Press, 2007.

Bacon, Frances. *Novum Organum. Cambridge Texts in the History of Philosophy*. Cambridge: Cambridge University Press, 2000 [1620].

Bakhtiar, Laleh. *Shari'ati on Shari'ati and the Muslim Woman*. Chicago: ABC International, 1996.

Balibar, Étienne. "La proposition de l'égaliberté." Les Conférences du Perroquet
22 (November 1989); "'Rights of Man' and 'Rights of the Citizen': The Modern
Dialectics of Equality and Freedom." *Masses, Classes, Ideas: Studies on Politics and
Philosophy before and after Marx*, 39–59. New York: Routledge, 1994.

Barium, Fawzia. "Malik Bennabi and the Intellectual Problems of the Muslim
Ummah." *American Journal of Islamic Social Sciences* 9 (fall 1992): 325–37.

Beck, Ulrich. "The Truth of Others. A Cosmopolitan Approach." *Common Knowledge*
10, no. 3 (2004): 430–49.

Becker, Marc, and Judy Hinojosa. "Nina Pacari." *Notable Twentieth-Century Latin
American Women: A Biographical Dictionary*, ed. Cynthia Tompkins and David
William Foster, 218–22. Westport, Conn.: Greenwood, 2001.

Bell, David. *China's New Confucianism: Politics and Every Day Life in a Changing Society*. Princeton: Princeton University Press, 2008.

Bello, Walden. "The World Social Forum at the Crossroad." ZNET: A Community of People Committed to Social Change. http://www.zcommunications.org/the-world-social-forum-at-the-crossroads-by-walden-bello.

————. "The Past, Present and Future of the World Social Forum." The Labor Community Strategy Center. http://www.thestrategycenter.org/radio/2009/03/09/walden-bello-past-present-and-future-world-social-forum.

————. *Deglobalization: Ideas for a New World Economy*. Dhaka: University Press, 2004.

————. *The Future in the Balance. Essays on Globalizaton and Resistance*. Oakland: Food First, 2001.

Benlahcene, Badrane. "A Metatheoretical Study of Malek Bennabi's Approach to Civilization." Ph.D. diss., Universiti Putra Malaysia, 2004. http://psasir.upm.edu.my/289.

Bennabi, Malik. *The Question of Culture*. 1971, ed., annotated, and with a foreword by Mohaber El-Tahir El-Mesawi. Trans. Abdul Wahid Lu'lu'a. Kuala Lumpur: International Institute of Islamic Thought, 2003.

————. *The Question of Ideas in the Muslim World*. 1970. Trans., annotated, and with a foreword by Mohaber El-Tahir El-Mesawi. Kuala Lumpur: International Institute of Islamic Thought, 2003.

Benveniste, Emile. "L'appareil formel de l'énonciation." *Problémes de Linguistique Générale*, 2:9–88. Paris: Gallimard, 1974.

Best, Lloyd. "Independent Thought and Caribbean Freedom." *New World Quarterly* 3, no. 4 (1967): 13–36.

————. "Independence and Responsibility: Self Knowledge as an Imperative." *The Critical Tradition of Caribbean Political Economy: The Legacy of George Beckford*, ed. Kari Levitt and Michael Witter. Kingston: Ian Randle, 1996.

————, and Kari Polanyi Levitt. *Essays on the Theory of Plantation Economy: A Historical and Institutional Approach to Caribbean Economic Development*. Kingston: University of West Indies Press, 2009.

Bisaha, Nancy. *Creating the West: Renaissance Humanists and the Ottoman Turks*. Philadelphia: University of Pennsylvania Press, 2004.

Blaut, J. M. *The Colonizer's Model of the World: Geographical Diffusionism and Eurocentric History*. New York: Guilford, 2003.

Bonilla, Heraclio, ed. *Los conquistados: 1492 y la población indígena de las Américas*. Bogotá: Tercer Mundo, 1992.

Boroujerdi, Mehrzad. "Ali Shari'ati: The Aspiring Luther." *Iranian Intellectuals and the West: The Tormented Triumph of Nativism*, 105–16. Syracuse: Syracuse University Press, 1996.

Bossi, Fernando, and Evo Morales. "Entrevista a Evo Morales: Vivir bien es vivir en igualdad y en justicia." *Rebelión*, 29 September 2007. http://www.rebelion.org/noticia.php?id=56736.

Bouysse-Cassagne, Thérèse, and Olivia Harris. "Pacha: En torno al pensamiento aymara." *Tres reflexiones sobre el pensamiento Andino*, ed. Thérèse Bouysse-Cassagne, Olivia Harris, Tristan Platt, and Verónica Cereceda, 11–60. La Paz: Hisbol, 1987.

Brague, Rémi. *Europe: La Voie Romaine*. Paris: Gallimard, 1999.

Bremmer, Ian. *The End of the Free Market: Who Wins the War between States and Corporations?* New York: Portfolio, 2010.

Brown, F. A., Jr. "Life's Mysterious Clocks." *Adventures of the Mind*, ed. Richard Thruelsen and John Kobler, 159–78. New York: Random House, 1962.

Brown, F. A., J. Hastings, and J. Palmer, eds. *The Biological Clock*. New York: Academic, 1970.

Buck-Morss, Susan. "Can There Be a Global Left?" *Thinking Past Terror: Islamism and Critical Theory on the Left*, 92–112. London: Verso, 2003.

———. *Thinking Past Terror: Islamism and Critical Theory on the Left*. London: Verso, 2003.

Buruma, Ian, and Avishai Margalit. *Occidentalism: The West in the Eyes of Its Enemies*. New York: Penguin, 2004.

Cairo Carou, Heriberto, ed. "Palestra." *Tabula Rasa* 8 (2007). http://www.revistata bularasa.org/numero8.html.

Cairo Carou, Heriberto, and Walter D. Mignolo, eds. *Las vertientes americanas del pensamiento y el proyecto des-colonial*. Madrid: Trama / Gecal, 2008.

Cajete, Gregory. *Look to the Mountain: An Ecology of Indigenous Education*. Asheville, N.C.: Kivaki, 1994.

Cantlie, James, and C. Sheridan Jones. *Sun Yat Sen and the Awakening of China*. London: General Books, 2009.

Cash, Richard. "Research Imbalances: Taking Science to the Problem." *International Health* 27.1 (spring 2005): 50–53.

Cassano, Franco. *Homo civicus: La ragionevole follia dei beni comuni*. Bari: Dedalo, 2004.

———. *Il pensiero meridiano*. Bari: Laterza, 1996. Trans. Norma Bouchard and Valerio Ferme as *Southern Thought and Other Essays on the Mediterranean*. New York: Fordham University Press, 2011.

Castells, Manuel. *The Rise of the Network Society: The Information Age: Economy, Society and Culture*. London: Blackwell, 1997.

Castro-Gómez, Santiago. *La hubris del punto cero: Ciencia, raza e ilustración en la Nueva Granada (1750–1816)*. Bogotá: Editorial Pontificia Universidad Javeriana, 2005.

———. "The Missing Chapter of Empire: Postmodern Reorganization of Coloniality and Post-Fordist Capitalism." *Cultural Studies* 21, nos. 2–3 (2007): 428–48.

Castro-Kláren, Sara. "Posting Letters: Writing in the Andes and the Paradoxes of the Postcolonial Debate." *Coloniality at Large: Latin America and the Postcolonial Debate*, ed. Mabel Moraña, Enrique D. Dussel, and Carlos A. Jáuregui, 130–57. Durham: Duke University Press, 2008.

Césaire, Aimé. *Discourse on Colonialism*, trans. Joan Pinkham with a new introduction by Robin D. G. Kelley. New York: Monthly Review, 2000 [1955].

Charleston, Steven. "From Medicine Man to Marx: The Coming Shift in Native Theology." *Native American Religious Identity: Unforgotten Gods*, ed. Jace Weaver, 155–72. New York: Orbis, 1998.

Chakrabarty, Dipesh. *Provincializing Europe: Postcolonial Thought and Historical Difference*. Princeton: Princeton University Press, 2000.

Chatterjee, Partha. "Democracy and the Violence of the State: A Political Negotiation of Death." Lecture delivered in the History Department, Harvard University, 18 November 1999.

———. "On Civil and Political Society in Post-colonial Democracies." *Civil Society: History and Possibilities*, ed. Sudipta Kaviraj and Sunil Khilnani, 165–78. Cambridge: Cambridge University Press, 2001.

———. *The Politics of the Governed: Reflections on Popular Politics in Most of the World*. New York: Columbia University Press, 2004.

———. "Talking about Our Modernity in Two Languages." *A Possible India: Essays in Political Criticism*, 263–85. Calcutta: Oxford University Press, 1998.

———. "Modernity and Indian Nationalism." *India Revisited: Conversations on Contemporary India*, ed. Ramin Jahanbegloo, 45–50. New Delhi: Oxford University Press, 2008.

Chen, Kuan-Hsing. *Asia as Method: Toward Deimperialization*. Durham: Duke University Press, 2010.

Chimalpahín, Francisco de San Antón Muñón. *Relaciones originales de Chalco Amaquemecan*, paleography, trans., and gloss by Silvia Rendón, preface by Angel María Garibay K. Mexico City: Fondo de Cultura Económica, 1965 [1650].

Ching, Leo T. S. *Becoming Japanese: Colonial Taiwan and the Politics of Identity Formation*. Durham: Duke University Press, 2001.

Choquehuanca, David, Rigoberta Menchú, et al. *Buen Vivir y Derechos de la Madre Tierra: Avances y Propuestas Hacia el Mundo*. www.fedaeps.org. IV Foro Social Américas, Setiembre 2010. http://www.fedaeps.org/cambio-civilizatorio-y-buen-vivir/buen-vivir-y-derechos-de-la-madre.

Chuji, Monica. "Modernidad, desarrollo, interculturalidad y Sumak Kawsay o Buen Vivir." Presentación en el Foro Internacional sobre Interculturalidad y Desarrollo, Uribia, Colombia, 23 May 2009. Published by Fundación Regional y Asesoría de los Derechos Humanos (INREDH, http://www.inredh.org), Ecuador. http://www.inredh.org/index.php?option=com_content&view=article&id=216:modernidad-desarrollo-interculturalidad-y-sumak-kawsay-o-buen-vivir&catid=58:informes&Itemid=86.

Churchland, Patricia Smith. *Brain-Wise: Studies in Neurophilosophy*. Cambridge: MIT Press, 2002.

Churchland, Paul. *Neurophilosophy at Work*. Cambridge: Cambridge University Press, 2007.

Clavero, Bartolomé. "¿Genocidios Afines? Bolivia—2003, Perú—2009." Bartolomé Clavero, 9 June 2009. http://www.clavero.derechosindigenas.org.

Coe, Michael D. *Breaking the Maya Code*. New York: Thames and Hudson, 1992.

Conrad, Joseph. *Heart of Darkness*. London: Penguin, 1995 [1899].

Consejo Nacional de Ayllus y Markas del Qullasuyu. "Constituido el 22 de Marzo de 1997." http://www.conamaq.org.

Coronil, Fernando. "Elephants in the Americas? Latin American Postcolonial Studies and Global Decolonization." *Coloniality at Large: Latin America and the Postcolonial Debate*, ed. Mabel Moraña, Enrique Dussel, and Carlos A. Jáuregui, 396–416. Durham: Duke University Press, 2008.

——. "Naturaleza del postcolonialismo: Del eurocentrismo al globocentrismo." *La colonialidad del saber: Eurocentrismo y ciencias sociales: Perspectivas Latinoamericanas*, ed. Edgardo Lander, 87–112. Buenos Aires: Consejo Latinoamericano de Ciencias Sociales, 2000.

Curran, James, and Myung-Jin Park, eds. *De-Westernizing Media Studies*. London: Routledge, 2000.

Dagenais, John. Introduction. "Decolonizing the Middle Ages." Special issue of *Medieval and Early Modern Studies* 30 no. 3 (2000) 431–48.

——. "The Postcolonial Laura." *Modern Language Quarterly* 65, no. 3 (September 2004): 365–89.

Dainotto, Roberto. *Europe (in Theory)*. Durham: Duke University Press, 2008.

De la Grange, Bertrand, and Maite Rico. *Subcomandante Marcos: La genial impostura*. Madrid: El Pais / Aguilar, 1998.

de Landa, Diego. *Relación de las Cosas de Yucatán*. 1556. Encyclopedia Britannica Online, 8 November 2010. http://www.britannica.com.

Deloria, Vine, Jr. *For This Land: Writing on Religion in America*. London: Routledge, 1998.

——. "Thinking in Time and Space." *God Is Red: A Native View of Religion*, 61–76. Golden, Colo.: Fulcrum, 1994.

Descartes, René. *Discours de la méthode, pour bien conduire la raison, et chercher la vérité dans les sciences*. Leyde: Ian Maire, 1637.

——. *Meditationes de prima philosophia, in qua dei existentia et animae immortalitas demonstratur*. Paris: Michaelem Soly, 1641.

De Sousa Santos, Boaventura. "O China o Sumak Kawsay." *America Latina en Movimiento* 441 (25 February 2009): 10–14.

——. *The World Social Forum: A User's Manual*. 2004. http://www.ces.uc.pt.

——. "The World Social Forum and the Global Left." *Politics and Society* 36, no. 2 (2008): 247–70.

Diawara, Manthia. "Pan-Africanism and Pedagogy." Black Cultural Studies, 1996. http://www.blackculturalstudies.org.

Dilthey, Wilhelm. *Introduction to the Human Sciences*. Princeton: Princeton University Press, 1991.

Dirks, Nicholas B. "Introduction: Colonialism and Culture." *Colonialism and Culture*, ed. Nicholas B. Dirks, 1–26. Comparative Studies in Society and History Book Series. Ann Arbor: University of Michigan Press, 1992.

Du Bois, W. E. B. 1903. *The Souls of Black Folk*. New York: Signet Classic, 1995.

Dussel, Enrique. "Ethical Sense of the 1994 Maya Rebellion in Chiapas." *Hispano-Latino Theology* 2–3 (1994): 41–56.

———. *Etica de la liberación en la edad de la globalización y de la exclusión*. Mexico City: Universidad Autónoma Metropolitana, 1998.

———. *20 Tesis de política*. Mexico City: Plaza, 2006.

———. *Twenty Theses on Politics*, trans. George Ciccariello-Maher. Durham: Duke University Press, 2008.

———. "World System and 'Transmodernity.'" *Nepantla* 3, no. 2 (2002): 221–44.

Eastman, Charles. *The Essential Charles Eastman (Ohiyesa)*, ed. Michael Oren Fitzgerald. Bloomington: World Wisdom, 2007.

Ebaugh, Helen Rose. *The Gülen Movement: A Sociological Analysis of a Civic Movement Rooted in Moderate Islam*. London: Springer, 2009.

Elden, Stuart, and Eduardo Mendieta, eds. *Reading Kant's Geography*. Albany: State University of New York Press, 2011.

El-Tahir El-Mesawi, Mohamed. "Religion, Society and Culture in Malik Bennabib's Thought." *The Blackwell Companion of Contemporary Islamic Thoughts*, 213–56. London: Blackwell, 2007.

Enloe, Cynthia. *Bananas, Beaches and Bases: Making Feminist Sense of International Politics*. Berkeley: University of California Press, 2001 [1989].

Enriquez Salas, Porfirio. "La concepción andina de la crianza de animales y plantas." *Volveré* 5, no. 31 (May 2008). http://www.unap.cl/iecta/revistas/volvere_31/edit.htm.

———. "Pachamama-Runa-Sallqa: La crianza de la vida." *Volveré* 2008. http://www.unap.cl/iecta/revistas/volvere_31/articulo2.html.

Equipo Nizkor. "Perú: Masacre en Bagua." Derechos/Human Rights. http://www.derechos.org.

Ernst, Carl W., and Richard C. Martin, eds. *Rethinking Islamic Studies: From Orientalism to Cosmopolitanism*. Columbia: University of South Carolina Press, 2010.

Escobar, Arturo. "Beyond the Third World: Imperial Globality, Global Coloniality and Anti-Globalization Social Movements." *Third World Quarterly* 25, no. 1 (2004): 207–30.

———. *Encountering Development: The Making and Unmaking of the Third World*. Princeton: Princeton University Press, 1995.

———. "Latin America at the Cross-Road: Alternative Modernizations, Post-Neoliberalism or Post-Development?" *Cultural Studies* 24, no. 1 (January 2010): 1–65.

———. "Worlds and Knowledges Otherwise: The Latin American Modernity/Coloniality Research Program." *Cultural Studies* 21, nos. 2–3 (2007): 179–210.

Escobar, Arturo, and Walter D. Mignolo, eds. *Globalization and the Decolonial Option.* London: Blackwell, 2010.

Espejo, Oscar Mauricio. "La izquierda Latinoamericana, la colonialidad del poder y la emergencia de actores sociales de 1989 al 2006." Ph. D. diss., Universidad Distrital "Francisco José Caldas," Bogota, 2009, http://www.scribd.com/doc/36850846/.

Euben, Roxanne L. *Enemy in the Mirror: Islamic Fundamentalism and the Limits of Modern Rationalism: A Work of Comparative Political Theory.* Princeton: Princeton University Press, 1999.

Eze, Emmanuel Chukwudi. "The Color of Reason: The Idea of 'Race' in Kant's Anthropology." *Postcolonial African Philosophy: A Critical Reader*, ed. Emmanuel Chukwudi Eze, 103–40. London: Blackwell, 1997.

EZLN. "First Declaration of the Lacandon Jungle." http://en.wikisource.org.

———. "Sixth Declaration of the Selva Lacandona." http://en.wikipedia.org.

Fabian, Johannes. *Time and the Other: How Anthropology Makes Its Object.* New York: Columbia University Press, 1983.

Fanon, Frantz. *Peau noires, masques blanches.* Paris: Maspero, 1952. Trans. Charles Lam Markmann as *Black Skin, White Masks.* New York: Grove, 1967. Trans. Richard Philcox as *Black Skin, White Masks.* New York: Grove, 2008.

———. *Les damnés de la terre.* Paris: Maspero, 1961. Trans. Richard Philcox as *The Wretched of the Earth.* New York: Grove, 1963.

Farriss, Nancy M. "Remembering the Future, Anticipating the Past: History, Time and Cosmology among the Maya of Yucatan." *Time: Histories and Ethnologies*, ed. Diane Owen Hughes and Thomas R. Trautmann, 107–38. Ann Arbor: University of Michigan Press, 1995.

Fell, Lloyd, and David Russell. "An Introduction to Maturana's Ideas." Autopoiesis Plus, 1994. http://www.univie.ac.at/constructivism/pub/seized/matsbio.html.

Ferguson, Niall. *Empire: The Rise and Demise of the British World Order and the Lessons for Global Power.* London: Allen Lane, 2002.

Fernández Osco, Marcelo. "Ayllu: De-colonial Critical Thinking and an (Other) Autonomy." *Globalization and Autonomy Online Compendium.* http://www.globalautonomy.ca.

———. *La ley del Ayllu: Práctica de jach'a justicia y jisk'a justicia (Justicia Mayor y Justicia Menor) en comunidades aymaras.* La Paz: Proyecto de Investigaciones Estrateticas de Bolivia, 2000.

Florescano, Enrique. *Memory, Myth, and Time in Mexico: From the Aztecs to Independence*, trans. Albert Bork with the assistance of Kathryn R. Bork. Austin: University of Texas Press, 1994.

Foucault, Michel. *Les mots et les choses.* Paris: Gallimard, 1966.

Freyre, Gilberto. *Casa-grande e senzala.* Rio de Janeiro: José Olympio, 1988 [1933].

Gabilondo, Joseba. Introduction to *The Hispanic Atlantic.* Special issue of *Arizona Journal of Hispanic Cultural Studies* 5 (2001): 91–113.

Galindo, Mario. "Los Aymaras ya tienen el modelo de sociedad comunitaria autonómica." La Paz: PIEB (Proyecto Investigación Experimental de Bolivia), 2006. http://www.pieb.com.bo/nota.php?idn=428.

García Linera, Álvaro. *La potencia plebeya: Acción colectiva e identidades indígenas obreras y populares en Bolivia*. Antología y presentación de Pablo Stefanoni. Buenos Aires: Prometeo Libros, 2008.

———. "El desencuentro de dos razones revolucianarias: Indianismo y Marxismo." *Barataria* 1 (2005): 4–16. Repr. in CLACSO, *eldiplo.info/docs/clacs03.pdf*, trans. in *International Journal of Socialist Renewal*. http://links.org.au/node/264.

Giddens, Anthony. *Beyond Left and Right: The Future of Radical Politics*. Stanford: Stanford University Press, 1994.

Girvan, Norman. "Lloyd Best: A Great Conceptualizer." Orig. pubd. in *Trinidad and Tobago Review*, November 2005. http://www.tntreview.com. *Caribbean Political Economy*. 22 October 2005. http://www.tntreview.com.

———. "Long Live Independent Thought." *Caribbean Political Economy*. 14 October 2010. http://www.normangirvan.info/wp-content/uploads/2010/10/new-world-book-launch2.pdf.

———. "New World and Its Critics." *The Thought of New World: The Quest for Decolonization*, 3–29. Kingston: Ian Randle, 2010.

Glissant, Edouard. *Caribbean Discourse: Selected Essays*, trans. with an introduction by J. Michael Dash. Charlottesville: University Press of Virginia, 1989.

———. *Poetics of Relation*, trans. Betsy Wing. Stanford: Stanford University Press, 1997.

González Casanova, Pablo. "Las razones del Zapatismo y la Otra Campaña." *OSAL* 6 (2006): 291–303.

Goody, Jack. *Capitalism and Modernity*. Cambridge: Polity, 2004.

Gordon, Lewis R. *Disciplinary Decadence: Living Thought in Trying Times*. Boulder: Paradigm, 2006.

———. *Existentia Africana: Understanding African Existential Thought*. London: Routledge, 2000.

———. "Fanon and Development: A Philosophical Work." *Africa Development* 29 (2004): 71–93.

———. *Fanon and the Crisis of European Man: An Essay on Philosophy and the Human Sciences*. London: Routledge, 1995.

Gould, Stephen Jay. *Time's Arrow, Time's Cycle: Myth and Metaphor in the Discovery of Geological Time*. Cambridge: Harvard University Press, 1987.

Grafton, Anthony. "Chronology and Its Discontents in Renaissance Europe: The Vicissitudes of a Tradition." *Time: Histories and Ethnologies*, ed. Diane Owen Hughes and Thomas R. Trautmann, 139–66. Ann Arbor: University of Michigan Press, 1995.

Greer, Margaret R., Walter D. Mignolo, and Maureen Quilligan, eds. *Rereading the Black Legend: The Discourse of Religious and Racial Difference in the Renaissance Empires*. Chicago: Chicago University Press, 2007.

Gresh, Alain. "Iran, vers une 'communauté internationale.'" *Le monde diplomatique*, 21 May 2010.

Grosfóguel, Ramón. "Developmentism, Modernity, and Dependency Theory in Latin America." *Coloniality at Large: Latin America and the Postcolonial Debate*, ed. Mabel Moraña, Enrique D. Dussel, and Carlos A. Jáuregui, 307–35. Durham: Duke University Press, 2008.

————. "Transmodernity, Border Thinking and Global Coloniality." *Eurozine* (2008). http://www.eurozine.com/articles/2008-07-04-grosfoguel-en.html.

Grovogui, Siba N'Zatioula. *Beyond Eurocentrism and Anarchy: Memories of International Order and Institutions*. New York: Palgrave, 2006.

————. "Mind, Body and Gut! Elements of a Postcolonial Human Rights Discourse." *Decolonizing International Relations*, ed. Branwen Gruffydd Jones, 179–96. London: Rowman and Littlefield, 2006.

————. *Sovereigns, Quasi Sovereigns and Africans: Race and Self-Determination in International Law*. Minneapolis: University of Minnesota Press, 1995.

Gudynas, Eduardo. "Evo Morales renueva las propuestas de integración regional orientándolas al 'buen vivir.'" *Peripecias* 25 (29 November 2006). http://www.peripecias.com.

Guha, Ranajit. *Dominance without Hegemony: History and Power in Colonial India*. Cambridge: Harvard University Press, 1997.

Gusdorf, Georges. *Les origines des sciences humaines et la pensée occidentale*. Paris: Payot, 1967.

Habermas, Jürgen. "The Inclusion of the Other." *Studies in Political Theory*, ed. Ciaran P. Cronin and Pablo De Breiff, 35–37. Cambridge: MIT Press, 1999.

Hardin, Garrett. "The Tragedy of the Commons." *Science* 162 (1968): 1243–48.

Hawking, Stephen. *A Brief History of Time: From the Big Bang to Black Holes*. Toronto: Bantam, 1988.

Hay, Denys. *Europe: The Emergence of an Idea*. Edinburgh: Edinburgh University Press, 1968.

Hegel, George W. F. *The Philosophy of History*, trans. J. Sibree. Buffalo: Prometheus, 1991 [1822].

Heilbron, Johan. *The Rise of Social Theory*, trans. Sheila Gogol. Minneapolis: University of Minnesota Press, 1995.

Heinze, Eric A., and Brent J. Steele. *Ethics, Authority and War: Non-State Actors and the Just War Tradition*. New York: Palgrave Macmillan, 2009.

Held, David. *Democracy and the Global Order: From the Modern State to Cosmopolitan Governance*. Stanford: Stanford University Press, 1995.

Hinkelammert, Franz. *El mapa del emperador*. Costa Rica: Instituto de Estudios Teológicos, 1996.

————. "The Hidden Logic of Modernity: Locke and the Inversion of Human Rights." *Worlds and Knowledges Otherwise*, vol. I, dossier 1, 2004. http://www.jhfc.duke.edu/wko/dossiers/1.1/contents.php.

————. *El asalto al poder mundial y la violencia sagrada del imperio*. San José de Costa Rica: Departamento Ecuménico de Investigaciones, 2003.

———. *The Ideological Weapons of Death: A Theological Critique of Capitalism*, trans. Phillip Berryman with a foreword by Cornel West. Maryknoll, N.Y.: Orbis, 1986 [1974].

Hodgson, Marshall G. S. *Rethinking World History: Essays on Europe, Islam and World History*. London: Cambridge University Press, 1993.

Horkheimer, Max. "Traditional and Critical Theory" (1937). *Critical Theory: Selected Essays*, trans. Matthew J. O'Connell et al., 188–243. New York: Continuum, 1999.

Horowitz, David. *Unholy Alliance: Radical Islam and the American Left*. Washington: Regnery, 2005.

Hountondji, Paulin J. "Recapturing." *The Surreptitious Speech:* Présence Africaine *and the Politics of Otherness, 1947–1987*, ed. V. Y. Mudimbe, 238–48. Chicago: University of Chicago Press, 1992.

Houston, Stephen, Oswaldo Chinchilla Mazariegos, and David Stuart, eds. *The Decipherment of Ancient Maya Writing*. Oklahoma: University of Oklahoma Press, 2001.

Hui, Wang. "An Interview Concerning Modernity: A Conversation with Ke Kaijun." *The End of Revolution: China and the Limits of Modernity*, 139–88. London: Verso, 2009.

Hunter, Shireen T. "Islamic Reformist Discourses in Iran: Proponents and Prospects." *Reformist Voices in Islam: Mediating Islam and Modernity*, ed. Shireen T. Hunter, 33–95. Armonk, N.Y.: M. E. Sharpe, 2008.

Huntington, Samuel. *The Clash of Civilizations? The Debate*. New York: W. W. Norton, 1995.

———. *The Clash of Civilizations and the Remaking of World Order*. New York: Simon and Schuster, 1998.

Indigènes de la République. "The Decolonizing Struggle in France. An Interview with Houria Bouteldja by Saïd Mekki," November 2009, http://www.indigenes-republique.fr/article.php3?id_article=763.

Innerarity Grau, Daniel. "Cronopolítica: Una teoría de los ritmos sociales." *El futuro y sus enemigos: Una defensa de la esperanza política*, 133–52. Barcelona: Paidós, 2009.

Jenning, Willie James. *The Christian Imagination: Theology and the Origins of Race*. New Haven: Yale University Press, 2010.

Jersild, Austin. *Orientalism and Empire: North Caucasus Mountain Peoples and the Georgian Frontier, 1845–1917*. Montreal: McGill-Queen's University Press, 2003.

Kale, Mahavi, *Fragments of Empire: Capital, Slavery, and Indian Indentured Labor in the British Caribbean*. Philadelphia: University of Pennsylvania Press, 1996.

Kant, Immanuel. *Anthropology from a Pragmatic Point of View*, trans. F. P. Van De Pitte. Carbondale: Southern Illinois University Press, 1996 [1798].

———. "The Conflict of the Faculties" (1798). *Religion and Rational Theology*, ed. and trans. Allen W. Wood and George Di Giovanni, 233–328. Cambridge: Cambridge University Press, 1996.

———. "The Contest of Faculties." *Kant: Political Writings*, 2nd edn., ed. Hans Reiss. Cambridge: Cambridge University Press, 1991.

————. *Géographie*, trans. Michèle Cohen-Halimi, Max Marcuzzi, and Valérie Se-
roussi. Paris: Aubier, 1999.

————. "Idea of a Universal History from a Cosmopolitan Point of View" (1784).
Kant on History, ed. Lewis White Beck, 11–26. New York: Macmillan, 1963.

————. *Lectures on Logic*, ed. J. Michael Young. Cambridge: Cambridge University
Press, 2004.

————. *Observations on the Feeling of the Beautiful and the Sublime* (1764), trans.
John T. Goldthwait. Berkeley: University of California Press, 1960.

————. *Political Writing*, ed. H. S. Reiss. Cambridge Texts in the History of Political
Thought. Cambridge: Cambridge University Press, 1970.

————. *Physische Geographie*. Mainz: Gottbrief Vollmer, 1801–5.

Keene, Edward. *Beyond the Anarchical Society: Grotius, Colonialism and Order in
World Politics*. Cambridge: Cambridge University Press, 2002.

Kellner, Douglas. "Critical Theory, Poststructuralism, and the Philosophy of Liberation." *Illuminations* (2001). http://www.uta.edu.

Keenan, Bernard. "Communism A Viable Alternative?" *The Guardian*, 16 March 2009.

Khaldun, Ibn. 1377. *The Muqaddimah: An Introduction to History*, ed. N. J. Dawood,
trans. Franz Rosenthal, introduction by Bruce Lawrence. Princeton: Princeton
University Press, 2004.

Khana, Parag. *How to Run the World: Charting the Course of the Next Renaissance*.
New York: Random House, 2011.

Kusch, Rodolfo. *América profunda*. Buenos Aires: Hachette, 1962.

————. *Esbozo de una antropología filosófica Americana*. Buenos Aires: Castañeda, 1978.

————. *Geocultura del hombre Americano*. Buenos Aires: García Cambeiro, 1976.

————. *Indigenous and Popular Thinking in America*. 1973, trans. María Lugones and
Joshua Price. Durham: Duke University Press, 2010.

————. *La seducción de la barbarie: Análisis herético de un continente mestizo*. Buenos
Aires: Raigal, 1953.

————. *Obras Completas*. Rosario, Argentina: Fundación Ross, 2000.

————. *Pensamiento indígena y pensamiento popular*. Buenos Aires: Hachette, 1971.
Trans. María Lugones and Joshua Price as *Indigenous and Popular Thoughts in
América*, prologue and introduction by Walter D. Mignolo. Durham: Duke Univer-
sity Press, 2010.

Laclau, Ernesto. *Emancipation(s)*. London: Verso, 2007.

Lafitau, Joseph François. *Moeurs des sauvages américains, comparées aux moeurs des
premiers temps*. Paris: C.-E. Hochereau, 1724.

Lamming, George. "The Occasion for Speaking." *The Pleasures of Exile*, 23–50. London: Allison and Busby, 1984 [1960].

Lander, Edgardo. *Desarollo, eurocentrismo y economía popular: Más allá del paradigma
neo-liberal*. Caracas: Mision Vuelvan Caras, 2006.

————. "Eurocentrism, Modern Knowledge and the 'Natural' Order of Capital."
Nepantla 3, no. 2 (2002): 245–68.

———. "Una profunda crisis civilizatoria." *Foro Social Mundial*, Dakar, 2011. http://fsm2011.org/es/estamos-viviendo-una-profunda-crisis-civilizatoria.

———. "Crisis civilizatoria. El tiempo se agota." www.fedaeps.org, March 2011, http://www.fedaeps.org/cambio-civilizatorio-y-buen-vivir/crisis-civilizatoria-el-tiempo-se.

———. "Estamos viviendo una profunda crisis civilizatoria." *Transnational Institute*, A *worldwide fellowship of scholar activists*, January 2010. http://www.tni.org/node/69522.

———. "How the Myth of Unlimited Growth Is Destroying the Planet." An interview with Nick Buxton. *Transnational Institute. A worldwide fellowships of scholar activists*, December 2009. http://www.tni.org/node/69522.

Lao-Montes, Agustín. "De-colonial Moves: Trans-locating African Diaspora Spaces." *Cultural Studies* 21, nos. 2–3 (March 2007): 309–38.

Lascano, Sergio Rodríguez, and Fernando Yáñez Muñoz, eds. *Rebeldía* 7, no. 65 (2009). http://revistarebeldia.org.

Latouche, Serge. *The Westernization of the World: The Significance, Scope and Limits of the Drive toward Global Uniformity*, trans. Rosemary Morris. Oxford: Polity, 1996.

Latour, Bruno. "Whose Cosmos, Which Cosmopolitics? Comments on the Peace Terms of Ulrich Beck." *Common Knowledge* 10, no. 3 (2004): 461.

Le Bot, Yvon, ed. *El sueño Zapatista: Entrevistas con el Subcomandante Marcos, el Mayor Moisés y el Comandante Tacho, del Ejército Zapatista de Liberación Nacional*. Barcelona: Plaza y Janés, 1997.

Lee Kuan Yew, and Fareed Zakaria. "Culture Is Destiny: A Conversation with Lee Kuan Yew." *Foreign Affairs* 73, no. 2 (March–April 1994): 109–26.

Lenkersdorf, Carlos. *Los hombres verdaderos: Voces y testimonios tojolabales*. Mexico City: Siglo Veintiuno, 1996.

Levander, Caroline, and Walter Mignolo, eds. "The Global South and World Dis/Order." Special issue of *Global South* 5/1 (2007).

Levitt, Kari. "From Development to Neo-Liberalism: What Have We Learned about Development?" *The Critical Tradition of Caribbean Political Economy: The Legacy of George Bedford*, 201–22. Kingston: Ian Randle, 1996.

———. "In Search of Model I." *Essays on the Theory of Plantation Economy*, ed. Lloyd Best and Kari Polanyi Levitt, 189–96. Kingston: University of West Indies Press, 2009.

LeSueur, James D. *Uncivil War: Intellectuals and Identity Politics during the Decolonization of Algeria*. Philadelphia: University of Pennsylvania Press, 2001.

Llanque Chana, Domingo. *La cultura Aymara: Desestructuración o afirmación de identidad*. Puno: Instituto de Estudios Aymaras, 1990.

Lovejoy, Arthur O. *The Great Chain of Being: A Study of the History of an Idea*. Cambridge: Harvard University Press, 1936.

Lugones, María. "The Coloniality of Gender." *Worlds and Knowledges Otherwise*, a web dossier of the Center of Global Studies and the Humanities, Duke University, 2008. http://jhfc.duke.edu/wko.

———. "Decolonial Feminism." *Hypatia* 25, no. 4:742–59.

Luhman, Niklas. *Social Systems*, trans. Eva M. Knodt. Stanford: Stanford University Press, 1984.

Lyell, Charles. *Principles of Geology: Being an Attempt to Explain the Former Changes of the Earth's Surface by Reference to Causes Now in Operation.* London: John Murray, 1830–33.

MacCormack, Sabine. "Time, Space, and Ritual Action: The Inka and Christian Calendars in Early Colonial Peru." *Native Traditions in the Postconquest World,* 295–344. Washington: Dumbarton Oaks, 1998.

Mahbubani, Kishore. *Can Asians Think? Understanding the Divide between East and West.* Singapore: Times Books International, 1998.

———. *The New Asian Hemisphere: The Irresistible Shift of Global Power to the East.* New York: Public Affairs, 2008.

———. "Peeling Away the Western Veneer." *New Perspective Quarterly* 25, no. 2 (2008). http://www.digitalnpq.org/archive/2008_spring/02_mahbubani.html.

Mahmood, Saba. *Politics of Piety: The Islamic Revival and the Feminist Subject.* Princeton: Princeton University Press, 2005.

Maldonado-Torres, Nelson. *Against War: Views from the Underside of Modernity.* Durham: Duke University Press, 2008.

———. "On the Coloniality of Being: Contributions to the Development of a Concept." *Cultural Studies* 21, nos. 2–3 (2007): 240–71.

———. "Topology of Being and Geopolitics of Knowledge." *City* 8, no. 1 (2004): 29–56.

Mangabeira Unger, Roberto. *Knowledge and Politics.* New York: Free Press, 1975.

Marcos, Sylvia. "The Borders Within: The Indigenous Women's Movement and Feminism in Mexico." *Dialogue and Difference: Feminisms Challenge Globalization,* ed. Marguerite Waller and Sylvia Marcos, 81–112. New York: Palgrave, 2005.

———. *Taken from the Lips: Gender and Eros in Mesoamerican Religions.* Leiden: Brill, 2006.

Marcos, Subcomandante Insurgente. "The Fourth World War," trans. irlandesa. http://www.inmotionmagazine.com/auto/fourth.html.

———. "Siete piezas sueltas del rompecabezas mundial." http://web.mit.edu/course/21/21f.707/SubcomandanteMarcos.html.

Masuzawa, Tomoko. *The Invention of World Religions.* Chicago: University of Chicago Press, 2005.

Maturana, Humberto. Interview. 1985. http://www.oikos.org/maten.htm.

———. "Reality: The Search for Objectivity or the Quest for a Compelling Argument." *Irish Journal of Psychology* 9, no. 1 (1988): 25–82.

Maturana, Humberto, and Bernhard Poerksen. *From Being to Doing: The Origins of the Biology of Cognition: A Conversation between Humberto R. Maturana and Bernhard Poerksen,* trans. Wolfram Karl Koeck and Alison Rosemary Koeck. Heidelberg: Carl-Auer, 2004.

Medina, Javier. "Forma Estado y Forma Ayllus. Ideas para rebobinar el proceso de cambio." *La Reciprocidad*, March 2011. http://lareciprocidad.blogspot.com/2011/03/forma-estado-y-forma-ayllus-ideas-para.html.

Menchú, Rigoberta. *Me llamo Rigoberta Menchú y así me nació la conciencia*. Mexico City: Siglo XXI, 1982.

Mignolo, Walter D. "Beyond Populism, Decolonizing the Economy." *Counterpunch*, 29 May 2006. http://www.counterpunch.org/mignolo05082006.html.

———. "Canon A(nd)Cross-Cultural Boundaries (Or, Whose Canon Are We Talking About?)." *Poetics Today* 12, no. 1 (1991): 1–28.

———. "Cartas, crónicas y relaciones del descubrimiento y de la conquista." *Historia de la literatura hispanoamericana* 1 (1992): 57–120.

———. "Citizenship, Knowledge and the Limits of Humanity." *American Literary History* 18, no. 2 (2006): 312–31.

———. "Colonial and Postcolonial Discourse: Cultural Critique or Academic Colonialism?" *Latin American Research Review* 28, no. 3 (1993): 120–34.

———. "Coloniality at Large: Time and the Colonial Difference." *Time in the Makings*, 106–49. Rio de Janeiro: Universidad Cándido Mendes, 2000.

———. "Coloniality of Power and Subalternity." *The Latin American Subaltern Studies Reader*, ed. Ileana Rodríguez, 424–44. Durham: Duke University Press, 2001.

———. "Commentary." *Natural and Moral History of the Indies*, by José de Acosta, ed. Jane E. Mangan, trans. Frances López-Morillas, 451–518. Durham: Duke University Press, 2002.

———. "The Communal and the Decolonial." *Turbulence: Ideas for Movement*, October 2009. http://turbulence.org.uk/turbulence-5/decolonial.

———. "Comprensión hermenéutica y comprensión teórica." *Revista de Literatura*, 90 (1983): 5–38. Madrid: Consejo Superior de Investigaciones Científicas.

———. "Cosmopolitanism and the De-Colonial Option." *Studies in Philosophy and Education* 29, no. 2 (March 2010): 111–27.

———. "The Darker Side of the Enlightenment: A Decolonial Reading of Kant's *Geography*." *Readings on Kant's Geography*, ed. Stuart Elden and Eduardo Mendieta. Stony Brook: Stony Brook Press, 2011.

———. "The Darker Side of the Renaissance: Colonization and the Discontinuity of the Classical Tradition." *Renaissance Quarterly* 45, no. 4 (winter 1992): 808–28.

———. *The Darker Side of the Renaissance: Literacy, Territoriality and Colonization*. Ann Arbor: University of Michigan Press, 1995.

———. "Decolonial Cosmopolitanism between Theology and the Spirit of Global Capitalism." Lecture for the project "Multiple Trajectories, Critical Interrogations," led by Kamari Clarke, Ariana Hernández-Reguant, and Moira Fradinger, Yale University, 2 November 2008.

———. "The Decolonial Option and the Meaning of Identity in Politics." *Anales Nueva Época*, nos. 9–10 (2007): 43–72.

————, ed. "Delinking: The Rhetoric of Modernity, the Logic of Coloniality, and the Grammar of Decoloniality." *Cultural Studies* 21, nos. 2–3 (2007): 449–514.

————. "Delinking Epistemology: An Interview with Marina Grzinick." *Reartiku-lacija* 4, no. 1 (summer 2008). Part I, http://www.reartikulacija.org/RE4/ENG/ decoloniality4_ENG_mign.html; part II, 5, http://www.reartikulacija.org/RE5/ENG/ decoloniality5_ENG_mign.html; part III, 6, http://www.reartikulacija.org/RE6/ ENG/decoloniality6_ENG_mign.html.

————. "De-linking: Globalization, Don Quixote and the Colonies." *Macalester International* 17, no. 1 (2006): 3–38.

————. "Dussel's Philosophy of Liberation: Ethics and the Geopolitics of Knowledge." *Thinking from the Underside of History: Enrique Dussel's Philosophy of Liberation*, ed. Linda Alcoff and Eduardo Mendieta, 27–51. Boulder: Rowman and Littlefield, 2000.

————. "The End of the University as We Know It: World Epistemic Fora toward Communal Futures and Decolonial Horizons of Life." Mignolo on the Web, weblog entry, 7 May 2009. http://waltermignolo.com. Repr. in *Campaign for the Public University*, Warwick, England. http://publicuniversity.org.uk/2010/11/23/the-end-of-the-university-as-we-know-it. Repr. in *The American-Style University at Large: Transplants, Outposts, and the Globalization of Higher Education*, ed. James Mc-Dougall and Kathryn Kleypas. Lanham, Md.: Rowman and Littlefield, forthcoming.

————. "Epistemic Disobedience and the Decolonial Option: A Manifesto." *Subaltern Studies and Interdisciplinary Study of Media and Communication*, 2 February 2008. http://subalternstudies.com/?p=193.

————. Interview with Imanel Galfalsoro http://criticalstew.org/?p=193.

————. "Los estudios culturales: Geopolítica del conocimiento y existencias/necesi-dades institutionales." *Revista Iberoamericana* 69, no. 203 (2000): 401–15.

————. "Evo Morales en Bolivia: Giro a la izquierda of giro descolonial?" *Democra-cias en Desconfianza: Ensayos en sociedad civil y política en América Latina*, ed. José de la Cruz, 93–106. Montevideo: Coscoroba, 2006.

————. "From 'El Derecho de Gentes' to 'La Dignidad Humana': The Zapatistas' Theoretical Revolution." Paper presented at "Comparative Colonialism: Pre-Industrial Colonial Intersections in Global Perspective," the thirty-first annual conference at the Center for Medieval and Renaissance Studies, Binghamton University, State University of New York, 31 October–1 November 1997.

————. "Geopolitics of Knowledge and the Colonial Difference." *South Atlantic Quarterly* 101, no. 1 (2002): 57–96.

————. "Globalization and the Geopolitics of Knowledge: The Role of the Humani-ties in the Corporate University." *Nepantla* 4, no. 1 (2003): 97–119.

————. "Human Understanding and (Latin) American Interests: The Politics and Sensibilities of Geo-Historical Locations." *Poetics Today* 16, no. 1 (1995): 171–224.

————. *The Idea of Latin America*. London: Blackwell, 2005. Span. trans. *La idea de América Latina. La herida colonial y la opción decolonial*. Buenos Aires: Gedisa, 2006.

———. "Introduction: Coloniality of Power and De-colonial Thinking." *Cultural Studies* 21, nos. 2–3 (2007): 155–67.

———. *Local Histories/Global Designs: Coloniality, Subaltern Knowledges and Border Thinking.* Princeton: Princeton University Press, 2000.

———. "The Many-Faces of Cosmopolis: Border Thinking and Critical Cosmopolitanism." *Public Culture* 12, no. 3 (2000): 721–48.

———. "El metatexto historiográfico y la historiografía indiana." *Modern Languages Notes* 96 (1981): 358–402.

———. "Nebrija in the New World: The Question of the Letter, the Colonization of Amerindian Languages, and the Discontinuity of the Classical Tradition," *L'Homme* 32, nos. 122–24 (1992): 185–207.

———. "On the Colonization of Amerindian Languages and Memories: Renaissance Theories of Writing and the Discontinuity of the Classical Tradition." *Comparative Studies in Society and History* 34 (1992): 301–30.

———. "La opción decolonial: Desprendimiento y apertura: Un manifiesto y un caso." *Tabula Rasa* (2008): 243–81.

———. "La opción descolonial: Desprendimiento y apertura: Un manifiesto y un caso." *Las vertientes Americanas del pensamiento y el proyecto des-colonial*, 175–208. Madrid: Trama, 2008.

———. "El pensamiento descolonial: Desprendimiento y apertura: Un manifiesto." Trans. Enrique Dussel. *El giro descolonial: Reflexiones para una diversidad epistémica más allá del capitalismo global*, ed. Ramón Grosfóguel and Santiago Castro-Gómez, 25–46. Bogotá: Universidad Central y Universidad Pontificia Javeriana, 2007.

———. "(Post) Occidentalism, (Post) Coloniality, and (Post) Subalternity." *The Pre-Occupation of Postcolonial Studies*, ed. Fawzia Afzal-Khan and Kalpana Seshadri-Crooks, 86–118. Durham: Duke University Press, 2000.

———. "Post-Occidental Reason: The Crisis of Occidentalism and the Emergenc(y)e of Border Thinking." *Local Histories/Global Designs: Coloniality, Subaltern Knowledges and Border Thinking*, 91–126. Princeton: Princeton University Press, 2000.

———. "Semiosis, Coherence and Universes of Meaning." *Text and Discourse Connectedness*, ed. Maria-Elizabeth Conte, János Petofi, and Emel Sozer, 483–506. Amsterdam: John Benjamins, 1989.

———. "La semiosis colonial: La dialéctica entre representaciones fracturas y herme-néuicas pluritópicas." *Foro Hispánico* 4 (1992): 11–27.

———. "Semiosis y universos de sentido." *Lexis* 7, no. 2 (1983): 219–38.

———. "Stocks to Watch: Colonial Difference, Planetary 'Multiculturalism' and Radical Planning." *Plurimondi: An International Forum for Research and Debate on Human Settlements* 2 (2000): 7–33.

———. "Teorías literarias of de la littérature. Qué son y para qué sirven?" *Teorias literarias en la actualidad*, ed. Graciela Reyes, 41–78. Madrid: El Arquero, 1989.

———. "Who Speaks for the 'Human' in Human Rights?" *Human Rights in Latin American and Iberian Cultures. Hispanic Issues on Line* 5, no. 1 (fall 2009): 7–24.

http://hispanicissues.umn.edu/assets/pdf/MIGNOLO_HRLAIC.pdf. Repr. in *Human Rights from a Third World Perspective: Critique, History and International Law*, ed. José-Manuel Barreto. Newcastle: Cambridge Scholars, 2011.

Mignolo, Walter D., and Tlostanova, Madina. *Learning to Unlearn: Thinking Decolonially in Eurasia and Latin/o America*. Athens: Ohio University Press, forthcoming 2012.

————. "The Logic of Coloniality and the Limits of Postcoloniality." *The Post-colonial and the Global*, ed. Revathi Krishnaswamy and John C. Hawley, 109–24. Minneapolis: University of Minnesota Press, 2008.

————. "On Pluritopic Hermeneutics, Trans-Modern Thinking and Decolonial Philosophy." *Encounters: An International Journal for the Study of Culture and Society* 1 (2009): 9–26.

————. "Theorizing from the Borders: Shifting to Geo- and Body-Politics of Knowledge." *European Journal of Social Theory* 9, no. 2 (2006): 205–22.

Mihesua, Devon Abbott, and Angela Cavender Wilson, eds. *Indigenizing the Academy: Transforming Scholarship and Empowering Communities*. Lincoln: University of Nebraska Press, 2004.

Miller, Arthur G. "Transformations of Time and Space: Oaxaca, Mexico, circa 1500–1700." *Images of Memory: On Remembering and Representation*, ed. S. Kuchler and W. Melion, 141–75. Washington: Smithsonian Institution Press, 1991.

Mohamad, Mahathir. "Speech by Prime Minister Mahathir Mohamad." Presented at the Tenth Islamic Summit Conference, Putrajaya, Malaysia, 16 October 2003. Anti-Defamation League. http://www.adl.org.

Montejo, Victor. *Maya Intellectual Renaissance: Identity, Representation and Leadership*. Austin: University of Texas Press, 2005.

Morales, Evo. "Speech of President Morales before the UN General Assembly on April 22nd, International Mother Earth Day." Permanent Mission of the Plurinational State of Bolivia to the United Nations in New York. http://www.workers .org/2009/world/evo_morales_0521.

Muñoz Ramirez, Gloria. ezln: *20 y 10, el fuego y la palabra*. Mexico City: Rebeldía / La Jornada, 2003.

————. *The Fire and the Word: A History of the Zapatista Movement*, ed. Greg Ruggiero and Elaine Karzenberger, trans. Laura Carlsen and Alejandro Reyes Arias. San Francisco: City Lights, 2008.

Murphy, Viren. "Modernity Against Modernity: Wang Hui's Critical History of Chinese Thoughts." *Modern Intellectual History* 3, no. 1 (2006): 137–65.

Nandy, Ashis. "The Beautiful Future of Poverty: Popular Economics as Psychological Defense." *Enchantments of Modernity: Empire, Nation, Globalization*, ed. Saurabh Dube, 482–99. London: Routledge, 2009.

————. "Looking in the Mirror of the East." *Talking India: Ashis Nandy in Conversation with Ramin Jahanbegloo*, 18–53. New Delhi: Oxford University Press, 2006.

————. "Gandhi and the Indiant Identity." *India Revisited: Conversations on Contem-*

porary India, ed. Ramon Jahanbegloo, 51–58. New Delhi: Oxford University Press, 2008.

Naquib al-Attas, Syed. *Prolegomena to the Metaphysics of Islam: An Exposition of the Fundamental Elements of the World View of Islam*. Kuala Lampur: ISTAC, 1995.

O'Gorman, Edmundo. *La idea del descubrimiento de América*. Mexico City: Universidad Autónoma de México, 1951.

———. *La invención de América: El universalismo en la cultura occidental*. Mexico City: Fondo de Cultura Económica, 1958.

Ortelius, Abraham. *Theatrum Orbis Terrarum*. Antwerp: Gilles Coppens de Diest, 1570.

Osamu, Nishitani. "Anthropos and Humanitas: Two Western Concepts of 'Human Being.'" *Translation, Biopolitics, Colonial Difference*, ed. Naoki Sakai and Jon Solomon, 259–74. Hong Kong: Hong Kong University Press, 2006.

Ottobah Cugoano, Quobna. *Thoughts and Sentiments on the Evil of Slavery*, ed. with an introduction and notes by Vincent Garretta. London: Penguin, 1999 [1786].

Owen Hughes, Diane. "Introduction." *Time: Histories and Ethnologies*, ed. Diane Owen Hughes and Thomas. R. Trautmann, 1–20. Ann Arbor: University of Michigan Press, 1995.

Oyesumi, Oyeronke. *The Invention of Women: Making African Sense of Western Discourses*. Minneapolis: University of Minnesota Press, 1997.

Pacari, Nina. "La incidencia de la participación política de los pueblos indígenas: Un camino irreversible." *Las vertientes Americanas del pensamiento y el proyecto descolonial*, ed. Heriberto Cairo Carou and Walter D. Mignolo. Madrid: Trama / Fecal, 2008.

Palermo, Zulma. *Desde la otra orilla: Pensamiento crítico y políticas culturals en América Latina*. Córdoba: Alción, 2005.

Pannikar, Raymond. "Aporias in the Contemporary Philosophy of Religion." *Man and World* 13, nos. 3–4 (1980): 357–83.

———. *Myth, Faith and Hermeneutics: Cross Cultural Studies*. New York: Paulist, 1980.

———. "What Is Comparative Philosophy Comparing?" *Interpreting across Boundaries: New Essays in Comparative Philosophy*, ed. Gerald James Larson and Eliot Deutsch, 116–36. Princeton: Princeton University Press, 1988.

Patzi Paco, Félix. *Sistema comunal: Una propuesta alternativa al sistema liberal*. La Paz: Centro Estudios Andinos, 2004.

Pérez, Laura. *Chicana Art: The Politics of Spiritual and Aesthetic Altarities*. Durham: Duke University Press, 2007.

Pletsch, Carl E. "The Three Worlds, or the Division of Social Scientific Labor, circa 1950–1975." *Comparative Study of Society and History* (1981): 565–90.

Poma de Ayala, Guamán. *Nueva corónica y buen gobierno*, ed. John Murra and Rolena Adorno. Mexico City: Siglo XXI, 1982 [1616].

Prior, Michael. *Bible and Colonialism: A Moral Critique*. London: Continuum International, 1997.

Pukara. *Historia, coyuntura y descolonización. Katarismo e Indianismo en el proceso politico del MAS en Bolivia.* La Paz: Fondo Editorial Pukara, 2010, www .periodicopukara.com/.../historia-coyuntura-y-descolonizacion.pdf.

Quijano, Anibal. "Colonialidad del poder, cultura y conocimiento en America Latina." *Anuario Mariateguiano* 9 (1997): 113–21.

———. "Colonialidad y modernidad-racionalidad." *Los conquistados: 1492 y la población indígena de América*, ed. Heraclio Bonilla, 437–47. Bogotá: Tercer Mundo / FLACSO, 1992.

———. "Coloniality and Modernity/Rationality." 1992. *Cultural Studies* 21, nos. 2–3 (2007): 22–32.

———. "Coloniality of Power, Ethnocentrism, and Latin America." *Nepantla* 1, no. 3 (2000): 533–80.

———. "Otro horizonte de sentido histórico." Special issue, "Mas allá de la crisis." *América Latina en Movimiento* 32 (February 2009): 441.

———. "'Raza,' 'Etnia' y 'Nación' en Mariátegui: Cuestiones Abiertas." *José Carlos Mariátegui y Europa: El otro aspecto del descubrimiento*, ed. Roland Forgues, 167–87. Lima: Empresa Amauta, 1993.

———. "América Latina: Hacia un nuevo sentido histórico." www.fedaeps.org, March 2011, http://www.fedaeps.org/cambio-civilizatorio-y-buen-vivir/crisis-civilizatoria-el-tiempo-se.

Quijano, Anibal, and Immanuel Wallerstein. "Americanity as a Concept, or the Americas in the Modern World-System." *International Sociological Association* 1, no. 134 (1989): 549–56.

Qutb, Sayyid. *The Islamic Concept and Its Characteristics.* Burr Ridge, Ill.: American Trust, 1992.

Rahman, Fazlur. *Islam and Modernity: Transformation of an Intellectual Tradition.* Chicago: University of Chicago Press, 1982.

Rahnema, Ali. *An Islamic Utopian: A Political Biography of Ali Shari'ati.* London: I. B. Tauris, 2000.

———. "Shari'ati's Audience and Discourse at the University of Mashhad." *An Islamic Utopian: A Political Biography of Ali Shari'ati*, 193–209. London: Zed, 2000.

Rawls, John. *The Law of Peoples.* Cambridge: Harvard University Press, 1999.

Readings, Bill. *The University in Ruins.* Cambridge: Harvard University Press, 1996.

Reinaga, Fausto. *La revolución India.* La Paz: PIB, 1969.

Rengifo Vázquez, Grimaldo. "The Ayllu." *The Spirit of Regeneration: Andean Culture Confronting Western Notions of Development*, ed. Fréderique Apffel Marglin with PRATEC, 89–123. London: Zed, 1998.

Roa Avendaño, Tatiana. "El Sumak Kawsay como expresión de la descolonialidad del poder." Censat Agua Viva, 19 January 2009. http://www.censat.org/noticias/ 2009/1/19/El-Sumak-Kawsay-como-expresion-de-la-descolonialidad-del-poder.

Rod, Thayne R. "Stranger in Foreign Land: José de Acosta's Scientific Realization in Sixteenth-Century Peru." *Sixteenth Century Journal* 29 (1998): 19–33.

Rorty, Richard. *Philosophy and the Mirror of Nature*. Princeton: Princeton University Press, 1979.

Rose, Nikolas. *The Politics of Life Itself: Biomedicine, Power, and Subjectivity in the Twenty-First Century*. Princeton: Princeton University Press, 2007.

Sabet, Amr G. E. *Islam and the Political: Theory, Governance and International Relations*. London: Pluto, 2008.

Safi, Omid, ed. *Progressive Muslims on Justice, Gender and Pluralism*. Oxford: Oneworld, 2003.

Said, Edward. *Orientalism*. New York: Vintage, 1978.

Sanjinés, Javier. "Mestizaje Upside-Down: Aesthetic Politics in Modern Bolivia." *Nepantla* 3, no. 1 (2002): 39–60.

Schmitt, Carl. *The* Nomos *of the Earth in the International Law of the* Jus Publicum Europaeum. 1950, trans. G. L. Ulmen. New York: Telos, 2003.

———. *Political Theology: Four Chapters on the Concept of Sovereignty*, trans. George D. Schwab. Cambridge: MIT Press, 1985 [1922].

———. *Théologie politique*, trans. Jean-Louis Schlegel. Paris: Gallimard, 1988.

Sebill, Nadine. *Ayllus y haciendas: Dos estudios de caso sobre la agricultura colonial de los Andes*. La Paz: Hisbol, 1989.

Seigel, Jerrold. *Marx's Fate: The Shape of a Life*. University Park: Pennsylvania State University Press, 1993.

Sen, Amartya. *Development as Freedom*. Oxford: Oxford University Press, 1999.

Shari'ati, Ali. "Extraction and Refinement of Cultural Resources." *Man and Islam*, trans. Fatollah Marjani, 29–45. Kuala Lampur: Islamic Publications International, 2005.

———. *Man and Islam*, trans. Fatollah Marjani. Kuala Lampur: Islamic Publications International, 1981.

———. "Modern Man and His Prison." *Man and Islam*, trans. Fatollah Marjani, 46–62. North Haledon, N.J.: Islamic Publications International, 1981.

Shiva, Vandana. "Monocultures of the Mind: Environmental Activist, Agricultural Researcher, Water Rights Campaigner, and Much More, Vandana Shiva Speaks with David Barsamian." *India Together* (April 2003). http://www.indiatogether.org.

———. *The Monocultures of the Mind: Perspectives in Biodiversity*. London: Zed, 1993.

Sigal, Pete. *Infamous Desire: Male Homosexuality in Colonial Latin America*. Chicago: University of Chicago Press, 2003.

———. *From Moon Goddesses to Virgins. The Colonization of Yucatecan Maya Sexual Desires*. Austin: University of Texas Press, 2000.

Silverblatt, Irene. "Becoming Indian in the Central Andes of Seventeenth Century Peru." *Imperial Aftermaths and Postcolonial Displacements*, ed. Gyan Prakash, 279–98. Princeton: Princeton University Press, 1995.

Slabodsky, Santiago E. "De-colonial Jewish Thought and the Americas." *Postcolonial Philosophy of Religion*, ed. Purushottama Bilimoria and Andrew B. Irvine, 251–73. New York: Springer, 2009.

Smith, Andrea. "Walking in Balance: The Spirituality/Liberation Praxis of Native

Women." *Native American Religious Identity*, ed. Joyce Weaver, 178–98. New York: Orbis, 1998.

Smith, Efrem, and Phil Jackson. *The Hip-Hop Church: Connecting with the Movement Shaping Our Culture*, foreword by Bakari Kitwana and Alton B. Pollard III. Nottingham: Inter-Varsity, 2006.

Smith, Linda Tuhiwai. *Decolonizing Methodologies: Research and Indigenous Peoples*. Dunedin: University of Otago Press / Zed, 1999.

Spence, Jonathan D. *The Chan's Great Continent: China in Western Minds*. New York: W. W. Norton, 1998.

Spivak, Gayatri. *In Other Worlds: Essays in Cultural Politics*. New York: Routledge, 1988.

Steger, Manfred. *Globalism: Market Ideology Meets Terrorism*. New York: Rowman and Littlefield, 2005.

Stengers, Isabelle. *Au temps des catastrophes: Résister á la barbarie qui vient*. Paris: La Découverte, 2009.

Suárez Navaz, Liliana, and Rosalva Aída Hernández, eds. *Descolonizando el feminismo: Teorías y prácticas desde los márgenes*. Valencia: Ediciones Cátedra, Universidad de Valencia, 2008.

Sugnet, Charles, and Baaba Maal. "I Sing All the Space." *Transition* 74 (1997): 184–98.

Suma Qamaña, Sumak Kawsay, Teko Kavi/For a Better Life. Directed collectively, produced by the Cinematography Education and Production Center, Bolivian Indigenous Peoples' Audiovisual Council, 2008.

Sun Yat-sen. *The Three Principles of the People: With Two Suplementary Chapters by Chian Kai-shek*, ed. J. T. Chen, trans. Frank W. Price. Shanghai: Commercial Press, 1927.

Thiry, Paul Henri, Baron d' Holbach. *Nature, and Her Laws as Applicable to the Happiness of Man, Living in Society, Contrasted with Superstition and Imaginary Systems*. London: Watson, 1834 [1797].

Tinker, George E. *Spirit of Resistance: Political Theology and American Indian Liberation*. Minneapolis: Fortress, 2004.

Tlostanova, Madina. *Gender Epistemologies in the Eurasian Borderlands*. Basingstoke: Palgrave Macmillan, 2010.

———. "The Janus Faced Empire Distorting Orientalist Discourses: Gender, Race and Religion in the Russian/(Post)Soviet Constructions of the Orient." Worlds and Knowledges Otherwise, a web dossier of the Center of Global Studies and the Humanities, Duke University, 2008. http://jhfc.duke.edu/wko.

Todorov, Tzvetan. "Problèmes de l'énonciation." *Languages* 17 (1970): 3–11.

Toulmin, Stephen. *Cosmopolis: The Hidden Agenda of Modernity*. Chicago: University of Chicago Press, 1990.

Trouillot, Évelyne. "Pour l'evidence des subjectivités: 'Anse à Fouler' au centre du monde." *Texte de Référence*, 583–96. Rio de Janeiro: Academy de la Latinité / UNESCO, Universidad Candido Mendes, 2006.

Trouillot, Michel-Rolph. "North Atlantic Universals: Analytical Fictions, 1492–1945." *South Atlantic Quarterly* 101, no. 4 (2002): 839–58.

UNESCO. "Historic Bridgedown and Its Garrison." World Heritage Convention, 7 October 2009. http://whc.unesco.org/en/tentativelists/1991.

Wallerstein, Immanuel. *The Capitalist World-Economy*. Cambridge: Cambridge University Press, 1979.

———. *The Modern World-System*. New York: Academic, 1974.

Wallerstein, Immanuel, et al. *Open the Social Sciences: Report of the Gulbenkian Commission of the Restructuring of the Social Sciences*. Stanford: Stanford University Press, 1995.

Untoja, Fernando. *Retorno al Ayllu*. La Paz: Cada, 1992.

Walsh, Catherine. "Interculturalidad, decolonialidad y el buen vivir." *Interculturalidad, estado, sociedad: Luchas (des) coloniales en nuestra época*, 213–36. Quito: Universidad Andina Simon Bolívar and Abya-Yala, 2009.

———. "Development as *Buen Vivir*: Institutional Arrangements and (De)Colonial Entanglements." *Development* 53, no. 1 (2010): 1521.

Walsh, Catherine, with Juan García. "El pensar del emergente movimiento Afroecuatoriano: Reflexiones (des)de un proceso." *Estudios y otras prácticas latinoamericanas en cultura y poder*, ed. Daniel Mato, 34–50. Caracas: CLACSO, Consejo Latinoamericano de Ciencias Sociales, 2002.

Walsh, Catherine, and interview with Laura Fano Morrissey. "Human Development and *Buen Vivir*." Society for International Development, March 2010, http://www.sidint.net/interview-with-catherine-walsh-human-development-and-buen-vivir.

Walsh, Catherine, and interview with Walter Mignolo. "Thinking and Doing in the Andes," *Reartikulacija* nos. 10–13. Electronic journal: Lujbjana, Slovenia. Part I: http://www.reartikulacija.org/?p=1468; Part II: http://www.reartikulacija.org/?p=1473.

Walsh, Sebastian J. "Killing Post-Almohad Man: Malik Bennabi, Algerian Islamism and the Search for a Liberal Governance." *North African Studies* 12, no. 2 (2007): 235–54.

Watkins, Ralph C., et al. *The Gospel Remix: Reaching the Hip Hop Generation*. Valley Forge, Penn.: Judson, 2007.

Weber, Max. *The Protestant Ethic and the Spirit of Capitalism*. London: Routledge, 1992 [1905].

Williams, Eric. *Capitalism and Slavery*. Chapel Hill: University of North Carolina Press, 1944.

Wiredu, Kwasi. "Formulating Modern Thoughts in African Languages: Some Theoretical Considerations." *The Surreptitious Speech: Présence Africaine and the Politics of Otherness, 1947–1987*, ed. V. Y. Mudimbe, 301–32. Chicago: University of Chicago Press, 1992.

Wynter, Sylvia. "Towards the Sociogenic Principle: Fanon, Identity, the Puzzle of Conscious Experience." *National Identities and Socio-Political Changes in Latin America*, ed. Mercedes F. Durán-Cogan and Antonio Gómez-Moriana, 30–66. New York: Routledge, 2001.

———. "Después del hombre, su última palabra: Sobre el postmodernismo, *Les Damnés* y el principio sociogénico." Trans. into Spanish by Alejandro de Oto. *La teoría política en la encrucijada descolonial,* ed. Walter D. Mignolo, 51–124. Buenos Aires: Ediciones del Signo / Duke Project in the Humanities, 2009.

———. "Unsettling the Coloniality of Being/Power/Truth/Freedom: Towards the Human, after Man, Its Overrepresentation: An Argument." *New Centennial Review* 3, no. 3 (2003): 257–337.

———. "The Re-Enchantment of Humanism: An Interview with Sylvia Wynter." With David Scott. *Small Axe* 8 (2000): 119–207.

Yampara Huarachi, Simón. *El Ayllu y la territorialidad en los Andes: Una aproximación a Chambi Grande.* La Paz: Inti Andino, 2001.

———. "La sociedad Aymara: Sistemas y estructuras sociales de los Andes." *Las cosmovisión aymara,* 221–40. La Paz: Hisbol-UCB, 1992.

Yampara Huarachi, Simón. "Debates sobre el Pachamamism, habla Simón Yampara." *Tani Tani. Boletín Electrónico* 4, no. 356 (9 June 2010). http://www.amigo-latino.de/indigena/noticias/newsletter_5/342_pachamamismo_sy.html.

Yavuz, M. Hakan, and John L. Esposito, eds. *Turkish Islam and the Secular State: The Gülen Movement.* Syracuse: Syracuse University Press, 2003.

Yehia, Elena. "Decolonizing Knowledges and Practices: A Dialogic Encounter between the Latin American Modernity/Coloniality/Decoloniality Research Program and Actor Network Theory." *Tabula Rasa* 6 (2007): 85–114.

———. "Towards Decolonizing Encounters with Social Movements' Decolonizing Knowledges and Practices." Center for Global Justice, 2006. http://www.globaljusticecenter.org/papers2006/yehiaENG.htm.

Young, Robert C. J. *Postcolonialism: A Very Short Intoduction.* New York: Oxford University Press, 2003.

Žižek, Slavoj. "A Leftist Plea for 'Eurocentrism.'" *Cultural Inquiry* 36 (1998): 988–1008.

———. "Closing Comments." Presented at the conference "On the Idea of Communism," Birkbeck Institute, 13–15 March 2009. YouTube, bigcasinodotorgdotuk channel, video, 4 min., 44 sec. http://www.youtube.com/watch?v=BotV8wHn4hQ.

———. *The Ticklish Subject: The Absent Centre of Political Ontology.* London: Verso, 1999.

Zuidema, R. Tom. *Inca Civilization in Cuzco,* trans. Jean-Jacques Decoster. Austin: University of Texas Press, 1990.

INDEX

Note: Page numbers in italics indicate illustrations.

WALTER D. MIGNOLO is director of the Center for Global Studies and the Humanities and William H. Wannamaker Professor of Literature and Romance Studies at Duke University, where he holds a secondary appointment in cultural anthropology. He is also Researcher Associated at the Universidad Andina Simón Bolivar in Quito, Ecuador. He is also the author of *The Idea of Latin America* (2005; winner of the Frantz Fanon Award from the Caribbean Philosophical Association in 2006, translated into Spanish in 2006 and Korean in 2010); *Local Histories/Global Designs: Coloniality, Subaltern Knowledges, and Border Thinking* (2000; translated into Spanish in 2003 and Portuguese in 2003, now being translated into Korean); *The Darker Side of the Renaissance: Literacy, Territoriality and Colonization* (1995; winner of the Katherine Singer Kovacs award from the Modern Language Association of America, being translated into Spanish and Chinese); *Teoría del texto e interpretación de textos* (1986); and *Elementos para una teoría del texto literario* (1978). In 2010 he published a monograph in Spanish, *Desobeciencia epistémica: Retórica del la modernidad, logica de la colonialidad y gramática de la descolonialidad*, translated into French and German. He edited *Capitalismo. El eurocentrismo y la filosofía de la liberación en el debate intelectual contemporáneo* (Buenos Aires: Ediciones del Signos, 2000). His co-edited books include, with Margaret R. Greer and Maureen Quilligan, *Rereading the Black Legend: The Discourses of Religious and Racial Difference in the Renaissance Empires* (2007); with Heriberto Cairo, *Las vertientes americanas del pensamiento y el proyecto des-colonial* (2008); with Arturo Escobar, *Globalizaton and the Decolonial Option* (2009); and, with Elizabeth Hill Boone, *Writing without Words: Alternative Literacies in Mesoamerica and the Andes* (Duke University Press, 1994). He is a co-editor of the series Latin America Otherwise. In 2010 he was appointed International Board Member for the six-year project "Time, Memory and Representation" at Sorderton University in Sweden. He also serves on the international advisory board of the Hong Kong Advanced Institute for Cross Disciplinary Studies (College of Liberal Arts and Social Sciences), at the City University of Hong-Kong. In October 2010 he lectured at the Bruno Kreisky Foundation in Vienna and he delivered the Annual Norbert Lerner's Lecture Series at the Universidad Diego Portales in Chile. Additionally, he was the 2010 Visiting Fellow at the Institute of Advanced Studies at Warwick University, Department of Sociology. He was also co-curator of the exhibit "Estéticas descoloniales," which opened in Bogotá, Colombia, on 10 November 2010, and co-curator of a follow-up exhibit, "Decolonial Aesthetics," at the Center for Global Studies and the Humanities, Duke University, that opened in May 2011. In 2011 he was the Brackenridge Distinguished Visiting Professor in the Department of English at the University of Texas, San Antonio. He was an Erasmus Mundus Fellow at the Institute of Europhilosophy, University of Louvaine–la-Neuve and Denkplatz Distinguished Professor at the Institute of Postcolonial and Transcultural Studies (INPUTS), University of Bremen. He delivered a keynote address at the Rhodes Forum for the Dialogue of Civilizations (6–9 October 2011) in the seminar on "Post Secular Dialogues," and has contracted to be visiting scholar at The Hong Kong Advanced Institute for Cross-Disciplinary Studies of the City University of Hong Kong from January to June of 2012.

Library of Congress Cataloging-in-Publication Data

Mignolo, Walter.
The darker side of Western modernity : global futures, decolonial options / Walter D.
Mignolo.
p. cm. — (Latin america otherwise: languages, empires, nations)
Includes bibliographical references and index.
ISBN 978-0-8223-5060-6 (cloth : alk. paper)
ISBN 978-0-8223-5078-1 (pbk.: alk. paper)
1. Civilization, Western. 2. Civilization, Modern 3. Decolonization. 4. Forecasting.
I. Title. II. Series: Latin America otherwise.
CB245.M495 2011
909'.09821—dc23
2011021956